THE WEHRMACHT

THE WEHRMACHT

HISTORY, MYTH, REALITY

WOLFRAM WETTE

TRANSLATED BY DEBORAH LUCAS SCHNEIDER

HARVARD UNIVERSITY PRESS
Cambridge, Massachusetts
London, England
2006

Printed in the United States of America

Originally published as *Die Wehrmacht—Feindbilder, Vernichtungskrieg, Legenden,*
© S. Fischer Verlag GmbH, Frankfurt am Main 2002.

Library of Congress Cataloging-in-Publication Data

Wette, Wolfram, 1940–
[Wehrmacht. English]
The Wehrmacht : history, myth, reality / Wolfram Wette ;
translated by Deborah Lucas Schneider.
p. cm.
Includes bibliographical references and index.
ISBN 0-674-02213-0 (alk. paper)
1. Germany–Armed Forces—History—20th century.
2. World War, 1939–1945—Germany. 3. World War, 1939–1945—Atrocities.
4. Nationalism—Germany—History. 5. Germany. Heer—Officers—History.
I. Title.

D757.W4313 2006
940.54'1343—dc22   2005052604

Contents

Preface

Peter Fritzsche

"HISTORY," GÜNTER GRASS has written, "the history we Germans have repeatedly mucked up" over the course of the twentieth century, "is a clogged toilet. We flush and flush, but the shit keeps rising." Grass despairs in the most exasperated language about the ability of Germans to come to terms with their Nazi past. He is certainly right to indicate that the German past has not gone away. Germans live every day with the consequences of World War II and the Holocaust. But Grass is wrong to insinuate that Germans today are trying to get rid of the past or have not learned from it. In the late 1990s, in a truly extraordinary demonstration of public interest, tens of thousands of Germans visited the photographic exhibition "War of Extermination: The Crimes of the Wehrmacht, 1941–1944." More effectively than any other work of history, the exhibit opened up a difficult and productive debate on the role of ordinary Germans in the murder of innocent civilians during World War II. Organized by the Institute for Social Research in Hamburg, "War of Extermination" showed photograph after photograph of German soldiers rounding up and killing Jewish men, women, and children in towns across Poland, the Soviet Union, and Yugoslavia. In the streets, on hastily erected gallows, along the edges of forest, perpetrators and victims occupied the same photographic space. After fifty years, a few dozen photographs eliminated at once the distance of time and place and of selective memory. Facsimiles of military documents as well as excerpts from the letters and diaries of Wehrmacht soldiers added to the powerful message that the organizers hoped to convey:

the German army was complicit in the murder of Jews and other civilians. The exhibit showed that it was more than just a few units that were guilty of war crimes, and that partisans were not the only civilians the Wehrmacht killed.

The Wehrmacht exhibit opened in Hamburg in March 1995 and eventually toured thirty-three cities in Germany and Austria before it was disassembled at the end of 1999. It prompted an extensive national debate about complicity and about the writing and rewriting of history. The outpouring of newspaper commentaries and letters to the editor, and sometimes tearful, sometimes defiant testimony by veterans themselves, followed by conferences, panel discussions, television shows, and finally some corrections to the installation itself, did not provide closure. Rather, the photographs and documents posed new questions about the German army and challenged widely held assumptions which distinguished between the millions of Germans in the "clean" Wehrmacht and the hundreds of thousands of culpable Nazis in the killing squads of the SS.[1] Even the German parliament debated the "War of Extermination" exhibit. In March 1997, lawmakers from all parties participated in a remarkably personal discussion in which they recollected family histories, exposed their own misunderstandings and distortions, and, most important, listened to one another. Thanks to the Wehrmacht exhibit, Germans broke the cycle of reiteration and repetition.

The exhibit touched a very raw nerve. Almost 20 million German men served in the Wehrmacht in the years 1939–1945. It was truly a people's army. Any indictment of what military units in the field did to civilians was an indictment of masses of ordinary Germans, the fathers of friends and neighbors. "Young and old may well have preferred to identify with the victims as they had done on other occasions," reflected Michael Geyer, "but here they recognized themselves as killers of unarmed men, women, and children."[2] Indeed, much of the evidence of the Wehrmacht's participation in atrocities came from soldiers themselves, who seemed eager to bear witness to their acts. A series of photographs held in the United States Holocaust Memorial Museum (but not featured in the exhibition) shows Wehrmacht soldiers assembling and shooting Jewish civilians and then browsing through the pictures they have taken of the grisly events. These snapshots may well have been tucked away in the personal belongings of soldiers at the front or sent back home to relatives as souvenirs.[3] Now they are evidence of the extensive criminal activity of the Wehrmacht and of the broad knowledge and acceptance of that activity in everyday life.

The exhibit provoked an uproar because it undermined the ways in which postwar Germans had managed to come to terms with the very difficult legacy of the Nazi period. While no one disputed the facts of the Holocaust, the record of the Wehrmacht was regarded as relatively "clean." The distinction between the many "good" Germans in the Wehrmacht and the far less numerous "bad" Germans in Nazi organizations had allowed the postwar generations both to recognize complicity and to contain complicity. Indeed, ordinary soldiers of the Wehrmacht were often perceived as victims themselves, the unwilling instruments of a Nazi-inspired race war and the bearers of its horrors on the eastern front. In the collective memory of the war, the accent fell not on "Barbarossa," the operational code name for the German invasion of Russia in June 1941, but on Stalingrad, the battle site everyone knew as the place where so many soldiers on both sides suffered and died in the winter of 1942–43 and the location from which so many German prisoners, more than one hundred thousand in all, were taken, the vast majority never to return home. The Wehrmacht exhibit disputed this vision of German soldiers as victims only by putting Stalingrad back in the context of Germany's race war against the Soviet Union and reconnecting it to "Barbarossa." It showed very graphically what the German Sixth Army did to civilians in Kiev and Kharkov in the autumn of 1941 on its way to Stalingrad.[4] Other photographs depicted the victims, civilian faces on identity papers confiscated in the war. As a result of the exhibition and the publicity surrounding it, the Wehrmacht was identified as a perpetrator. The immensity of that judgment fell hard on the contemporary Germans who crowded the exhibit. Questions of participation in wartime atrocities proved to be far more vexing than simply establishing who had or had not been a Nazi, because it was not official party members but young army recruits in their twenties who were the killers. The Wehrmacht exhibit forced the issue of war crimes into German homes, often for the first time. One newspaper ran an article titled "The Catastrophe and the Family" as the exhibit traveled to Bonn, the "twenty-eighth station" of this difficult journey.[5] No new consensus emerged, but thousands upon thousands of Germans were prompted to question ready-made stereotypes and cherished assumptions both about the Nazi past and about the way they had come to explain it in the decades since 1945.

Wolfram Wette's new book on the Wehrmacht in World War II helps to clarify these murky images from the German past. It is a sober, angry indictment of the German army and its involvement in atrocities against Jews and other civilians. It is also an analysis of why this evidence was denied and replaced by the myth of the "clean Wehrmacht." Wette exposes the lies of the past and explains how the general silence about the war crimes was finally shattered by the Wehrmacht exhibit. He reveals the Wehrmacht to have been a willing partner in the Nazi regime's genocidal plans for the racial restructuring of Europe. First in Serbia and then in the Soviet Union, the Wehrmacht classified Jews as partisans and thereby made them acceptable military targets. To retaliate against the killing of its own soldiers by partisans, the Wehrmacht wiped out whole villages, executed men and, soon enough, women and children, and otherwise destroyed the means of survival for millions of people. Moreover, relations between the killing squads of the SS and the units of the Wehrmacht were generally good, and the Wehrmacht earned the praise of Nazi ideologues for assembling Jewish civilians and cordoning off killing sites. Wehrmacht soldiers were often among the crowds of spectators who watched the gruesome murders carried out by the SS. By 1942–43, the Wehrmacht had created huge death zones in the Soviet Union in order to destroy the "racial" enemy.

Wette's indictment goes beyond the horrible events of World War II, which he surveys with precision and clarity. He analyzes how the Wehrmacht became such a willing partner of the Nazis and explores the long-term political and social consequences of the army leadership's attitudes. Long before the Nazis arrived on the political scene in the mid-1920s, the German army held highly prejudicial views of Jews, Slavs, and Bolsheviks and anticipated the Nazi Weltanschauung by turning them into the demonic amalgam "Jewish Bolshevism." Wette begins his book with an analysis of German perceptions of Russia precisely in order to counter notions of Germany's "fateful entanglement" in the East with precise facts about Germans' prior political views about Russia and the Soviet Union. He argues that the invasion of the Soviet Union in June 1941, in combination with the determination to fight the war as an all-or-nothing race war, was not simply a demented Nazi mission but was co-produced by the German army. Wette traces the long record of anti-Semitism in the army, which not only disdained Jewish officer candidates all along but also initiated in the middle of World War I the notorious "Jew count" in order to determine whether or not Germany's Jews were dying at the same rate as Christians (they were). Even before Hitler's prophecies in *Mein Kampf,* the restless war hero Erich Ludendorff imagined the next world war, drawing attention to both the future demands of total war and the necessity for racial cleansing in order to triumph. In short, terse, precisely formulated paragraphs, Wette presents the unassailable evidence, making a compelling argument for the long-term military preparation for fighting a racial war to guard Germany's future. There is no longer a credible foundation for the myth of a "good" Wehrmacht. And, as Wette shows, there is more and more willingness not simply among scholars but among ordinary German citizens to confront this record of complicity and of deeply rooted anti-Semitism in early-twentieth-century Germany. *The Wehrmacht* is a sobering argument for confrontation, not evasion, for history, not myth.

To try to understand "Barbarossa" as well as Stalingrad, and to begin to make sense of the actions of German murderers in Babi Yar, outside Kiev, on the way to Stalingrad, Wette plunges the reader into two chapters on how the German military viewed Russians and how it viewed Jews. This is the essential historical context for understanding the racially motivated violence on the eastern front. Then Wette presents the evidence for wide-ranging complicity of the army in crimes against civilians during World War II. He pursues the establishment of the myths that protected the "clean" Wehrmacht from indictment and finally the work of dismantling those myths. Wette's history is written in the active voice. This means that the Wehrmacht soldiers analyzed here did not merely find themselves in the Soviet Union, in inhospitable circumstances. Rather they put themselves there. They knew why they were on the eastern front and had been carefully trained for the work they set out to do. Wette's exposé has forced a new generation of Germans to confront the truth about the army's criminal activity in Nazi Germany's racial war. This book is an awful indictment of soldiers who are mostly dead now, but it is also a powerful statement of how Germany today acknowledges the crimes of the Wehrmacht.

Foreword

Manfred Messerschmidt

WOLFRAM WETTE'S AIM in this book is not just to provide a new description of the Wehrmacht's so-called "entanglement" in the campaign of annihilation on the eastern front in World War II, but rather to expose what this euphemistic term covers up: namely, the development of an ideology and perceptions of the enemy that set in long before 1933 and made the ideological solidarity between the Wehrmacht and National Socialism appear to nationalist circles as a plausible way to advance German power.

The transformation of Germans' perceptions of Russia into a threatening representation of "Jewish Bolshevists" cannot be ascribed to the National Socialists alone. The Reichswehr,[1] circles within the educated bourgeoisie, and even some voices within the churches played a role. It is here that root causes of the German army's participation in the Holocaust are to be found. Hitler did not need to compel the Wehrmacht to adopt his goals for the war on the eastern front. The generals were not "seduced" or "led astray."

Wette does not limit his discussion to abstractions or political theory, however. He shows how political ideology was connected with the course of events and decisions made by officers at various levels of the military hierarchy, and how this connection turned the Wehrmacht into co-perpetrators of the mass killings along with special units designed for that purpose.

Wette also covers one aspect of the war omitted in most accounts, namely, the attitudes and actions of the "average" German soldier—enlisted man and draftee—within the constraints of the National Socialist system and the requirement to obey orders. It emerges that the men impelled to resist on the basis of their Christian faith could not count on support from either of the major churches (Roman Catholic and Lutheran), whereas Jehovah's Witnesses knew that fellow members of their denomination would stand by them if they refused to serve in the Wehrmacht. The perspective of the "little guy" reveals in an especially vivid manner both the Wehrmacht's share in the Holocaust as part of the regular division of labor and the documented efforts of the generals to instill ideology. This represents an important dimension of Wette's research, which he has been pursuing for some time now, into the Second World War "as seen from below."

Such an approach has a bearing, furthermore, on the second major theme of this book, as the author traces how the role of the Wehrmacht was addressed after the war—a history of misrepresentation, concealment, and falsification the influence of which has not been eradicated to the present day. In this case we are dealing with the "achievement" of a broad conservative coalition that was made easier by the climate of the Cold War, and to which the military, the courts, and politicians interested in German rearmament made decisive contributions. Wette documents this history with persuasive examples of a strategy of concealment that has had lasting effects not only on the development of a military tradition within the Bundeswehr[2] but on German historiography as well, with the result that research on military history and on the Holocaust proceeded along independent tracks. Only in recent years has the taboo been shattered that permitted no connection to be made.

Wette's book thus represents a necessary step in the early stages of reconceiving the past. It demonstrates how the findings of earlier critical studies can be incorporated into a new overall picture, and does so impressively, as it is clearly organized and notably well written. Few books prove as thought-provoking as this one.

Abbreviations

CDU	Christlich-Demokratische Partei, Christian Democratic Party
DDP	Deutsche Demokratische Partei, German Democratic Party
DNVP	Deutschnationale Volkspartei, German National People's Party
DVLP	Deutsche Vaterlandspartei, German Fatherland Party
IMT	International Military Tribunal
NMT	Nuremberg Military Tribunal
OKH	Oberkommando des Heeres, Army High Command
OKW	Oberkommando der Wehrmacht, Armed Forces High Command
SA	Sturm Abteilung, Storm Troops
SD	Sicherheitsdienst, "Security Service" (i.e., Intelligence Service of the SS)
SPD	Sozialdemokratische Partei Deutschlands, Social Democratic Party of Germany
SS	Schutzstaffel, SS
USPD	Unabhängige Sozialdemokratische Partei Deutschlands, Independent Social Democratic Party of Germany

THE WEHRMACHT

CHAPTER ONE

Perceptions of Russia,
the Soviet Union, and Bolshevism as Enemies

IN 1941 THE GENERALS of the Wehrmacht were prepared to wage an unprecedented kind of war against the Soviet Union, motivated by ideology and designed to exterminate specific ethnic groups within the population. Today these facts are no longer in dispute. What we still need, however, is an explanation of the underlying causes of their behavior. How did it come about that the generals of the Wehrmacht were willing to embrace Hitler's plan for a war based on racial ideology and use their powers of command to carry it out? A study of the period immediately preceding the German attack on the Soviet Union cannot provide a fully satisfactory answer to this question, for several strands of the ideology behind the war of annihilation against the Soviet Union originated much earlier. One consists of the traditional attitudes regarding war and the necessity for it that characterized first Prussian and then German military history; a second strand comprises the traditions of the authoritarian state and the corresponding submissive attitude inculcated in the population. Third is the tradition of anti-Semitism, and fourth and last the perceptions of Russia and attitudes about the Soviet Union and Bolshevism prevalent in Germany.

Our first task will be to reconstruct German perceptions of Russia at that time. It is necessary to understand that what the Wehrmacht generals knew about the Soviet Union in the year 1941 and how they viewed its inhabitants had considerable political significance. This is because the military elite represented an essential source of power within the National Socialist state.

Descriptions of the Wehrmacht as the "second pillar" of the National Socialist state and its "guarantor of steel" indicate not only that the Wehrmacht was an enormous instrument of force, but also that the officers at the top could have played an independent role in power politics, had they wished to do so. It is the fact that as a rule they showed no inclination to make use of this power that needs to be explained.

The military leaders rejected democracy because they regarded it as a weak form of government, and they welcomed the reestablishment of an authoritarian state under Hitler. They had failed to grasp the significance of the fact that countries with democratic governments had been able to defeat Germany in World War I because they were better able to motivate and mobilize their populations. Prejudice against pluralism in politics prevented the German military leaders from drawing any connection between the two.

And, finally, one obvious fact is often overlooked: even though Hitler was a dictator who succeeded in making himself supreme commander of the Wehrmacht in 1934, he could not plan, prepare, and wage his wars alone; he needed the close cooperation of the military elite, that is, the generals of the army and the air force, the naval leadership, and their general staffs. In fact, if we leave aside concerns about technical feasibility occasionally voiced by military experts, the plans for war were supported by a far-reaching consensus.

German Perceptions of Russia in the Twentieth Century

Views of Foreign Countries and Their Political Significance

Do the images that inhabitants of one country create about another country have any lasting influence on the way the two nations get along? Or does no such political significance exist in reality? In general terms, one can say the following: under certain circumstances the ideas that people develop about other nations can have significantly greater political import than does reality. Often the real conditions prevailing in a foreign country are unknown, and thus the images that people have stand in for the reality. Such images provide an orientation for people's thinking, and sometimes for their actions as well. Even if these images bear only a very small resemblance to reality, they can represent an important factor in politics. The power of images lies not in the degree to which they reflect reality but in that fact that people believe them. Vivid proof of this is available, in the conflict-laden history of Russo-German relations, in the perceptions of Russia that can be documented on the German side.

Naturally such observations do not answer the question of how a particular image of Russia became established in people's minds. And indeed there is no single answer, since many very diverse influences play a role in forming ideas about another country, and only rarely can one assign a precise identity to them. Nevertheless, in the development of German images of Russia in the twentieth century, certain driving forces existed which can indeed be named and described. By this I mean the political elites in Germany who devised the aggressively exaggerated images of Russia that were then disseminated as propaganda before and during the two world wars. That this occurred in a context of specific political and economic interests goes without saying. The function of such images was to convince Germans of the correctness and necessity of their leaders' political agenda, especially if it could be implemented only by using military force.

In these historical situations the images of foreign peoples took on the character of images of an enemy, and thus the degree to which they corresponded to reality meant even less than before. Images of foes distort reality. They serve not so much to provide information about other peoples as to motivate one's own side to prepare for and participate in a military conflict. The means by which images of the enemy are conveyed to the target audience is propaganda.

Mirroring in East and West

German images of Russia—and conversely Russian images of Germany—are the subject of ongoing research initiated by Lev Kopelev, the Russian writer and scholar of Germany who died in 1997. Founded in the 1980s, the Wuppertal Research Project on German-Russian Perceptions is an interdisciplinary investigation into the history of such images from earliest times to the twentieth century. Since 1985 the results have been published in the series *West-östliche Spiegelungen* (West-East Reflections).[1] The scholars participating in this undertaking want to find out not only "what Germans and Russians knew about each other in past centuries" but also "what German writers, scholars, diplomats, trade and research partners, and journalists thought and wrote about Russia and Russians; what their Russian contemporaries thought and wrote about Germany and Germans; and what image of the foreign nation developed from their writings."[2] In other words, the investigators' goal is to determine, in addition to the images themselves, the circumstances in which the images developed, who produced them, and how they were spread.

As far as the twentieth century is concerned, an additional aspect should be considered, for in this phase the writers, scholars, traders, and diplomats no longer played the major role in determining German perceptions of Russia. Instead, the political elites and their aides within the civil service entered the picture. They began working systematically to influence public opinion in Germany through decidedly politicized notions about Russia. This politicization is characteristic of twentieth-century German perceptions of Russia. Taking the form of a negatively tinged image of the Soviet Union, it became superimposed on—and at times even replaced—perceptions of Russia as the homeland of the Russian people and their culture. This politicized picture of the Soviet Union, however, was not specifically limited to Germany. It was developed in a similar manner by the political elites of all Western countries that opposed Communism.[3] Important new insights have arisen from research on specific aspects of German attitudes toward Russia during the Third Reich.[4] For an overview, however, it will be necessary to take a broader approach. Hence in what follows I consider several more general questions: What different perceptions of Russia existed in Germany in the twentieth century? Which of them represent the main trend that had a real effect, and which remained minority views without any influence on history? And in addition, we must consider whether particular perceptions emerged as focal points and how existing tendencies could be consolidated and intensified. Next, I try to provide a systematic summary of German perceptions of Russia in the twentieth century and identify the main categories into which they fall: cultural, Social Democratic, Communist, nationalistic and imperialistic, and racist.

Perceptions of Russia among the German Bourgeoisie

At the beginning of the twentieth century, no clearly defined image of czarist Russia existed in Germany. Germans regarded it as a "distant land," as puzzling, mysterious, and "Asiatic,"[5] and vague ideas circulated about the "Russian soul."[6] In Hermann Meyer's *Konversations-Lexikon* for 1866 the article on the Russian Empire states: "The common people are in the main cheerful, carefree, frugal, good-natured, but also gluttonous and intemperate; in some cases they can be cruel, suspicious, and sly. There is a strong tendency to thievery."[7] And an encyclopedia article of 1907 informed contemporaries that Russians were open and hospitable "but also indolent, disorderly, and given to drink." The article continues, "On its dark side the Russian character displays a love of material pleasures and an inclination to guile, thievery, and graft."[8] It is evident that this characterization hardly bothers to conceal an attitude of assumed cultural superiority.

Political relations between Prussia, and later Germany, on the one hand and Russia on the other during the nineteenth century tended more toward cooperation than enmity, despite tensions arising now and again from German nationalism and Russian pan-Slavism.[9] In particular, Bismarck's foreign policy (up to 1890), which emphasized Prussian/German and Russian joint action at the expense of the Poles, tended to favor the positive patterns of perception. Within the framework of these political conditions, the educated German middle class developed an image of Russia in which that country's cultural achievements predominated. This way of seeing the country was characterized by interest and understanding—the very opposite of the perceptions of Russia that would come to play such a role in the history of the twentieth century—although at the same time it was connected with a sense of superiority, as we have seen. The German admirers of Russia's culture, however, were not especially interested in political conditions there or in the misery of working people, choosing instead to emphasize Russian literature, philosophy, and art, and the long tradition of cultural ties between the two countries.[10] The tradition was exemplified by the great German philosopher Gottfried Wilhelm Leibniz (1646–1716), who suggested the founding of the Imperial Academy of Sciences in St. Petersburg in the seventeenth century and collaborated effectively with Peter the Great on the czar's reforms.[11]

The list of great Russians who were and are admired in Germany includes the names of Aleksandr Pushkin, Nikolay Gogol, Ivan Turgenev, Fyodor Dostoyevsky, Leo Tolstoy, Anton Chekhov, Maksim Gorky, Boris Pasternak, and Aleksandr Solzhenitsyn. It is important to recall, in the words of the German historian Fritz Fischer, that "for more than a hundred years, from the 1870s and 1880s to the present day, the great works of Russian literature had a profound emotional and intellectual impact on the educated German bourgeoisie, creating a sense of connection with Russia that remained constant throughout all the changes of governments and even wars and revolutions."[12]

Prior to the First World War, whole communities of Russian university students were to be found in Berlin, Heidelberg, Dresden, Leipzig, and Jena.[13] Russian artists and scholars served on the faculties at German academies and universities. The First World War put an end to most of these activities, and the Bolshevist revolution in October 1917 dealt a further blow to perceptions of Russia as the home of intellectual and cultural elites. When the revolutionaries deprived the never very numerous Russian bourgeoisie of what power they had been able to exert, their German counterparts viewed it quite understandably as a potential political threat.

Nevertheless, a German-Russian cultural exchange resumed in the 1920s, though on a limited scale. German writers traveled throughout Russia, as did thousands of Communist workers, and reported their impressions at home. The pictures of Russia that they developed would make an interesting research topic, since one would assume that they came very close to reality.

Scholarly contacts in the period between the world wars reached a certain peak when the prominent German scientist Max Planck led a delegation to Leningrad on the occasion of the two hundredth anniversary of the Academy of Sciences and gave a speech on the unifying effect of science.[14] A conference of German and Soviet historians was held in Berlin in 1928. But the links between scientists and scholars were only part of a far larger cultural network that also included theatrical presentations, films, and exhibits. All of this ceased when Hitler came to power in 1933.[15]

It must be said, however, that the mostly well-educated Germans whose image of Russia was dominated by its cultural achievements did not represent a particularly powerful interest group. It was very different in the case of groups who viewed Russia through other lenses—especially imperialist, racist, and anti-Bolshevist ones. Thus the cultural image remained a relatively minor factor in terms of its influence in Germany.

The Social Democrats' View of Russia

There is good reason to speak of a distinctive Social Democratic perception of Russia. Its outstanding characteristic was its emphasis on politics. Conditions in Russia were viewed in each instance through the lens of German Social Democrats' own convictions and assessed accordingly. Such perceptions were, as a rule, not imperialist, militaristic, or racist. The Social Democrats developed positions on the changing political systems in Russia, first on the czarist autocracy, and then on the no less autocratic Communist system in the form of Stalinism.[16] Within Germany they recognized the Communists as a political party in competition with Social Democratic ideals and hence, in the abstract at least, as a political opponent.[17]

Before the First World War, German Social Democrats tended to have anti-Russian attitudes only to the extent that they rejected the rule of the czars, who sought to seal the country off from all democratic impulses, as autocratic and socially unjust. During the Russian revolution of 1905, the Social Democrats' sympathies lay with the revolutionaries. Their leader August Bebel was even prompted to make martial statements, though already an old man. He announced that if there should ever be a war against czarist Russia and its brutally repressive system, he himself would be ready to "shoulder his rifle." He regarded the country as the "stronghold of reaction" in Europe and held its political system responsible for Russia's failure to develop a modern economy.[18]

The anti-czarist views of the Social Democratic deputies in the Reichstag strongly influenced the stance they took at the start of the First World War. If the aim was now to defeat the "stronghold of reaction," they would not stand idly by. The question is whether the leaders of the German Social Democratic Party (SPD) were sufficiently aware that the troops on the other side of the front lines consisted of the very same Russian peasants whom they in principle wished to liberate from the yoke of the czars. Rosa Luxemburg addressed precisely this danger of a breakdown of solidarity between

ordinary working people in the countries at war when she commented, "The dividends are rising while the proletariat falls."[19]

The mood following the outbreak of war caused some Social
Democratic politicians to use phrases that could have originated
with the Kaiser's own propagandists. For example, Gustav Noske, an
SPD deputy in the Reichstag, wrote in the Chemnitz newspaper the
Volksstimme (Voice of the People) that "at this moment we all recognize it as our first duty to fight against the repressive yoke of Russian rule. We will not allow German women and children to become
the victims of Russian bestiality nor permit Cossacks to ravage German fields . . . We will defend every last inch of German culture and
German freedom against a ruthless and barbaric foe."[20]

Such a statement signaled a tendency to adopt the negative image
of Russia prevailing in Germany now that the country was at war.
The outbreak of open hostilities thus represents one of the key mo-
ments in which a primarily negative German perception of Russia
became dominant.[21] After the two Russian revolutions of 1917—the
Menshevik uprising in February and the Bolshevik revolution in October—the Social Democrats found themselves with mixed feelings:
many sympathized with the Russians as they tried to shake off the
oppressive czarist regime; but they also roundly rejected Lenin's
autocratic and undemocratic manner of governing. Furthermore,
the SPD from then on feared the Russian Communists' calls for
world revolution, since it was directed at their own voter base in the
working class and threatened to provide serious competition for the
party's own reform program. Nevertheless, the SPD retained a fundamentally positive attitude toward Russia in the decade after the
revolution, a circumstance that was for a short time reflected in
the German government's foreign policy. The same political and
ideological view of Communist Russia also characterized the Social

Democrats' policy after 1945, albeit with a clear renunciation of the use of force. Overall, the history of the Social Democratic Party reveals no racist tendency to disparage Slavic peoples.

"A Peaceful Power": German Communists' Pro-Russian Image

Among all twentieth-century perceptions of Russia that included the political and social system and were not restricted to cultural matters, the only positive image emerged from German Communists. Their image of the young Soviet Union of the 1920s drew on idealizations of the Russian Revolution and the insurgent proletariat. Lenin's success in power politics also played a major role in German Communists' perceptions of Russia. In the process they failed to reflect sufficiently on the actual differences that existed in economic development between Germany, an industrialized country, and the Russian agrarian state, which in 1917 contained only a small population of industrial workers. The Communists' relatively uncritical views stressed German-Soviet friendship instead.[22]

During the Weimar Republic the image of Russia represented by the German Communist Party (KPD) and its associated organizations was entirely dominated by efforts to support the role of revolutionary Russia in world politics. At the same time, the voter base of the KPD between the world wars represented only about 10 percent of the population.

Perceptions of Russia in Nationalist and Imperialist Circles

The nationalistic view of Russia had a far greater degree of influence in Germany. It consisted essentially of two trains of thought. The first ran: Russia is immense, but structurally weak. Contemporary propaganda expressed this idea in the image of the "colossus with feet of clay." The second was extremely aggressive in nature. It was located in the context of a German "striving toward the East," a euphemism for German desires to seize eastern territories from Russia by force. Soon after the turn of the twentieth century—but by 1912 or 1913 at the latest—Germans began speaking of an "inevitable final struggle" for land between Slavic and Germanic peoples.[23] A wave of propaganda was created "against pan-Slavism and against the flood of Slavs threatening the Germanic peoples, but also against the Germans' archenemy, France."[24] Such an interpretation of a possible situation for future conflict was, however, once again connected less with a fear of being outnumbered by Slavs than with an interest in expansion for both strategic political and economic reasons, particularly into the Ukraine, the "breadbasket" of eastern Europe.

The first signs that this nationalistic and imperialist view of Russia was having an effect on policy can be identified in the period before the First World War. It became more influential in the years 1914–1918 and reached its peak in Germany's war of annihilation against the Soviet Union under Hitler in 1941–1945. Its advocates were German nationalists, from the extremist Pan-German League around the turn of the century to the fascist National Socialist German Workers' Party (NSDAP). But the crucial factor in historical terms is that this perception of Russia was represented within highly influential elite circles. It really did consist in part of a smug and condescending attitude toward the different levels of development in the two countries, which went hand in hand with racist comments even in the early days. A popular postcard from the year 1914 with a text about cleanliness is a typical example: "Little Father, your country is a disgrace! We're coming to cultivate you—and to disinfect while we're at it!"[25]

This sort of perception of Russia was shared by the fifty-six university professors who signed the famous appeal in October 1914 addressed to "the civilized people of the world." It presented the war as a struggle for survival that had been forced on a peace-loving Germany, and contained the following passage: "In the East the land is soaked with the blood of women and children butchered by the Russian hordes, and in the West our soldiers are being ripped apart by dumdum bullets. The nations with the least right to call themselves the defenders of European civilization are those which have allied themselves with Russians and Serbs and offer the world the degrading spectacle of inciting Mongols and Negroes to attack the white race."[26]

One characteristic of the nationalistic and imperialist view of Russia was the assumption that Germans were superior to the Russians and, more generally, to all Slavic peoples in terms of politics, economics, military might, and intellectual ability. This thinking, however, did not lead the German nationalists to act like German admirers of Russian culture and initiate constructive exchanges that might conceivably have reduced the disparities in economic development. Instead, it was given a belligerent twist: since the distribution of territory had left the Germans at a disadvantage, they were entitled to conquer "the East" by force, govern it, and exploit it economically. As the supporters of this kind of German power politics perceived the situation, the Russian Empire was enormous but at the same time weak. They assumed that if it were invaded by what they took to be a superior German army, it would quickly collapse. The course of the First World War seemed to confirm this belief. After the German government dictated the terms of the Brest-Litovsk peace treaty in the spring of 1918, Germany's expansionist ambitions were able to be fulfilled for a brief period.

Although Germany's real political possibilities were drastically curtailed by the peace treaty of Versailles in 1919, the nationalistic-imperialist view of Russia persisted below the surface in the period between the world wars.[27] At this point it began to take on the contours of an image of the Soviet Union. The nationalists of this era presented a new defensive variation, in which Germany represented a "wall" or "bulwark" against Bolshevism. The fact that nationalistic-imperialist perceptions of Russia lived on in Germany in this temporarily defensive form even during the Weimar Republic should not be overlooked in assessing the treaty of Rapallo.[28] At the same time, it should be stressed that anti-Bolshevist ideology was exploited in the 1920s in German domestic policy and used to hold disparate groups together.

It is striking that the right-wing nationalists' anti-Bolshevism was compatible with short-term efforts to cooperate, such as in joint exercises of the Reichswehr and the Red Army.[29]

Using the "bulwark" claim as a point of departure, Hitler was later able to implement his own program for seizing *Lebensraum* in the East. And Hitler built on older perceptions of Russia in other respects as well. Not least important among them was the utterly false assumption that Russia was "a colossus with feet of clay," which, as is well known, still characterized the thinking of the National Socialist leadership and top echelons of the Wehrmacht in 1941.[30] It is apparent that carryovers existed from one government to the next.

National Socialists' Perceptions of Russia: "Jewish Bolshevism"

Racist perceptions of Russia represent a specific, exaggerated form of the nationalistic view. They were particularly dangerous because they interpreted the disparate stages of economic development in Germany and Russia in racial terms. As a result, the Germans' sense of superiority toward Russians—in which they were not unique—acquired a "biological" foundation. In its simplest form, this view held that differences between the Germanic and Slavic races existed in nature, and that the former were more advanced.

Some early signs of a sense of superiority based on racist thinking had been present in Germany even before the First World War. It did not begin to play a role on the stage of world history, however, until the Hitler era,[31] or, more precisely, the Russian campaign from 1941 on.[32] The racist viewpoint formed the ideological core of Hitler's perceptions of Russia. Hitler was convinced that the Slavic race was incapable of forming its own state and hence had to be ruled by others. This was the reason why international "Jewish Bolshevism"—Hitler's term—had been able to establish its foreign-dominated rule in Russia in 1917.[33] The phrase of course implied that many or most of the leading figures in the Bolshevist regime were Jewish. To eradicate Jews and seize *Lebensraum* in the East were Hitler's two main goals.

Hitler's perceptions of Russia thus identified two enemy groups. First, they led him to oppose Russian Jews within the context of his program to annihilate the Jews of Europe. In addition to this anti-Semitic strand, they had an anti-Slavic component. In the views of the time, which were promoted by Hitler and by SS propaganda in particular during the war, Germans were supposed to regard not only Jews, or "Jewish Bolsheviks," as racially inferior—*Untermenschen*[34]—but Slavs as well. National Socialist ideology declared that these two groups did not deserve to be treated in accord with international law. In the German empire of the future, "the greater German Reich," which would reach from the Atlantic Ocean to the Urals, Slavs were to play the role of slave labor and serve the master race.[35]

This, in a nutshell, was the National Socialist image of Russia. Its most striking feature was the way it gathered together all the negative clichés about Russia and the Soviet Union current in Germany at the time and assembled them into a single portrait of the enemy. The image of Russia devised by National Socialist propaganda had several components which could be applied in various configurations depending on the tactical needs of the moment.[36] It combined the traditional nationalistic sense of German superiority with a violently aggressive anti-Bolshevism that could be turned on and off like a recording and correspondingly exploited. It also created a connection to the racist elements mentioned earlier, that is, anti-Semitism and anti-Slavism. These facets of the German image of the enemy were further interwoven with German fears of the great power to the east and its supposedly "Asiatic" nature, which, the propagandists claimed, threatened the continued existence of the West.

In this manner a diffuse complex of perceptions about the enemy arose that made it possible to combine the waging of war with racial policies.[37] The function of the images of Russia put forward in National Socialist propaganda is obvious: it was to inculcate in German soldiers, both members of SS units and the regular troops in Russia, attitudes that would enable them to carry out the program of racial ideology whose core elements consisted of the "final solution" and a German empire in the East.[38]

What was new in these perceptions, and what had been carried over from earlier times? Fritz Fischer stresses the continuity between the older pan-German form of expansionism under Kaiser Wilhelm and Hitler's policy of conquest, while at the same time drawing certain distinctions as follows: "A new aspect attributable to Hitler is the intensification of this policy to a degree that made it criminal— treating the Polish and Russian population as slave laborers, and allowing millions of Russian prisoners of war to starve to death, a crime for which the Wehrmacht shares a good deal of the blame. And the murder of millions of European Jews should probably be ascribed to Hitler alone."[39]

The specific way, described earlier, in which the National Socialists gathered together several older images of Russia, intensifying them and making them more pointedly aggressive, and combined them with an anti-Semitism bent on annihilation made this the most momentous of all twentieth-century German views of Russia, and the one with the greatest consequences for history.

The view expressed in the National Socialists' propaganda phrase "Jewish Bolshevism" must be clearly distinguished from attitudes toward Russia or the Soviet Union that, while also anti-Communist or anti-Bolshevist, contained no racist elements. Those who took the latter position concentrated on criticism of the political and social system. Political perceptions of the Soviet Union along these lines formed part of the Social Democratic image of Russia from 1918 on, and were also typical of non-socialist images of Russia throughout the West.[40] The typical National Socialist conflation of anti-Semitic and anti-Slavic elements came to an end in 1945 with the Allied victory over Germany, but perceptions characterized by anti-Communism or anti-Bolshevism lived on after the end of the war.[41] For West Germans it formed one of the few ideological links between the wartime and postwar eras.

Perceptions of Russia among the Wehrmacht Generals

The Reichswehr and the Wehrmacht before 1940

If the aim is to identify the intellectual and political milieu of the officers in the Reichswehr and later the Wehrmacht, one can hardly

go wrong in seeking them first among the proponents of the nationalistic-imperialist view. But recent research has enabled us to make
some interesting differentiations.[42] It is known that during the years
of the Weimar Republic, the Reichswehr and the Red Army at one
point conducted joint maneuvers. The Soviet Union—like Germany
one of the defeated powers in the First World War—provided the
Reichswehr with an opportunity to carry out intensive testing procedures and exercises on Russian soil that were forbidden in Germany
itself. The weapons training connected with these exercises later
enabled Hitler's Wehrmacht to assemble the first armored units
(panzers) and Luftwaffe squadrons by the mid-thirties. The intensive cooperation over a period of several years between Reichswehr
and Red Army officers[43] resulted in perceptions of Russia on the
Germans' part that were by no means purely negative.[44] In addition,
the cooperation between two groups with such different ideological
orientations can be interpreted as an indication that a sense of international professional solidarity existed among career officers, as in
other professions, even when the nation-states to which they belonged were waging war on one another.

Furthermore, one finds that among the younger Reichswehr officers in the 1920s there were a good many who did not transfer
their domestic political antipathies—to liberals, Communists, or Social Democrats—to the international arena. Specifically, this might
mean that they were primarily hostile not toward the Soviet Union
but rather toward the Treaty of Versailles, the newly established republic in Germany, and Poland. In some cases, officers' prevailing
attitudes were even anti-western and anti-liberal, which made them
quite well suited to conduct joint exercises with the Soviet Union.
From "Thoughts on War in the Future," which Lieutenant Colonel
Joachim von Stülpnagel, a planner for the Reichswehr, wrote in

1924, for example, it emerges that he regarded France and Poland as Germany's main enemies.[45] Pragmatic thinkers accepted the dictum of power politics that foreign policy took precedence over all other areas. Hence one could be opposed to Bolshevists, socialists, and pro-democracy groups at home but still advocate military cooperation with the Bolshevist Soviet Union. This position could be found within the Reichswehr, too.

When German officers had an opportunity to get to know a country as vast as Russia on their many official visits, what were the main impressions they brought home with them? Clearly they shared one overall impression, namely, that the Communist leadership had been successful in eliminating Russia's traditional inferiority complex in dealing with foreigners, and that the country was experiencing a dynamic phase with accompanying hopes for both cultural and economic development.[46] Colonel Wilhelm Keitel expressed himself in much the same terms in 1931, when he was serving as head of the Organization Department in the Troop Office; this is the same man who as field marshal and chief of staff of the Armed Forces High Command signed criminal orders and brusquely rejected all criticism of Hitler's plans for a war of annihilation.[47]

More than a few German officers were favorably impressed by what they called "the healthy militarism" of the Soviet state. By this they meant "its whole-hearted propagation of defense and the great value of the military for society,"[48] that is, a high regard for career military men, both in society at large and in the political sphere, which the officers of the Reichswehr sorely missed at home, given that the climate in the Weimar Republic tended to be antimilitary and Germany was limited to a 100,000–man army.

It is important to recall that it was the young staff officers of the Reichswehr in the 1920s who became the Wehrmacht generals of the 1940s and led the war of annihilation against the Soviet Union. The generals on the other side were not their old comrades from the earlier joint exercises, however, for most of those men had fallen victim to Stalin's purges in 1937 and 1938.

Occasionally one finds a Reichswehr officer voicing extreme racist views about Russian officers even before 1933. When the Soviet general and politician Mikhail Tukhachevsky visited Berlin in 1932, a captain named Hans Krebs described official guests in the delegation as "a sly and cunning Jew, . . . [and] a Jewish half-breed . . . insincere, with a suspicious and treacherous nature, apparently a fanatic Communist."[49] Language of this sort clearly belongs to the ideological prehistory of the racist war of annihilation that followed. As an expert on Russian affairs and a loyal National Socialist, Krebs was posted to the German embassy in Moscow in 1936 as acting military attaché in place of General Ernst August Köstring; as such he played a not unimportant role in the grossly inaccurate estimation of the Red Army, mentioned earlier.[50] In the final phase of the war (on March 29, 1945), Hitler made Krebs, by now an infantry general, acting chief of staff of the army. After Hitler's death, Krebs tried unsuccessfully to open negotiations with the Red Army. He then committed suicide in the Reich chancellery on May 1, 1945.

In 1933 Hitler's new government broke off the joint activities of the Reichswehr and the Red Army, to the regret of more than a few officers. Among them was Colonel Walter von Reichenau, who, having just been named head of the Ministerial Office of the Reichswehr Ministry, occupied a key political position under Hitler's devoted minister of defense, General Werner von Blomberg. Interestingly, Reichenau assured a member of the Soviet embassy staff in Berlin in June 1933 that the Reichswehr stood behind "developing and intensifying German-Soviet friendship, just as in the old days."[51] Eight years later, when the Soviet Union was attacked, Reichenau—

by then a field marshal and commander of the Sixth Army—would act as one of the most ardent proponents of racial ideology and the war of annihilation.[52]

In the 1930s the German military's perceptions of Russia began to be affected by the diminishing flow of information about the Soviet Union and its armed forces. This deficit encouraged a tendency to fall back on old clichés, and they replaced reality to an ever greater degree as time passed. Stalin's purges were interpreted within German military circles as a "beheading" of the Red Army, depriving it of leaders and weakening even further a force that lacked modern technology in any case.[53] In fact, the purges wiped out virtually the entire top leadership. According to one Russian military historian, the army was lacking 120,000 senior officers in June 1941 as a result.[54] From this perspective the traditional image in Germany of the "colossus with feet of clay" could gain new currency.[55]

Ideological Solidarity in 1941

In the 1970s the well-known military historian Andreas Hillgruber decided to investigate the Wehrmacht generals' ideas about Russia in the period from July 1940 to June 1941, that is, during the planning phase of the Russian campaign. His study appeared in 1978.[56] In it he focused on the circle of people directly concerned with the preparations for war,[57] and his conclusions largely confirmed what had been known before. According to Hillgruber, the following elements typified the perceptions of Russia among the German military elite in 1940–41:

1. They had relatively little current information about the Soviet Union, its armed forces, or its industrial potential.

2. Hence, they fell back on the traditional notion that Rus-

sia remained a "colossus with feet of clay," which would quickly collapse if attacked by a strong force from outside.

3. They viewed the entire country from a relatively narrow military perspective, which in the absence of specific intelligence also tended to increase reliance on older stereotypes.

4. These included a tendency to underestimate the military capabilities of the Red Army, particularly within the leadership, although ordinary Russian soldiers were credited with being tough and dogged fighters.

5. At the same time, they overestimated the capabilities of the Wehrmacht, particularly in the euphoria following the rapid fall of France in 1940.

6. As a result, they predicted that the Wehrmacht could win a war against the Soviet Union in six to eight weeks.[58]

In Hillgruber's view, even though most of the military was caught up in a rather traditional view of Russia, Hitler was able to push through his concept of a war of annihilation based on racial ideology with the help of "several military leaders."[59] More recent research suggests the related hypothesis that in 1941 a genuine ideological solidarity was achieved between Hitler and the generals of the Wehrmacht. In order to explain how this could come about, it will first be necessary to discuss currents of anti-Semitism already existing within the German military.

At this point, however, we can already say that in the spring of 1941 the staff officers of the Wehrmacht and the army had accepted and "identified themselves with Hitler's intentions to a large extent."[60] There can be no doubt that the perceptions of Russia dominated by racial ideology were now in the mainstream, and that they and not others shaped history. The scattered protests that occurred—against the decree to execute civilian political commissars who fell into German hands, for example—had no real possibility of affecting the course of events. In other words, from the time of the attack on, an image of Russia couched in terms of racial ideology (along with notions of annihilation and "criminal orders") determined the character of military actions, and not the remnants of a less radical, more traditional image that continued to exist among some segments of the military elite. A comparison can help to sum up the situation: unlike the Red Army, the Wehrmacht in 1941 needed no political commissars to provide the troops with an ideological indoctrination; the German generals were taking care of this need themselves.

Of course, it should not be overlooked that opposition existed within both the German diplomatic corps[61] and the Wehrmacht. Those who spoke out remained isolated, however, and were unable to change the course of official policy in any phase of the war. Furthermore, one historian who studied the attitudes of the German resistance toward Hitler's Russian policy and the war in the East[62] reached the conclusion "that even during the war many of Hitler's opponents could not let go of the anti-Bolshevism—sometimes of a militant kind—that had been stressed so much in Nazi propaganda of the 1930s."[63] Even in these circles the Soviet Union was accepted as the "proper" enemy, on the basis of a "fundamentally anti-Bolshevist unanimity" and probably also to some extent a racist attitude toward the Slavic population.[64]

The ideas about Russia that had become firmly fixed in the minds of the Wehrmacht elite thus continued the tradition of nationalistic currents present in certain circles of German society since the turn of the century. This image already had racist or anti-Slavic tendencies and was framed and propagated in the context of an "Asian peril" threatening the West. After the Russian Revolution of October 1917 and the German Revolution of 1918, a highly emotionally charged picture of the enemy arose among right-wing nationalists and in parts of the educated German bourgeoisie, which could be mobilized against the Soviet Union. These two strands of the nationalistic perceptions of Russia were characteristic of officers of the Reichswehr in the 1920s and later of the Wehrmacht. It was Adolf Hitler who then fused the idea of an "Asian peril" with anti-Semitism, anti-Bolshevism, and anti-Slavic racism.

CHAPTER TWO

Anti-Semitism in the German Military

WAS THERE A PARTICULARLY VIRULENT FORM of anti-Semitism circulating in the Wehrmacht between 1935 and 1945 that would explain why soldiers were willing to participate in murdering Jews? Or is it more likely that the levels of anti-Semitism in the Wehrmacht were similar to those found in German society at large? The forms that such an attitude could take varied widely, ranging from a vague feeling that Jews were an alien people to a belief that it would not be wrong to exclude them from public life altogether, and culminating in the "eliminationist anti-Semitism" of which Daniel Jonah Goldhagen has written.[1] We do not know how many Germans espoused this last murderous belief. Were there 100,000 of them, or perhaps more?

What seems more important than numbers, however, is the fact that the most extreme form of anti-Semitism was able to gain ground only because a general prejudice against Jews existed in the first place. Clearly the killers could count on many people who sympathized in secret simply to look the other way. In this context, what is crucial is that the authorities—in this case the National

Socialist government and the agencies responsible for soldiers, the Armed Forces High Command (OKW) and the Army High Command (OKH)[2]—opened the way for the murders to be committed; they made it possible for the killing of Jews to be organized and carried out as official acts of the state.

From Anti-Semitism to the Holocaust?

Any scholar researching the subject of anti-Semitism in the German military, and trying to ascertain how much of a role it played in events, will soon encounter a rather odd situation. Although some research exists on the history of anti-Semitism in Germany in general (most of it done by Jewish scholars, incidentally),[3] there are virtually no studies on anti-Semitism within the military in particular. Hence we still know relatively little today about possible continuity in anti-Semitic attitudes that might have extended from the nineteenth century up to the Second World War. The best introduction to the subject remains Manfred Messerschmidt's 1996 article with the somewhat misleading title "Jews in the Prussian and German Armies."[4] His essay contains a whole series of observations about anti-Semitism in the German armed forces before the Second World War. Apart from this, however, it is striking that even such an outstanding study of the Reichswehr as the article by Rainer Wohlfeil in the *Handbuch zur deutschen Militärgeschichte* (Handbook of German Military History) omits all mention of the subject.[5] The English historian F. L. Carsten, by contrast, has quite a few things to say on the topic in his political history of the Reichswehr.[6]

On the whole, the subject of anti-Semitism in the Reichswehr has not been much investigated up to now. What does exist is a whole series of studies on Jews who served in German armies in various periods, in which the pervasive theme is their willingness to perform military service in order to gain recognition from German society at large. Horst Fischer studied this phenomenon in connection with the wars of liberation against Napoleon in the early nineteenth century.[7] Several other studies date from before the First World War or from the Weimar Republic. Most of the authors were Jewish, and their aim was to provide documentary evidence of Jewish Germans' patriotism as expressed by their military service (in many cases voluntary).[8] Various publications of the Reichsbund jüdischer Frontsoldaten (League of Jewish Front Soldiers),[9] which represented these veterans' interests in the public sphere, should also be mentioned. The authors of studies on Jewish soldiers in the First World War[10] and the Jewish Veterans' League[11] strive to make the same point.

A perspective similar to that of this early pro-Jewish scholarly literature is displayed by German publications of a certain type from the 1960s onward. Here the authors' goal—certainly praiseworthy in itself—is to refute the anti-Semitic slogans of previous decades and confirm what Jewish organizations had always claimed and documented with statistics, namely, that Jewish Germans were no less patriotic than Germans of other faiths. This tendency is apparent in the documentation titled *Kriegsbriefe gefallener deutscher Juden* (Wartime Letters of Fallen German Jews), first published in 1935 and reprinted in 1961.[12] The political significance of the new edition was heightened through the addition of commentary by Franz Josef Strauss, then the German federal minister of defense. Strauss noted that the soldiers' letters from the First World War offered "wonderful proof of the patriotic attitude of German Jews and an incontrovertible refutation of Nazi propaganda, which strove to depict Jewish fellow citizens as cowardly, corrupt, and treacherous by nature."

In another passage Strauss explained that it was his wish "to show our Jewish fellow citizens and soldiers in Germany in the right perspective again, after their memory was desecrated by the National Socialists." He admitted, however, that such an attempt could have only a modest effect in view of "the great problem of anti-Semitism and the atrocities connected with it."[13]

When the Federal Ministry of Defense commissioned a traveling exhibition, "German Jewish Soldiers, 1914–1945," the result (assembled by the Military History Research Office) took a similar line.[14] The catalogue for this exhibition, published in 1982, also contains informative accompanying texts. Richard Stücklen, president of the Bundestag at the time, explained that the exhibit was linked with a "national policy concern," insofar as its goal was "to contribute to the rehabilitation of Jewish soldiers" who had fought bravely for their German fatherland as a matter of course.[15] The head of the Military History Research Office, a Bundeswehr officer, emphasized for his part that "the declared aim of the exhibit . . . [was] to serve in rehabilitating German Jewish soldiers who had hoped to achieve full recognition as citizens by their military service for the fatherland, but who were denied the fruits of their efforts by the National Socialists."[16]

The German Jewish soldiers were thus to be "rehabilitated," a term that can only mean retroactively defending them from slanderous attacks. One wonders what audience was being addressed. The sponsors did not answer this question explicitly. In any case, it did not include Germans who had never denigrated Jews, for they had never needed convincing that anti-Semitic propaganda did not describe the Jewish soldiers. But it remains an open question: Were the accusations of slander directed at modern-day anti-Semites, perhaps the members of the older generation who had never shaken off the influence of pre-1945 patterns of thinking? Or did the exhibitors mean those Germans who, in Franz Josef Strauss's words, had defamed Jews as "cowardly, corrupt, and treacherous" during the First World War, that is, declared anti-Semites? In other words, was the exhibit more of a retrospective and theoretical exercise, intended to highlight an earlier current of right-wing thinking? Did it mean to identify as slanderers those officers in the Prussian Ministry of War who in 1916 ordered the "head count" of Jews in the Prussian-German army that caused such enormous outrage? Or the free corps officers[17] who assassinated prominent Jewish politicians during the Weimar Republic? Or only the anti-Semites of the Nazi period in the SS and the Wehrmacht who carried out the extermination of Jews?

One can recognize in all of this an attempt to limit responsibility for the extermination of the Jews of Europe during the Second World War, and to assign it solely to the National Socialists. The question of whether their racial anti-Semitism had any prior history was avoided for the most part, and the question of the extent to which anti-Semitism existed in the German military before Hitler (and of course during the Third Reich) has also remained unaddressed. Instead, the title of the exhibition, "German Jewish Soldiers," places the emphasis on the demonstrable existence of such men within its ranks, not on the presence of anti-Semitism. It is only consistent, then, that the 1982 catalogue ends with an essay on the rare but naturally gratifying instances in which German officers came to the aid of Jewish and "half-Jewish" comrades-in-arms.[18] The existence of such cases cannot and should not be disputed. Nevertheless, a historical approach that fails to place such noteworthy instances of personal courage in the overall context of the war and the Holocaust runs the risk of appearing defensive.

In 1997 the radical right-wing newspaper *Deutsche National-Zeitung* published a series of articles documenting the "patriotism of German Jews" to combat the "erroneous impression of an allegedly lasting antagonism between Germans and Jews." Citing Professor Herbert Weichmann, a "patriotic Social Democrat of Jewish origin," one article warned that "a dozen years of Hitler should not be made the permanent standard by which a people is judged."[19] The newspaper made the argument that the Hitler years should be viewed as a "historical accident" and cited a "flaming pro-German" article from the *Jüdische Rundschau* (Jewish Review) of August 7, 1914, "which could not have been outdone in its attitude by the Pan-Germans." It quoted further an article from the newsletter of the "Central Association of German Citizens of the Jewish Faith" from March 30, 1933, in which "patriotic German Jews" contradicted foreign press reports on outbreaks of anti-Semitic violence in Germany. Here, too, the message is that such "occurrences" aimed against Jews took place only during the Hitler era, and excludes the question of continuity. If one is looking for genuine explanations, however, this question must be faced.

Germany under the Kaiser and the First World War

The Officer Corps: Jews Need Not Apply

If one compares anti-Semitism in the pre–World War I German Empire with the anti-Semitic attitudes of earlier centuries, it is possible to identify several significant new developments.[20] First of all, it was the period when the pseudoscientific doctrine of fundamental biological differences among races was spreading and finding acceptance. As a consequence, attempts were made to provide existing prejudices with a scientific foundation and thereby give them additional importance (in a period when faith in science was enormous). Second, it must be noted that for the first time anti-Semitism now became organized. Political associations were founded—such as the Deutscher Handlungsgehilfenverband (German Clerks' League, a nationalist trade union), the Bund der Landwirte (Union of Agricultural Workers), and the Alldeutscher Verband (Pan-German League)—which made anti-Semitism part of their official program and treated Jews as if they were a distinct political interest group within the country. Among the publications used to further these goals was the *Kreuz-Zeitung*. Their anti-Semitic propaganda, which made use of all the modern media techniques of the day, was aimed first and foremost at people who feared a decline in their social status. Anti-Semitism gained a foothold in the parties on the right; in the (Catholic) Center Party and among German Social Democrats it found fewer supporters.

Since the Prussian officer corps was located on the far right of the political spectrum of the day—generally monarchist, in favor of an authoritarian state, anti-liberal, and opposed to the Social Democrats—the attitude of most of its members toward Jews can easily be guessed. And in fact the officer corps of the Prussian army under the Kaisers did display a fundamentally anti-Semitic bias. This manifested itself most clearly in the army's personnel policies. At the time neither a law nor official directives dictated that Jews—who were then defined primarily as members of a religious faith rather than as members of a race—were to be excluded as candidates for career officer.[21] On the contrary, their equal rights were protected by the constitution of the German Empire. Consequently, it represented a clear breach of fundamental law when in practice, Jewish civil servants and employees regularly experienced discrimination in promotions. The practice of excluding Jews from promotion to the officer corps in the Prussian army was equally unconstitutional, as was their exclusion from the ranks of reserve officers from 1885 on.[22]

Jews did not belong to the groups considered "desirable" within the exclusive caste of Prussian career officers.[23] The identity of these "desirable" groups was defined by Kaiser Wilhelm II in an order regarding additions to the officer corps of March 29, 1890: "In addition to the sons of noble families of the country, and the sons of my loyal officers and civil servants, who according to old tradition constitute the main pillars of the officer corps, I see the future standard-bearers of my army in the sons of those honorable bourgeois families in which love for their king and fatherland and respect for the military and Christian morals are cultivated and handed down."[24] In the case of Jews, such a policy permitted those in charge of personnel within the military to cite their lack of "Christian morals." The same lack was attributed to Social Democrats, who were unwelcome in the Prussian officer corps for political reasons. The latter were also charged with possessing an insufficient degree of "love for king and country." They were "unpatriotic fellows," and Prussian officers wanted nothing to do with them.[25] Since they feared that socialist ideas might nonetheless seep into military bases through the presence of draftees, they developed a system of surveillance methods.[26]

The main factor in Prussian officers' refusal to accept members of the Jewish faith was clearly anti-Semitic prejudice. It existed in rather distinct forms among the military leadership, who tended to be members of the aristocracy, and among reserve officers, whose origins were usually the middle and higher levels of the bourgeoisie. The American historian Werner T. Angress described the difference: "The anti-Semitism of the former was based on a traditional, deep-rooted and widespread antipathy toward a religious minority felt to be an alien element in a monarchical Christian state. The top officers regarded Jews as socially inferior, classed them politically as members of the democratic opposition or revolutionaries, and held their military abilities in low esteem. Such an attitude toward Jews was particularly prevalent in Prussia, the state within Germany that had the largest Jewish population." It was a "conventional" kind of anti-Semitism, according to Angress, "based largely on a long-standing sense of class superiority and rarely amounted to a blind, fanatical hatred." In some cases, officers from the aristocracy married wealthy Jewish women. The reserve officers from the bourgeoisie adopted the aristocrats' attitudes as a rule; but "on the eve of the First World War they belonged to a generation that had grown up in the 1890s and been shaped in their political thinking by the extremely nationalistic and anti-Semitic movement of that era. Furthermore, the reserve officers were far more susceptible than their superiors to the new kind of racially motivated anti-Semitism that had been introduced into German politics around the turn of the century."[27] In other words, there existed in the Prussian officer corps a rather moderate, conventional anti-Semitism as well as a more radical variant, a modern form based on racial ideology, which a few decades later, in the National Socialist era, would be raised to the level of official government ideology.

It should be noted that somewhat different conditions prevailed in Bavaria and Saxony than in Prussia. In the royal Bavarian and Saxon armies, Jews were able to become officers in the reserve until the turn of the century, and in isolated cases even active officers. This possibility led quite a few affluent Jewish families to leave Berlin, capital of both Prussia and the German Empire, and move to the other states so that their sons could acquire an officer's commission in the reserves. In the militarized society of that time, it was a seen as a highly desirable distinction.[28]

How did the exclusion of Jews from the Prussian officer corps work in practice? A decisive factor is that no order from the central command was needed to achieve the desired goal. Rather, the system which gave each regiment the right to select its own officers ensured that Jewish applicants for either the active professional military or the reserves had no chance of success.[29] In other words, anti-Semitism within the Prussian officer corps was a constant. Speaking to the Reichstag as part of the debate on the "Jewish question" on February 10, 1910, Colonel-General Josias von Heeringen admitted openly that a certain antipathy existed to the idea of promoting Jewish one-year volunteers to officers in the reserves. Avoiding the question of anti-Semitic prejudice within the officer corps, he stated "that among the common people the opinion can be found here and there that a Jew would not command the respect necessary for an officer's authority, and we have to take that into account."[30]

It represents no contradiction to the foregoing that when the Association of German Jews published a study titled "The Jewish Faith as an Impediment in Promotion to the Rank of Officer in the Prussian Reserves" in 1911, the author noted that twenty-six sons of Jewish parents had achieved that status.[31] It was because in all twenty-six cases the men had converted to Christianity to promote their assimilation. Despite the widespread aversion to Jews, the Prussian officer corps placed no obstacles in the way of converts. This fact confirms that before the First World War, Jews were defined far more by the religion they practiced than by heritage or race. Although the radical racial anti-Semitism of the bourgeois nationalists existed at that time, it did not set the general tone.

The Jewish "Head Count" of 1916

In the war years 1914–1918, the total Jewish population in Germany numbered about 500,000. Almost 100,000 men of Jewish background served in the armed forces—in the ranks, as noncommissioned officers, and a very small percentage as officers and medical officers. Twelve thousand German Jewish soldiers lost their lives in the First World War.[32] Thirty-five thousand Jewish soldiers received decorations of various kinds, including the medal "Pour le Mérite," the highest honor awarded.[33] These figures demonstrate that the Jewish citizens of Germany participated in the war and shared its burdens in the same way as other Germans. Many of the soldiers were volunteers. They wanted to establish themselves as loyal German patriots, as a way of promoting equal rights for Jews and their integration into German society.[34] A statement by a Jewish air force lieutenant from Württemberg named Josef Zürndorfer is typical of this group: "I joined up as a German, to protect my threatened country—but also as a Jew, to fight for full equal rights for the members of my religion."[35] Ludwig Frank, a noted Social Democratic member of the Reichstag from Mannheim, made a point of volunteering for the army very publicly in 1914;[36] he was killed in his first battle at the front. In the 1950s he was honored for his participation by West Germany when an army barracks in Mannheim was named after him.

When Kaiser Wilhelm II announced in 1914, at the start of the war, "I do not know parties any longer, I know only Germans," Jewish citizens felt included as part of the German nation. They rallied around the flag as quickly as other Germans, and the tone in the Jewish press was no less nationalistic than elsewhere. In fact, anti-Semitism in the Prussian-German army appears to have been on the decline during the first few months of the war. This can be explained first by the mood of euphoria pervading the nation and second by the fact that the army needed millions of men and was not prepared to exclude any group in the population, including Jews. But only a few months later, in the fall of 1914, this aspect of the domestic "truce" was threatened when the right-wing press—especially the organs of the Pan-Germans and the Reichshammerbund —resumed their anti-Semitic propaganda.[37] What disturbed the Jews in Germany even more than this, however, were the "unmistakable signs that anti-Semitism was noticeably on the rise in the army, namely, in the officer corps, where it was particularly the reservists who were setting the tone."[38]

Jews were forced to conclude that their efforts to prove themselves good patriots by participating in the war effort were not being appropriately honored everywhere. In the army itself, discrimination continued as Jewish soldiers were regularly passed over for pro motion.[39] Furthermore, the propaganda of the radical nationalists specifically targeted at Jews began to seep into the wider society; the claim—entirely without foundation—that Jews were not fighting at the front, that they were "cowards," "shirkers," and "war profiteers," gained wider acceptance when there were no military successes to report and economic and political problems related to the war arose within the country. Anti-Semitic propaganda could offer some relief from these adverse developments by providing a distraction and a scapegoat.

This was the situation when the Prussian Ministry of War initiated its notorious "Jewish head count" in the autumn of 1916. On October 11 General Wild von Hohenborn, the minister of war, issued an order for statistics to be gathered on the number of soldiers of the Jewish faith in the units of the Prussian army.[40] While the decree stated that no discriminatory intention lay behind the measure, contemporaries did not accept the claim, showing that even at the time the anti-Semitic impetus of the investigation was perceived. Many Jews regarded it as defamatory, and they were entirely correct. The *Israelitisches Familienblatt* (Israelite Family News) commented:

"Officials have declared that inflammatory articles in the press are the reason why statistics on Jews are being gathered. The official assurance that the Ministry of War is not pursuing any anti-Semitic goal with its head count cannot alter the shameful fact that these articles have appeared. The collection of statistics is in itself a concession to anti-Semites, who will be well aware of how they can exploit it. It is for just this reason that Bavaria has not taken the same step as Prussia and collected data on religious affiliation."[41]

The resulting statistics did not confirm the anti-Semites' expectations or provide fodder for their continuing propaganda. Hence the Prussian Ministry of War opted simply not to publish them, although several members of the Reichstag had demanded publication. As for the political effects of the defamatory head count of 1916, one must conclude that it drove a wedge between Jewish and non-Jewish soldiers. It also caused German soldiers who until then had not been exposed to anti-Semitic agitation to adopt a wait-and-see attitude, if not an even more distant one, toward their Jewish comrades in arms.

After the war the sociologist Franz Oppenheimer studied the "head count" and published a brochure titled "The Statistics on Jews Collected by the Prussian Ministry of War."[42] His results showed that relative to their numbers in the population, just as many Jews were fighting at the front as non-Jews. Oppenheimer was able to refute empirically all the talk about cowardice and shirking, but only after the fact: the head count of 1916 had long since affected political developments.

Ludendorff, Bauer, Tirpitz, Gebsattel, Keim, and Others

After Field Marshal Paul von Hindenburg took charge as the third supreme commander of the German army during the war, General

Erich Ludendorff and Lieutenant Colonel Max Bauer occupied politically powerful positions on his staff: Ludendorff was quartermaster general, and Bauer functioned as his political adviser. At the
same time, Bauer was liaison officer between the government and
the army supreme command, as well as a spokesman for the extreme right-wing Pan-German Party. Ludendorff and Bauer were
committed anti-Semites. They considered Jews to be shirkers and
profiteers, although they knew full well that the statistics collected
in 1916 had provided no foundation for such beliefs.

Bauer used the same anti-Semitic arguments that had led the
Prussian Ministry of War to gather data. In a memo sent to the Kaiser, the Crown Prince, and General Ludendorff, Bauer noted that the
army's strength was beginning "to crumble." Among the reasons for
this, he asserted, were poor morale on the home front, which was beginning to affect the army; the soldiers' concerns for the welfare
of their families at home; the lack of proper care for the war
wounded—and the Jews. "Lastly," he wrote, "there is a huge sense
of outrage at the Jews, and rightly so. If you are in Berlin and go to
the Ministry of Commerce or walk down the Tauentzienstrasse, you
could well believe you were in Jerusalem. Up at the front, by contrast, you hardly ever see any Jews. Virtually every thinking person
is outraged that so few are called up, but nothing is done, because
going after the Jews, meaning the capital that controls the press and
the parliament, is impossible."[43]

In the right-wing officers' hostile anti-Semitic view, Jews were
not only contemptible shirkers but also a powerful lobby in domestic
politics, able to direct the flow of capital and manipulate the press
and legislature. Hence Bauer, instead of offering rational arguments
against left-leaning liberals' and Social Democrats' support for a negotiated peace, tried to stir up emotions against them as "Jewish
freethinkers and international comrades."[44]

Max Bauer's ideological viewpoint was by no means an isolated case in the milieu of the armed forces. Lieutenant Colonel Hans Helfritz, chief of staff of an army corps, saw liberals through the same set of lenses. Writing to Erhard Deutelmoser, head of the war press office, he declared that the "hateful Jewish attacks" printed in the *Frankfurter Zeitung* "undermined the morale of all those who do not support the same disgraceful pacifistic goals." He demanded that these articles be "ruthlessly eliminated from the press."[45] Clearly, as we can see, journalists who supported a negotiated peace were characterized as Jewish, pacifist, disgraceful, and subverters of social unity. The term "eliminate" had also been introduced.

For Bauer, an officer whose thinking followed the political categories of the right-wing nationalists, the political situation within Germany in the spring of 1918 appeared polarized: on one side he saw loyal German idealists, especially in Prussia, who had not wavered in their desire to fight on to a victory, on the other the weak-kneed advocates of peace negotiations, "as flabby as old women." Bauer perceived them as the enemy within, so to speak. From this perspective several factors appeared as threats to continued prosecution of the war: the relatively weak national government, the majority parties in the Reichstag (the Social Democratic Party, the Center Party, and the left-of-center Progressive People's Party), the labor unions and people calling for strikes, along with "pigheaded or crooked legislators and agitators." What had an especially subversive effect was "the spread of a *Jewish* mentality (since this is in fact the dominant outlook of the Social Democrats, the *Berliner Tageblatt* [Berlin Daily News], the *Frankfurter Zeitung*, and so on)."[46] One can also recognize the function of this anti-Semitic propaganda: the powerful economic circles, political parties, media, and journalists who stood "on the other side" on domestic political issues were characterized as either "Jewish" or influenced by "a Jewish mentality." The picture of the enemy was therefore not in sharp focus but blurred around the edges; it was motivated at its core by anti-Semitic prejudice, but it could be expanded and exploited to include other groups as necessary. In other words, leading figures in the German military began using anti-Semitism as a tool for manipulation as early as 1917–18.

Ludendorff and Bauer may well have been among the inventors of the *Dolchstosslegende*, the legend of the "stab in the back," but at the very least they profited from it, since it drew attention away from their own responsibility not just for the war in general but for its prolongation and the ultimate defeat: "It was the pillars of the *Kaiserreich* (the army, bureaucracy, industry, the churches and universities) who, with the aid of the press, sermons, memoirs, lawsuits on trumped-up issues, and the historical profession (particularly official historiography), created this legend in order to distract attention from the locus of responsibility for the war and the military defeat, and to place the burden of these on Jews and Social Democrats."[47] The legend of the stab in the back had a genuinely anti-Semitic thrust, for the men alleged to be shirkers, both the munitions workers who went on strike and politicians from the socialist parties, were labeled "Jews" themselves or their ideas were called "Jewish-inspired." From this source arose the anti-Semitic verse that became popular in 1918: "Überall grinst ihr Gesicht, nur im Schützengraben nicht!" (Everywhere you see them grin, except in the trenches to help us win!)[48]

Ludendorff and Bauer believed that Jews had created a secret international organization to promote revolutionary movements in several countries, first Russia in 1917 and then Germany in 1918.[49] In 1919 Ludendorff "devoted himself to destroying the 'internationalist, pacifist, defeatist' Jews and the Vatican, people who 'systematically destroyed' our 'racial inheritance and national character.'"[50]

Such statements reveal few if any fundamental differences from Hitler's anti-Semitic perceptions of Jews as the enemy. Hence it is anything but an accident that the celebrated commander of the First World War, Erich Ludendorff, allied himself with Hitler in 1923 in an attempted putsch against the Weimar Republic, that he agreed to run for the Reichstag as a candidate of the National Socialist Party, and that in 1924 he succeeded in winning election. In his book *Kriegführung und Politik* (Warfare and Politics, 1922; revised edition 1923), the proclaimed anti-Semite wrote that Germany must be made *judenrein*—"free of Jews"—before the next war.[51] This idea anticipated Hitler's policies in the years 1933–1939. General Ludendorff's opinions on "total war" in the 1930s would be adopted by the National Socialist Party and most of the leadership of the Reichswehr.[52]

In 1917 the Pan-German politician Wolfgang Kapp founded a new party, the Deutsche Vaterlandspartei (German Fatherland Party, DVLP), which he hoped would attract all the various groups demanding that Germany fight on until victory and become a kind of "collective movement." A further goal of the party was to preserve the political dominance of the nobility and upper-middle class in the face of growing working-class strength.[53] The first chairman of this pre-fascist group was a naval officer, Grand Admiral Alfred von Tirpitz, who until March 1916 had been state secretary of the Imperial Navy Office. Tirpitz was revered by the entire nationalistic right wing and also idolized by the navy. Kapp tried several times to establish a military dictatorship with Tirpitz as chancellor,[54] and most career officers would have welcomed him as a political "strongman."

Close ties existed between the Fatherland Party and the Third Supreme Command of the army. A large number of former officers joined the DVLP; those on active duty were not permitted to be members of any political party. While Tirpitz appears to have distanced himself from anti-Semitism,[55] Ludendorff and Bauer were strongly prejudiced, as noted earlier. In the Pan-German League, anti-Semitism was used consciously as a political tool beginning in October 1918 at the latest; former officers participated as leaders in this effort. One of them was a retired general of the Bavarian cavalry named Baron Konstantin von Gebsattel, who was deputy chairman of the Pan-German League from 1914 on and, after the war, chairman of the radically anti-Semitic Deutschvölkischer Schutz- und Trutzbund (German Ethnic Defense Alliance). After Germany's military defeat he urged at one meeting that the organization "exploit the situation to arouse opinion against the Jews and use them as lightning rods for all the wrongs we have suffered." August Keim, another retired general and influential editor of the *Militär-Wochenblatt* (Military Weekly), had expressed the same idea in the last weeks of the war: "If we lose this war, it will only be because the German people have been poisoned by the Jews; their heads are spinning and they no longer know where they are going."[56] To the members of the Pan-German League, the "Jewish question" now appeared to be the most promising means for attracting the hoped-for masses of supporters to their "collective movement."

The Revolutionary Era of 1918–19

Perceptions of the Enemy as "Jewish Bolsheviks"

Although National Socialist propagandists of the 1940s are usually thought to be the source of the catchphrase "Jewish Bolshevik" as a characterization of one of Germany's enemies, this is erroneous; the term was already in use in some military circles during the German Revolution of November 1918.[57] On November 11, 1918, an officer of the Imperial Navy, a commander named Bogislaw von Selchow, noted in his diary: "This morning I went to the Navy Office, and the red flag was hoisted above it. At the entrance a Jewish Bolshevik in civilian clothes was standing guard with a shotgun. It was all like a bad dream."[58] Presumably the guard belonged to the Berlin division of the "People's Navy," a revolutionary unit whose political loyalties lay with the Independent Social Democrats or the radical left-wing Spartacists. Such fine political gradations did not interest a man like Selchow. For him everything to do with revolution was "Bolshevist," and that was a term he equated with "Jewish." This is the same identification or reduction later propagated by Hitler. It was probably based on the notion (inspired by a basically anti-Semitic attitude) that the German revolutionaries must be Jewish since the Russian Bolsheviks were. So even at this early date some considered the two identical.

This perspective is of some significance, for it makes clear that the propaganda phrase "Jewish Bolshevism"[59] used to disparage officials of the Communist Party and Russian Jews after the attack on the Soviet Union on June 22, 1941, was not invented by Hitler or Goebbels, but had been in circulation among radical right-wing German officers since 1918. In Captain von Selchow's diary there are certainly passages foreshadowing an eliminationist form of anti-Semitism, as in this excerpt from the entry for November 15, 1918: "We passed all sorts of people, the dregs of the city. Jews and deserters—gutter scum, in the vilest sense of the word—now rule Germany. But as far as the Jews are concerned, their day will come, and then woe to them!"[60]

The Officers Who Assassinated Luxemburg, Liebknecht, and Eisner

The men who killed the two charismatic political leaders of the radical left in Germany, Rosa Luxemburg and Karl Liebknecht, in Berlin on January 15, 1919, were young officers in the Imperial Navy. Among the participants in the officers' plot led by Captain Waldemar Pabst of the general staff were Lieutenant Hermann W. Souchon—a nephew of Admiral Wilhelm Souchon, governor of the Kiel naval base—Lieutenant Horst von Pflugk-Harttung, Captain Heinz von Pflugk-Harttung, Lieutenant Kurt Vogel (ret.), as well as Lieutenants Bruno Schulze, Heinrich Stiege, and Ulrich von Ritgen, and Captain Rühle von Lilienstern. Lieutenant Wilhelm Carnaris was also involved.[61] All these officers belonged to the Ehrhardt naval brigade, attached to the Cavalry-Guards-Rifles Division under Lieutenant General Heinrich von Hoffmann. The officers committed the murders, and judges then shielded them from prosecution.[62] The right-wing nationalists regarded the antiwar position of the two leaders of the Spartacists "as more evidence of the 'Jewish Bolshevik' conspiracy. It did not matter in the least that both were atheists with an overwhelmingly Gentile following, or that the vast majority of Jews were appalled by their revolutionary ideas."[63]

The man who gave the order for Rosa Luxemburg and Karl Liebknecht to be killed was Captain Pabst,[64] first officer of the general staff of the Berlin Cavalry-Guards-Rifles Division. He later boasted, "I had them executed." In the next few years Pabst, a right-wing fanatic with a love of intrigue, would turn up wherever a military putsch against the government of the Weimar Republic was in the works. He played just as important a role in the Kapp putsch of 1920 as General von Lüttwitz, Colonel Max Bauer, and Captain

Hermann Ehrhardt, whereas Ludendorff preferred to remain in the background and wait to see whether the plan would succeed.

The Communist newspaper *Rote Fahne* (Red Flag) ran an article on February 12, 1919, naming Lieutenant Pflugk-Harttung and his associates as the men who had assassinated Karl Liebknecht, accusing Lieutenant Vogel of the murder of Rosa Luxemburg, and identifying Captain Pabst as an accessory. Thus the author of the article, a Jewish journalist and politician named Leo Jogiches, came remarkably close to the truth, despite all the attempts of the military and legal authorities to hush the matter up. In March, Jogiches was taken into police custody and then shot dead by a police officer "while trying to escape," as the report put it.[65]

In Munich an officer by the name of Anton Arco-Vally had previously assassinated Kurt Eisner, the new Jewish premier of Bavaria (a founding member of the Independent Social Democratic Party, USPD), in January 1918. In May 1919 soldiers of the Reichswehr mounted an attack on the revolutionary Bavarian government of workers' councils, killing 161 people in what was felt at the time to be an "extension" of the First World War.[66] It was in 1919, in the milieu of the Reichswehr, that Corporal Adolf Hitler, who had served in the war, embarked on his political career as an "'expert' on the Jewish Bolshevik menace."[67]

Opposing Anti-Semitism in the Reichswehr: Noske and Reinhardt

At the time of the November revolution of 1918 in Germany, positive efforts were also being made to improve conditions for Jewish soldiers. Walther Reinhardt from Württemberg, who became Prussian minister of war in 1918, generally backed "full rights" for Jews, including access to officers' commissions[68]—a position that de-

manded some courage, given the background of anti-Semitic prejudice already described. Reinhardt's stance anticipated the equal civil
rights guaranteed by the constitution of the Weimar Republic in
1919.

After the Prussian Ministry of War was dissolved, General Reinhardt, who was loyal to the republic, became the first army chief of
staff for a time and then assumed command of a mixed training brigade in Döberitz outside Berlin. At Easter 1921 he gave a farewell
address to these troops, among whom there existed not only a generally nationalistic attitude but also a strongly anti-Semitic one. In his
remarks Reinhardt spoke out clearly: "The German Jews who loyally stand with us and fight alongside us must be recognized and re-
spected. The love of mammon and excessive greed for profit deserve
contempt, and we must reject them in Gentiles as well as Jews; first
and foremost, we must not let dissipated habits or irresponsibility
make us dependent on moneylenders and hence often on Jews. This
defensive kind of anti-Semitism is praiseworthy; it does not express
itself in animosity toward Jews, but is rather a form of self-disci-
pline."[69] At a time when another officer could describe the Weimar
government as a "Jew republic" and use an obscenity in referring to
the newly created Supreme Court without fear of dismissal,[70] it
probably took some courage to oppose anti-Semitism as openly as
Reinhardt did.

Article 3 of the Weimar constitution declared the national colors
to be black, red, and gold, in place of the black, white, and red flag
of the German Empire created in 1871. The framers of the constitution were intentionally returning to the colors associated with the
democratic movements of the nineteenth century, particularly the
revolution of 1848–49. A good many officers and noncommissioned
officers of the Provisional Reichswehr, who had fought under the

old imperial flag, felt that the new colors failed to express enough national pride. They showed their disapproval by ridiculing the new flag, often in combination with anti-Semitic slogans. In officers' clubs the new colors were sometimes referred to as "black-red-mustard," and the black eagle on the new seal of the republic was called the *Pleitegeier*.[71] At the end of August 1919, officers at the Pinneberg garrison in Holstein called the national flag the "black-red-gold Jew flag"; their regimental commander was Colonel Leopold von Ledebur, a right-wing radical and member of the aristocracy. The Social Democratic newspaper *Vorwärts* (Forward), which reported the incident, also noted that soldiers who refused to go along with the shift to the right were being pushed out of the regiment bit by bit.[72]

Gustav Noske, Reichswehr minister at the time and a Social Democrat, was aware that "anti-Semitic incidents" had frequently occurred within the army; he had been forced to admit as much in July 1919 to the German National Assembly, to his great—and sincere—regret. Therefore, he continued, "all commanding officers must be reminded that it is their duty at all times to respond forcefully to any kind of anti-Semitic propaganda or incitement of hatred among their men." Noske agreed with the head of the Independent Social Democratic Party, Hugo Haase, that anti-Semitic agitation within the army was "extraordinarily dangerous," and promised to "clamp down" on it when an occasion presented itself.[73]

Nevertheless, only a month later, in August 1919, it became evident that the minister's orders had met with no success at all in suppressing anti-Semitic remarks by officers in the Reichswehr. At this time it was reported that Colonel Wilhelm Reinhardt, commander of the Berlin brigade of the Reichswehr and an authoritarian former leader of one of the free corps (not to be confused with the

Prussian minister of war, Walther Reinhardt, mentioned earlier), had disparaged the flag of the republic as a "Jew flag," and had referred to Matthias Erzberger, the minister of finance, and the government as "riffraff" and "the dregs of society." He had also summarily discharged soldiers known to have republican sympathies.[74] Once again a high-ranking army officer had revealed perceptions of a political enemy within the country that imperceptibly combined both anti-Semitic and anti-republican attitudes. The parallels to the Nazi propaganda slogan of "Jewish Bolshevism" introduced later are immediately obvious. Colonel Wilhelm Reinhardt, it should be said, had a typical career for a man of his political convictions. He joined the National Socialist Party, became a *Gruppenführer* in the SS (equivalent to the rank of lieutenant general in the Wehrmacht), and achieved the rank of general of the infantry in the Wehrmacht.

Back in the summer of 1919, when Reinhardt's right-wing invective against the symbol and leaders of the Weimar Republic was made public by a courageous soldier representing the Veterans' Association of Noncommissioned Officers and Men, Noske could not find the courage to remove the colonel from the Reichswehr. At that point the former Social Democratic prime minister Philipp Scheidemann delivered a stirring speech at a rally in Kassel attended by more than ten thousand people. Scheidemann warned that monarchist propaganda was being disseminated openly in army garrisons, and that anti-Semitism was once again rearing its head as the perennial favorite issue in radical right-wing agitation.[75] Scheidemann's speech implies that in the first year of the Weimar Republic the real political power lay not in the hands of the elected government but in the hands of the military. In a speech to the National Assembly in October 1919, later regarded as "historic," Scheidemann declared to the leaders of the government, "The enemy is on the right!"[76] This warning, which proved only too well justified, was taken up again in 1922 in a vehement speech by Chancellor Joseph Wirth after the murder of the foreign minister, Walther Rathenau. It is obvious that the assassination attempt on Scheidemann in June 1922[77] represented one response to those speeches of 1919 by certain officers who were prepared to use violence.

The Postwar Period: War Continued by Different Means

Anti-Semitic Extremism

The nationalist propaganda issuing from the radical right influenced not only the political attitudes of officers who had fought in the war but also their actions. Some were incited by it to mount attacks on prominent left-wing politicians. Acts of political violence committed by the radical right were mainly the work of military officers, either still on active duty or retired.[78]

A whole series of assassinations and attempted killings took place between 1919 and 1922; they were committed by junior officers who experienced the end of the war as a loss of status. The huge wartime army was disbanded, and many men had difficulties returning to civilian life. Since they would have preferred to remain on active duty in the military, they joined the new free corps in 1919 and hoped to serve in the future Reichswehr, which had yet to be created. The Treaty of Versailles of June 28, 1919, however, limited the German army to a maximum strength of 100,000 men and the navy to 15,000, making it inevitable that many units would be dissolved.

Two of these units, the Ehrhardt and Loewenfeld naval brigades, had already played a prominent role in efforts to suppress the revolutions of 1918–19; now they participated actively in the Kapp-Lüttwitz putsch of March 1920, with the goal of preventing the brigades' dissolution, which had already been ordered. When the putsch failed and they were forced to disband, the commander of one of the brigades, Captain Hermann Ehrhardt, with members of his former brigade founded a new secret organization called Organization Consul (OC). It developed into a radical right-wing terrorist group. The officers and men of the organization carried out a whole series of political assassinations during 1921–22. The statistician Emil Julius Gumbel, who made a systematic study of right-wing radicalism in the Weimar era, had by 1924 reached the conclusion that the OC was carrying out a program of planned murders: "There has probably not been a single assassination in Germany in recent years in which the Organization C[onsul] was not involved, either directly or indirectly."[79] And in fact a study confirmed not long ago that the assassination attempts on Matthias Erzberger, Philipp Scheidemann, and Walther Rathenau were planned, led, and carried out by officers who had belonged to the Ehrhardt naval brigade.[80] As will be shown, anti-Semitic motives played a decisive role in these murders and others as well.

The free corps veteran and writer Ernst von Salomon claimed that Organization Consul was "a very loose association of former officers and men of the naval brigade, who . . . remained in touch and on good terms with one another and out of personal loyalty to their commander . . . occasionally carried out tasks assigned to them by the captain's 'headquarters' in Munich."[81] In fact, however, the OC was an underground military organization, which maintained strict secrecy and operated as a command structure in which orders were given and carried out. The "consul" was the commander, Captain Hermann Ehrhardt. He had an adjutant and a staff, and a right-hand man, Lieutenant Alfred Hoffmann. Below the rank of the commander and his deputy there were other former naval officers with precisely defined tasks and subordinates to whom they could issue orders. In contrast to the real military, the members of an assassination squad were chosen by lot, and everyone in the organization knew that any betrayal would be punished with death. The military character of Organization Consul was later confirmed by the Wehrmacht during the Nazi years, incidentally, for the time a man had spent in the organization counted fully in calculating his years of military service.[82] Already in the summer of 1921 the OC had adopted a decidedly anti-Semitic program. Membership was open to "patriotic Germans" but not to Jews or members of other "alien races."[83] The bylaws also threatened traitors to the organization with death. The OC identified as its targets the constitution of the Weimar Republic, the Social Democratic Party, and Jews.

In the scholarly literature on the subject, these terrorists who attacked the Weimar Republic in the postwar years are usually characterized as right-wing radicals and ultra-nationalists.[84] Certainly they were both, but a further point should not be overlooked, namely, their profession: all these extremists were either former career servicemen or men who had been so profoundly influenced by their experiences in the military that they could not return to civilian life in peacetime. Their thinking revolved around the use of force; they viewed the world in terms of a stark division between friend and foe, and they employed the tools of the trade they had been taught to use during the war, namely, handguns and grenades. Psychologically they remained in a state of war, even after the armistice and the signing of the peace treaty. They referred to the first few years after World War I as the *Nachkrieg*, which means something like the "postwar war" or the "war extension." In this combat the enemy was no longer a foreign nation but domestic political opponents. Jews, pacifists, and socialists became the scapegoats for all the problems Germany faced at the time. What the extremists feared most was the outbreak of a genuine peace, in which they would no longer be able to practice their trade of violence. For this reason they attacked the republic and hoped for the establishment of a military dictatorship, which would apply the rules of military life, so transparent and easily grasped, to society as a whole.

The killings committed in the early twenties by active and former military officers with political opponents as their victims—Jews, left-wingers, supporters of the republic, and pacifists—need to be looked at against the backdrop of the National Socialist period as harbingers of the Nazis' tactics against their political opponents.

The Attempt to Assassinate Hugo Haase

After the revolutionary government in Munich had been brought down by troops loyal to the national government acting on the orders of defense minister Gustav Noske in May 1919, a degree of calm returned to Germany, which had been disrupted for the previous six months by outbreaks of unrest amounting almost to civil war. In October 1919, however, the German public was alarmed by a new attack on one of the country's leading politicians. The target was Hugo Haase, then the chairman of the Independent Social Democratic Party. In the years from 1914 to 1917, before the Independents had split off from the main party, Haase—who was Jewish—had served as co-chairman with Friedrich Ebert as successors to the legendary leader and party founder, August Bebel. The Independents' party newspaper, *Die Freiheit* (Freedom), drew a connection with previous attacks on left-wing politicians and speculated that this assault too had been mounted by organized militarists: "Our party chairman, Comrade Haase, was wounded by a man who fired several shots at him in front of the Reichstag, an hour before he was to give a major speech against the government's criminal policies in the East and the violence committed by Noske's troops. Murder squads from the militarists' headquarters have already killed Luxemburg and Liebknecht, Eisner, Dorrenbach, Landauer, Jogiches, and many others in cities throughout the country."[85]

In fact the man who fired at Hugo Haase, inflicting the wounds from which he died a month later, acted alone. He was a French worker in the leather trade named Voss, and was described as a "mentally retarded monomaniac" and an "idiot";[86] clearly he had not been in contact with the extremist officers of the Ehrhardt naval brigade.

Gustav Noske, the defense minister, who had frequently been attacked by Haase and the Independent Social Democrats as a "bloodhound" for cooperating with the free corps and officers hostile to the republic, described Hugo Haase in his memoirs as an outstanding man and took the opportunity to describe the generally good relationship between Gentiles and Jews within the Social Democratic Party:

> His outlook and character will probably never be fully understood by outsiders, because they were shaped by his Jewish faith. Haase was a thoroughly good and decent person. No one can doubt the integrity of his political aims. He sincerely believed that he was serving the best interests of the German people and beyond that all of humanity. I have known a good many Jews in my time, and there was hardly one who did not suffer from the social discrimination they experienced. Some were extremely sensitive when the subject of Judaism came up. Such treatment as second-class citizens turned some of them into pessimists and cynics, while

many others became consumed with hatred. Many of them joined the Social Democratic movement, where anti-Semitic attitudes were expressed only on very rare occasions, although beneath the surface they were never entirely absent.[87]

Officers Assassinate Matthias Erzberger

In early 1920 Matthias Erzberger, the German finance minister and member of the Zentrum (Center Party), was seriously injured in an assassination attempt by a cadet named Oltwig von Hirschfeld.[88] A few months later, in May 1920, an unidentified attacker lobbed a hand grenade at him during a campaign appearance in the Württemberg town of Esslingen.[89] Erzberger did not survive the third attempt on his life on August 26, 1921; while out walking one day in the Black Forest with Karl Diez, a Center Party deputy to the Reichstag, he was killed by several revolver shots fired at close range.

The two assassins both turned out to be former officers and members of the Ehrhardt naval brigade: Lieutenant Heinrich Tillessen (born in 1884) and Heinrich Schulz (born in 1893). They had received their instructions to kill Erzberger from Manfred von Killinger, head of a so-called "Storm Company Killinger" within the brigade, and Captain Ehrhardt had approved the order.

Erzberger was marked for assassination because he had supported the peace resolution of 1917 and then signed the armistice agreement at Compiègne in November 1918 as a member of the German delegation. Right-wing radicals also despised him for urging acceptance of the Versailles peace treaty and the payment of reparations to the victorious Allies; Erzberger was regarded as a leading representative of the Weimar Republic, so was hated by the right. Nationalist politicians mounted a campaign of inflammatory attacks on him, led by the German National Party politician Karl Helfferich, who published a leaflet in 1919 titled *Erzberger Must Go!*[90] Characteristically, the extremist circles that regarded Erzberger's support for the peace treaty and reparations as "crimes" depicted the finance minister, who was a Catholic, as "a puppet of the Jews."[91] The results demonstrate yet again what damage this kind of unchecked demonizing of enemies could do.

Manfred von Killinger, a leading figure in Organization Consul, had a not untypical career as a right-wing extremist and anti-Semite.[92] His career path led from one of the free corps to the National Socialist Party and the SA (Sturm Abteilung, or storm troopers), and from there to the higher ranks of Nazi policymakers. He held the rank of lieutenant in the Ehrhardt naval brigade; then after the Kapp-Lüttwitz putsch failed, he founded the Union of Front-Line Veterans, a group of men prepared to "report for duty in the event of a crisis."[93] Simultaneously, Killinger joined another secret society, the "Germanic Order," founded in 1912, to which Erzberger's killers also belonged. This society was open only to men prepared to take a "blood oath" and swear that "only Aryan blood flows in his veins and that his own and his wife's parents and forebears include no members of the colored or Hebrew race." The goals of this organization were to "reestablish and strengthen the role of the Germanic peoples as masters over other races."[94]

Obviously we are dealing with a direct precursor of the National Socialists' racial policies, which became binding on members of the Reichswehr in 1934 with the introduction of the "Aryan clause."[95] As we have seen, Killinger himself participated in the assassination plot against Matthias Erzberger. In the OC he was entrusted with "military" assignments. After joining the NSDAP in 1927, he joined the SA in 1932 and was elected to the Reichstag as a Nazi Party deputy. From May 1933 until 1935 he served as premier of the state of Saxony; later he represented Hitler's Germany as a diplomat in San Francisco and Romania.

Assassins Attack Scheidemann and Kill Rathenau

The name of labor leader Philipp Scheidemann, a Social Democrat, was also on the extremist officers' list of targets. Scheidemann, who had served as the first prime minister of the republic in 1919 and after his resignation became mayor of the city of Kassel, had assailed anti-republican and anti-Semitic tendencies within the military on several occasions. The plan was to kill Scheidemann in Kassel in 1922 using prussic acid, but by a stroke of luck the politician escaped with his life.[96]

This latest attack on a leading politician of the Weimar Republic was carried out by two former soldiers who had fought in the First World War, Hans Hustert (born in 1900) and Karl Oehlschläger (born in 1893). Both were supporters of the DNVP (German National People's Party) who had met as members in the Upper Silesian Defense Force, one of the free corps fighting the Poles in 1919. In 1920 they joined Storm Company Killinger within the Ehrhardt naval brigade and then Organization Consul, which issued the order to assassinate Scheidemann. Even though he had resigned as prime minister in 1919 out of protest over the harsh conditions of the Treaty of Versailles, the nationalists still regarded Scheidemann as the personification of the republic they detested so much. At their trial the two assailants attempted to justify their crime with references to a polemic written by Colonel Max Bauer, an associate of General Ludendorff.[97] Even though anti-Semitism played no role in this case, Scheidemann nevertheless fit the category of "November traitors" as a perceived enemy of the nationalists; this category lumped together all socialists, Jews, and pacifists without distinction.

Walther Rathenau, like Erzberger one of the political leaders of the Weimar Republic, was the next victim of the extremists. Rathenau, a wealthy Jewish industrialist and writer, had risen to prominence during World War I as head of the government board for overseeing the distribution of essential raw materials. He performed this task so well that during the latter half of the war even conservatives in Germany hailed him as a "savior of the fatherland" and "an inspiring leader, Hindenburg's counterpart in the economic sector."[98] After the war Rathenau was first appointed minister of reconstruction and then German foreign minister.

Because he adopted a policy of consultation and negotiation with the victorious powers, German nationalists began attacking Rathenau, who was essentially a conservative, as a hireling of the Allies and singling him out as a target of their vicious propaganda. In a striking characterization Arnold Brecht, an expert on constitutional law and a senior official at the Ministry of the Interior, declared Rathenau to be the quintessential "Weimar German" and hence in the category of perceived enemies known as "Potsdam Germans," that is, the politicians alleged to have—cravenly and unnecessarily—betrayed the brave soldiers in the field.[99] Testifying before an investigating committee of the Reichstag after the war, General Ludendorff, a pronounced anti-Semite, attempted to forge a link between Rathenau and the legend of the "stab in the back." His defamatory statements would have far-reaching effects, and several scholars regard Ludendorff as in large measure morally responsible for Rathenau's later assassination.[100] The *Neue Preussische Zeitung* (Prussian News) attacked Rathenau in May 1921 as a Jewish enemy of the country who had driven it to the edge of ruin.[101] This marked the end of the period when the nationalists on the right took the view that the foreign minister's Jewish origins were offset by the service he had rendered to the nation during the war. They put him down on the list for assassination.

Rathenau could never grasp why someone who had done as much as he had for his country should be so hated by nationalists. When he once posed the question to Hellmut von Gerlach, a pacifist journalist and political associate, Gerlach offered this revealing reply: "Precisely because you are Jewish and at the same time successfully shaping Germany's foreign policy. You are living proof that the anti-Semites' theory about the harm Jews cause to Germany is totally wrong."[102] John Weiss, who has written on German and Austrian anti-Semitism, also interprets the hatred for Rathenau in terms of the deeply rooted perception of Jews as the enemy. In his *Ideology of Death* (1996) he observes: "Nothing Rathenau could do would protect him from the fury of the right . . . Pan-Germans despised him for denouncing war profiteering without raising the false issue of 'Jewish' profits, and they were furious when he called for heavy taxes on inherited wealth and a high income tax to pay reparations. Ludendorff joined in, denouncing the 'Jewish traitor and defeatist.'"[103]

When he was a young man, Rathenau's chances of advancing in the Prussian army had been as slim as those of other Jewish soldiers. He served as a one-year volunteer in a Prussian regiment, but his Jewish origins made even a promotion to officer in the reserves impossible.[104] In 1921 Rathenau told an English officer about the constant threats to his life: "In some parts of my country companies of men march to the rhythm of the words, 'Schlagt tot den

Walther Rathenau / die gottverdammte Judensau!'" (Kill that Walter Rathenau, the god-damned Jewish sow!).[105] And it was true: this couplet inciting to murder *was* being sung in free corps units in Upper Silesia at the time.[106]

The former Ehrhardt naval brigade continued to publish a newsletter, *Der Wiking* (The Viking); it ran an article in 1922 after Rathenau had been named foreign minister that referred to the republic as a "synagogue congregation" and to the role of Jews as the "cardinal question" of all German foreign and domestic policy. The article concluded: "As surely as there is a German God in heaven, so surely shall we destroy the net in which the Jews have caught us. With a single blow we will smash the Jewish yoke that now oppresses a nation of 60 million. The path to this goal of liberation will be found when the time is ripe, and then let the chips fall where they may. *How* the goal is achieved will be of small concern."[107] The wait turned out to be a short one.

Former members of the German navy who later became free corps officers murdered Walther Rathenau on June 24, 1922, using an army-issue pistol and a hand grenade.[108] The assassins were twenty-four-year-old Erwin Kern, from Breslau, where his father was a civil servant, and Hermann Fischer, age twenty-six, the son of a professor of art in Dresden. Kern had not been demobilized from the navy until the previous year. Like the other assassins from the Ehrhardt naval brigade, to which they belonged, both young men came from affluent middle-class families. Both were also members of various other right-wing organizations, include the German Ethnic Protection Alliance. They were acting on orders from OC member Karl Tillessen, a former naval lieutenant and later officer in the SS, and the brother of Heinrich Tillessen, the man who had killed

Erzberger.[109] In delegating the assignment to assassinate Rathenau, Tillessen was following orders delivered personally by Captain Ehrhardt.[110]

It emerged that on the night before the assassination, Kern had made some muddled remarks providing clues about the killers' motives: "They believed that the removal of Rathenau would incite the left to attack, and that would result in the nationalist political parties coming to power. Furthermore, the foreign minister was an adherent of 'creeping Bolshevism' who was pursuing the goals of international Jewry as one of the three hundred Elders of Zion. He had also married off his sister to the Russian communist Karl Radek and had achieved his appointment as head of the Foreign Ministry through threats and extortion."[111] As is evident, Kern's statements included several different catchwords that added up to a complex identification of the enemy as consisting of Jews, leftists, Russian Communists, and Bolsheviks. Inflammatory anti-Semitic slogans played a role in them, as did a strategy of provocation designed to bring about the overthrow of the republic.

The prosecutor later summarized the motives for the assassination as follows: Rathenau's killers had "committed the crime out of fanatic anti-Semitism and under the illusion . . . that by eliminating an outstanding member of the government, whose policies they regarded as disastrous, they could bring about a working-class revolt that would then . . . be suppressed and bring the radical right wing to power."[112] Ludendorff and Ehrhardt were the figures they could imagine in the role of a military dictator, and in the minds of the nationalistic extremists in uniform, a military dictatorship corresponded far better to the traditions of Prussian and German militarism than the Weimar Republic, committed to the goals of democracy and peace.

During the National Socialist era Konstantin Hierl (a former officer of the general staff and commander of a free corps) became leader of the Reich Work Service and named the posts in Bad Schmiedeberg and Doberschütz "in honor of" the two assassins.[113] With this gesture Hitler's government ennobled the tradition of political assassination and at the same time legitimated its own policy of violence against political opponents and minorities declared to be enemies on "racial" grounds.

Rathenau's assassination led to massive protests by pro-republic groups, passage of a bill "to protect the republic," and the banning of organizations whose purpose was anti-Semitic propaganda. Yet not quite two weeks after the killing, another prominent German Jew became the target of an assassination attempt by right-wing extremists. The intended victim was Maximilian Harden, editor of a journal devoted to politics and literature that shifted from a pro-war to an ardently antiwar stance, reflecting Harden's own views.[114] Since he had endorsed President Woodrow Wilson's idea of world peace, the German right wing viewed Harden as a traitor.

The perpetrators—Paul Ankermann, Albert Grenz, and Herbert Weichardt—did not belong to the Organization Consul but were associated with other right-wing military groups dominated by racist and anti-Semitic attitudes. Ankermann was corps leader of the Jungmannenbund (roughly, League of Young Knights) and had met Grenz and Weichardt in the local chapter of the veterans' organization Stahlhelm (Steel Helmet) in their town of Oldenburg. Grenz, the owner of a bookstore, was also secretary of the Oldenburg branch of the German Ethnic Protection Alliance, and belonged to the National Federation of German Soldiers and the German Herald.[115] During his trial Ankermann told the court that Harden was particularly dangerous "because of his writings and his change of attitude about national questions . . . It outraged us that he dared to attack everything as a Jew." Grenz saw himself as acting, so to speak, on behalf of many German anti-Semites; he testified, "I do not regret my action . . . Two percent of the German people may support the other side, but 50 percent of them stand behind me."[116]

The Weimar Republic

Veterans Introduce an "Aryan Clause"

From its founding in 1919, "Steel Helmet" attracted veterans of the First World War with conservative, nationalistic attitudes. By the mid-1920s the organization's membership numbered about 300,000, a figure that grew to 500,000 in 1930, if one includes its youth organization.[117] These veterans regarded themselves not as right-wing radicals, but rather as solid citizens still loyal to the values of the Prussian military who, because of that loyalty, could accept neither the limitations imposed by the Treaty of Versailles nor the "unsoldierly" democracy and republican form of government established by the Weimar constitution. Those they regarded as their domestic opponents were the "Reich Flag Black-Red-Gold," an organization dedicated to protecting the republic, and Jews and the Catholic Church (both of which were seen as too "international" to be truly patriotic).

In its early years the shared experience of the war in the trenches dominated, insofar as every man who had served at the front had a right to join the "Steel Helmet," regardless of origin, class status, or religious affiliation. Accordingly a number of Jewish veterans became members, even though an alternative existed in the form of the Federation of Jewish Veterans, also founded in 1919. According to Volker Berghahn, author of a history of the "Steel Helmet," however, "soon a growing number of members began voicing the political, cultural, and economic forms of anti-Semitism that had little to do with the racism of the National Socialists but was quite widespread in the German middle class."[118]

Discussion of the "Jewish question" appeared on the official program of the annual meeting for the first time in 1922. A stormy debate took place when one group of delegates argued that this point should be dropped from the agenda because it had no relevance for the organization, while another faction insisted that it was a "burning question." The president of the "Steel Helmet," Franz Seldte, attempted to mediate by declaring that all the members were "neither Jews nor Gentiles, but 'Steel Helmet' men." The debate continued for several hours without a decision being reached.

Two years later the anti-Semites in the organization again seized the initiative. This time they proposed the introduction of an "Aryan clause" in the qualifications for membership, so that Jewish candidates could be rejected and current Jewish members expelled. The main spokesman for this group was Georg Ludwig Maercker, a retired general who only a few years earlier had received instructions from the Social Democratic minister of defense, Gustav Noske, to guard the sessions of the National Assembly in Weimar as it drafted the new constitution. The fact that Maercker and his volunteer corps carried out their orders shows that, at least at that time, he was not openly hostile to the republic. After leaving the Reichswehr, he joined the "Steel Helmet" and was immediately named chairman of the chapter in Saxony, as befitted his high rank. Maercker adopted the position that "no Jews may be admitted to membership" and was supported by Lieutenant Colonel (ret.) Theodor Duesterberg, national vice chairman of the "Steel Helmet" and Seldte's deputy. At a meeting of regional chairmen in March 1924, Seldte had little choice but to accept the "Aryan clause," and it was accordingly added to the bylaws. The few Jewish members gradually dropped out of the organization, which from then on strove, in its own words, to keep at bay all "influences of non-German races." This included urging members to boycott Jewish-led businesses.[119] The exclusion of Jews from the largest and most influential veterans' organization in 1924 must be regarded as an immediate precursor of the "Aryan clause" introduced for the Reichswehr by Minister of War Werner von Blomberg ten years later. In this way the ground was prepared.

Theodor Duesterberg, Seldte's rival within the "Steel Helmet" as well as his deputy, espoused a strongly racist ideology and acted as spokesman for the racist wing within the organization. He supported Maercker, as noted, and often expressed his anti-Semitic attitudes in the years that followed. Hence it must have come as a serious blow to him to learn from a fellow member in 1932 that he himself had Jewish forebears. It emerged that his grandfather, a Jewish physician, had converted to Christianity in 1818. "Both his grandfather and father had been loyal Prussian subjects and received both military and civilian honors. Their descendant had every reason to be proud of them, but the news came as a great shock. He nearly suffered a breakdown and immediately submitted his resignation to the board of directors."[120]

Several leading figures within the "Steel Helmet" attempted to dissuade Duesterberg from resigning, but others feared the reaction of numerous members of the organization with anti-Semitic attitudes if they learned the truth about his origins. Duesterberg made a last-ditch effort to stay on by proposing a list of four requirements that every member or candidate should fulfill before criticizing his family origins. Each member of the "Steel Helmet" should be able

(1) to present a notarized copy of church records showing that both parents, as well as grandparents and great-grandparents on both sides, were members of the congregation and, furthermore, to identify any and all ancestors of foreign blood (e.g., Polish, Italian, French, Czech, or otherwise non-German); (2) swear on his word of honor that he had no professional, familial, or personal dealings with Jews, that he had not borrowed money from Jews and had no Jewish patients or clients, or any Jewish in-laws; (3) furnish proof that his ancestors participated in the nineteenth-century wars of liberation and German unification, and on which side; and (4) furnish proof that he himself served in the First World War, and in what capacity, whether at the front or at home.[121]

As soon as Duesterberg's Jewish antecedents became public, the National Socialists mounted a campaign against him in which Joseph Goebbels, future Reich propaganda minister, and R. Walther Darré, the Nazi Party agricultural expert, played leading roles. Darré declined when Duesterberg challenged him to a duel, saying that he could not engage in one with an opponent of "Jewish blood." So instead the two met before the court of honor of the Association of Former Officers of the Field Artillery Regiment of Scharnhorst (First Hannoverian) no. 10, to which Darré belonged. The court decided against Duesterberg, indicating how widespread anti-Semitic attitudes were among right-wing officers. (When Darré accepted the post of minister of agriculture in Hitler's "national cabinet" in 1933, by contrast, the officers' association refused to condemn him.) Ultimately, German president Paul von Hindenburg and Minister of Defense Werner von Blomberg intervened in Duesterberg's dispute with the "Steel Helmet" and urged him to resign. In April 1933 Duesterberg finally capitulated and left the organization.[122]

No Jews in the Reichswehr

In the years from 1920 to 1926, the dominant figure in the Reichswehr was Hans von Seeckt. He kept the armed forces of the republic insulated to a large extent from social and political pressures and strove to shape them in accord with his own ideas. His thinking was influenced primarily by Prussian military traditions, meaning that despite all the limitations imposed by the Treaty of Versailles, Seeckt believed that the country would need a strong army in the future. Only on that basis could Germany achieve its primary policy goal, which was to regain the status of a major power in Europe.

Seeckt's ideas were shared at the time by the nationalists on the right; they were represented politically chiefly by the German National People's Party (DNVP), which had been founded as a successor to the German Fatherland Party after the First World War. During the last years of the war, the Fatherland Party had been located at the right end of the political spectrum, with an emphatically anti-Semitic orientation even at that time.[123] The DNVP was closely associated with several groups that had taken decidedly anti-Semitic stances in the past, such as the Reichslandbund, the nationalistic German Clerks' League, and the Pan-German League, which had spawned the more recent German Ethnic Protection Association. The DNVP and these other organizations took up not only anti-democratic and nationalistic slogans but also radically racist ones. Among the older conservative groups anti-Semitism was a long-standing tradition.[124] The most extreme professed a racially based anti-Semitism of the type the NSDAP would later adopt.

It is possible that a man like Seeckt, who in his role as army chief of staff could, more than anyone else, shape the Reichswehr to his liking, was at home in these patterns of thinking, even though his wife was Jewish. A passage in a letter he wrote to her on May 19, 1919, makes his fundamentally anti-Semitic attitude clear. In expressing his opinion of the new prime minister of Prussia, Paul Hirsch, a Social Democrat, Seeckt wrote: "[He] is not so bad and is an old parliamentarian. For this post he seems quite unsuitable, especially as a Jew; not only because this is in itself provocative, but because the Jewish talent is purely critical, hence negative, and can never help in the construction of a state. This is no good."[125]

The constitution of the Weimar Republic provided a foundation for the complete emancipation of Jews. According to the constitution, at least, Jews could now become army officers on active duty. In the nationalistic right-wing camp, however, this obligation was not accepted. The basically anti-Semitic attitude in the officer corps of the Reichswehr was carried over into the republic. The right-wingers continued to slander and persecute Jewish candidates as they strove to prevent any further emancipation. In nationalistic circles German Jewish soldiers continued to be characterized in defamatory terms as "cowards, deserters, and traitors"—long before Hitler came on the scene.[126] And during the 1920s they continued to be barred from joining veterans' organizations, which tended to espouse nationalistic views.[127] They were excluded, in other words, on the basis of an anti-Semitic orientation. The right-wing and radical-right nationalists persisted in blaming Jews for the defeat of 1918, for the movement to create soldiers' councils during the revolutionary period, and for the weakness of the Weimar Republic.

As we have seen, the "Steel Helmet" introduced an "Aryan clause" into its qualifications for joining; Jewish soldiers could not become members even if they had served at the front and won decorations for bravery. As a result of such attitudes, in the 100,000-man army that the Allies had agreed to permit in the Weimar Republic, there were no Jewish officers and only a few Jewish enlisted men, who were forced to fight—usually in vain—to be granted equal rights.

In 1919 Jewish veterans of the First World War founded their own organization, the League of Jewish Front Soldiers. Its chairman was Dr. Leo Loewenstein, a former captain in the reserves, and their newsletter was called *Der Schild* (The Shield). For the next decade its main task was rebutting the vicious slanders and anti-Semitic attacks of the other veterans' groups.[128]

After the economic collapse of 1929 and the ensuing political crisis, not all the attempts to find causes for the dramatic downturn were rational and analytic; people were also looking for scapegoats. The capitalistic system appeared to have broken down entirely. The old resentments of the middle class and educated professionals against modern industrial society rose to the surface again, and nationalistic ideas gained in influence. Increasingly, calls were heard for a "strong man" to head the government, as Hans Mommsen has written:

> Such attitudes almost invariably went hand in hand with a subliminal anti-Semitism, which under the prevailing conditions was expressed more and more openly. By contrast, organized anti-Semitism was not particularly widespread. Following the ban of the German Ethnic Protection Association it was most evident in the NSDAP, without, however, having been the primary factor on the part of its sympathizers in their decision to join the party. Anti-Semitic excesses like the assaults that had taken place in Berlin's Scheunen neighborhood in November 1923 remained isolated incidents. On the other hand, anti-Semitic feelings, particularly toward non-

assimilated Jewish groups, began to pervade German public life as a whole.[129]

In addition to the NSDAP, the creators and spreaders of anti-Semitic propaganda included the DNVP and several student organizations, especially the German Student National Socialist League. The last-named organization aspired to prohibit any Jew from studying at a German university, and it acquired majority support in the student bodies at many universities long before Hitler came to power.

The National Socialist Era up to 1939

From 1934 on, the Reichswehr increasingly adopted and applied ideas borrowed from the National Socialists' views on race. This was not done by virtue of any special order Hitler had given. It was the minister of defense, General Werner von Blomberg, who took the initiative, just as he had earlier decided to issue an order requiring all soldiers of the Reichswehr to wear a swastika (the symbol of the National Socialists) as a sleeve patch on their uniforms. This was an extraordinary first step in creating a positive attitude toward the Nazis within the army.[130] During the Weimar years the Reichswehr had remained politically neutral and committed to serving the republic, but now the NSDAP was accepted as a virtually ideal embodiment of a nationalistic authoritarian state.

On April 7, 1933, Hitler's government issued the Law for the Restoration of the Professional Civil Service. This measure created a legal basis for dismissing all officials whose political or religious affiliation was viewed by the Nazis as undesirable. This group consisted first and foremost of supporters of democracy and the Weimar constitution, but also included all Jews. Paragraph 3 of the new law

stated, "Civil servants of non-Aryan origin are to be placed on re-
tirement status."[151] It made no mention at all of soldiers serving in
the Reichswehr. Nevertheless, General von Blomberg seized the initiative; in an act of proactive obedience, he gave instructions that the
"Aryan paragraph" be applied to all ranks of the Reichswehr.[152]
Blomberg ordered company commanders to obtain proof of "Aryan
origins" from all the men under their command. In cases where the
necessary documents could not be furnished, the order named specific officers who were then to determine "whether sufficient documentation existed to certify Aryan origins" for the man in question.
If not, such soldiers could "not be retained in the Wehrmacht," and
were to be discharged immediately. The only exceptions permitted
were soldiers who had fought at the front in the First World War or
who had lost a son or father in the war.

This voluntary adoption of the "Aryan paragraph" for the Reichswehr was a momentous step, as it gave Nazi racial ideology official
status within the military. Simultaneously, the defense minister intervened in an area that top army officers had jealously protected up
to that time, namely, personnel decisions. Before Blomberg's order,
such matters had been largely the privilege of regimental commanders. As noted earlier, during the empire this had led to the exclusion of certain groups from the officers' ranks even without a specific law, such as Jews, Social Democrats, and members of religious
sects. During the Weimar period the Reichswehr had circumvented
the provisions of the republican constitution guaranteeing equal
civil rights for all citizens in the same unofficial manner and had not
admitted Jewish candidates to the officer corps. Now, one year after
Hitler had come to power, anti-Semitism was formally introduced
into the language of a military order.

What motive could have prompted Blomberg to issue this racist order? The military historian Klaus-Jürgen Müller notes that in 1933 members of the NSDAP and its subsidiary organizations had begun publicly voicing their doubts about the "racial purity" of the Reichswehr officer corps. Since in this period the SA and Reichswehr were rivals, Müller argues that Blomberg probably wanted to block such criticism and demonstrate that the army could be relied on politically and ideologically. Hence, he concludes, the extension of the "Aryan paragraph" to the army should be viewed in the context of an intra-German struggle for military dominance.[133] Interpreting the order primarily in terms of power politics, however, leaves one question open, namely, how willingly or unwillingly the Reichswehr carried it out. In other words, to what extent was the army already pervaded by anti-Semitic attitudes and thus open to racism as a policy of the National Socialist state even before the "Nuremberg Laws" were adopted in 1935?

Once the order was given, it is evident that the leadership of the Reichswehr were prepared to do as they had been told. They required soldiers to submit the necessary documents, looked them over, and decided which of the men had to be placed in the category of "non-Aryan" and discharged. In the course of the purge, which took only a few weeks, at least seventy officers, noncommissioned officers, and enlisted men were dismissed from the Reichswehr. It must be stressed, however, that the men affected were neither practicing members of the Jewish faith themselves nor sons of observant Jewish parents. (No one fitting this description was serving in the officer corps at that time in any case, as the Ministry of Defense expressly declared in October 1933.)[134] Rather, for the first time the racist definition characteristic of Nazi ideology was officially applied within the German armed forces. The officers and men discharged were declared "non-Aryan" because one or more of their parents or grandparents had been registered as Jewish at birth. It made no difference whether the soldiers themselves practiced the religion or even whether their parents or grandparents had converted to Christianity years earlier.

The documentary evidence reveals that seven officers, eight officer candidates, thirteen noncommissioned officers, and twenty-eight enlisted men were expelled from the army, as well as three officers, four officer candidates, three noncommissioned officers, and four enlisted men from the navy, making a total of seventy.[135] At the same time, however, the goal of a "Jew-free" military was not achieved with this single purge, since additional "non-Aryan" soldiers were discharged in succeeding months and further purges were ordered and carried out, especially after the draft was introduced.

Although this first anti-Semitic purge within the Reichswehr represented a significant curtailment of autonomy in personnel matters and could not help but have a negative effect on loyalty and esprit de corps, it was not met with a storm of protest. Reactions varied.[136] In the majority of cases the order was obeyed and occasionally welcomed. Some commanders expressed their regret to the men affected by it and did what they could to retain them. Nevertheless, they did not raise any objection on principle to this racist exclusionary measure. This was true of both General Werner von Fritsch, commander in chief of the army, and Admiral Erich Raeder, the supreme naval commander. Their reserve suggests that either the officers accepted this form of anti-Semitism,[137] or at least did not consider it opportune to oppose it openly as the National Socialists were creating an authoritarian state. It has been correctly pointed out that during this early phase of cooperation between the Wehrmacht and the NSDAP it was not yet possible to foresee the Holocaust. It is also correct to say, however, that with regard to anti-Semitism, traditional military values did not offer a foundation on which a policy for opposing Hitler could develop.[138]

Colonel von Manstein Objects

It is all the more remarkable that in 1934 one officer did protest the introduction of the "Aryan paragraph" in the Reichswehr on general principle, namely, Colonel Erich von Manstein of the army general staff. A few weeks after Defense Minister von Blomberg had issued his order, Manstein wrote a memorandum, titled "Applying the Aryan Paragraph of the Civil Service Law to the Wehrmacht,"[139] and sent it to a number of senior officers, including General Ludwig Beck, chief of the general staff of the army; General von Fritsch, commander in chief of the army; and General von Blomberg himself. Manstein argued that Blomberg's order infringed on the military's autonomy in personnel matters, thereby placing the high social status of the officer corps in doubt. In Manstein's view this status was justified by the particular nature of the profession and the strict military code of honor. Considered in such terms, the expulsion of soldiers who had committed no offense, solely because of their Jewish origins, was incompatible with the requirement of loyalty to comrades in arms. As is evident, Manstein's arguments drew upon the traditional officers' code.

Yet there is no clear evidence that Manstein had any fundamental objections to racist anti-Semitic ideology as such. On the one hand, he expressed his incomprehension that men who had already "offered proof of their Aryan convictions" would suddenly no longer be regarded as Germans, whereas many other men had not offered such proof, even though they might have "an Aryan grandmother." But on the other hand, Manstein declared it fundamentally appropriate "that the entire army endorse the idea of racial distinctions and in future not tolerate anyone in its ranks who does not meet the criteria or offends against them."[140]

The historian Klaus-Jürgen Müller has examined this statement and Manstein's polemics elsewhere against "Jews and half-Jews" and "left-wingers in the civil service" and concluded that they do not amount to explicit racism; rather they represent "popular prejudices" and "unexamined stand-ins for the hated 'Weimar system,'" expressing a general aversion to "leftist elements" and "representatives of the system."[141] Müller thus assumes that an officer such as Manstein would have made a fundamental distinction between common anti-Semitism and a rejection of the colors "black-red-gold" and all they stood for. It is precisely their vagueness and lack of sharp contours, however, that characterize the nationalistic perceptions of opponents and enemies.

One further factor should be considered in any interpretation of Manstein's objections to the "Aryan paragraph." Erich von Manstein was born the tenth child of Eberhard and Helene von Lewinski but was adopted by an uncle. The king of Prussia granted special permission for Erich to take his uncle's name. The Lewinski family had Jewish origins, including a distant forebear named Levi.[142] His own familial background probably motivated him to take a stand against an anti-Semitic policy within the Reichswehr in 1934 and to reject the modern, National Socialist form of racism which could pose a danger to him personally one day.

The question of the extent to which knowledge of his own Jewish ancestors may have influenced Manstein's thinking and actions has not been investigated; he would rise to the rank of field marshal and is widely regarded as the best strategist among the generals of the Wehrmacht. In view of later developments, particularly the war of extermination from 1941 to 1944, it should be noted that even in the war years the enemy was not conceived in terms of some official doctrine but rather consisted of a conglomeration of popular prejudices and was correspondingly vague in character. If we want to acquire an accurate grasp of the actions of senior Wehrmacht officers in the war and the Holocaust, creating somewhat artificial categories is probably less helpful than pointing out the fluid boundaries between traditional anti-Semitism and its modern racist form. It was the similarities between the two that made it possible to cluster together various prejudices and perceptions of who the enemy was. General von Manstein exploited this possibility in 1941 when he used the phrase "Jewish Bolshevism."[143]

The facts of the case—namely, that the Protestant Christian general had Jewish antecedents—are firmly established. Manstein informed a small circle of officers on his staff (the High Command of the Army Group Center), perhaps after one of them mentioned a similar case in his own family. Lieutenant Alexander Stahlberg, Manstein's ordnance officer, revealed that he was the great-grandson of Wilhelm Moritz Heckscher, who had helped to write the Pan-German constitution of 1848 and served briefly as German minister of justice. Since his own great-grandfather was Jewish, Stahlberg told Manstein, he felt "involved with the fate of the Jews quite personally, as well as on principle."[144]

During the campaign against the Soviet Union, when Special Action Group D of the SS was attached to the Eleventh Army, Manstein repeatedly received precise reports about their systematic murder of Jews.[145] His reaction to the reports is unclear. On the surface, he either ignored them or declared the information on the scale of the killings to be unreliable.[146] Despite full knowledge of the murders and, in his view, catastrophic strategic errors on Hitler's part, his motto was, "Prussian field marshals do not mutiny."[147] His views on the duties of a soldier, and in particular on the absolute loyalty a Prussian officer owed to a legitimate government, were such that he could not take action against them, even when he was aware of war crimes being committed on a mass scale.[148] He must have dealt with the knowledge that he himself had Jewish forebears by repressing it.

Anti-Semitic Measures before the "Defense Law" of 1935

After 1933 the *Militär-Wochenblatt* (Military Weekly) began to repeat the old claims—long since disproved—that German Jews had failed to do their part in World War I and had avoided service at the front.[149] Dr. Leo Loewenstein, chairman of the League of Jewish Front Soldiers, had already rebutted such claims in a book titled *The Jewish War Dead* (1932), based on careful research and accurate statistics.[150] But the anti-Semites in the Reichswehr and the general population were more interested in expressing their prejudiced views than in facts. The *Military Weekly* ran several racist articles in late 1933, including one titled "Soldiers and Improving the Race."[151] They offer further proof that army leaders were now interested in spreading the radical version of NSDAP racial doctrine within the military and implementing it by purging soldiers with Jewish antecedents from the army and navy. Manfred Messerschmidt sums up the anti-Semitic measures of 1933–34 as "the climax of a long slow process."[152] They closed a chapter of German-Jewish history that had spanned some 120 years, beginning with the participation of Jews in the wars of liberation in the early nineteenth century.

During this whole period, German Jews had hoped that their readiness to perform military service, first in Prussia and other German states, then in the empire, would be recognized and rewarded with equal civil rights and integration into German society. In certain periods "progress" of a kind was made toward these goals. The German military at least took in Jewish soldiers in wartime and sent them to the front lines along with everyone else; it just denied them promotion into the officer corps. Then in times of peace Jewish soldiers were forced out, as occurred in the Reichswehr during the Weimar Republic, even though the constitution prohibited discrimination on religious grounds. Now, in the early years of the National Socialist government, the latent anti-Semitic attitudes within the German officer corps became radicalized, and the Reichswehr abruptly ejected all its members whose Jewish background they had been able to discover. The only exceptions made—at least for the time being—were for Jewish soldiers who had demonstrated bravery at the front in the First World War and received the corresponding military commendations. Here the traditions of the Prussian-German military state clashed with the new racist ideology, especially the notion of a "racially pure" population.

Thus it was not the case that passage of the "Nuremberg Laws" in 1935 forced the Reichswehr to fall into line and adopt analogous measures within the military. On the contrary, it had already acted independently in 1933–34. Reintroduction of a general draft—in violation of the Treaty of Versailles—and the increased demands for personnel, armaments, and the attendant equipment then gave rise to a further process aimed at keeping Jews out.

The Defense Law of May 21, 1935,[153] brought about enormous social change in Germany. As a result of its passage, some 18 million men were pulled out of the civilian labor force and called up for military service. From the perspective of the National Socialist regime and military leaders, it also posed "racial" questions for which new answers had to be found, since applying the "Aryan paragraph" to a much smaller force had offered only a provisional solution. In the

Wehrmacht, as the Reichswehr was henceforth to be known, only persons of "Aryan" descent were to be placed on active service (and hence be eligible for military careers). Paragraph 15 of the law declared in addition that "positions of command in the Wehrmacht can be exercised solely by persons of Aryan descent." Furthermore —probably with an eye to Jewish veterans of the First World War who had served at the front—the Defense Law stated that "whether exceptions can be admitted, and to what extent, will be decided by a commission on the basis of guidelines to be established by the Reich minister of the interior and the Reich minister of defense." Requirements for marriage earlier proposed by General von Fritsch now acquired the force of law: "Members of the Wehrmacht who are themselves of Aryan descent are forbidden to marry persons of non-Aryan descent. Violations of this regulation will result in demotion to the rank of private."[154] The question of whether "non-Aryans" should perform service in the event of war was raised and, like the question of Jewish veterans, reserved for a special commission to decide.

In a separate decree, "The Concept of Race and the Leadership Elite," dated May 13, 1936, Hitler as the supreme commander demanded that the leadership of the Wehrmacht use the concept of race as a basic principle of orientation, above and beyond the legal requirements. The officer corps should consist "of men of pure German blood or a related type." The Wehrmacht was further obligated to select men for a career in the military "according to the strictest racial standards, so as to have our soldiers taught and trained by the best representatives of the German *Volk*."[155] Hitler assigned the task of ensuring that these guidelines were applied uniformly throughout the armed forces to the head of the OKW (Armed Forces High Command).

In June 1936 the Defense Law was modified to conform to the Reich Citizenship Law of September 15, 1935, which established citizenship on the basis of racial criteria: "Only those persons are to be considered citizens of the Reich who are German citizens or members of a related blood type who demonstrate by their behavior that they are suitable persons willing to serve the German people and Reich loyally."[156] Paragraph 15 of the new version of the Defense Law now ran: "(1) No Jew may perform active military service. (2) Jewish half-breeds cannot serve as officers in the Wehrmacht. (3) The service of Jews during wartime is to be governed by special regulations."[157] Thus Jewish "crossbreeds" of the first and second degree would be required to perform military service, but without the possibility of advancing in the ranks.

Exemptions Granted to "Half-Jews" and "Quarter-Jews"

The intention of Hitler and the Wehrmacht leaders to exclude Jews from the Wehrmacht was unambiguous. At the same time, however, it was not possible to make this racist principle a reality in pure form. From the beginning, exceptions to the rule were granted, primarily for veterans with service at the front in World War I. Now the Defense Law introduced further special regulations for "Jewish half-breeds," although they proved difficult to implement in practice. Within the Wehrmacht, lists or tables were in circulation in which an individual's amount of "Jewish blood" was listed in percentages. These data were intended to make it easier to decide who was to be classified as a "full Jew" (equivalent to three or four Jewish grandparents), a "half-Jew" (equivalent to two Jewish grandparents), or a "quarter-Jew" (one Jewish grandparent).

Little is known, however, about how the exclusion of draftees with Jewish forebears was handled in practice. "Full Jews" were not

allowed in the Wehrmacht. "Half-Jews" were at first permitted to
serve, and even to volunteer, but could not be promoted to the rank
of officer. "Quarter-Jews" could not become officers but were allowed to serve as enlisted men until 1944. At this point a decree was
issued ordering that they be discharged, but at such a late stage in
the war, it was very seldom carried out.[158] In 1940, after the war had
begun, the OKW issued a secret decree on Hitler's orders outlining
how "Jewish crossbreeds" in the Wehrmacht were to be dealt with.
It required that "half-Jews" be discharged from active duty and assigned to the second-line reserves with the notation "not to be
used."[159] Two years later, on September 25, 1942, the OKW ordered
the discharge of "50 percent crossbreeds." In October 1944 the military department of personnel, acting on instructions from Hitler,
discharged officers who had previously been declared "of German
blood" or registered as "crossbreeds in the first degree."[160]

Any exemptions required specific permission from the Fuehrer.
Hitler reserved to himself the right to declare soldiers from Jewish
backgrounds "of German blood," that is, to "Aryanize" individuals
by personal fiat. And in fact he is thought to have studied a considerable number of applications for "Aryanization"—as an amateur "racial biologist," so to speak—and made recommendations based on
such superficial criteria as hair color or facial expressions. These applications were then processed by Major (later Lieutenant General)
Gerhard Engel, Hitler's army adjutant, or another adjutant. Thousands of men applied for racial exemptions. The evidence from the
files of the Reich chancellery indicates that Hitler approved more
than 60 percent of the petitions from quarter-Jewish applicants but
approved only 10 percent of half-Jewish applicants. The exact figures are not known, but they also number in the thousands.[161] One
strange circumstance in this context is the fact that when a Jew-

ish "crossbreed" fell at the front, Hitler displayed his gratitude by posthumously certifying him to have been "of German blood." Hermann Goering is also reported to have declared, "I decide who is Aryan!" Clearly, in addition to a systematic policy of racist discrimination and exclusion from the military, the National Socialist regime permitted a number of arbitrary decisions.

Since approvals of applications were on the whole exceptional and rare events, however, many more soldiers from Jewish backgrounds forged their papers or concealed documents to prevent their ancestry from becoming known in the first place. Their actions, taken together with the small number of officially approved "Aryanizations," meant that a certain number of men with Jewish forebears did serve in the German armed forces. The American historian Bryan Rigg estimates that there were some 2,000 to 3,000 Jews and 150,000 to 200,000 "half-Jews" and "quarter-Jews" in the Wehrmacht, most of whom were not identified. The vast majority were draftees, although hundreds of officers, including about twenty generals, are thought to have been part Jewish. A portion of them remained in the Wehrmacht even after the outbreak of the Second World War.[162] These soldiers of Jewish ancestry performed their military service even though most knew that Jews were being murdered and some were even aware of the fates of their own families.

On the one hand, the National Socialist regime had millions of Jews murdered. On the other, it could not prevent—and clearly did not want to prevent—a number of Jews and a larger number of Jewish "crossbreeds" from serving in the Wehrmacht and even achieving high rank, contrary to the Defense Law of 1935 and the Nuremberg racial laws. One of them, the Luftwaffe officer Erhard Milch, who enjoyed the personal protection of Hermann Goering, even attained the rank of field marshal.[163]

How can this situation be explained? It is undeniable that the National Socialist state's principle of anti-Semitism applied to the Wehrmacht—particularly to the Wehrmacht—and was spelled out in specific laws and regulations. In practice, however, the removal of Jews and "crossbreeds" from its ranks could not be carried out as strictly as the political and military leadership deemed necessary. For one thing, a person's ancestry could often not be determined conclusively; furthermore, a good number of the men affected by the racial laws chose not to reveal their identity as the state had now defined it. Third, both the state and the Wehrmacht themselves made distinctions between full, half-, and quarter-Jews. Fourth, commanders protected the men under them who were of Jewish ancestry and endeavored to keep them in the Wehrmacht. And finally, there existed the possibility that Hitler could "Aryanize" individuals, as mentioned earlier, and thus preserve them from the threat of extermination.

From this it follows that the Wehrmacht derives no credit as an institution from the fact that a certain number of soldiers from Jewish backgrounds served in its ranks; it was not due to any lack of radicalism by the army in carrying out anti-Semitic measures. Rather it resulted from the practical impossibility of ending a long process of assimilation and intermarriage with one swift stroke. In the preceding century Jews had become assimilated into German society at an increasingly rapid pace; there were thousands of mixed marriages that by 1933 had produced more than 100,000 sons eligible for the draft. Even with extreme measures it was not possible to undo these developments entirely.

In addition, matters were affected by the military's own traditions. German soldiers of the Jewish faith had fought at the front in the First World War, and by so doing had acquired—at least temporarily—a recognized degree of status in German society. Thus, despite the new regime's regulations, in the eyes of some officers in the Wehrmacht they remained comrades in arms, who could not simply be treated in the same way as Jewish civilians. This was the attitude taken by the new president of the Reich and former field marshal Paul von Hindenburg, who sent the League of Jewish Front Soldiers greetings in 1933. Following his example, some Wehrmacht officers clearly continued to distinguish between "ordinary Jews" and veterans even during the Second World War.

General Werner von Fritsch

The attitudes of career officer Werner von Fritsch may be taken as typical of many Reichswehr officers of the 1920s. In 1924 he wrote to his fellow officer Joachim von Stülpnagel about his hope that Colonel-General Hans von Seeckt would establish a dictatorship. He reported his total opposition to another "black, red, and gold cur" as head of the German government, and went on to attack political leftists and the "propaganda of the Jewish papers." Fritsch concluded his letter with a list of all those he perceived as enemies: "For in the last resort Ebert, pacifists, Jews, democrats, black, red, and gold, and the French are all the same thing, namely the people who want to destroy Germany. There may be small differences, but in the end it all amounts to the same."[164]

Fritsch lumped together all political currents of the Weimar era that ran counter to his own wishes for a military dictatorship, thereby exhibiting extreme disloyalty to the republic to which he had sworn an oath. The Social Democrat Friedrich Ebert was president of the country, and black, red, and gold were the national colors. Fritsch attacked pacifists, Jews, and democrats all in the same breath as those responsible for all the political misfortunes of the present day: the war, lost because the forces fighting at the front had been stabbed in the back; the "shameful" Treaty of Versailles; and the hated Weimar Republic. He attributed to all of them a desire to "destroy" Germany. How would he deal with these politicians and members of these political and religious communities if he ever acquired power within the country?

In 1935 Fritsch became commander in chief of the Wehrmacht. Even before his promotion he had devised a policy that prohibited officers from marrying Jewish women. On December 31, 1934, he formally announced to the men under his command a view that amounted to an order: it "goes without saying that an officer [should seek] a wife only within Aryan circles."[165]

The Aryan paragraph of 1934 gave rise to repeated instances of soldiers snooping and spying on comrades to discover their ethnic ancestry, both in the Reichswehr and later in the Wehrmacht. In any event, the commander in chief (from 1935 to February 1938) felt compelled to issue the following statement in January 1936, designed to combat the consequences of the racist legislation: "I expect officers to display a spirit of comradeship and to refrain from spreading any rumors about the non-Aryan ancestry of a fellow officer or his wife or speculating on the subject. Commanding officers are to treat information regarding the non-German blood of a subordinate as strictly confidential. All communications pertaining to the non-Aryan ancestry of an officer are to be treated as classified documents."[166]

Fritsch's aim was to prevent turmoil within the officer corps. In other respects he belonged to the group of hardened anti-Semites who expected Hitler to carry out an extensive campaign against Jews. A great deal of light is shed on his attitudes by a private letter Fritsch wrote on December 11, 1938; it can be considered a key document. Fritsch wrote to his correspondent: "Soon after the war I came to the conclusion that three battles would have to be fought and won if Germany was to become powerful again. 1. The fight against the working class, in which Hitler has been victorious; 2. Against the Catholic Church, or to put it better, against ultramontanism; and 3. Against the Jews. We are still in the midst of the last two battles. And the struggle against the Jews is the hardest. I hope it is clear to people everywhere what a battle it will be."[167] It is indisputable that the conservative and nationalistically minded General von Fritsch affirmed the National Socialist state, and he accepted Hitler as a dictator fully and completely. Given this compatibility of outlook, one may doubt whether Fritsch's pronounced anti-Semitism reflects "political naïveté," as the historian Klaus-Jürgen Müller has asserted.[168] By December 1938 the process of denying their civil rights to German Jews was well advanced, and the pogrom of November 9–10, Kristallnacht, the "night of shattered glass," had already claimed dozens of Jewish victims. As we have seen, however, Fritsch believed that this was only the beginning, and that the real "battle against the Jews" still lay in the future.

Wehrmacht Indoctrination in Anti-Semitism

The beginnings of a training course in national political issues, dominated by National Socialist ideology, were developed in the Reichswehr during the winter of 1933–34.[169] In 1939, the year in which the war began, the supreme commanders of the army, navy, and Luftwaffe concurred "that in future greater importance should be attached to instruction on the National Socialist worldview and national policy goals." Accordingly, they decided to introduce teaching materials on these two subjects for use within the military, which company commanders, officers in charge of recruits, and platoon leaders could draw on. Beginning in February 1939 such instructional manuals were distributed throughout the armed forces in order "to achieve the most uniform instruction possible."[170]

The fifth booklet issued that first year contained a nearly forty-page-long article on the topic of "Jews in German History," written by a Dr. C. A. Hoberg.[171] Since political instruction in all units of the armed forces was probably based on this text among others, it may be considered an essential document of anti-Semitic indoctrination within the military. Written in accessible language, the essay draws on historical arguments to present a summary of National Socialist views on "the Jewish question." As Manfred Messerschmidt has observed, its systematic vilification of Jews anticipated the propaganda of the "ideological war."[172]

In his opening sentence Hoberg asserts, "Jews have no share in Germany's great and unique history."[173] In support of this claim he trots out the old suspicions connected with the "Jewish head count" of 1916, namely, that German Jews had avoided service at the front, and that many Jewish businessmen had profited handsomely from the war. He then recounts the legend of the "stab in the back": "Worst of all were the Jewish propagandists who undermined the will of those on the home front to persevere, while soldiers bled and died at the front."[174] Hoberg asserts that the book *J'accuse*—written by the German pacifist Richard Grelling[175] about Germany's responsibility for the war and published anonymously in 1915—caused as much damage to Germany as a lost battle. The "Jewish propaganda" then reached its height in the revolution of November 1918, insofar as Jews assumed leading positions in governments all over Germany, including Hugo Haase and Otto Landsberg in the Council of People's Deputies and Paul Hirsch as prime minister of Prussia. In Bavaria, according to Hoberg, Kurt Eisner headed a Communist government "at the head of a horde of Jews (Levien, Leviné, Toller, Axelrod, etc.)," and in Austria Julius Deutsch and Foreign Secretary Viktor Adler worked hand in hand with "the other Jewish Communists." The first parliamentary cabinet in Germany after the war contained five "non-Aryans," namely, Hugo Preuss, the principal author of the Weimar constitution, Otto Landsberg, Bernhard Dernburg, Georg Gothein, and Eugen Schiffer. Another particularly conspicuous figure was the Jewish minister of finance from 1923 to 1929, Rudolf Hilferding. German foreign minister Walther Rathenau, also Jewish, is alleged to have initiated the "fatal policy of fulfilling the demands of the Western powers"; he also concluded the treaty of Rapallo with the Russian Bolshevists in 1922, but died "from the bullet of an avenger whose cause was at heart just."[176] In the postwar period the "Jewish Reds" betrayed the workers, just as the "moneyed Jews" had earlier betrayed the Kaiser. To Hoberg this added up to a Jewish monopoly on power: "The members of the race active on both sides met in the middle and assumed rule over the German people."[177] The "alien domination of Jews in the postwar period" did not merely reduce "the economic prosperity, the intellectual creativity, and political independence of the German people"; it also threatened their "biological existence." While mixed marriages had been a rarity at one time, the author claimed that in the 1920s almost one-quarter of German Jews had married Christian partners, a circumstance he interpreted as a "dishonoring of German blood."[178]

In his eyes Jewish blood was harmful because it was not only alien to German racial stock but also biologically inferior, producing mental illness, moral depravity, and criminality. Furthermore, Jewish propaganda had exerted a harmful effect on every sphere of German culture. It was necessary to shift from a Christian opposition to Judaism to a modern form of racism, Hoberg asserted, because of the large number of Jews who had converted to Christianity during the nineteenth century. In the modern day only an investigation of racial origins could provide information about who was Jew-

ish and who was not. He then introduced the Nazi program by declaring, "No Jew can be a member of the German people." The
conclusion that soldiers were to embrace was the following: "National Socialism does not intend to segregate the Jewish people and
preserve them, as the old empire did, nor absorb them into the German people, as the nineteenth-century wanted to do. Rather it wants
to eliminate them from German life, as is the only correct way to
deal with an alien entity, with parasites and carriers of diseases."[179]
By 1939, Hoberg continued, Adolf Hitler had succeeded in creating a dividing line between the German and Jewish populations
through legislation, yet this was not enough. The "defensive struggle" against Jews would continue even after the last Jew had left
German soil, for two major tasks would still remain: "1. The eradication of all ill effects of Jewish influence, above all in the economy
and intellectual life; and 2. The struggle against world Jewry, which
is endeavoring to stir up hatred against Germany all around the
world."[180]

The material for instructing members of the armed forces on the
"Jewish problem" ends with ideological slogans designed to justify
the coming campaigns against Jews: "We combat world Jewry in the
same way that it is necessary to combat a poisonous parasite. And
when we strike, we strike not only an enemy of our nation, but a
plague of all nations. The struggle against Jews is a moral struggle
for the purity and health of the racial communities that God intended, and for a new and more just world order."[181]

To the soldiers who were fed such information by their commanders, the statement that Jews had to be combated like a poisonous parasite, that is, done away with, offered a quite specific perspective.
With the knowledge that the Wehrmacht provided this kind of indoctrination in mind, it is worth noting that the full series title for

this and similar works was "Instruction Manuals on the National Socialist Worldview and National Policy Goals." Probably there was
some thought given to the parallelism between "National Socialist"
and "national policy"; some of the older officers, at least, considered
it important to link the two ideas. Since the instruction manuals
were published by the Supreme Command of the Armed Forces and
the preface stressed the common initiatives taken by the commands
of the army, navy, and air force to produce them, it is unlikely that
anyone protested their anti-Semitic content. In any event, no protest
is known to have occurred. The fact that the officer corps accepted
this aggressive form of anti-Semitism, and indeed probably agreed
with it for the most part, is highly important.

In conclusion, the portrayal of the enemy in strongly anti-Semitic
terms prepared millions of soldiers for the possible forms that a future war might take—forms that were in no way connected with
facing the soldiers of enemy nations in battle. A direct path leads
from this material for indoctrinating racial hatred to the orders issued in the spring and summer of 1941 at the highest levels of the
German military. The orders given to the German forces on the
eastern front in fact concerned not just the defeat of the Red Army
of the Soviet Union but also the extermination of large groups of
noncombatants, who had been declared enemies on the basis of racist and political criteria. The period in between—namely, the campaign against Poland—gave soldiers time to become accustomed to
the new expectations. There they could learn for the first time how a
military campaign and the mass murder of civilians could be combined under the ideological banner of an "ethnic struggle," that is, a
racially motivated war of extermination.

CHAPTER THREE

The Wehrmacht and the Murder of Jews

THE MAIN MEANS the Wehrmacht had at its disposal for conducting the war consisted of issuing direct orders and disseminating propaganda. The military leadership—that is, the Supreme Command of the Wehrmacht and the High Command of the army—was responsible for both. The combination of orders and propaganda created a climate in which the murder of Jews could be carried out.

Issuing Orders and Propaganda in the Wehrmacht

The Generals' Position: Solidarity with Hitler

In the spring of 1941, Hitler seized several opportunities to confer with senior generals and army troop commanders and impress on them his conviction that the approaching campaign against Russia would be a "purely ideological war."[1] By this he meant both a racial war and a war of extermination. At the same time, Hitler demanded that the generals regard him not only as the supreme commander of the armed forces but also as the "supreme ideological leader."[2]

In the framework of preparations for this campaign one event plays a key role, as it marked the final step in the military leadership's progress toward solidarity with Hitler. This was a secret meeting at the Reich chancellery on March 30, 1941—two and a half months before the invasion of the Soviet Union—at which Hitler addressed some 250 generals who would later command the German forces on the eastern front, numbering 3 million men. These men had not been specially chosen for this assignment on the basis of their ideological soundness; rather they represented—to paraphrase Christopher Browning—"ordinary generals."[3]

In a speech that lasted nearly two and a half hours, Hitler rehashed his ideological convictions and spoke openly about his plans. He denounced Bolshevism, declaring that it was "identified with asocial criminality" and that the forthcoming conflict would be a "war of extermination," with an aim of eliminating both Bolshevist commissars and the Communist intelligentsia. The German armed forces would have to "forget the concept of comradeship between soldiers," he warned. "This war will be very different from the war in the West. In the East, harshness today means leniency in the future." From the notes taken by General Franz Halder, chief of the army general staff, it is not clear whether Hitler also made reference to Jews.[4] We can assume he did, however, for in the propaganda published by the National Socialist regime from late June 1941 on, the phrase "Jewish Bolshevism" became ubiquitous.

For historians trying to determine how the Wehrmacht reacted, the following question is crucial: How did the generals gathered at the chancellery react when Hitler demanded they wage a kind of war that—as all of them undoubtedly realized—clearly violated both prevailing international law and their own military code of honor?

After the war, in the trial against the Supreme Command of the

Wehrmacht in Nuremberg, men who had attended the meeting on March 30 made some noteworthy statements. In their judgment, the members of the American military court reported that

> [Hitler's pronouncement seemed] to have caused quite a bit of excitement among those present who, of course, recognized it as being brutal, murderous, and uncivilized. After Hitler had made his speech and had departed to his inner sanctum, protests were uttered by the commanders to the effect [that] the extermination planned by Hitler would violate their soldierly principles and, further, would destroy discipline. Brauchitsch [commander in chief of the army] agreed with them and promised to express their opinion to the OKW and Hitler, respectively. He tried through Keitel [chief of staff of the OKW] to obtain a change in the plans but was unable to do so.[5]

Nevertheless, later and more thorough research has shown that no particular significance can be attached to these protests. The historian Heinrich Uhlig, who went through all the documents available in the 1960s and compared them with the postwar statements by Wehrmacht generals, reached a conclusion that is hardly surprising: the statements were self-justificatory in character, and anyone intent on getting at the historical truth would do well to disregard them.[6]

The investigations undertaken in the Military History Research Institute (Potsdam) established that the generals offered no concerted opposition to Hitler's plans to attack the Soviet Union. Some individuals expressed their displeasure and disapproval, but on the whole their reactions did not have much effect.[7] Instead, Hitler's intentions were passed down the chain of command and translated into specific orders in the OKW and OKH. In this way the series of orders came to be given that were later correctly termed "criminal."[8]

The results thus show that in the spring of 1941, the leaders of the Wehrmacht and army fell into line with Hitler because there was "a substantial measure of agreement of ideological questions"; they, too, held a view of Russia dominated by racial ideology.[9] The scattered protests against the order concerning Russian commissars and others did not alter the course that had now been set.

The "Criminal Orders"

The division of responsibilities and areas of cooperation between the Einsatzgruppen of the SS and the army were settled entirely in accord with Hitler's wishes before the June 1941 attack on the Soviet Union. The two sides were represented at the discussions by SS-Obergruppenführer[10] Reinhard Heydrich, chief of the Sicherheitsdienst (the security and intelligence service of the SS), and General Eduard Wagner, quartermaster general of the army.[11] This agreement was then passed on to the troops on April 28, 1941—about a month after Hitler's speech to the generals of the eastern forces and almost two months before the invasion of the Soviet Union—in the form of a secret order from the army High Command. Its title read: "Regulations for the Employment of the Security Police and Sicherheitsdienst in Army Units."[12]

It was agreed that special commandos of the Security Service would carry out certain "security missions" within areas where German forces were operating. After the Polish campaign it was clear to all participants that these missions involved the execution of specific enemy groups. General von Brauchitsch's order employs the typical euphemistic vocabulary, stating that the Einsatzgruppen and Security Service commandos would be responsible for "carrying out measures with respect to the civilian population." Precise regulations were drawn up for the ways in which the Wehrmacht and SS units would cooperate both near the front and at some distance behind it. As far as the division of responsibility was concerned, the order read: "The special commandos of the security police and Security Service have sole responsibility for carrying out their mission. They report to the regular armies for marching orders, food, and shelter."[13] In other words, the military commanders had a degree of authority over the SS units. For their part, the SS units were instructed to cooperate with the intelligence officers of the armed forces.

Shortly before the approximately 3 million soldiers of the German eastern forces began their invasion of the Soviet Union on June 22, 1941, they received a key order. Titled "Guidelines for the Conduct of the Troops in Russia," it depicted Bolshevism as a "mortal enemy of the National Socialist German people." The campaign against Bolshevism would require German forces "to crack down hard" and "completely eliminate all resistance, both active and passive." It is important to note that Jews were expressly mentioned in this OKW order, which depicted the campaign as also targeting "Bolshevist propagandists, partisans, [and] saboteurs."[14] These descriptions of the enemy were purposely kept vague. The intended message was: Attack and "eliminate" everyone connected with Bolshevism and Judaism. As for the "treatment" of political commissars within the Red Army (who were presented to German soldiers as the incarnation of "Jewish Bolshevism"), the "commissar decree" of the OKW gave instructions that they were to be shot on the spot. Franz Halder, chief of the army general staff, was largely responsible for the language in which this order was couched.[15]

Yet another order considered "criminal" today dealt with questions on the exercise of war jurisdiction for the upcoming campaign.[16] Essentially, this order provided instructions for dealing ruthlessly with the civilian population. It was formulated in such a way that officers must inevitably have read it as authorizing virtually all kinds of violence against civilians in the USSR. Concern for discipline among German troops led to the contents of these orders being revealed to enlisted men only gradually, but ultimately everyone grasped the implications: In Russia I can do whatever I like, and I will not be held responsible by the German military justice system.

Racist Orders and Speeches by Hoepner, Manstein, and Reichenau

It is not only the "criminal orders" emanating from the OKW and OKH that document the solidarity between Hitler and the military leaders. The commanders in the eastern theater also issued orders that—most untypically for this form of communication with troops in the field—contained lengthy ideological statements. In addition, copies of speeches that high-ranking commanders delivered to their officers have survived, revealing efforts to prepare the latter psychologically and ideologically for the Russian campaign. Reading the speeches and orders from 1941 of Generals Erich Hoepner, Erich von Manstein, and Walter von Reichenau today, one cannot avoid the impression that they represent a direct echo of Hitler's speech of March 30.

General Hoepner commanded Panzer Group 4, which was scheduled to participate in the eastern campaign. At the beginning of May 1941—that is, more than a month before the invasion—he explained to his officers how it would be run. His written order offers a perfect example of how various elements of German propaganda could be combined to create an explosive mixture: "Every military

action must be designed and executed with an iron resolve to annihilate the enemy utterly and mercilessly. In particular there is to
be no mercy for officials of the present-day Russian Bolshevist system."[17]

In 1941 General von Manstein,[18] whose abilities as a strategist
were much praised even after the war, commanded the Eleventh
Army in the southern sector of the eastern front. He, too, passed on
to his soldiers the aggressively anti-Semitic ideology of the National
Socialists.[19] An order dated November 20, 1941, to be distributed to
all regiments and battalions—meaning that it reached all lower-
level officers at the very least—included this statement: "The Jewish-Bolshevist system must be eradicated once and for all. It must
never be allowed to intrude on our European sphere again." Manstein went on to say that German soldiers were participating in this
battle "as bearers of an ethnic message and to avenge all the acts
of brutality committed against them and the German people." Manstein does not make entirely clear here what he meant by "brutality," but probably he intended to evoke the revolution of November
1918, so traumatic for German nationalists. He further urged his
troops not to condemn the murders committed by the SS Einsatzgruppen: "Soldiers must show understanding for the necessity of
harsh measures against Jews, who have been the moving force behind Bolshevist terror and must pay the penalty for it. These measures are also necessary to suppress uprisings, which in most cases
are instigated by Jews, at the first sign of unrest."[20]

In October 1941 Field Marshal Walter von Reichenau, commander of the Sixth Army in Army Group South, considered it necessary to issue an order specifying how much force was permitted or
desired in dealing with the Bolshevist system, since so many soldiers
had "unclear ideas" on the subject. In this order, which was in-

tended to reach every soldier in the Sixth Army, Reichenau presented ideological arguments for the goal of extermination: "The
most important goal of the campaign against the Jewish-Bolshevist
system is the complete destruction of its grip on power and the elimination of Asian influence from our European cultural sphere. This
means that soldiers will have to carry out missions that go beyond
the traditional one-sided military duties. Here in the East our soldiers must not only engage in battle according to the rules of war,
but also be the bearers of a relentless ethnic message and ruthlessly
avenge the bestialities committed against us and ethnically related
peoples." The order went on to mention the mass executions carried
out by the Einsatzgruppen of the SS: "Hence soldiers must fully accept the necessity for the harsh but just expiation exacted from Jewish *Untermenschen*. This punishment serves the further purpose of
suppressing uprisings behind the German front lines, which experience has shown are always instigated by Jews." Reichenau concluded
his order with an intentionally vague call to continue the war of
extermination: the mission of German soldiers was "ruthlessly to
eliminate the treachery and brutality of non-German individuals
and thereby secure the lives of German military personnel in Russia."[21]

General Reichenau, a fervent National Socialist, had either observed or been informed that the murders of Jews had by no means
met with the approval of all officers and soldiers in Army Group
South. In one case, Lieutenant Colonel Hellmuth Groscurth of the
general staff had attempted to intervene in the killings at Belaya
Tserkov', and it is likely that some Wehrmacht officers expressed
criticism or even outrage over the mass executions at Babi Yar near
Kiev on September 29–30, 1941 (see the discussion later in this chapter). General Reichenau's order thus represents a response to the

behavior of the troops during and after these mass killings. At the time of the Babi Yar massacre, Reichenau had executive authority in the Kiev area. His radical and racist order was adopted, incidentally, by Field Marshal Gerd von Rundstedt, commander of Army Group South. It was also approved by Field Marshal Walther von Brauchitsch, commander in chief of the army, and ultimately the operation was expressly commended by Hitler himself.

Racist Wehrmacht Propaganda for Enlisted Men

Did these messages reach ordinary soldiers in the ranks? What did they believe? As citizens of the National Socialist state, members of the armed forces had been subjected to daily doses of propaganda since the early 1930s. With the start of the Russian campaign, however, the propaganda concerning Jews became more and more aggressive. Messages now spoke of Jews as "the global enemy" who had to be "annihilated." Hitler repeated several times his absurd claim that Jews had begun the war against the German Reich. And the propagandists set out to strengthen the sense of superiority that Germans had long felt with respect to the Slavic peoples to the east, and to found it on racist ideology.

Another way of influencing enlisted men was through propaganda that the High Command itself produced in Department Wpr (Wehrmacht propaganda). Major General Hasso von Wedel, who had built up the propaganda office within the OKW from 1939 on, remained at its head until 1945. Despite stories to the contrary, spread mainly by Wedel himself after the war, the department's task was to convey the anti-Jewish, anti-Bolshevist, and anti-Slavic messages and the concepts of the war of annihilation down the chain of command to the enlisted men. The following passage taken from the department's newsletter, *Mitteilungen für die Truppe* (News for the

Troops), illustrates how it was done. This newsletter was designed to be read aloud to the men of a company, or otherwise brought to their attention. The first issue after the attack on the Soviet Union contained the following information on the aims of the war: "The goal is to wipe out the species of subhuman Red represented by the rulers in Moscow. The German people stand before the greatest mission in their history. The world will see how this mission is accomplished to the letter."[22] These few sentences clearly contain virtually the entire propaganda message about the Russian campaign that the National Socialists wished to send: anti-Bolshevism, racism, and the plan for extermination.

If one attempts to acquire an overview of what the issues of the propaganda department's newsletter contained during the German-Soviet war,[23] the following trends are striking. Anti-Bolshevist propaganda is ubiquitous, as is anti-Semitism. The soldiers were informed quite openly that this campaign was "racial in character," "in order to rid Europe of Jews."[24] It was directed against "Stalin's Bolshevist-Jewish system," but not "against the people of the Soviet Union."[25] There was no directly racist propaganda against ethnic groups in the East other than Jews, but it was implied, especially from 1942 on. The propagandists made it clear to German soldiers, for example, that they were members of a *Herrenvolk*, a "master race."[26] At the same time, they also tried to define the term *Herrenmensch* (racially superior person, member of the master race) in somewhat milder terms and link it to virtues such as a strong sense of duty.[27]

It is true that no direct path led from such vague descriptions of the enemy and prejudices imbued with racism to the ideological war of annihilation that commenced on June 22, 1941. The intent of the military orders cited is clear, however: the soldiers were to be persuaded at least to tolerate the systematic killings by the SS, and to show no mercy in fighting their own battles. At the same time, the language was intended to blunt their scruples and the feelings of guilt likely to surface in conjunction with such brutality. Thus the main function of the racist propaganda consisted in creating a psychological distance between German soldiers and enemies through continual denigration and dehumanization of the latter in order to make killing them easier.

Some Theaters of War

Poland

The chronology of events shows that the killings of Jews began not in the wake of the Russian campaign but much earlier, in 1939–40, in Poland. There Hitler tried out not only the tactics of the Blitzkrieg but also exterminating groups defined by racial ideology as enemies[28]—as if in preparation for the war of annihilation against the Soviet Union. It should not be forgotten that Poles were also murdered on Stalin's orders. More than four thousand Polish officers were shot by Soviet secret police at Katyn, near Smolensk, in the spring of 1940,[29] in an action clearly analogous to the "decapitation" of the Soviet Red Army during the purges of 1937–38. The Russian government did not admit to this crime until the 1990s.[30]

Even before the Germans attacked Poland, the leaders of the armed forces and the head of the SD, Reinhard Heydrich, had reached an agreement that after the military conquest of Poland some thirty thousand people would be arrested, based on lists of names the Security Service had compiled in advance. On September 7, 1939, Heydrich spoke of murdering the Polish ruling class, which consisted in his view of the aristocracy, Catholic clergy, and Jews. Hitler ordered that "all members of the Polish intelligentsia" be killed.[31] According to the agreement, the Einsatzgruppen would be responsible for the "suppression of all elements hostile to Germany and the Reich in enemy territory behind the front lines."[32] The chief of the army general staff, General Franz Halder, was aware of the dimensions of the National Socialist plans for extermination in Poland.[33]

After conquering Poland, the German occupying forces carried out these plans, and the actual killings—the liquidation of the Polish intelligentsia, to which many Jews belonged—were carried out by the Einsatzgruppen of the SS. The murder of Jews took place "in public view," as General Johannes Blaskowitz reported[34]—and hence also in view of the German troops. It was in Poland that the Germans initiated their policy of enslavement and extermination, their offences against human dignity and international law,[35] and not in the Soviet Union as is often assumed.

The Wehrmacht did not participate directly in the liquidation of entire population groups in Poland, but neither did it insist on a policy of occupation that conformed to international law. The Wehrmacht could have intervened in the mass murders being committed by SS units, since officially the latter were police units under Wehrmacht jurisdiction.[36] Nothing of the kind occurred, however. Thus the conclusion is justified: "After the Polish campaign the Wehrmacht had no further right to feel it was innocent of the crimes of the Hitler state."[37]

In some cases individual officers lodged complaints. The previously mentioned General Blaskowitz,[38] head of the Eighth Army in Poland, protested repeatedly against the liquidations carried out by the SS forces that had marched into Poland with the German army.[39] His objections, however, seem to have been based not so much on fundamental moral concerns as on pragmatic and tactical considerations. Blaskowitz thought that "slaughtering" ten thousand Jews and Poles in mass shootings was inefficient and would also have an adverse effect on discipline among his troops.[40] When Brauchitsch, the commander in chief of the army, failed to respond to these protests, Blaskowitz and other generals did not oppose him openly, much less take the spectacular step of resigning. Instead they conformed. Even so, Blaskowitz fell out of favor with Hitler for having protested at all, and received no further promotions during the war, although he continued to be given assignments. Due to stand trial as one of the defendants in the OKW case before the Nuremberg Military Tribunal, Blaskowitz committed suicide in prison in 1948.

Another general, Field Marshal Georg von Küchler, also protested against the killings in Poland and was removed from his command as a result.[41] The other commanders and high-ranking officers of the Wehrmacht followed the advice of the OKW simply to steer clear of the "racial measures" being undertaken—that is, the murders of civilians—and not get involved. Lieutenant Colonel Helmuth Stieff, who in 1939 was serving as head of Group 3 in the Operations Department of the general staff in Berlin, wrote to his wife from Warsaw about the mass killings of Polish intellectuals in November 1939, saying: "I am ashamed to be a German! The minority that are dragging our good name through the mud by murdering, looting, and torching houses will bring disaster on the whole German people if we don't put a stop to it soon." He continued, "The wildest imaginings of propagandists who make up atrocity stories are tame compared to the crimes that an organized gang of murderers, robbers, and looters is really committing here, supposedly with the tacit consent of the highest levels."[42] Stieff would later join the resistance circle that attempted to assassinate Hitler on July 20, 1944.

Serbia

After making a thorough study of the military sources, the Viennese historian Walter Manoschek was able to show that in 1941–42 the Wehrmacht developed a regional model for "the solution to the Jewish and Gypsy question."[43] His study caused a considerable stir, and for good reason, since he demonstrated that the leadership of the Wehrmacht had in principle approved the National Socialist policy regarding Jews even before the campaign against the Soviet Union began. Franz Halder, chief of the army general staff, drafted an order in early April 1941 for the security police and Security Service during "Operation Marita" that defined the enemy in highly significant terms; in addition to "emigrants, saboteurs and terrorists," in Serbia this group was to include Communists and Jews.[44]

In the Serbian theater of war the Wehrmacht not only created the political and logistical conditions for murdering Jews—as became the rule in the Soviet Union—but also planned their extermination itself and then proceeded to carry it out. Beginning in the fall of 1941, the Wehrmacht shot thousands of Jews, disguising the measure as the "execution of hostages," even in the absence of specific orders "from above." As far as the motives of the commanding general are concerned, one must conclude that Franz Böhme, who was Austrian by birth, acted in anticipation of orders that had not yet been issued.

A propaganda troop of the Wehrmacht was also working in Serbia. The events and speeches it sponsored, which emphasized the superiority of the German "master race" over the Slavs of Serbia, demonstrated in an exemplary manner "how firmly National Socialist racial ideology was anchored in the Wehrmacht."[45] Under the effect of such influences, enlisted men and officers carried out their orders to kill Jews without protest. In their letters home they wrote openly about the massacres and even included photos of the mass shootings and hangings, despite strict prohibitions.[46] According to Manoschek, the equation of Jews with Communists matched the view of the troops. This shows that the propaganda had achieved its goal and that the attitude could be converted into action.

The murderous practice of the Wehrmacht commanders in Serbia resulted in the extermination of all Jews there within a year, making it unnecessary to call in the commandos of the SS for assistance.

Kaunas, Lithuania

As they murdered the Jews of Kaunas (present-day Lietuva) in 1941, Wehrmacht units and SS commandos employed a division of labor that would be duplicated later in many places. The historian Helmut Krausnick offered a detailed account of these events in his book *Die Truppe des Weltanschauungskrieges* (The Troops of the Ideological War), first published in 1981.[47] The killings of Jews in Kaunas, at that time the provisional capital, began within three days of the start of the eastern campaign, on June 25, 1941. When the advance troops of Army Group North took and occupied Kaunas, they were immediately followed by SS Einsatzgruppe A, headed by Brigade-führer[48] Franz Stahlecker. Himmler's deputy Heydrich had instructed Einsatzgruppe A to incite the Lithuanian population to carry out a pogrom against Jews that was supposed to appear spontaneous. In Kaunas this succeeded on the night of June 25–26. According to Stahlecker's report, "more than 1,500 Jews were eliminated by the Lithuanian partisans,[49] several synagogues were set on fire or destroyed by other methods, and a Jewish quarter of about sixty houses was burnt down."[50]

The reaction of the officers of the Wehrmacht who were present in Kaunas to this bestial massacre is described by Krausnick as "one of the most distressing in the annals of the German army." He continues:

> Normally the most basic duties of an occupying force, even in the first few days after entering a large city, was to guarantee a minimum of public order and take responsibility for the safety of the *entire* population. What happened in Kaunas makes a mockery of the traditional standards of an occupation by the German military, and a former staff officer of the Army Group North testified that it was the most appalling thing he had experienced in both world wars. In full public view, in the streets and squares of the city, the Lithuanian "partisans" killed the Jews they had herded together. Two eyewitnesses reported that hundreds were clubbed to death at a gas station, one after the other. This last atrocity took place only about two hundred yards away from the headquarters of the Sixteenth Army, before a large crowd that included a great many German soldiers in uniform, as the surviving photographs make revoltingly clear.[51]

Ernst Klee, Willi Dreßen, and Volker Rieß published some of these photographs, now in the collection of the German Federal Archives in Ludwigsburg, in their volume *"The Good Old Days."* The editors added several eyewitness reports from German soldiers, including a colonel, as well as a corporal and sergeant major from a bakers' company.[52] They show that German soldiers watched the public killings but made no attempt to intervene, even when the massacres continued over the next few days, claiming thousands of additional lives. How can this behavior be explained? Didn't the SS commandos who organized these massacres expect that officers of the Wehrmacht would intervene and put a stop to them? Krausnick argues, based on Stahlecker's report, that there existed not only an agreement between General Ernst Busch, commander of the Sixteenth Army and a loyal follower of Hitler, and Stahlecker himself, but also strict military orders, delivered verbally, to keep out of what would be disguised as "spontaneous self-cleansing actions."[53]

When Franz von Roques, commander of the Army Group North Rear Area, received an account of the massacres, he first inspected the sites and then went to his superior, Field Marshal Wilhelm von Leeb, who, as commander in chief of Army Group North, had executive authority in the occupied portions of Lithuania. Leeb listened to Roques's complaints and responded that he had no influence over such measures; all one could do was keep one's distance. Then Leeb and Roques discussed whether it might not be better to sterilize Jewish men rather than killing them. In other words, two high-ranking Wehrmacht generals considered sterilizing millions of innocent men as a more humane alternative to the plans for mass murder, the beginnings of which were already under way.[54]

In early July 1941 Hitler's chief adjutant, Colonel Rudolf Schmundt, was on a visit to the headquarters of the Army Group North in Kaunas. When he was informed of the "spontaneous" pogroms and the liquidation of Jewish men by Einsatzkommando 3 in the city, Schmundt replied, "Soldiers should not be burdened with these political questions; it is a matter of a necessary cleaning-up operation." Clearly he was acting as Hitler's mouthpiece.[55]

In sum, we can conclude that both Wehrmacht officers in occupied Lithuania and their superiors had precise information about the killings of Jews in Kaunas between June 25 and June 29, 1941. By doing nothing to stop it, they offered de facto protection for the SS commandos and their Lithuanian accomplices. This case set a precedent for later events.

Belaya Tserkov': The Children's Massacre of August 1941

Belaya Tserkov' lies not far from the Ukranian capital city of Kiev. The town became the scene of a barbaric massacre only a few weeks after the German invasion of the Soviet Union when the German occupiers murdered ninety Jewish children there. Those responsible were officers from both SS commandos and the regular army. This massacre offers further proof that the murder of Russian Jews began in the first few months of the eastern campaign, everywhere the Wehrmacht had created the necessary conditions. At the same time, the events in Belaya Tserkov' and Babi Yar show how closely the army and SS were working together.

What distinguishes the children's massacre from many comparable killings in Poland and the Soviet Union is the detailed information we possess about it. This is owing in large measure to one German officer, who courageously intervened but was unable to prevent the children's deaths in the end. This was Lieutenant Colonel Helmuth Groscurth, who did not survive the end of the war; he died as a Russian prisoner of war in April 1943. He succeeded in preserving seven important documents, however, which describe what happened in Belaya Tserkov' between August 20 and 22, 1941. They reveal the preliminary events, Groscurth's clash with the SS and army authorities who were responsible, and finally the course of the massacre itself. First published in 1970, the documents also received commentary from scholars in the field.[56] The massacre they described did not attract wide public attention, however, until the 1995 exhibition assembled by the Hamburg Institute for Social Research, titled "War of Annihilation: Crimes of the Wehrmacht, 1941–1944."

What exactly happened in Belaya Tserkov'? The historians Bernd Boll and Hans Safrian describe the central events:

> The post headquarters in Belaya Tserkov' ordered the registration of Jews in mid-August. The Secret Field Police turned the adults over to Sonderkommando [special commando] 4a, which had them shot by a platoon of Waffen-SS. Ninety children remained under guard in a building outside the city.
>
> On August 20, two chaplains alerted the First General Staff Officer of the 295th Infantry Division, Lieutenant Colonel Groscurth, to the misery of the children, who had been locked in the house for days without food, waiting for their execution. Groscurth convinced the commander of military administration headquarters that he should postpone the murders by demanding a decision by superiors with the Sixth Army. The Commander of the Sixth Army, von Reichenau, responded: "Immediately after the telephone inquiry from the Division and after consulting with SS Colonel Blobel (head of Sonderkommando 4a), I delayed the execution because it had not been properly arranged. I ordered that on the morning of 8/21 Blobel and the representative of the Army High Command should go to Bialacerkiev to assess the situation. As a matter of principle, I have decided that the operation, once begun, is to be carried out in a proper manner."

The army leadership thus issued the death sentence for

more than ninety children. They were executed as planned on the next day.[57]

As is evident, a whole series of members of the Wehrmacht and SS were involved in this deadly operation.[58] The headquarters of the town commander of Belaya Tserkov', which had been established after the advance of the Sixth Army into the area southwest of Kiev, was a Wehrmacht field post. It was from these headquarters that the order was issued in mid-July for the Jews of the town to be registered. And it was the Secret Field Police, a unit of the Wehrmacht, who took the Jews who showed up to register to a school building outside the town and turned them over to an officer of the SS from Sonderkommando 4a, one of the units known to have murdered Jewish men, women, and children systematically in areas occupied by the Wehrmacht. The head of the Sonderkommando had the prisoners shot by members of a Waffen-SS platoon. Over the following days several hundred more Jewish men and women in Belaya Tserkov' were identified and murdered. In these actions the staffs of the town commander and field commander worked in close cooperation.

After the adults who had presented themselves for registration had been shot, their children remained in the school, where enlisted men heard them crying. They reported their observations to two military chaplains, expressing their "vehement indignation" at the situation.[59] The chaplains made an inspection and then turned for help to Lieutenant Colonel Groscurth, who was attached to the staff of the 295th Infantry Division, then stationed in Belaya Tserkov'. When Groscurth entered the school, he encountered an SS sergeant who informed him that the parents of the children had already been shot and that the children themselves were about to be "eliminated." Groscurth then went to the field commander, who was himself an officer of the Wehrmacht, and also an army lieutenant colonel. He explained to Groscurth that the SS officer was correct, and that he was carrying out his assignment with the field commander's knowledge. Groscurth, hoping to prevent the children from being killed for the time being, placed a telephone call to the staff headquarters of Army Group South and spoke with an officer there, who told him that the supreme command of the Sixth Army was the responsible authority. The intelligence officer there promised Groscurth that he would obtain a decision from the commander, General Walther von Reichenau, by that evening. At that point the staff officers began to debate the matter. Reichenau spoke by telephone with SS Colonel Blobel, the leader of Sonderkommando 4a, and ordered him to proceed to the site with an officer from Reichenau's staff. On principle, the general decided that the ninety children should be murdered. The next day Groscurth received a message to this effect. In a meeting attended by several Wehrmacht and SS officers, he was rebuked for having needlessly held up the "elimination" of the children, for, as Field Commander Riedel mentioned several times, they were "spawn" that had to be "eradicated."[60]

It emerges that a relatively large group of people knew about the killings of the children in Belaya Tserkov'. In addition to the enlisted men, officers, chaplains, and SS men already mentioned, probably all the German soldiers stationed in the town had heard about them. Furthermore, it becomes clear how closely the various staffs and headquarters of the army were working with the SS special commando already operating in the region at that point, only about two months after the war against the Soviet Union had begun. In the person of Reichenau, the Sixth Army made itself "a willing accomplice to genocide," even in the absence of a specific order from Hitler for the Wehrmacht to participate in the killings of Jewish men, women, and children.[61]

The murder of the children in Belaya Tserkov' was not an isolated incident, nor was it an act of excessive brutality arising from specific circumstances. On the contrary, the murder of Jews in the Ukraine by Einsatzgruppe C,[62] with "active support" from the Sixth Army,[63] had been proceeding systematically for weeks by that time. Fifteen hundred Jewish men had been killed in early July 1941 in the town of Lutsk in the western Ukraine.[64] In Tarnopol, Sonderkommando 4b instigated pogroms against the Jewish inhabitants.[65] Members of the Wehrmacht participated in them, clubbing innocent people to death. In Zhytomyr, Sonderkommando 4a hanged two victims in public and shot hundreds of Jewish men.[66] Here as elsewhere a large number of spectators were present at the mass killings. And in any event, Sonderkommando 4a, a unit of Einsatzgruppe C numbering about seventy men in all, would never have been capable of murdering many thousands of people on its own.

As we have seen, the man chiefly responsible for the murders of ninety Jewish children in Belaya Tserkov', Field Marshal von Reichenau, commander of the Sixth Army, found it necessary to spell out once again for his troops the requirements of a war of extermination; obviously, reluctance to follow orders still existed in some quarters. Lieutenant Colonel Groscurth, who back in August 1941 had not been able to imagine that the Wehrmacht would support and cooperate in the murder of defenseless children, now learned what the commander of the Sixth Army meant when he spoke of "a relentless ethnic message" and "eradication." At the end of the first year of the campaign against the Soviet Union, Groscurth wrote about Reichenau and his ilk in a letter to his brother: "One can't view the responsible people with anything but the deepest contempt. Because this is so, Germany will be destroyed; I no longer have the slightest doubt of that."[67] Nevertheless, this officer's attitude and his courageous act were rarities: "He was one of the very few officers in the German armed forces who intervened in an execution by the Einsatzgruppen with the threat of force—unsuccessfully in the end, but through no fault of his own."[68]

The circumstances of the killings of the ninety children in Belaya Tserkov' on August 22, 1941, make it clear that the German machinery of extermination had been set in motion on the eastern front and could no longer be stopped from within.

The Massacre at Babi Yar

The massacre at Babi Yar, near Kiev, which claimed the lives of more than thirty thousand Jewish victims on September 29 and 30, 1941, was the largest single mass killing for which the German army was responsible during its campaign against the Soviet Union. The military official in charge was Field Marshal von Reichenau, commander in chief of the Sixth Army. Just as the name "Auschwitz" has become a symbol for the mass killing of Jews by poison gas in quasi-industrial procedures (and in a broader sense for the murder of European Jews in general), so "Babi Yar" stands for the mass executions carried out by mobile SS units in the first two years of the war against the Soviet Union. In this phase the Einsatzgruppen of the SD were still killing their victims with bullets, and in carrying out their "operations," they cooperated closely with the Wehrmacht.

As far as historical research on Babi Yar is concerned, it must be noted that up to now no German historian has undertaken a comprehensive study of the massacre. When Erhard Roy Wiehn, a sociologist at the University of Konstanz, edited a memorial volume for the fiftieth anniversary of the massacre in 1991, he had to admit that the voluminous collection of essays could provide only "a fragmentary survey of events leading up to the killings, the massacre itself, and its consequences."[69] In the 1990s research on this war crime was advanced considerably by the studies of Bernd Boll, Hans Safrian, and Hartmut Rüss, and through the work of Klaus Jochen Arnold on some secondary aspects.[70]

The German invasion of the Soviet Union and the capture of the Ukrainian capital city of Kiev by the troops of the Sixth Army under Field Marshal Walter von Reichenau created the conditions for the murder of Kiev's Jews. The Twenty-ninth Army Corps took Kiev on September 19, 1941, and placed it under occupation law. An advance group of Sonderkommando 4a of Einsatzgruppe C, about fifty men strong, arrived with the corps, followed a few days later by the rest of 4a and the Group C staff.[71] The Sixth Army established a military administration for the occupation and named Major General Kurt Eberhard, Field Commandant 195, as city commandant for Kiev.[72]

In order to understand how the German crimes in Kiev could be committed with so few obstacles, it is necessary to know the background. Reichenau and the commanding officer of Sonderkommando 4a, SS Colonel Paul Blobel, had worked closely together on carrying out murders of Jews in the preceding months of July and August.[73] Kuno Callsen, who was Blobel's liaison officer to Sixth Army headquarters, reported that Blobel himself was in close contact with Reichenau during this period.[74] Clearly the views of both men about the role of racial ideology in the war, and the necessity of killing Jews, were nearly identical. Five weeks earlier, on August 22, Reichenau had decided that the Jewish children of Belaya Tserkov', temporarily spared when their parents were murdered, should also be shot.[75]

After Kiev had fallen to the Germans and the Babi Yar massacre had taken place ten days later, Einsatzgruppe C filed a report describing the cooperation of the Wehrmacht in glowing terms: "From

the very first day the group succeeded in creating an excellent working climate with all Wehrmacht duty stations. This also meant that
from the start of its operations the group never had to remain in the
rear area; instead we were repeatedly asked by the Wehrmacht to
keep our commandos as far forward as possible."[76] The commander
of Einsatzgruppe C, SS Major General Otto Rasch, stressed several
times how closely he had cooperated with Reichenau, who for his
part repeatedly expressed appreciation for the work of the special
commandos, including the massacre at Babi Yar.[77]

Kiev had become the capital of the Ukrainian Soviet Socialist Republic in 1934; at the time of the German attack in 1941 it had a
population of about 930,000. About half of the city's residents were
ethnic Ukrainians, and one quarter were Russians. The Jewish residents of Kiev numbered around 220,000. Two thirds of them were
able to flee eastward as the Wehrmacht neared the city, so that according to German estimates some fifty thousand Jews remained
in Kiev under the occupation.[78] Since the younger and relatively
healthy Jewish men had been drafted into the Red Army,[79] this
group consisted largely of old men, women, and children. When the
Wehrmacht marched in, the response of the population was mixed:
some welcomed the Germans, but others were distinctly hostile. In
any event, it rapidly proved more difficult to implement the planned
occupation policy than the Wehrmacht leaders had originally expected.

Only a few days after the Germans had taken Kiev—sometime
between September 24 and 26—powerful explosions rocked the city
center, destroying a number of buildings in which the Wehrmacht
had installed headquarters and duty stations. Several hundred of the
occupation troops and a number of local inhabitants were killed.[80]
The German officers now felt an urgent need to "find a guilty

party."[81] It was in this mood that they gathered to discuss the situation and seek what the SS documents misleadingly called appropriate "retaliatory measures." The meeting took place on September 26 in the office of the city commandant, Major General Kurt Eberhard, the "little palace" of the czar.[82] In addition to the general and several SS officers, it was attended by Major Gerhard Schirmer, an intelligence officer representing the Twenty-ninth Army Corps. At this meeting it was decided that a large number of the Jews of Kiev should be killed. It was also determined that "the Jews of the city should assemble for the purposes of a so-called evacuation."[83] Given the policy of extermination carried out in the preceding months, the participants could sense that they had the backing of Field Marshal von Reichenau, the highest-ranking representative of the Wehrmacht in the region.[84] It is possible that the plans to murder the Jews of Kiev involved direct consultations between Blobel and Reichenau.

This meeting and others that followed were also attended by SS First Lieutenant August Häfner, who belonged to Sonderkommando 4a of Einsatzgruppe C. He later recalled the respective assignments of the SS and Wehrmacht as follows: "We had to do the dirty work. I will never forget how Major General Eberhard said to us in Kiev: '*You* have to do the shooting.'"[85] Not only did the general have no objections to the plan for the massacre as such, but, given the ongoing arson attacks, he was actively promoting it, as an SS report to Berlin confirms: "The Wehrmacht welcomes the measures and requests a radical approach."[86]

The agreement that the Jews of Kiev had to be killed in "retaliation" for the bombings and arson amounted to a diversionary maneuver. The German officers merely seized on them as a justification for the murders, which had been planned in advance on ideological grounds. The term "retaliation" was intended to create the impression of military necessity and thus justify it in the eyes of soldiers and members of the SS.[87]

Carrying out the "operation" was assigned to Sonderkommando 4a under Colonel Blobel. The unit had already proved its murderous efficiency over the previous few months in a number of mass shootings. It was made up of members of the security police and the SD (most of whom had formerly belonged to the Gestapo or police detective squads), as well as one company of a Waffen-SS battalion on special assignment and two detachments from Police Regiment South.[88] Two further police battalions and units of Ukrainian auxiliary police were brought in as reinforcements.

The operation began with the posting of notices around the city in Russian, Ukrainian, and German ordering the Jewish population to assemble at a specific place at eight o'clock in the morning on the following day, September 29.[89] Failure to comply was punishable by death. The text was formulated by members of Propaganda Company 637, and the posters themselves were produced in the print shop of the Sixth Army.

The next morning a far larger number of Jews appeared at the gathering point near the Kiev cemeteries than the Germans had expected: more than thirty thousand. According to survivors' reports, most of them believed the Germans' assurances that they were to be evacuated and "resettled." It was also reported, however, that some old men among the Jews remaining in the city had warned, "Children, we are going to our deaths. Prepare yourselves!"[90] One Jewish mother who did not believe in the "resettlement" plans found no other way out but to poison herself and her children. One girl threw herself from a window of the Kiev Opera. Most of those who obeyed the summons to gather probably expected that the Germans would load them onto trains and transport them to Russian territory. The attempts to prevent panic by making misleading announcements seem to have succeeded in large measure.[91]

Next the German occupation authorities ordered the Jews to start walking toward the part of town where the Jewish cemetery and a section of the Babi Yar ravine were situated. The route was guarded by Wehrmacht soldiers under the command of Commandant Eberhard.[92] The site of the shootings itself had been cordoned off with barbed wire, with members of Sonderkommando 4a and Ukrainian police standing guard. When they arrived, the Jews were made to surrender their valuables, undress, and proceed to the ravine, where they were shot. According to the official reports of Einsatzgruppe C, 33,771 people were murdered on September 29 and 30, 1941.[93] Accounts of how the shootings proceeded, from both members of the special commando and survivors of the massacre, have been preserved.

One German participant, Kurt Werner, reported:

> The terrain was sandy. The ravine was about 10 meters deep and 400 meters long, about 80 meters wide at the top and 10 meters wide at the bottom. Immediately after arriving at the execution site I had to climb down into this gully with my fellow soldiers. It didn't take long before the first Jews were led down the sides of the ravine to us. They had to lie down with their faces to the ground. In the gully there were three groups of soldiers, with about twelve men in each. New groups of Jews were being sent down constantly. The new arrivals had to lie down on top of the corpses of the Jews who had just been shot. The soldiers stood behind them and killed them with shots to the base of the skull. I still remember today the horror that struck the Jews when they reached

the edge of the ravine and got their first sight of the bodies below. Many of them started screaming with fright. You can't imagine what strong nerves it took to go on with that filthy job down there . . . The whole process must have lasted until about five or six o'clock at night.[94]

The participation of army engineers in concealing the massacre has been documented.[95] As far as getting rid of the evidence is concerned, the killers were always intent on hiding their crimes.[96] This is true of the German perpetrators who acted on official orders in Kiev in 1941 and could cite that fact in their defense. Covering up the evidence of the murders served several purposes. First, it would have made preparing and carrying out further massacres more difficult if word had got out. And second, the leaders wanted to prevent reports about the killing of Jews in Kiev from being used in enemy propaganda to denounce the German occupying forces and sway both the Russian population and world opinion against them.

The German authorities involved in the massacre at Babi Yar made every possible effort to hide the events from local people as well as the German population and the rest of the world. A week later the SS recorded its impression that both the killings and the attempt to hush them up had been generally successful: "The operation itself went smoothly, with no unforeseen incidents. The measures to 'relocate' Jews were definitely regarded favorably by the population. Hardly anyone is aware that the Jews were in fact liquidated, but past experience indicates that if it were to become known, it would probably not meet with disapproval. The Wehrmacht also expressed its approval of the measures carried out."[97]

The only place where the liquidations were not hushed up but instead were documented precisely was in the top secret reports of the

Einsatzgruppen to the Reich Security Main Office in Berlin. They were regularly sent as coded messages by radio. The Security Office collected them and made them available to a strictly limited circle of leaders under the title "Event Reports, USSR." As we know today, however, the British Secret Service was able to listen in on and decode these radio messages from 1941 on. Einsatzgruppe C boasted in its reports of the extraordinary efficiency of its special commandos in the systematic killing of nearly 34,000 people in only two days. The group also presented itself to its superiors as a unit that attached great value to orderliness in matters of precise bookkeeping. Thus the massacre at Babi Yar was fully documented from the perspective of the perpetrators by Sonderkommando 4a and Einsatzgruppe C.

By contrast, the fact that the Wehrmacht was informed and involved finds practically no mention in its records. How can this finding be explained? For one thing, only a few records of the army units present in Kiev in 1941 have survived. In particular, the war diary of the Kiev city commandant's headquarters, which would be of great value in reconstructing the course of events, has never been found. And even those records which are preserved contain striking gaps. In the records of the Sixth Army and the Twenty-ninth Army Corps, for example, the intelligence officers' reports are missing for precisely the days at the end of September and beginning of October 1941. Yet despite this lack of documentation, one must try to envision how large an "operation" this mass killing was, and how meticulously it had to be planned and carried out. Many German authorities participated in it either directly or indirectly.

In interpreting the silence about the massacre at Babi Yar in the Wehrmacht records, we must assume that a systematic attempt was made to erase all traces of guilty knowledge and participation. It began on the day itself, went on long after the end of the war, and continues to cast its shadow up to the present day.[98] There must have been a tacit agreement among the officers of the Wehrmacht units stationed in Kiev to keep all mention of this crime and their participation in it out of the official records as far as possible so as not to sully the army's reputation. The condition that Major General Eberhard required from the SS—"*You* have to do the shooting"— offers a key to the cover-up efforts that began on the spot.

It was possible, however, to find one "leak" in the surviving documents. This is a report, located in an obscure file, by an officer named von Froreich, who served as an administrator in the 454th Security Division.[99] It proves that it was not difficult for a member of the Wehrmacht in Kiev at the time to acquire information about the main facts of the massacre. On October 1, 1941, Froreich had a conversation with several other officers, including men from the headquarters of Field Commandant 195. What he heard there he wrote down as follows: "The Jews of the city had been ordered to assemble at a particular place in order to be registered and relocated in a camp. Approximately 34,000 of them appeared, including women and children. All of them were killed after turning in their valuables and clothing, a process that took several days."[100]

Froreich's entry represents the only known instance in which a member of the Wehrmacht mentioned the massacre at Babi Yar in writing. He was presumably a lawyer who had worked in some bureaucracy before the war, one of the "civilians in uniform" too unfamiliar with military customs to know not to put on paper what he had heard. The news that Froreich picked up on his visit to Kiev spread rapidly to other Wehrmacht units, too—as was inevitable, given the scale of the atrocity.

Information about the massacre at Babi Yar soon found its way beyond the limits of the Ukrainian capital. In early October several foreign journalists turned up in Kiev and began researching. In this context it is of interest that news of Babi Yar was already circulating among the staff officers of the German military commander's head-quarters in Paris that same month. An officer just transferred from the eastern front to Paris had been able to provide accurate details of the mass murder to people he encountered.[101] And even Victor Klemperer, the professor of Romance languages living in Dresden, got word of the horrible events on the edge of Kiev in the spring of 1942. A corporal serving as a driver for a troop of police had reported to Klemperer's wife, Eva: "Ghastly mass murders of Jews in Kiev. The heads of children smashed against walls, thousands of men, women, adolescents shot down in a great heap, a hillock blown up, and the mass of bodies buried under the exploding earth."[102] Accounts of the shootings in Babi Yar spread like wildfire, mainly through soldiers home on leave or transferred to other posts.[103]

In 1943, after the Germans lost the battle of Stalingrad and the possibility began to emerge that the Red Army might force the Wehrmacht to keep on retreating, the idea was born in Berlin to eradicate the evidence of crimes against civilians committed on Soviet territory. That summer Himmler ordered Blobel to remove all traces of the killings in the occupied areas of the Soviet Union before the expected advance of the Red Army. So Blobel returned to Babi Yar with another unit, Sonderkommando 1005, which had been created especially for this assignment. Its members included more than three hundred prisoners who had been requisitioned from a concentration camp, many of them Jewish themselves. Under the supervision of German SS men, they "unearthed" *(enterdeten)* the bodies—allegedly between 40,000 and 45,000 of them—and burned them on pyres made of railroad ties soaked in gasoline. After four weeks of labor, which was treated as "top secret," all traces of the mass graves were completely gone. What remained was to remove those who knew how the evidence had been destroyed—namely, the members of the special commando. The prisoners had an inkling of the fate intended for them and tried to flee. About three hundred of them were shot, but a few succeeded in escaping and after the war were able to provide eyewitness accounts of how the corpses were burned.[104]

It is to be presumed that in the interests of their own image, the officers of the Wehrmacht prevented information about the massacre at Babi Yar from being entered in units' logbooks. And in addition they had an opportunity after the war to undertake a systematic cleansing of the files of the army and SS units involved. When the war ended, the U.S. Army seized the Wehrmacht files but did not use the material in preparing the charges for the Nuremberg war crimes trials. The Americans did, however, make the material available to German officers who were prisoners of war and were doing research in the U.S. Army's "Historical Division" on the Wehrmacht's strategy in the campaign against the Soviet Union. General Leo Geyr von Schweppenburg has confirmed that it was quite possible "to ensure that bits of incriminating evidence, which could have been used at the Nuremberg trials, disappeared here and there. The Americans even helped out."[105]

After the war it was lawyers and jurists who first began dealing with the massacre at Babi Yar in the framework of the Nuremberg trials. Among the accused was Paul Blobel, the head of Sonderkommando 4a. He had formerly studied architecture and worked as an architect, making him one of the highly educated men—"SS intellectuals"—that Himmler preferred as leaders of Einsatzgruppen and their special commandos. At the very least they had a university degree, and thus came by no means "from the fringes or dregs of German society, but rather from its middle or upper strata."[106] The American military court appeared impressed by the biographies of the SS mass murderers:

> The defendants are not untutored aborigines incapable of appreciation of the finer values of life and living. Each man at the bar has had the benefit of considerable schooling. Eight are lawyers, one a university professor, another a dental physician, still another an expert on art. One, as an opera singer, gave concerts throughout Germany before he began his tour of Russia with the *Einsatzkommandos*. Another of the defendants, bearing a name illustrious in the world of music, testified that a branch of his family reached back to the creator of the "Unfinished Symphony" . . .
>
> It was indeed one of the many remarkable aspects of this trial that the discussions of enormous atrocities . . . [were] constantly interspersed with the academic titles of the persons mentioned as perpetrators.[107]

The defendants cited "orders from above," situations of self-defense, and their duties as soldiers as mitigating circumstances. Feelings of guilt, shame, or remorse were lacking, and it would be wrong to conclude that they carried out the murders of Jews against their will: "Hatred against the Jews was great; it was revenge, and people wanted money and gold."[108]

The military court found Blobel guilty on all three counts of the indictment (crimes against humanity, war crimes, and membership in a criminal organization) and sentenced him to death by hanging.[109] He spent the next few years in the prison at Landsberg and filed an appeal for clemency, but in the eyes of John J. McCloy, the American high commissioner for Germany, Blobel's crimes represented one of the few cases in which "clemency has no meaning . . . no mitigating circumstances whatever have been found."[110] Other defendants in Case 9 for whom the death sentence was not commuted were SS leaders Werner Braune, Erich Naumann, and Otto Ohlendorf. As grounds for his refusal to grant clemency to Blobel, McCloy summed up his crimes, noting, "The Military Tribunal at Nuremberg found him guilty of ordering the killing of 60,000, including over 30,000 Jews who were murdered in the notorious two-day massacre at Kiev in September, 1941, and sentenced him to death."[111] Blobel and the three other leaders of Einsatzgruppen were hanged at Landsberg on June 8, 1951.

In the 1960s the Central Bureau for the Prosecution of National Socialist Crimes that had been established in the city of Ludwigsburg opened investigations on eleven more members of Sonderkommando 4a. In the "Callsen trial," the county court of Darmstadt pronounced eight of them guilty of "jointly aiding and abetting to murder 33,771 people" on November 29, 1968, and sentenced them to long prison terms.[112]

Field Marshal von Reichenau had died of a stroke in 1942, and General Eberhard died in Stuttgart in 1948. The other officers of the Wehrmacht, however, who participated in the preparation, oversight, and cover-up of the Babi Yar massacre in one way or another were never placed on trial. The background of this scandalous omission remains murky.

Two motives are discernable, one of them political and the other legal. The political motive is connected with the fact that in 1955 a new military organization was established in West Germany with a leadership that consisted entirely of former Wehrmacht officers.

The government did not want a renewed spate of war crimes trials to impede the development of the Bundeswehr. And in the legal area a lobby of former National Socialists, who had ties to the Federal Ministry of Justice and included several members of the Bundestag, found a way to protect former officers by reinterpreting the definitions of "murder" and "accessory to murder," and through the statute of limitations.[113] This was the final stage (to date) in the long process of removing almost all traces of evidence that could have led to a more accurate historical clarification of the German war crimes at Babi Yar.

The Wehrmacht and SS in the Russian Campaign

How the agreement between the Wehrmacht and SS to cooperate functioned in practice was uncovered long ago. The well-known historian Andreas Hillgruber described it in 1984:

> The practical cooperation of the regular army and the Einsatzgruppen with regard to Jews took this form: Immediately after gaining control of an area the army commander issued orders for the Jews there to be registered. Instructions for Jewish residents to come forward and identify themselves were provided on large-format posters, making it easy for units of the security police and SD to place them under arrest—unless some of them, having learned of their intended fate, fled to the woods or otherwise "went underground" . . . Just like the Einsatzgruppen in the Rear Army areas, in the parts of the Soviet Union placed under German civilian administration the "higher SS and police leaders" had a prescribed set of duties—that included the systematic killing of Jews.[114]

In principle, this distribution of labor between the two remained in force throughout the war, and in fact they grew closer over time. In the framework of the campaign of annihilation, which led to an increase in barbarity,[115] members of the SS and the Wehrmacht came to view the official distinction as artificial.

This is confirmed by a report to the OKW filed by Lieutenant General Hans Leykauf, who was assigned to inspect armaments in occupied Ukraine.[116] In this document Leykauf recounted his experiences in the previous six months on the subject of "settling the Jewish question in the Ukraine." On the details of the operation in which units of the police shot Jews, he wrote, "It took place in full public view, with reinforcements from the Ukrainian militia, and unfortunately in many cases with the voluntary participation of members of the Wehrmacht." Leykauf was aware of the scale of the killings: "In terms of the number of executions the operation is more gigantic than any similar measure undertaken in the Soviet Union previously. A total of some 150,000 to 200,000 Jews [have been] executed so far in the part of the Ukraine belonging to the Reich Commissariat."[117]

Leykauf, an economic expert in the military, then began bemoaning the fact that while this murderous "solution of the Jewish question" did in fact mean the "elimination of superfluous mouths to feed," it also had drawbacks from an economic point of view. Using language that associated the Wehrmacht with SS units, he wrote to his superior: "If we shoot the Jews, let the prisoners of war die, and condemn a considerable part of the urban population to starvation, and if we are further going to lose a part of the rural population to hunger next year, then the question that must be answered is: Who exactly is supposed to produce economic value here?" In the Ukraine the murder of Jews was certainly also carried out in the main by

Einsatzgruppen and police units of the SS. Nevertheless Leykauf, an officer of the Wehrmacht, rightly used the first-person plural: "we," the German invaders and occupiers, the Wehrmacht and SS, are responsible for killing the Jews, for letting so many prisoners of war die, and letting countless Ukrainian civilians starve.

When the noted scholar of the Holocaust Raul Hilberg wrote on the topic of "the Wehrmacht and the extermination of the Jews," he stressed not a few spectacular incidents but rather the way the Wehrmacht took part "in the process of extermination like every other branch of authority in the Third Reich": "The involvement of the Wehrmacht in the annihilation of European Jews occurred in wartime and often in the name of the war. It was easy to stigmatize 'the Jews' collectively as opponents of the Third Reich and a threat to the army."[118]

Furthermore, the campaign against the Soviet partisans was also seized upon to a considerable extent as a pretext for murdering Jews. In two case studies of the German occupation in Belorussia, the historian Hannes Heer has decoded the meaning of the then-common phrase "mopping up the countryside"—in other words, killing the Jews—with the active participation of the Wehrmacht.[119] And so in October and November 1941 the first major ghetto massacres were carried out under the orders of Major General Anton von Bechtolsheim, the Wehrmacht commander in Belorussia, which the Germans had now renamed the "General Commissariat of White Ruthenia."

In the Army Group Rear area the "security divisions" murdered countless Soviet civilians and burned Russian settlements to the ground under the pretext of suppressing partisan resistance. In Wehrmacht documents these operations were concealed as the "elimination of partisan nests, partisan camps, partisan bunkers."[120]

Admittedly, Stalin had issued a call on July 3, 1941, for the partisan war to be unleashed,"[121] but there were many delays, and the partisan movement did not become a significant force until 1943. What really happened in the first phase of the occupation in 1941–42 under the cloak of fighting partisans is revealed clearly in the reports of the Wehrmacht commanders. They record that for every German soldier killed, approximately one hundred Russian "partisans" had died. Heer refers to this lopsided result, which requires an explanation, as "the bizarre situation of an anti-partisan war without partisans."[122]

The Jewish population represented the most significant group of victims in these operations. This was barely concealed by the slogan "Jews and partisans are the same thing." The war logbooks of the infantry divisions assigned to the area provide evidence, and Raul Hilberg offers confirmation: "It was almost an automatic mechanism to suspect that [the Jews] were helping the partisans—particularly in the 'flat land.' Even the utterly helpless Jewish prisoners of war, soldiers in the Red Army, were transferred without further ado to the SS and police for 'special treatment.'"[123]

Some critics of the exhibition "The German Army and Genocide" took offense at the stark phrase "partisan struggle without partisans" and in this context expressed doubt more generally about whether or not the Wehrmacht had carried out a war against the civilian population of Belorussia in violation of international law, under the pretext of combating partisan attacks. Since then this point has been carefully studied once more by a commission of experts, who looked in particular at the provisions of the Hague Convention regarding the laws and customs of war on land. As the commission concluded, there can be no doubt that the German leaders, with the approval of the Wehrmacht leadership, had "decided months before the attack that no consideration whatsoever should be given to international laws of war, including the Hague Convention."[124]

Furthermore, plans to decimate the Russian population were also drawn up prior to the attack on the Soviet Union. The leaders then sought plausible arguments to persuade the Wehrmacht to accept such a war aim. The commission had the following to say on this subject:

> It was fully accepted that the planned exploitation of Soviet food resources, in which the Wehrmacht cooperated and for which it bears partial responsibility, would involve the deaths from starvation of untold millions of Soviet citizens . . . The military leadership reckoned with the foreseeable consequences of such a policy, meaning not only a partisan movement led by Communists but also hunger revolts among the general population. This is reflected in the blanket permission to carry out executions on a large scale, as provided by the "War Jurisdiction Decree" of May 13, 1941. Not only could partisans as defined by the Hague Convention be shot on the spot, but also "suspicious elements" and "attackers" of all sorts, whereby the decree defined "attack" so broadly as to include distributing leaflets or failing to follow German orders.[125]

This background explains why the Wehrmacht claimed to be fighting a "struggle against partisans" as early as 1941, when—despite Stalin's call to arms—no serious threat by partisans appeared to exist yet. The German advance aroused fear and dread, causing Russian soldiers who had been cut off from their units to flee into the forests, but it did not lead to an organized resistance movement. People driven by the German policy to roam the countryside searching for food were shot as "vagabonds" or for "aiding the partisans." On the subject of the scale of these killings, the commission reported that in the Rear Army area center 80,000 partisans and "suspected partisans" were liquidated between June 1941 and May 1942, while German casualties numbered 1,094.[126] This disproportion certainly justifies calling the campaign a war against civilians, in this case the population of Belorussia, in violation of international law. At the same time, it should be noted that among the German troops a subjective sense of being threatened by partisans was widespread. On this point the commission observed: "Before the war against the Soviet Union began, the German leadership stoked a fear of partisans quite intentionally, not least because it seemed to guarantee that the chosen policies would be carried out in radical form. Hitler himself had declared to his inner circle that a war against partisans had 'one advantage: It makes it possible for us to exterminate whatever opposes us.'"[127]

Why did it take so long for these connections to be recognized? First of all, a new school of military and contemporary historians had to uncover the fact that the highest military authorities, in particular the OKW and the OKH, issued a series of criminal orders before the attack on the Soviet Union in which Jews, among other groups, were fated for annihilation. Then scholars could prove that arrangements to cooperate had been made at the highest levels of the SS and Wehrmacht, according to which the military would create favorable conditions for the SS to carry out the killings and also provide logistical support. Research on special topics made it increasingly apparent that the murderous operations of the SS units had not remained secret, but rather had taken place in full public view, at least in 1941–42. Regular army soldiers played roles as spectators, bystanders, and photographers, and occasionally took part in the shootings themselves. By cleverly manipulating and exploiting familiar military concepts, Wehrmacht commanders in different regions contributed to members of their own troops becoming perpetrators of the Holocaust themselves. In Serbia, killings of Jews were labeled shootings of "hostages," and in Belorussia and elsewhere, accounts of suppressing "bandits" and "partisans" served a similar purpose. Recent studies on the liquidation of Jews in specific areas under German occupation in eastern Europe have established that the operations were carried out in very different ways, but that the Wehrmacht cooperated actively everywhere.

Anti-Semitism as a Soldier's Duty

General Rudolf Schmundt's Directive of 1942

The anti-Semitic propaganda and policy goal of exterminating the Jews of Europe did not provoke serious or extensive opposition in the officer corps of the Wehrmacht even after the killings of the SS Einsatzgruppen became widely known and the subject of frequent discussions in various units. One such discussion is documented for the officers of the Army Group Center.[128] The fact that these murders prompted individual officers from this army group to join a nascent resistance movement did not become known in Berlin, of course, until after the assassination attempt of July 20, 1944. Hence their deliberations cannot have been the reason why the Armed Forces High Command felt it necessary to declare a radical anti-Semitic attitude to be virtually a German soldier's official duty.

There were a few cases that made it clear to the Wehrmacht leadership that the attitudes of its officers did not always meet expectations, although these were hardly of a spectacular kind. One regimental commander serving on the eastern front, for instance, had for years exchanged annual birthday letters with a childhood friend and former schoolmate who was Jewish. Once he had even tried to send a letter to the man—without including a return address—via an officer under his command who was going on leave. Another officer had appeared in public several times in a German city in the company of a Jew who, "although he had served as an officer in the world war, was now recognizable as a Jew by virtue of the Star of David he wore."[129] At a time when the extermination campaign was in high gear, the leaders of the Wehrmacht showed themselves to be so loyal to Hitler that they felt obliged to pursue even cases as trivial as these. Both officers were discharged because of the behavior described.

The head of personnel for the army, Colonel (later General) Rudolf Schmundt, publicized both cases and treated them as an opportunity "to make unmistakably clear the demeanor of officers with respect to Jews." He issued a secret directive requiring unambiguously anti-Semitic deportment:

> Every officer must be fully aware first that the Jewish lobby has challenged the German people's claim to *Lebensraum* and standing in the eyes of the world, and second has forced our nation to prevail against a world of enemies by spilling the blood of our best young men. Officers must therefore adopt a clear and totally uncompromising stance on the Jewish question. There is no difference between supposedly "decent" Jews and the rest. Nor may any consideration be given to relationships of whatever nature that existed before the threat posed by Jews was common knowledge among the German people. Hence no connection, even of the most ca-

sual sort, may exist between an officer and a member of the Jewish race. The present decisive struggle against the international enemy Jewish Bolshevism has clearly revealed the true face of Jewry. Every officer must therefore oppose it on the basis of firm inner conviction and refuse all association with it. Any infraction against this uncompromising stance will make him unviable and result in expulsion from the army. All officers under your command are to be instructed accordingly.[130]

Like his fellows generals Blomberg, Keitel, Jodl, Reichenau, and Burgdorf, Schmundt was a committed National Socialist. In 1939 he was appointed the Wehrmacht's chief adjutant in the OKW to the "Fuehrer and Chancellor of the Reich," Adolf Hitler; to this was added on October 1, 1942, the influential position of chief of personnel for the army. Schmundt has been characterized as "a willing tool of Hitler."[131] In his directive he took as his model an officer committed to a struggle based on a belief in racism. Consequently, any officer who deviated in any manner from the position of extreme anti-Semitism was guilty of dereliction of duty. The term "unviable" made it clear beyond all doubt that an officer who behaved like those described could be relieved of duty and discharged from the army.

Admirals Erich Raeder and Karl Dönitz

After World War II, the German navy succeeded in even greater measure than the army in deflecting suspicion that it could have borne any responsibility for the Holocaust. In fact, however, naval units took part in the killing of Jews,[132] and senior officers espoused decidedly anti-Semitic views.

The commander in chief, Admiral Erich Raeder, claimed to have set the navy on a National Socialist course even before January 30, 1933.[133] According to a statement made by air force general and air commander of the Atlantic theater Ulrich Kessler in 1945, Raeder was an outspoken anti-Semite and had informed him in early 1933 that he could not be "indifferent" to Jews but had to "hate" them.[134]

According to the same source, Raeder's successor, Admiral Karl Dönitz, was "a picture-book Nazi and confirmed anti-Semite."[135] It was partly for this reason that Hitler later appointed Dönitz as his successor. In a radio address broadcast on Heroes' Day—March 12, 1944—the admiral spoke of the "corrosive poison of Jewry."[136] In another speech in 1944 he declared, "I would rather eat dirt than have my grandchildren raised in the Jewish outlook and poisoned by that filth."[137] In his own defense Dönitz later asserted that he had saved some officers from the concentration camps, retaining them under his command even though their Jewish forebears meant that they, like Lieutenant Commander Schmidt di Simoni, fell under the Nuremberg Laws.[138]

Officers Find the Italians Not Anti-Semitic Enough

There is another, little-known chapter in the history of the Wehrmacht: in the years 1941–1943, considerable conflict arose between German and Italian officers because the latter were unwilling to make Italy a staging ground for the Germans' murderous anti-Semitism. Admittedly, racial laws were passed in Italy in 1938 that turned Jews into second-class citizens, but so many Italians withheld their support and refused to cooperate that the laws' effectiveness was reduced. Actual extermination was favored by no one.[139] In any event, the officers of the Italian armed forces completely rejected the Germans' racist ideas and offered active resistance to the campaign of persecution.[140]

As a result, an unbridgeable gap opened up between the treatment of Jews in the Italian-occupied areas of Yugoslavia and Greece and those controlled by the Germans. When they marched into Greece in April 1941, the Germans immediately began persecuting the Jews of that country (although deportations did not start until March 1943). The Italians, by contrast, introduced measures to protect them. In Salonika, for instance, the Italian consul general liberally dispensed certificates of Italian citizenship to the Jews of the city, thereby rescuing them from the clutches of Italy's German ally.[141] In the Libyan city of Tripoli, which was occupied by Italian troops, members of the Wehrmacht reported with disgust that Italian officials were protecting the roughly sixteen thousand Jewish inhabitants and allowing them to go about their business undisturbed. Some of them expressed the opinion that the Jews of Libya were fundamentally "decent fellows." When they revealed through their behavior that they made no distinction between Italians and Jews, they were met with total incomprehension on the German side.[142] Wehrmacht officers exerted pressure on their ally to stop the flight of Greek Jews into the Italian zone of occupation and to follow the German model by requiring them to wear the yellow star. But once again the Italians turned them down flat.[143]

At the beginning of 1943, Commander in Chief Southeast, General Alexander Löhr, tried to persuade the Italian commander in chief in Greece (from April 1941 to May 1943), General Carlo Gesolo, to follow the German model in dealing with Greek Jews. Gesolo turned him down.[144] Thereupon Löhr criticized the Italians' approach as weakness, a policy of trying to ingratiate themselves with the local population. "Clearly the Italians failed in his eyes by displaying human compassion, by being too soft, and showing more willingness to negotiate than a master race should."[145]

In the Croatian region of occupied Yugoslavia, Jews sought and received protection from the Italian armed forces. When the German government demanded that they turn over the Jews, the Italian government declared it to be a question of honor and refused. Lieutenant General Edmund Glaise von Horstenau, then the German plenipotentiary general in Croatia, reported to Berlin in August 1941 that Jews in the Italian-occupied areas were given preferential treatment. In Dubrovnik, he wrote, Italian officers had appeared in public accompanied by Jewish women, and socialized with Jews without the slightest embarrassment. He had also heard that they had conducted some five hundred Jews from Sarajevo to Dubrovnik, where the Italians supplied them with false passports.[146]

The chief of staff of the Italian infantry division "Murge," stationed in Mostar, declined to take action against the Jews in the city, who, according to the Wehrmacht, were fomenting rebellion. He declared that any special measures against Jewish citizens were incompatible with the honor of the Italian army.[147]

Angered by the pro-Jewish behavior of Italian officers, General Löhr and General Glaise von Horstenau joined forces with the German envoy in Zagreb, SA Obergruppenführer (Lieutenant General) Siegfried Kasche, and wrote Hitler an account condemning the actions of the local Italian military authorities. According to their report, "implementation of the Croatian government's laws concerning Jews is being so undermined by Italian officials that in the coastal zone—particularly in Mostar, Dubrovnik, and Crikvenika—numerous Jews are protected by the Italian military, and other Jews have been escorted across the border to Italian Dalmatia and Italy itself. Through these actions the Jews receive assistance and can carry on their subversive work against the government, i.e., work counter to our common war aims."[148]

Not long afterwards, on December 13, 1942, propaganda minister Joseph Goebbels made an entry in his diary concerning the problem of fundamental differences in Italian and German attitudes toward Jews and treatment of them: "The Italians are extremely lax in the treatment of Jews. They protect the Italian Jews both in Tunis and in occupied France and won't permit their being drafted for work or compelled to wear the Star of David. This shows once again that Fascism does not really dare to get down to fundamentals, but is very superficial regarding most important problems. The Jewish question is causing us a lot of trouble. Everywhere, even among our allies, the Jews have friends to help them, which is a proof that they are still playing an important role even in the Axis camp."[149]

It remains to be noted that, acting on orders from Generals Franz Böhme, Edmund Glaise von Horstenau, and Alexander Löhr (all of whom were from Austria), troops of the Wehrmacht systematically murdered the Jewish males of neighboring Serbia, starting in the summer of 1941—unhindered by the more compassionate and less racist Italians. This operation began independently, without the support of the SS, which only later, from the end of 1941 on, killed the Jewish women and children of Serbia.[150]

In sum, we can say that the officers of the Italian armed forces refused to hand over Jews to the Germans for extermination in the years from 1941 to 1943, during which time they were allies of the Wehrmacht in the war. German officers responded to this resistance not only with incomprehension and disgust but also with growing animosity. Such hatred would then find expression in physical attacks on Italian soldiers after Italy pulled out of the war in the fall of 1943. In the context of the racism that stood uppermost in Wehrmacht officers' minds and made them a "master race," the Germans now began to regard Italians as inferior too, and treated them in a manner hardly less degrading and inhumane than their treatment of Jews and Russian prisoners of war. Between Italy's withdrawal in 1943 and the end of the war in 1945, German killed approximately 46,000 Italians, among them many soldiers and about 7,000 Jews.[151]

CHAPTER FOUR

Generals and Enlisted Men

The Military Elites in the Grip of a War Ideology

IT TRANSPIRES THAT THERE was a not inconsiderable overlap of interests and opinions between Hitler and the German military elite. If we want to delve more deeply into the question of why this was so, we would do well to investigate how both Hitler and his commanders understood the role of war in international relations, both in historical terms and in their own time. Hitler and the National Socialist leaders on the one hand and the representatives of the military elite on the other shared a belief that great political questions are always ultimately decided by war and the force of arms. Hence one can speak of a shared conviction that was fundamentally militaristic in nature. Within this ideology of war, issues of national defense served as a superficial rationalization at best. In actual fact, the expansion of Germany's boundaries was a given in this kind of thinking, and the potential goals of war—such as achieving hegemony in Europe, building an empire, making Germany a great power or even a world power—were debated solely in terms of their practical feasibility.

Of course, one could say that thinking about armed conflict is the military profession's job, and hence it is hardly surprising to find senior members of the military performing their assigned task. Yet one can also argue that it is possible to think about armed conflict without emphasizing conquest and wars of aggression. And it was through its aggression and campaigns to conquer territory that the Wehrmacht became "the single greatest cause of misery" for the people and nations of Europe in the period in question.[1] The German military's traditional orientation, which had been shaped by history, prevented its leaders from developing any fundamental criticism of Hitler's expansionist policy (although they often criticized the plans for specific campaigns from a technical standpoint).

The unified Germany created in 1871 was an authoritarian state based on Prussian traditions, and the thinking of its officers was characterized by the belief that armed conflict between nations represented the natural state of affairs. Either separately or together, God, history, and nature were called upon to justify this view. Waging war was considered normal. The military had to be prepared to engage in armed conflict from time to time, and its leaders did not expend much thought on the political distinction between aggression and defense.

This thinking was reflected in their actions, in both domestic and foreign affairs. Because the main pillars of the German Empire desired an authoritarian state whose destiny was to achieve victories in war, military leaders were disinclined to leave foreign policy to diplomats and civilians. They intervened in it as readily as they did in internal matters. Justification for this was provided by reports and policy papers that intentionally stressed military solutions to conflicts and downplayed possible peaceful measures. Such interference reached a peak during the First World War, when Paul von Hindenburg and Erich Ludendorff headed the High Command between

1916 and 1918. Since the generals also occupied key political offices themselves, historians have quite accurately characterized the German government of the time as a military dictatorship, the most extreme form of Prusso-German militarism that had ever existed up to that time.

The decisive element in the whole edifice of military thinking was the idea that force played a positive role in history, a notion espoused not only by German nationalists, incidentally, but also by Karl Marx, Friedrich Engels, and other leaders of the workers' movement in Germany.[2] Otto von Bismarck had earlier captured the essence of this attitude in the striking phrase "blood and iron." The pacifist educator Friedrich Wilhelm Foerster had called it *Schwertglauben*, "faith in the sword,"[3] a characterization taken up by the peace movement after World War I. Foerster spoke as well of the "warlike Prussian spirit," "militaristic and nationalistic delusion," the "vice of war," a "militaristic attitude," and the widespread "idolization of power" in Germany;[4] he considered the last to be something like a national disease. Foerster was not alone; Paul von Schoenaich, Franz Carl Endres, and other officers who became pacifists considered militarism to be primarily a matter of the country's "mental outlook."[5]

In fact, the phenomenon confronting us here represents the ideological core of Prusso-German militarism. The continuity evident as the German state changed from a monarchy to a republic to the National Socialist regime is as striking as it is disturbing. One finds the same outlook reflected in remarks by such diverse figures as the Prussian field marshal Helmuth von Moltke in the year 1875, the Württemberg politician and supporter of the republic General Wilhelm Groener in 1919, Army Chief of Staff General Hans von Seeckt in 1922, and General Ludwig Beck (who was prepared to criticize Hitler on some points) in 1938. The attitudes of these four men, whose thinking typifies various versions of this militarism, are presented briefly in what follows.

Field Marshal Helmuth von Moltke

Field Marshal Helmuth von Moltke (1800–1891) served for thirty years as chief of staff of the Prussian army, from 1858 to 1888. In this role he led the military campaigns that resulted in the unification of Germany under its first Kaiser, the former King Wilhelm I of Prussia. Moltke summed up his metaphysical vision of the place of war in the world in 1880 in a letter to Johann Kaspar Bluntschli, a professor of constitutional law at the University of Heidelberg. It contained a passage that has been cited repeatedly ever since: "Peace is a dream, and not even a good one; war is a link in God's world order. War develops the noblest human virtues, such as courage and renunciation, devotion to duty, and the willingness to make sacrifices, even at the risk of one's own life. Without war the world would degenerate into a swamp of materialism."[6]

Moltke's thinking may well have been more multi-layered and flexible than that of other Prussian generals, a group in which he stood out for the breadth of his education. All the same, his view of war as part of a divinely ordained world order was standard among the officers of the era. In the same letter to Bluntschli, incidentally, Moltke contemplated the possibility of the maximal war that could be waged with the weapons of the time, which he characterized as a "struggle for existence."[7]

Dreams of peace were thus for other people; the officers themselves, used to thinking in terms of Realpolitik (as they saw it), meaning the exercise of power and waging war, inhabited a fundamentally different mental world. It was an attractive one for them, too, to the extent that it offered them a chance to win honor, glory, and prestige—as peace did not.

The ridicule that authoritarian politicians in Kaiser Wilhelm's Germany heaped on pacifists must be understood in this context. They regarded pacifism as a mixture of "stupidity, cowardice, and treason."[8] At best, pacifists were naïve idealists. They threatened to become dangerous crackpots, however, when they dared to question—and hence potentially to weaken—the authoritarian nation-state and thereby the ideological and material foundations of life in the officer corps as well.

General von Moltke's war ideology was a common theme among the soldiers of the era. This is demonstrated, for example, by the views of August von Mackensen, then a student and lieutenant in the reserves, whose later career as a Prussian field marshal in the uniform of the Death's Head Hussar Regiment became the stuff of legend. Mackensen's answer to the question of what caused wars was simple: "As long as boys get into fights, nations will go to war against each other."[9] A passage from a letter Mackensen sent to his mother a few years after the Franco-Prussian war of 1870–71 can also be considered thoroughly typical of its time. In it he expressed his "secret" hope that there would not be another fifty years of peace, and that the "good time" of the recent war would come to "blossom" for him once again. Like many of his contemporaries, Mackensen believed that war ennobled men and kept them from going soft. This was one more reason why war had to be viewed as a necessity from a "moral" point of view.[10]

General Hans von Seeckt

In 1920 General Hans von Seeckt (1866–1936) was chosen chief of the army command. He remained the political and military leader of the Reichswehr until his dismissal in 1926. After Friedrich Ebert's death in 1925, Seeckt debated whether to seek the office of president of the new republic, but decided not to run against the great hero of the First World War, Field Marshal Paul von Hindenburg.

In the early phase of the Weimar Republic, Major General von Seeckt, then serving as head of the General Troop Office in the newly created Reichswehr ministry, issued a directive to the general staff of the Provisional Reichswehr. He wanted to articulate for them his view of the times and the tasks that the German military elite would face in the future. He began with several skeptical observations on the peace treaty of Versailles, the League of Nations, and that organization's goal "of achieving international peace through general disarmament." He appended this decidedly anti-pacifist statement: "My own training in history prevents me from seeing in the idea of permanent peace anything more than a dream— whereby it remains an open question whether one can consider it, in Moltke's phrase, a 'good dream' or not."[11] For his part, Seeckt was unwilling to rely on the protection of the League of Nations, that is, on outside assistance. In his view, two old German sayings would remain valid in the new era: "Selbst ist der Mann" (A man relies on himself) and "Wehrlos—ehrlos" (without defense—without honor).

It was true that the limitations on rearmament dictated by the Treaty of Versailles could not be circumvented. Nevertheless, as the general argued in a restatement of "faith in the sword," no treaty could forbid men from "thinking like men" and making Germany ready to defend itself, at least in psychological terms. The following passage is quoted in full, as it reflects the warrior who has recognized, so to speak, that peace cannot be trusted, and that the state and nation remain in need of defenders:

German officers, and especially members of the general staff, have never sought a fight for its own sake or been warmongers. And they should not do so now, but they should also never forget the great deeds achieved by German warriors. Keeping the memory of them alive in ourselves and our people must be a sacred duty. For then neither officers nor people will lapse into enfeebling illusions of peace, but will remain aware that in the moment of truth only personal and national stature counts. If fate once again calls the German people to arms—and who can doubt that day will come?—then officers should not have to call on a nation of weaklings, but of strong men ready to take up familiar and trusted weapons. The form these weapons take is not so important if they are wielded by hands of steel and hearts of iron. So let us do our utmost to ensure that on that future day there is no lack of such hearts and hands; let us strive tirelessly to strengthen our own bodies and minds and those of our fellow Germans.

It was, Seeckt continued, "the duty of every member of the general staff to make the Reichswehr "not only a reliable pillar of the state, but also a school for leaders of the nation. Beyond the army itself, every officer will sow the seed of manly attitudes throughout the population."[12]

In sum, Seeckt was issuing a warning against "enfeebling illusions of peace" that could produce only a "nation of weaklings." Only German military might would count in the future war that fate would send, and the task fell to the officers of the general staff to train the men and lead the nation.

It was Seeckt who, confronted with the necessity of reducing the numerical strength of the German army, responded by creating a professional military of greatly increased efficiency. His elite officers were recruited from the most promising sons of aristocratic military families. He saw no room in the army of the new republic for Jews, Communists, Social Democrats, or outspoken democrats,[13] for none of them had shown much enthusiasm for embracing the proper kind of "faith in the sword." In 1923 Seeckt complained accordingly in a memorandum to Chancellor Joseph Wirth and other leading German politicians that the "German nation, with its Socialist majority," would be averse to "a policy of action, which has to reckon with the possibility of war." While he had to admit that the foolish cry of "No more war!" continued to find broad support, what was needed instead was a leader whom the people would follow "in the struggle for their existence," despite their "widespread and understandable need for peace."[14] What Seeckt envisioned specifically was anti-French and anti-Polish policies and military cooperation with Russia.

During the years in which Seeckt was in charge, he found a number of ways to sidestep the conditions of the peace treaty and prepare the buildup of the army of the future. And he certainly did not restrict his thinking to the requirements of national defense. Instead, carrying on the pre–World War I tradition, he aspired to world power status for Germany. In 1925 he confessed once again openly that this was the goal: "We must become powerful, and as soon as we have power, we will naturally take back everything we have lost."[15] Striking in this formulation is the lack of an economic motive in favor of power politics, which had earlier dominated the policies of both Bismarck and Albrecht von Roon, the Prussian minister of war, when the German Empire was founded.[16]

General Wilhelm Groener

General Wilhelm Groener (1867–1939), who came from Württemberg, figures among the most intelligent men in the top military echelon under the Kaiser and in the Weimar Republic, and also among the most sophisticated in his political thinking. In 1918 he succeeded Ludendorff as first quartermaster general in the High Command under Hindenburg. After the German Revolution broke out in November, he assured Friedrich Ebert, leader of the revolutionary government of People's Deputies, that the High Command was willing to cooperate. Ebert decided to work with Groener for the purpose of demobilizing the enormous army.[17] A personal relationship began to develop between the leading Social Democratic politician and the flexible general. Groener later served in the government of the Weimar Republic as minister of transportation (1920–1923) and as Reichswehr minister (1928–1932).[18] In 1931–32 he also served simultaneously as minister of the interior. He was a moderate among the generals of his generation, and his political sympathies are said to have lain with the liberal German Democratic Party (DDP). In terms of military ideology, however, he must be regarded as another supporter of "faith in the sword," and thus part of the continuing tradition.

In 1919, the first year of the republic, Groener grew alarmed at the mass protests by antiwar and pacifist demonstrators and felt compelled to warn the head of the government about what he regarded as a dangerous development. He summarized his views to Friedrich Ebert, who was by now the president, as follows: "We must never succumb to the self-deception of pacifist ideologists, as if eternal peace and human bliss could be achieved by suppressing every trace of national and martial spirit in a nation . . . Only in a *permanent* struggle for life are those mental and moral powers strengthened and steeled which alone can elevate a people, forming the wings by which they rise. Any nation that violates this law of nature is inwardly diseased and doomed to decline. They are false prophets who urge the people to renounce the development and use of their physical powers in the struggle for survival." In the coming years of peace, General Groener told the president, Germany would have to develop its muscle "as a great people that *refuses* to go under, that has the will to fight for its survival and once again takes up this struggle with the nations of the earth, to the extent and with the means that its condition reasonably allows."[19]

The underlying social Darwinism of the message is evident: Natural law ordains a never-ending struggle to survive, and for that reason maintaining the martial spirit of a nation and readying its defenses constitute a government's chief tasks. A commitment to preserving peace amounts to self-deception on the part of pacifist ideologues, and anyone taken in by their arguments will be guilty of causing his own country's ruin. It should be added that the resemblance of this argument to Hitler's is striking. I say this without any polemical intent, but in order to make clear how close this conservative, nationalistic ideology of war stands to the biological doctrine of the radical right. In the sequel to *Mein Kampf,* known as his *Second Book,* Hitler wrote in 1928 that "politics is in truth the implementation of a people's struggle for survival," and "life is the eternal stake for which it fights and struggles." The constant task of "all truly great legislators and statesmen of this earth was never the limited preparation for a war but rather the unlimited inner development and education of a people"—for war.[20] In both places we find social Darwinist thinking of an unceasing struggle between different populations which manifests itself in different forms of warfare; a nation can withdraw from it only at the price of its own downfall.

General Ludwig Beck

General Ludwig Beck (1880–1944) was a typical officer of his time to the extent that he approved Hitler's plans to rearm Germany on a large scale. He hoped that they would not merely result in "reestablishing Germany's military parity," as the propaganda of the time put it, but in fact lead to military supremacy. Beck was chief of the army general staff from 1935 to 1938. When he realized that Hitler intended to use the new armaments for wars of aggression, he wrote memoranda expressing opposition, but his concern was based on a lack of adequate preparation. Since his point of view did not prevail, Beck resigned in 1938. He later played a leading role in the resistance movement whose members attempted to assassinate Hitler on July 20, 1944. If the attempt had succeeded, the plan foresaw General Beck as the new head of state.

Beck is quoted here in order to make it clear that he, too, espoused the traditional ideology of war and the Prussian "faith in the sword." In the late 1930s General Beck wrote, "The ultimate instrument in nations' dealings with one another will remain their force of arms." Omitting mention of the Kellogg-Briand Pact of 1928, which called for renunciation of war as an instrument of national policy, he continued, every country was "entitled in principle to make use of the sword." Beck created a connection to Moltke's views by stating that war represented "a link in God's world order." Hence it was pointless to rack one's brains over how to prevent war: "We cannot abolish war. All reflection on the imperfection of human beings as God has made them will inevitably lead to this conclusion."[21]

Despite all the genuine differences that existed among the leading thinkers of the Prusso-German military tradition, they inhabited the same ideological neighborhood, and we can assume that the average officer of that era regarded pacifists as despicably weak, decadent, or even pathological. Not infrequently pacifism was linked with treason, and thus criminalized.[22] At the same time, the average officer thought of himself in categories such as strong, manly, coura-

geous, realistic, loyal to the monarch, and martial. He was filled
with a sense that he belonged to a special and socially elevated caste.

Hitler and the Generals

Those who speak of "the Wehrmacht" and mean the power structure of the institution as a whole are referring mainly to the responsible group of military leaders. It cannot be doubted that the top
level—that is, the ranking officers in the high commands and the
troop commanders—were largely responsible for converting into
specific military orders Hitler's general ideas about race and waging
an ideologically based war of extermination. This was demonstrated
in the preceding chapter. By comparison, the responsibility of millions of German enlisted men, many of whom were drafted for
military service against their will, is incomparably smaller, even
though, over the course of the war, many of them became accessories to crimes, or even accomplices in them.

But how much military and political influence did the military
elite possess, beyond the confines of the institution, within the overall power structure of the National Socialist regime? While National
Socialists persecuted their political opponents and achieved the
Gleichschaltung (Nazification) of most political and social organizations, they handled the Wehrmacht with kid gloves, and even favor-
itism. The military was strengthened enormously, in terms of both
personnel and materiel, and Hitler declared it to be the "second pillar" of the state, alongside the Nazi Party itself. In comparison with
the treatment of military affairs under the Weimar governments,
Hitler's policies brought about the restoration of the authoritarian
state for which the military had been longing. And that in turn
brought officers immense gains in social prestige and possibilities for
professional advancement.

One development with significant consequences for the relationship between the new government and the military leadership occurred on February 3, 1933, only a few days after Hitler had been named chancellor. The new head of government met for the first time with the commanders of the army and navy in a secret meeting at the Berlin home of General Kurt von Hammerstein-Equord, chief of the Army High Command. In a speech that lasted two and a half hours, Hitler laid out his new policies. Lasting relief for the present crisis, he explained to them, could be found only "by seizing new *Lebensraum* in the East and Germanizing it relentlessly." In order to achieve this, the first requirement would be a "complete reversal" of current domestic policies, entailing "the strictest kind of authoritarian government, eliminating the cancerous tumor of democracy, . . . [and] eradicating Marxism root and branch." It would further be necessary to make Germany ready to defend itself again, that is, to attack pacifism and strengthen the resolve of the population to fight "by all possible means." Germany would need to build up its armed forces and existing arsenal, freeing up the Nazi Party storm troopers (SA) to concentrate on domestic political issues. It would also be necessary for the army to refrain from all intervention in the domestic struggle.[23]

Hitler thus announced to the commanders of the armed forces in unmistakable terms his agenda for establishing an authoritarian state, and also for militarizing the government, the economy, and society. He even mentioned his goal of conquering new territory as *Lebensraum*. The generals and admirals in his audience were pleased by the "strong will and ideological energy" in Hitler's speech.[24]

Hitler's program for making the entire nation "ready to defend itself again" corresponded to the ideas then current in the armed forces that the wars of the future would be "total" in character.[25]

Werner von Blomberg, the new Reichswehr minister, was thus probably speaking for the commanders as a whole when he declared on
the same day, February 3, that Hitler's cabinet had turned the aspi-
rations of many of Germany's finest into a reality because the cabinet represented the first step in readying the average citizen for
"self-defense."[26] In this case, then, the interests of the National Socialist government and the military coincided. The same holds for
the long-term prospect of a future war. The officers could have had
no doubt that when Hitler spoke of expanding the military and
building new weapons, he did not mean strengthening the country's
defenses—a goal that in itself represented a violation of the Treaty
of Versailles—but rather preparations for an extensive campaign of
conquest.

All this indicates that Hitler and the military leadership were in
agreement from this early date on about a policy to militarize German society as a necessary first step on the path to later wars of aggression. A not insignificant circumstance in the solidifying of this
alliance was the way Hitler repeatedly emphasized his sense of obligation to the traditions embodied by Paul von Hindenburg, the former field marshal of the First World War and current president of
Germany. Adolf Hitler's public gesture on Potsdam Day, March 21,
1933,[27] could not have failed to make a lasting impression on military leaders of a conservative Prussian stamp and leaders from industry, the churches, the civil service, the legal system, and the aristocracy: in a well-calculated symbolic gesture, the old field marshal
had appeared at the military ceremony in full uniform, with all his
medals and a spiked helmet, and the man who had served in the war
as a private bowed to him before the eyes of the assembled soldiers
in a gesture of respect.[28]

Hindenburg died in 1934, and after that Hitler became, at least pro forma, "supreme commander of the armed forces." The military leadership now saw to it that all soldiers swore an oath of loyalty to Adolf Hitler personally. Such an oath may not have meant much to the average enlisted man, but for career officers it was a different matter. Up to 1918 they had sworn loyalty to the Kaiser as their supreme commander; he had been the central figure from which everything else took its orientation, and the new oath to the Fuehrer and chancellor of the Reich, Adolf Hitler, appeared to stand in the same tradition. Certainly the oath the generals had sworn to Hitler played a critical role during the Second World War, in particular when they struggled with the question of whether to join the resistance movement.

In the scholarly literature on the Wehrmacht, much has been made of Hitler's distrust of the generals, most of whom were Prussian and members of the aristocracy, and of various crises in which they were involved. Both the distrust and the crises were real, and have been well documented. Hitler was in fact by no means always certain that he had the generals' support, and he remained suspicious of them to the very end. Members of the military elite expressed doubts about Hitler's radical war strategy, as General Ludwig Beck did, for example, in 1938. Objections of this kind were raised during the preparations for war against France. But when the Blitzkrieg against France was waged exactly as Hitler wanted and ended in triumph, the generals were reduced to silence. From that point on they accepted the priority of Hitler's political leadership more than ever. In their eyes the military success had proved particularly convincing. And with few exceptions, they had no objections on principle to the fact that Hitler's radical kind of warfare violated international law. As we have seen, they accepted both the planning of the Russian campaign and the events at several sites.

The weight of the events referred to as the "generals' crises" has often been overemphasized since 1945. It is true that a number of generals were recalled, replaced, or transferred to the so-called "Fuehrer's reserve," and often this occurred against their will, of course. The resulting anger and resentment, however, never rose to levels that could have threatened the survival of the regime. The sole event amounting to a direct political attack on the dictatorship was the assassination attempt against Hitler on July 20, 1944.[29] In sum, the relationship between Hitler and the generals who did not participate in the conspiracy was one of trust, approval, and subordination; it was not characterized by conflicts, let alone fundamental differences of opinion on how the war should be waged.[30]

The fact is that a basic consensus developed early on between the military leadership and Hitler, given their similar political interests and their views on war as an instrument of policy—even a policy of aggression, conquest, and extermination. Through the oath they swore to the "Fuehrer and supreme commander of the Wehrmacht," career officers saw themselves as the latest link in the long Prussian tradition of unconditional obedience to military orders. The victories of 1939–40, which National Socialist propaganda ascribed to Hitler's genius as a military strategist, further reduced the officers' independence and political clout, binding them even more closely to the country's political leaders and their party.

Given so much consensus, it is almost surprising to find that Hitler made systematic use of bribes to keep the leaders of the Wehrmacht on his side. Hitler did not invent the use of gifts (in this case mostly cash or real estate) as a tool of leadership; it had existed earlier under rulers like Frederick the Great in Prussia and Napoleon in France.[31] The goal always remained the same: to bind the generals more closely to the ruler by giving them valuable presents.

Hitler marked special occasions such as military victories, but also birthdays, with gifts of money or land (tax free) as well as expensive objects, such as works of art, that had been seized by revenue officials. Occasionally politicians like Robert Ley and Joachim Ribbentrop or the staff of the architect Albert Speer were rewarded in this way,[32] but as a rule such gifts flowed to the top echelon of the military. As early as 1935 Hitler thanked August von Mackensen, the prominent elderly field marshal, for his services to the regime with a country house, which came with three thousand acres of land and a staff of two hundred. Field Marshals Gerd von Runstedt, Erhard Milch, and Hans-Günther von Kluge each received 250,000 reichsmarks, and General Heinrich von Kleist got the lavish sum of 480,000 marks, while Admiral of the Fleet Erich Raeder and Luftwaffe General Hugo Sperrle were given paintings valued at 38,000 and 90,000 marks, respectively. Field Marshal Wilhelm Keitel even took the initiative in this area, asking for and receiving from Hitler 250,000 reichsmarks in cash and a tract of land valued at 730,000 marks, from tax money and confiscated property.[33] The book *Dienen und Verdienen* (Serving and Earning) by Gerd R. Ueberschär and Winfried Vogel documents the extent to which members of the top echelon were dependent on the regime for their standard of living, and how Hitler ensured their gratitude, continued compliance, and support through his material gifts—buying it, in effect. The fact that generals allowed themselves to be rewarded in a manner smacking of corruption remained "largely unknown" to the German public during the war.[34]

In the final phase of the war, when it had become clear that Germany could not win it, the generals did not distance themselves from their supreme commander, Hitler, even though more people died from war-related causes than in the previous four years.[35] They remained devoted—one could even say chained—to him, and let the soldiers entrusted to their oversight fight on until the unconditional surrender of May 8, 1945.

The "Little Guy" in Uniform

Conscription: Providing Fresh Supplies of Cannon Fodder

In 1935 Hitler reintroduced the military draft in Germany, flouting the provisions of the Treaty of Versailles.[36] In doing so he could count on the support of all Germans who favored nationalistic policies aimed at reacquiring power. They all believed that reintroducing conscription was a necessary first step for waging the war of the future, in which Germany would regain its position as a world power. This war would have to be fought at some point. And the government needed the draft if the German "ethnic community" *(Volksgemeinschaft)* was to be successfully prepared for battle on the broadest possible scale. Hitler's earliest political writings reflect this fundamental conviction,[37] and he never altered it.

When, only a few days after being named chancellor in 1933, Hitler spoke to representatives of the military and stressed his intention to toughen up the population for battle "by all possible means," they could have had no doubt that these means included the reintroduction of conscription.[38] It was also clear that this measure was only a steppingstone on the way to Hitler's openly stated aims, "seizing new *Lebensraum* in the East and Germanizing it relentlessly." In other words, the military potential represented by future conscripts would be systematically and efficiently exploited to build up an army capable of going on the offensive.[39] Over the next two years the National Socialist government and the military leaders collaborated in the closest imaginable way to create a political and organizational basis for reintroducing general conscription[40] as quickly as possible. Their aim was realized with the defense law passed on March 16, 1935.[41]

It is not possible here to go into the foreign reactions this step produced.[42] Instead the emphasis will be on the ideological grounds for it publicized by the chief propagandist of the regime, namely, Adolf Hitler himself. In his proclamation "To the German People,"[43] Hitler presented the familiar revisionist arguments having to do with foreign policy, providing endless figures and adding repeated assertions of his desire for peace. He added that these measures would ensure the honor and security of Germany.[44] In a speech delivered to the "soldiers of the new German Wehrmacht" during the party conference in September 1935, Hitler went even further, claiming—falsely—that for Germans, "the service of arms was never an enforced service, but a service of the highest honor in every period of our history." And in a truly odd rhetorical flourish, given that the topic was his reintroduction of universal conscription, he asserted, "Throughout the centuries, German men have done this voluntarily, and they were proud of their accomplishments."[45]

An instinctive response to such claims is to ask why, if this was the case, it had been necessary to pass a conscription law at all. Yet the intention of this kind of rhetoric about conscription was clear: it was to tar anyone who opposed compulsory military service as a pacifist without honor or a traitor, to mark the place of such people as outside the bounds of the socially acceptable. As is well known, conscientious objectors were not recognized during the Third Reich; there was no legal way to refuse military service.

Men who nevertheless did refuse—like Hermann Stöhr, a Lutheran pacifist and secretary of the German branch of the International League for Reconciliation—were sentenced to death by the

Reich War Court and executed. During the Third Reich this court sentenced approximately three hundred conscientious objectors to death.[46] Most of them were Jehovah's Witnesses.[47]

Rhetorically and ideologically inflated descriptions of military service were common under the National Socialists. They must be understood as part of a strategy to militarize German society. One of the organizations that took up this task enthusiastically was the German Society for Defense Policy and Defense Studies.[48]

A few figures may help to clarify what the Defense Law of 1935 meant for Germany. During the Second World War, approximately 20 million German men—that is, roughly 50 percent of all male citizens—performed military service.[49] Precise figures are hard to come by, but if one assumes that between 1 and 2 million of them were volunteers, that leaves between 18 and 19 million who were drafted, in other words, forced to serve. This means that the armed forces of the Third Reich were overwhelmingly an army of conscripts, with a relatively small percentage of career soldiers and volunteers.

In the prewar period German men were confronted with the totalitarian oversight and registration mechanisms of the National Socialist state and co-opted into the community of the German *Volk*. Once they were drafted, they were subjected to an even more rigid system in which orders were given and obedience was required, and they were trained with a view to their future tasks of military aggression.

Even more than their basic training, however, it was the war itself that would rob conscripts of their natural inhibitions about killing. In wartime conditions that imposed both physical and psychological burdens on soldiers, the military's demands of absolute, unquestioning obedience—even to criminal orders—caused many of them to lose most of their sense of individual responsibility and personal guilt. Soldiers' sense of humanity and justice became dramatically deformed. The militarization of Germany, achieved on the basis of general conscription, led during the war to a disturbingly far-reaching loss of humane standards of behavior that had previously been viewed as a hallmark of civilized societies.[50]

It should not be necessary to stress here that none of the democratic ideals professed by proponents of universal conscription in the nineteenth and early twentieth centuries had survived in the Wehrmacht of the decade 1935–1945. The earlier optimistic assumptions that citizen-soldiers would serve as guarantors of peace had nothing to do with the actual conditions of the Third Reich. The reality of a militarized German *Volk* under fascist leadership was utterly different. The course of the battle of Stalingrad is a fitting symbol. Outwardly the Germans were aggressive and effective enough toward foreigners to advance all the way to the distant Volga, but inwardly they were virtually paralyzed by a military discipline that suppressed all rational reflection.[51] "Citizens and soldiers were degraded to the status of materiel, never more so than in the Third Reich, when universal conscription and democracy represented the most drastic opposites imaginable."[52]

Toward the end of World War II, soldiers are reported to have deserted or acted "subversively" by the hundreds of thousands.[53] Nevertheless, it will probably prove impossible to dislodge the hypothesis that the thoroughly militarized German *Volksgemeinschaft*, whose armed members consisted overwhelmingly of conscripts with no other options than to serve, fought to the bitter end and failed to revolt, as their fathers had in 1918. There was no draftees' uprising in 1944–45.

In other words, the worst fears of the Allies, and in particular the British, after World War I were realized, although they had done what they could to prevent it. For this reason, they did not debate in Potsdam in 1945, as they had in Versailles in 1919, the question of whether Germany ought to maintain a professional or a conscripted army. Instead they decided on a far more radical solution: "the complete disarmament and demilitarization" of Germany.[54]

During the November uprisings of 1918, conscripts of the German Imperial Navy took the initiative, sending the signals that would lead to revolutionary political changes and thereby fulfilling the fears of the professional military and the hopes of radical democrats at the same time. If one disregards this brief episode, however, there is no indication whatsoever that conscription led to a more democratic, let alone more pacifist, attitude within the German armed forces. During the National Socialist regime it is much more the case that attempts to frame conscription in authoritarian terms succeeded.

The armed forces were defined and shaped from the perspective of the career officers, not by the conscripts who stood at the bottom of the hierarchy and were granted no role beyond carrying out orders. Hopes of a more democratic kind, once espoused by no less a figure than Friedrich Engels, proved again and again to be illusory. In reality, universal conscription in the nineteenth and twentieth centuries, up to 1945 at least, was an instrument of various governments for compelling young men to military service; the political and military leadership could then do with them what it liked.

Conscientious Objectors: The Jehovah's Witnesses

The only group who resisted all the pressure exerted by Hitler's government to serve in the armed forces were members of a religious community, the Jehovah's Witnesses. The authorities treated them with the greatest severity possible. In 1933 this group had only between twenty and thirty thousand members in Germany, yet the new government placed it on the list of forbidden organizations in June 1933, and sent approximately ten thousand of its members to prison or to concentration camps.[55] One wonders why the National Socialists were not simply able to ignore such a relatively small minority. It is a fact, however, that they treated them like influential political opponents. This was the case although the Jehovah's Witnesses did not regard themselves as a political group in the least. Their own view of themselves was as professing Christians who sought to maintain their distance from all political issues. Nevertheless, their belief in a genuine kingdom of God on earth, which transcended all earthly governments, presented sufficient grounds for trouble in an authoritarian state. The Jehovah's Witnesses came into conflict with the totalitarian government's demands for unquestioning obedience.

The Jehovah's Witnesses displayed a distinct tendency to resist, which could be considered political even though the impulse behind it was religious in nature. The group's publications characterized the Third Reich as "the rule of the Devil" and Hitler as the "Antichrist." Members refused to say the normal greeting of the period, "Heil Hitler!," insisting instead on the traditional "good morning" or "good day"; this was a stance that required considerable courage under the new regime. Far more serious, however, was their refusal to swear an oath to Hitler as the supreme commander of the armed forces. From the perspective of the regime, this behavior represented disloyalty in a whole variety of forms and was treated as a declaration of open defiance. In the 1930s SS and Gestapo officers indeed categorized Jehovah's Witnesses as enemies of the state.[56]

The situation worsened with the reintroduction of universal conscription in 1935, for now every man in a particular age group was required to perform military service, without exception. Finally, once the war began in 1939, the Jehovah's Witnesses had to face the most difficult choice imaginable: either they bowed to the "necessities of wartime," meaning the demands of the totalitarian state, and renounced their convictions, or they remained true to their beliefs and resisted the draft. Choosing the latter, however, meant an almost certain death sentence. The number of community members who accepted martyrdom as their fate has remained a little-known fact to the present day.

Detlef Garbe's research has shown that some 250 German and Austrian Jehovah's Witnesses were sentenced to death by the Reich War Court for conscientious objection and were executed, usually by guillotine. As Hanns Lilje, a Lutheran bishop in Hannover observed in 1947, the Jehovah's Witnesses can "claim to be the only group that refused military service on a large scale during the Third Reich openly and on grounds of conscience."[57] In fact they were the only group that promoted and practiced conscientious objection during this period. The sense of cohesion within the group was extremely significant, for men who belonged to the Jehovah's Witnesses and refused the draft could be sure that their religious community backed them completely and would provide moral support at every point along the difficult path they had chosen.

Conscientious objectors from the two main churches in Germany could not count on the same solidarity, and this helps to explain why so few of them came from these groups. A total of twelve Roman Catholics and four Lutherans were executed for refusing to renounce their convictions. One of them, Franz Jägerstätter, was an Austrian farmer and a Catholic from St. Radegund, not far from Hitler's birthplace in Braunau on the Inn.[58] Jägerstätter objected to serving for religious and political reasons and was guillotined, without ob-

taining any assistance from church authorities. The Lutheran pacifist Dr. Hermann Stöhr, who before 1933 had served as secretary of
the International League for Reconciliation, received no more support or protection from his church leaders when he cited religious
belief as the grounds for his refusal to join the army. A death sentence was passed on Stöhr by the Reich War Court in the spring
of 1940 and carried out immediately.[59] Even after 1945 the two
churches did not honor or commemorate the conscientious objectors
in their ranks, and the postwar legal system offered them no posthu-
mous recognition either. It was not until 1997, for example, that the
conviction of Franz Jägerstätter was formally overturned.[60]

One question that has been much discussed is whether the Jehovah's Witnesses were actually pacifists. Is it necessary to distinguish
them from pacifists whose motives were political? First of all, it
must be noted that the latter group as a rule did not openly refuse to
serve in the military. Some prominent pacifists recognized the coming danger even before 1933 (or at the latest soon thereafter) and
emigrated. Others, like Carl von Ossietzky, were arrested and suffered in concentration camps. During the war some supporters of
banned pacifist organizations tried to find niches in the military that
promised a chance to avoid combat. These circumstances deserve
mention for two reasons: they show, first of all, how unique the behavior of the Jehovah's Witnesses was, and second, that it would be
wrong to categorize them as part of the pacifist movement of the
time without further differentiation. German pacifists may have
been led by various motives to the join the movement, but they always understood it as openly political, whereas the Jehovah's Witnesses were "not motivated by politics or pacifism, or at least not primarily."[61]

In that case, why were the military courts of the Third Reich so hostile to the members of the denomination who became conscientious objectors? What caused the military to treat them with such extreme harshness and brutality? It can't have been their numbers, since the few hundred draftees from the ranks of the Jehovah's Witnesses were insignificant in an army of 20 million men. Why did the judges consider them so dangerous, when all they wanted was to practice their faith and avoid politics as far as possible? How could they sentence these men to death? In some cases, judges appear to have had scruples. But why didn't more of them?

To answer this question it is necessary to step back and view it from a broader perspective; then it becomes evident that the National Socialist regime punished others who offered resistance, such as deserters and those accused of "undermining morale," with equal severity. All the participants in the plot of July 20, 1944, were killed, regardless of whether they were civilians or in the military, or only indirectly involved. Germany was then a totalitarian military dictatorship that brooked no deviation from the party line. It inflated the idea of military service ideologically, calling it "honorable service to the German people,"[62] thus sending a signal that no one would be able to evade the regime's grasp. Significantly, the National Socialists did not use the term "conscientious objection" that is so familiar to present-day Germans, largely because it numbers among the basic rights specifically guaranteed by our constitution. Instead the regime spoke of "underminers of morale," and the legal system dealt with them under this heading, whereby "undermining morale" was viewed as a hostile act directed against the whole community of the *Volk*. From the beginning of the war on, it constituted a capital offense.[63]

The Nazis' harsh treatment of Jehovah's Witnesses who became conscientious objectors can be explained partly as a result of this totalitarian mentality, but the political leadership also feared, strangely enough, the "propagandistic effect" of these "stubborn resisters," that is, their potential to serve as role models.[64]

Deserters and "Underminers of Morale"

How many members of the German armed forces deserted in the course of the Second World War is unknown; a great many cases certainly went unrecorded. As the army retreated and Germany approached collapse in 1944–45, men may have deserted in the hundreds of thousands. Entire units disintegrated in the weeks and months before the capitulation, and no one was keeping written records anymore. We possess a more exact figure on the sad topic of the number of death sentences imposed on soldiers by military courts during the war, however: 30,000.[65] More than 22,000 of these men were sentenced for the crime of desertion, and in some 15,000 cases the sentences were actually carried out.[66]

This toll of lives provides further evidence that those who tried to resist the war in any form were treated with the greatest possible severity. It was the murderous excess of a military justice system unleashed against its own troops, and it has no parallel in history.[67] In the democracies of the English-speaking world, exactly one soldier was executed for desertion during the Second World War, a man from Detroit named Eddie Slovik.[68] His case made headlines, whereas for a long time the German public did not even register what was being done to deserters from the Wehrmacht.

The treatment of deserters and so-called "underminers of morale" *(Wehrkraftzersetzer)* can be understood properly only in the context of the First World War,[69] or, more precisely, the way the experiences of this war were interpreted during the 1920s. Servicemen at the front, "in the trenches," came to be surrounded with an almost mythological aura, at the opposite end of the scale from "cowards," "shirkers," and, worst of all, deserters, who were detested as morally inferior. Hitler touched on the subject in *Mein Kampf:* "The deserter must know that his desertion brings with it the very thing that he wants to escape. At the front a man *can* die, as a deserter he *must* die."[70]

During the Second World War, just as German military psychiatrists offered their full support to the goals of the National Socialists,[71] so too did the justice system of the Wehrmacht (with some exceptions).[72] Military judges did not just interpret Hitler's dictum literally; they even exceeded expectations, so to speak, in their eagerness not to be criticized by the right, as had occurred after the First World War. At that time radical nationalists had faulted the courts and the legal system for not having prosecuted the underminers of morale on the home front, whom they associated with the legend of the "stab in the back." Hence military judges in the Second World War did not spend much time looking into the motives of individual defendants; their aim was rather to use harsh sentences to instill fear among the population and so counteract their growing unwillingness to keep on fighting, especially toward the end of the war.[73]

It is largely because the war courts took so little interest in this question that we still know very little about the motives of deserters from the Wehrmacht.[74] For their part, the defendants accused of desertion could naturally not mention to the court any political or moral motives they might have had, as it would have robbed them of any slight hope of escaping a death sentence. And last but not least, since they were executed, they were not around to explain their motives after the war. We cannot assume that their motives for trying to escape the machinery of the National Socialists' war were all the same; most likely they represented a whole spectrum: attempts to gain personal advantage; moral scruples and revulsion at the Germans' actions and extermination practices; shattered nerves as a result of unbearable pressures; realization that the German cause was lost (particularly in the final phase of the war); recognition of the unjust character of the National Socialist regime and the need for political resistance; and perhaps, in extreme cases, a conviction in the minds of a few that in order to fight Hitler they should join the other side.

One should probably picture the Wehrmacht deserter as a man torn by conflicting feelings and divided loyalties, seeking a way out, someone who did not want to share in the guilt for what was going on. In sociological terms, deserters were "average guys" in uniform who used one of the very few options remaining to them in the completely militarized society of that time to refuse to serve in the armed forces. It took more than fifty years after the war ended in 1945 for the realization to spread within the German public that desertion from the Wehrmacht needed to be reappraised in order to reflect the perspective that, in view of the criminal dimensions of this war, "any form of resistance at all [was] a morally appropriate act that merited respect."[75]

The charge of "undermining morale" should not be understood today as referring primarily to specific acts of resistance such as sabotage in armaments factories or openly calling for resistance to conscription. As a rule, it was based on remarks made by German citizens in public that did not conform to National Socialist propaganda. People who expressed doubt about Germany's "final victory," made jokes about the Fuehrer, or questioned the point of the war soon found themselves accused of this crime.[76] Others willing to denounce them for such remarks could clearly be found in all sectors of society.[77] In democratic nations such behavior is protected by the right of free speech, but it had been declared a capital crime in a society that in terms of both ideology and production was entirely focused on war.

How extensive were desertion and "undermining morale" during the Second World War? The former Wehrmacht general Günther Blumentritt dealt with the subject somewhat indirectly in response to a question put to him by American officers in 1947: "Why did German soldiers go on fighting in a hopeless situation?" It obviously did not occur to Blumentritt that desertion could be seen as a form of resistance on the part of enlisted men. He wrote that Germans could take pride in the fact that their army continued to fight even when the outlook was hopeless; it showed they had learned the lessons of 1918. Whereas the revolution had "been on the march" back then, the German population in 1945 was united in its opposition to Bolshevism. There were no red flags, no "indiscipline," no class hatred or party divisions, but instead a "community united by its suffering" and soldiers prepared to do their duty.[78]

Looking at the final phase of the war objectively, one must concede that at least General Blumentritt described the overall situation accurately. The National Socialist regime and the Second World War came to an end only with the Wehrmacht's unconditional surrender. Ultimately the "other soldiers" (in the title of one recent study)[79] who refused in one way or another to fight for Hitler amounted at best to sand in the gears of the war machine. A small number of individual resisters were dealt with by the military justice system, army prisons, and so-called punishment battalions (Strafbataillone), but they never represented a politically significant group. This fact makes their willingness to buck the tide appear all the more courageous. For decades after the war, the great majority of soldiers who had followed orders also refused to grant any recognition to those who had not. Demanding any more from the majority and their families would have been problematic, for it would have forced them to examine their own behavior, and the underlying values of military obedience and duty.

The Effect of War Propaganda on Enlisted Men

National Socialist propaganda always portrayed Russia as essentially an enemy nation, as was discussed earlier. This meant that the image was based less on knowledge of the country and its people than on negative stereotyping and prejudice. It was comparatively easy to spread such notions, for at that time few Germans had visited Russia. The information gap was filled by propaganda messages. As far as Hitler's plans to wage a war for *Lebensraum* was concerned, limiting knowledge about Russia to a few negative clichés had its advantages; his goal was not to stimulate informed discussions but to persuade the recipients of the propaganda that Russia should be attacked and its land annexed. Propaganda aimed at the military had the specific tasks of reducing soldiers' inhibitions about killing Russians and any scruples they might have about the war's legitimacy, and increasing their sense of their own superiority. At the same time, it was directed against the Red Army as "*Untermenschen* infected with Bolshevism."[80] The extermination practice of the war[81] showed the terrible extent to which it succeeded.

The question remains whether, when the image encountered reality, the experience made Germans more skeptical about their own government's propaganda. Were civilians at home affected by personal encounters with Russians performing forced labor, or soldiers by contacts in the Soviet Union with Russians, their culture, and the landscape? Did the propaganda image of the enemy turn into perceptions of reality? One would also like to know whether the National Socialist propagandists were forced to alter their strategy, and if any changes can be identified in their depiction of Russia and Russians.

In her book *Hitler's War and the Germans*, Marlis G. Steinert investigated these questions in detail, using reports from the SD (Sicherheitsdienst), the SS intelligence service, and other documents in which the mood of the public was reported. The results of her research are surprising, for they suggest that after some initial success, the anti-Soviet propaganda had less and less effect. Steinert summarizes the development as follows:

> Rank and file Germans, inundated with anti-Bolshevik propaganda for years, were nevertheless more inclined to interpret this agreement [i.e., the Hitler-Stalin pact] positively because fear of a two-front war and of an onslaught from the east was more deeply rooted than ideological antipathy. Bismarck remained the ideal of the gifted statesman, which Hitler was not beginning to approach. The rupture of the agreement and the attack on Russia could only be made acceptable to the broad masses by using the argument of an inevitable military confrontation between Bolshevism and National Socialism and by playing on atavistic fears. Thus the picture of Asiatic "sub-humans" *(Untermenschen)* was incessantly drummed into the public. As early as the winter of 1941–42, however, cracks appeared in this artificial caricature, and doubt began to creep in as to its authenticity. Men who fought so doggedly for their fatherland and their political system, who were able to bring such military potential into play, could not operate exclusively under the lash of their commissars and be completely primitive. The daily

contact with the eastern worker, who showed himself to be intelligent, technically talented, and likeable, caused the real breach in this carefully created image of the enemy. Collective stereotype and personal experience clashed increasingly, and despite all official propaganda efforts the fear of Bolshevism vanished, especially among certain strata of the working class and among those who had nothing more to lose as respect grew for the tremendous accomplishments of the eastern foe. The view began to spread that it was only the establishment—old and new—that had to fear for its existence, and not the mass of the working people. However, the Red Army's conduct on German soil painfully confirmed Goebbels' worst invectives concerning the "Asiatic hordes." Towards the end of the war this almost-vanished fear of eastern savagery, combined with the concept of a despotic Bolshevik system in comparison to which National Socialism seemed positively benign, emerged stronger than ever. The wretched mass of refugees became the vehicle for this terror and had to atone vicariously for the Teutonic mania and German atrocities. Next to the repercussions of renewed totalitarian developments in East Germany, these people remained the strongest motive force of a rapidly spreading anti-Communism in West Germany during the postwar period.[82]

Can one conclude that in the end the propaganda failed to win out over reality? One would have to ask to what extent the anti-Bolshevist stereotypes, which were drummed into people for years during the Third Reich, became a permanent part of Germans' view of the world, and particularly of soldiers who had served in the eastern campaign. Letters sent home from the eastern front by enlisted men show that personal experience could be interpreted according to the negative clichés they had previously learned. (Several editions of these letters have been published,[83] and there are additional collections in the archives that are gradually being studied and evaluated.)[84]

Here is one example that, although it certainly cannot be regarded as representative for the men and noncommissioned officers of the Wehrmacht,[85] does reveal what National Socialist propaganda achieved in some soldiers' heads. The following passage is taken from a letter written by a member of a Naval NCO Training Department at Eckernförde on January 31, 1943. This was one day after Hermann Goering had delivered a "funeral oration" on the radio for the doomed Sixth Army in Stalingrad.[86] Petty Officer Second Class A.M. wrote:

> In his speech yesterday our Reich Marshal expressed in very moving words to all of us, no doubt, that we Germans would lose everything that makes life worth living for us if Bolshevism should win. But we still have millions of soldiers in reserve, who are prepared to give their all. I'm sure I don't need to tell you that—you know it as well as I do. But what else can one write, when one's thoughts are with our heroic comrades on the eastern front and the brothers are dying cheerfully so that our homeland and everything we love can be preserved? It is hard for a soldier to be on a base at home when out there every comrade is giving the utmost he can. But I also believe that the decisive moment is coming in this struggle, and every man will have to do his duty, wherever he is sent. After all, I have seen those dehumanized hordes

myself, and I can imagine what would happen to our beautiful country if the Bolshevists came flooding in.[87]

Even more revealing is a letter containing a reaction to Goebbels's notorious speech of February 18, 1943, on "total war."[88] It shows that all the elements of anti-Bolshevist ideology had taken root in the writer's thinking, and that he was among those Wehrmacht soldiers who were convinced of the necessity of the war of annihilation against the Soviet Union. The NCO W.F. wrote to his wife on February 19:

In the meantime we heard Goebbels's big speech last night. I don't think any of his other speeches was as stirring as yesterday's, the way it roused the crowd. We've known about the danger of Bolshevism for years, but we didn't know its full, true danger until this winter . . . Now we have to be utterly ruthless. The war has reached its highest pitch; it is merciless, and the Bolshevists, those tools of Judas, have forced us into this situation. If we were not equal to it, it would mean our destruction. But since we have recognized this diabolical threat for what it is, it stops being a threat. It becomes instead the realization that we must just fight back with the same means, or maybe even more brutally, because we know that it is what God wants. For the time being we must abandon our lofty ideas about the value of human life, not because we want to, but because we must. We attach more value to our lives, they are more valuable to human civilization than those of the Asiatic hordes. This is a hard and bitter realization, no question, but it is what Nature demands. Any other course of action would be terrible for us and result only in what you describe in your letter, dear wife—whereby forced labor in Siberia or some other place would be getting off easy.

Then a fellow would still be alive, even if his life was miserable. It's more probable that he would lose his life. The best thing then would be if he put an end to it himself first. But that is not what we want, not with a single thought. We want to fight, fight to our last breath, until God's justice is victorious. That is our unflinching and unalterable resolve.

We believe that our cause is good, to be fighters and martyrs in order to save Western civilization. We believe unconditionally in the strength of our Fuehrer, who has been chosen by a higher power to shape the destiny of nations. For that reason we also believe in our victory, which is ordained by nature! Or else it is God's will that the human race should perish. But we are all the more convinced of victory, since we know God is not a figure but Nature.

Nature is God. We know there is a higher power in Nature, and that is God. He created life, He created death, and He created what lasts. Nature was and is eternal and will remain for eternity. Bolshevism is unnatural; it uses force to intervene in natural human development and leads it into paths that can only result in chaos and annihilation. But those who sin against Nature and against God will be annihilated.[89]

Any analysis of the possible mutual influences of propaganda images of the enemy and direct personal experience will fall short, however, if it does not take account of the particular situation in which such changes of perspective and consciousness took place.

This situation was a war and the constant dangers to which soldiers were exposed. These circumstances made them crave reassurance in the form of messages that gave meaning to what they were doing, and such messages were offered by the anti-Bolshevist, anti-Semitic, and anti-Slavic ideology behind Nazi propaganda. Whereas the characterization of the last two groups as inferior races was relatively short-lived and did not outlast the Third Reich, the ideology that depicted Bolshevism as a threat could not be exposed as false through personal experience, since the "enemy" was so abstract. This may help to explain why the anti-Russian propaganda images in their anti-Bolshevist form remained unaffected by the political realignment after 1945 and continued to exert an influence for decades in the new configurations of the Cold War.

Soldiers of the Wehrmacht in Light of Recent Research

The "Average Joe": Enlisted Men

Enlisted men made up more than 90 percent of the armed forces of the National Socialist state. Historical scholarship in Germany has lagged far behind that in the English-speaking countries in paying attention to the experience of ordinary servicemen. This is especially true of the majority of soldiers, meaning those who functioned obediently as cogs in the war machine and drew no negative attention to themselves. Since the 1990s a trend has arisen to focus intently on marginal groups of resisters, such as conscientious objectors, people convicted of "undermining morale," and deserters.

In the records of the Wehrmacht, the "little guy" or "average Joe" tends to exist only in anonymous form, as an unnamed statistic in reports of losses and troop strength. The logs of military units of varying sizes and other official sources generally make no mention

of enlisted men by name. The same applies to "regimental histories" written after the war and the diaries and accounts published by
officers. The men under their command remained nameless, and
their ordinary hardships and battle experiences went unreported.
This explains why the historical archives contain so little material on the subject. It has been estimated that the source material
on enlisted men in the German Federal Archives–Military Archives
in Freiburg amounts to less than 1 percent of the total holdings.
The Library for Contemporary History in Stuttgart, by contrast, has
made a priority of buying up collections of soldiers' letters and
makes them available to researchers.

If one surveys the research on military history with this in mind,
it becomes evident that for a long time scholars concentrated on a
tiny percentage of the total military, namely, generals and admirals
and their aides, the officers of the army and navy general staffs.[90]
Behind this perspective, which remains overwhelmingly dominant,
a few interests can be identified. For one thing, the proponents of a
focus on general staffs believe that research on military leadership
in wartime can be of service to the military at the present time and
in the future—the argument of "practical use." Second, depictions
of the role played by elites are likely to promote respect for the military as a profession. Manfred Messerschmidt's call for research on
the role of Germany in the Second World War, to be written as
"a history of the German people in wartime,"[91] has not yet been
heeded to the extent that it needs to be.

Of course, some good reasons can also be cited for the continuing
concentration of military historians' interest on elite groups. The
first concerns the system by which power is exercised within the
military. More than in other areas of society—including industry,
the churches, educational institutions, or political parties—the top

leadership in the military determines what happens wholly and completely. Nowhere else is the hierarchy so highly developed or the formulation of objectives so controlled from the top down (or, to put it more precisely, the imposition of the leadership's decisions through orders they expect to be obeyed); nowhere else does this constitute the absolutely dominant principle by which the institution functions. This means in turn that researchers seeking to understand what goes on in a military organization can in large measure limit their investigation to the thinking of the top echelon—how it assesses a given situation, what orders it gives, and last but not least, how it presents itself in historical accounts and memoirs written after the fact. Soldiers who do not belong to this elite function in this system, and in the thinking of those who run it, act merely as agents executing commands—essentially, that is, as parts of a machine.

A second good argument involves a political and historiographic challenge. If, from the 1960s on, many military historians in West Germany concentrated on subjecting the role of the Wehrmacht leadership in the National Socialist state and the Second World War to critical investigation, one of their main aims was to correct a lopsided view. This overly positive view was spread—just as it had been after the First World War[92]—through memoirs by officers intent on defending their reputations, and works of fiction that depicted soldiers as heroes and war as an adventure, including millions of popular booklets of stories for young people *(Landserhefte)*.[93] In view of all these publications, the important task fell to military historians as scholars to write truthful accounts based on the sources that had become available in the meantime.[94]

As necessary as these new emphases and the dismantling of certain legends may have been, however, they did not encourage the study of the military from the perspective of social history in general, or research on the experiences of enlisted men in particular. In order to highlight the magnitude of this deficit once more, it should be pointed out that the armed forces of the Third Reich numbered overall around 20 million men.[95] Plans called for officers to make up about 3 percent of this total. This goal was never achieved, however, owing to the high mortality rate of young officers holding the ranks of lieutenant to captain, that is, those who served at the front. The military elite in the narrower sense—generals, admirals, and their aides—constituted at most one tenth of the officer corps, meaning that they represented less than 0.3 percent of the total armed forces. The remainder, 99.7 percent of the Wehrmacht, consisted of enlisted men, NCOs, and junior officers not serving as aides to the top echelon, and until recently military historians had hardly studied them at all. Little work has been done on the group of noncommissioned officers.[96] The history of German enlisted men in the Second World War has remained largely uncharted territory.[97] For a long time, ordinary servicemen, popularly referred to in German as *Landser*, were simply overlooked.

Usually the story of their suffering was summed up with a reference to the memorials to "unknown soldiers," and that was that. The best known is probably the tomb of the unknown soldier under the Arc de Triomphe in Paris. In almost every European country there are similar war memorials where one unidentified soldier represents the many war dead of the nation. In Germany, however, no such national monument was erected after either the First or the Second World War; instead many towns created their own. Although these memorials were certainly constructed with the best of intentions, little thought appears to have been given to the idea that their anonymity could be a form of disrespect. Research on the victims of National Socialism, by contrast, has stressed the importance of shedding light on individuals' fates.

We also need examples of individuals among the ordinary servicemen who, as so often, found themselves in the double role of perpetrator and victim—during the Third Reich as well as in preceding centuries. In the war memorials of many German towns and villages this need has long been met, as they record the names of the fallen.[98] Nevertheless, such monuments are no substitute for historical accounts of their lives. We serve the end of assembling a truthful and specific picture of the war only when we can give back to the unknown soldier his face, his name, and his story. This does not mean that a telling of military history "from below" can replace the perspective "from above," but it can make an essential contribution to a new synthesis, in which the whole becomes visible, including the darker side.

Representative Experiences at the Front

In 1995 Stephen G. Fritz of East Tennessee State University published a book whose title begins with the German word *Frontsoldaten*. It refers to Hitler's soldiers in the Second World War.[99] This excellent work paints a clear but depressing picture of the ordinary serviceman that is full of stark contrasts. At the same time it testifies to what can be achieved by a modern military history "from below." Fritz states that his purpose was "to allow average German soldiers to speak . . . to hear their words and see the war through their eyes so as to get at the reality of the combat experience as lived by the men in the bunkers and foxholes."[100] How could such a book be written? On what sources could the author draw? It emerges that he went through thousands of letters, diaries, memoirs, and oral accounts by Germans who served at the front in the Second World War and studied their accounts of daily life. He then noted recurring themes and created a systematic frame of reference for them. Because the author does not place his own analysis in the foreground but lets these "average men" speak for themselves, a high degree of authenticity is achieved.

Those of us who have read collections of battlefield letters cannot avoid the impression at times that many of the *Landser* were not capable of finding adequate words to describe the events swirling around them. They could not accurately describe what it was like to live on the borderline between life and death, in a chaos that shattered nerves and wore bodies to the bone.[101] Yet it was by no means due to a lack of intelligence, nor merely consideration for the feelings of the recipients of the letters, whom the soldiers did not want to alarm. Many enlisted men were simply struck dumb by the hideous reality of battle; what they were experiencing was an inferno that defied description. Nevertheless, Fritz furnishes proof that the history of everyday life can extend even to the battlefield, for the relatively few soldiers who ignored the prohibitions against keeping diaries and sought to capture the real quality of their experience in letters home enable us today to grasp what war at the front was like. As Fritz observes, "The picture that emerges from their personal observations is therefore subtle, complex, and contradictory in its message." The author sums up this ambiguity as follows: "War is vile, but the chronicle of the *Landser* shows that not all who fight wars are vile."[102]

The self-image of many Wehrmacht soldiers—that despite all the death and destruction they had remained "decent fellows"—dominated the memoirs written after 1945: they had not deserted their comrades when they were in trouble (and on whom they depended); that in situations of confusion, fear, pain, and horror they had continued to do their duty; that they did not shrink from danger and were proud of their willingness to sacrifice themselves if need be.[103] "Decent behavior" was defined chiefly terms of a soldier's own unit, the small group who depended on him and with whom he was trying to survive. At the same time, his treatment of the enemy could be lawless; it could lack all humane orientation and become wantonly cruel in ways that are described in the most drastic yet accurate terms imaginable in letters from the eastern front.[104] Soldiers shot prisoners of war and partisans, men trying to give themselves up, commissars, and Jews; they destroyed entire villages and wiped out their inhabitants, "always conscious," as one *Landser* wrote after the war, "that as good soldiers we had to fulfill our hard duty."[105] Another confessed after the war, "I had unquestioningly accepted the brutal philosophy that might makes right."[106]

Based on his reading of letters and diaries, Fritz reaches the conclusion that "there existed among the troops in Russia such a striking level of agreement with the Nazi regime's view of the Bolshevik enemy and the sort of treatment that should be dealt them that many soldiers willingly participated in murderous actions."[107] He concludes further that a surprisingly large number of servicemen had adopted the complete National Socialist view of the world. These soldiers fought not only because the machinery of war left them no alternative, but also because they believed in the declared political goals of the war and the higher meaning ascribed to the struggle by Nazi propaganda.

In what is perhaps the strongest chapter of the book, "Trying to Change the World," Fritz uses a broad range of sources to demonstrate the degree to which most German servicemen believed that their mission was not only to preserve Germany and Europe from Bolshevism, but also to impose change in accordance with the National Socialists' concept of the "ethnic community" and racial ideology. After the war they remembered the dangers and hardships of all kinds that they had endured, but either lacked or had repressed the knowledge of the injustices they and their fellow soldiers had committed. This resulted in a belief that German soldiers on the eastern front had been victims rather than perpetrators. The bitter truth, however, was that for all their idealism, they had been tools of Hitler.

In order to compensate for the relative lack of sources for writing military history "from below," the anthropologist Hans Joachim Schröder took a different approach and decided to interview World War II veterans, in a sense creating the source material himself.[108] He asked participants in the war to tell their life stories, and then interpreted the results with a specific set of analytic tools.[109] This was the first time so much material had been collected from enlisted men who had fought in the Second World War, systematically sorted, and provided with commentary. The interview technique had clear limitations, however. While the veterans had some general inhibitions in bringing up their war experiences, they were even less forthcoming about taboo subjects such as killing others, instances of cruelty, and war crimes. Nearly all his informants, Schröder reported, either were unwilling to speak openly and in specific terms about the terrors of war, or were very hesitant.[110] He therefore concluded that while the interview technique yielded new insights into the basic phenomenon of fear, it provided little information on the crimes that made the Second World War the most hideous in human history.[111] The interviewees simply remained silent on this aspect of their war experiences.

The Will to Survive in the War's Final Phase

"To be or not to be!" "Final victory or doom!" "Triumph or death!" These were the terms in which National Socialist propaganda described the alternatives for the future of the German people. The commanders of the Wehrmacht responded to such dramatic proclamations not with the hardened realism one might expect; rather they guaranteed through the orders they issued that the battle the propagandists depicted as "heroic" would actually be fought.

The last nine months of the Second World War were not just one more phase in a long struggle; it was the bloodiest and most destructive of all. After the Allies landed in Normandy in June 1944, they stepped up their bombing of German cities.[112] These aerial raids were by no means limited to military targets, but consisted of carpet bombings of residential areas; by targeting civilians, the aim was to break the German population's will to fight on. The next spring the British and Americans continued their bombardments with attacks on Dresden—at that time crammed with almost a million refugees—on February 13–14, 1945, and again on April 17. They bombed Würzburg on March 16, Hildesheim on March 22, followed by Potsdam, the town which symbolized German militarism, on March 27, and Paderborn on April 14. In this last stretch of the war, between 300,000 and 400,000 Germans died every month, soldiers and civilians alike.[113] Of the approximately 5.3 million German soldiers who lost their lives in the Second World War, some 2.6 million were killed in this last phase between July 1944 and May 1945. The fact that more and more fighting was taking place within the borders of German territory contributed to this, and the ground battles grew increasingly fierce. Both troops and the civilian population were now caught up in violence that the Wehrmacht had unleashed from 1939 on in its attacks on neighboring countries.

By this time it was clear to most thinking people that the war could not end in victory for Germany. Why did it then continue? Why did Hitler not end it earlier? Or why didn't the military leadership demand that the government begin peace talks, or even force it to, as the third High Command under Hindenburg and Ludendorff had done in the fall of 1918? Why didn't the more than 10 million soldiers serving in the Wehrmacht in 1944, whose service had become so exceedingly dangerous, exert pressure on their leaders? And finally, why didn't the German civilian population protest against the prolongation of the war, carrying out strikes or even mounting a revolution, as they had at the end of the previous world war? Questions of this kind have been raised again and again, although as yet no convincing answers have been found.

Outwardly during the final nine months the political and military leaders of Germany displayed confidence and optimism. They tried to give the impression that a military victory still lay within the realm of possibility.[114] In view of the military crisis that was developing, however, as even they could not deny, National Socialist propagandists stopped referring to a victory that was imminent in the summer of 1944. Instead they now spoke of a distant future when the "final victory" would occur. At the same time, Joseph Goebbels, the minister for propaganda, announced that Germany would soon deploy "miracle weapons," which would tip the balance. In secret, Hitler and his loyal inner circle hoped that the Allied coalition might soon break apart.

During this period the message was hammered home ever more forcefully that the German population would have to hold out with fanatic determination. Propaganda began depicting in the most lurid colors imaginable what dangers threatened in the event of a military defeat. The German people would be "exterminated," a claim that can be recognized without difficulty as a projection of the Nazis' own policies onto their opponents. Using this scenario as a basis, the propagandists could then proclaim that in the current situation the only alternatives were "victory or doom." They could not and would not envision any other possible path to ending the war, such as an early capitulation.

As a result of this unmovable stance, the specter of "total war" that Goebbels had invoked in February 1943, after the defeat at Stalingrad, became more and more of a reality. The regime forced old men and boys, even women and children, into "voluntary" forms of service in militias and auxiliary organizations. The militarization of the *Volksgemeinschaft* reached its peak.

Simultaneously, military tactics grew increasingly brutal. Continuation of the war against a stronger enemy was forced with every possible means and in the face of all resistance, even as the Allies began penetrating into German territory. The Nazi leadership called upon Germans to oppose the advancing forces "everywhere, unflinchingly and implacably," and "down to the last bullet." Martin Bormann, Hitler's right hand and head of the Reich chancellery, proclaimed the watchword: "Win or die!"[115] The armed forces, the SS, and the justice system proceeded even more radically against defeatists and deserters.

Despite this terror, signs occurred here and there that things were beginning to fall apart.[116] Such events did not crystallize into an organized political opposition that could have demanded and forced a swift end to the war. Since both leading National Socialists and the generals had long feared a repetition of the revolutionary unrest that had manifested itself in 1918, they did everything they could to nip resistance in the bud.

Hence the final months of the war appear as one gigantic excess of violence, a fanatic escalation of the last-ditch effort evoked in Nazi propaganda. Was there no hesitation in unleashing it? In fact the German war machine stopped running only when the territory of the Reich was completely occupied by Allied troops and the Wehrmacht was forced to sign an unconditional surrender.

Here the views of General Günther Blumentritt should be recalled, as he expressed them in 1947. To the question of why German soldiers kept on fighting even though their situation was hopeless, he responded with allusions to 1918: their continuation of the war all the way to an unconditional surrender proved that the Germans had learned the lessons of that year, and instead of attempting a revolution, they had stood solidly against "Bolshevism" in 1945. Blumentritt left no doubt of his opinion that obeying Hitler to the bitter end had represented a sensible course of action.

This kind of thinking is difficult to understand today. It is striking that the political goals for which Germany was fighting play no major role in the general's argument, nor did the millions of war dead and the incalculable destruction prompt any self-criticism. Instead Blumentritt focused on an ideal that was closer to being realized in 1945 than at any previous time: Germany presented itself as a determined and united people that had adopted military patterns of organization from top to bottom and whose discipline could be relied on even when the outlook was hopeless. The path of unconditional surrender quite obviously struck the former general not as a politically and morally blameworthy end but as an honorable process in which the weaker had succumbed. Blumentritt apparently regarded total defeat as more acceptable than the conclusion of the First World War, which in objective terms was far more favorable for Germany. How is this strange perspective to be explained?

The myth of an honorable defeat had played a role at the end of the First World War. When news leaked out of an impending truce, the German navy entertained the idea of sending the fleet on a suicidal "final sortie" against Britain.[117] Given the two countries' respective military resources, this action would necessarily have ended in utter defeat, meaning the sinking of the ships with their crews. Influential career officers in the Imperial Navy believed that "going down with honor" *(ehrenvoller Untergang)* was preferable to accepting a truce. As is well known, enlisted men then prevented the fleet from embarking on this doomed course. On the five large warships that had been selected for this mission, with a combined crew of more than five thousand men, a mutiny occurred on October 29–30, 1918. The sailors, refusing to follow orders, put out fires in the engine rooms, thereby saving many lives. The plans of the officers to stage a sacrifice to the god of war were completely rejected by the crews, most of whom were skilled workers in civilian life.[118] Nevertheless, the senior officers refused to give up the idea of "going down with honor"; instead they sought and found an opportunity to bring it about. On June 21, 1919, Rear Admiral Ludwig von Reuter gave his sailors the order to scuttle the ships of the German High Sea Fleet that had been interned in the British harbor of Scapa Flow.[119] The order was carried out; the ships went down, but the crews survived.

In the summer of 1919 most German politicians were outraged at the harsh conditions imposed on their defeated country by the victorious Allies. A cabal of officers held a "council of war" to discuss whether Germany should break the armistice agreed upon at Compiègne on November 9, 1918, and initiate hostilities again.[120] Vice Admiral Adolf von Trotha, who had helped devise the plan to send the German fleet to certain destruction, repeated his rallying cry: "The Navy wants to preserve its honor."[121] At the same time, the best known of the German military commanders, Field Marshal Paul von Hindenburg, entered the political debate with a similar suggestion. In a telegram to Gustav Noske, a Social Democrat and Reichswehr minister, on June 17, 1919, Hindenburg began with a sober analysis of the military situation, stressing that reopening hostilities was hopeless, and pointing out that the likely consequence would be having to sign the peace treaty. Nevertheless, Hindenburg informed Noske, "As a soldier I must favor an honorable end over an ignominious peace."[122] Certainly one of his motives was a hoped-for propaganda effect. The field marshal had refused to go to Compiègne himself months earlier, and now his aim in mentioning an "honorable end" was to recommend himself to German nationalists who attached more importance to heroic phrases than to a sober view of what was politically possible. It was going to be the politicians who would have to bear the guilt for signing the peace treaty in Versailles, just as they had earlier in Compiègne. To this extent Hindenburg's telegram represented encouragement to avoid facing reality.

In the final phase of World War II, many of the older members of the Wehrmacht may have had vague memories of the heroic phrases in circulation during 1918 and 1919. The younger soldiers and civilians recalled something else, however: namely, the similar tone of Nazi propaganda after the devastating defeat of the Sixth Army in Stalingrad. In that case, too, the mythologically laden concept of *Untergang* played an important role. There can be no doubt that Hitler, Goering, and Goebbels did indeed associate this term with the idea of a sinking ship, a ship whose crew was doomed to die by drowning. They expected the soldiers of the Sixth Army to fight "to the last man" and "to the last bullet" and then go to their deaths.[123] Once they were encircled and could not win, they were not to make a risky attempt to break out, much less capitulate and become the Russians' prisoners of war. To accept death—be it at the hand of the enemy, from hunger or cold, or through suicide—was a "fate" that the Nazi leaders regarded as heroic. Hence they set out to conceal the hideous reality of mass death in Stalingrad from the German people and transform it into a heroic myth.[124]

By elevating the military disaster of Stalingrad to the rank of sacrificial death of historic proportions, the Nazi propagandists moved into an abstract, noble, and supposedly loftier world of make-believe.[125] Through their use of quasi-religious terms such as "holy awe," "reverence," "omnipotence," "providence," and "faith," Hitler, Goering, and Goebbels pursued a systematic strategy of "de-realization."[126] It becomes particularly evident in Goering's speech on January 30, 1943, a few days before the remnant of the Sixth Army in Stalingrad finally capitulated.

Those German soldiers still alive in Stalingrad regarded it as their own "funeral oration." Goering made use of two historical events that had long since achieved mythical status; they were probably familiar to many Germans of that time from their school days. The one story took place in ancient Greece. In 480 BCE a troop of three hundred Spartans under their leader Leonidas had defended the Greek pass of Thermopylae against the Persians to the last man, giving their lives for the larger goal of the war. Goering described this "heroic sacrifice" as an example of "the noblest military tradition."[127] In addition, he recalled "a magnificent heroic epic of an unparalleled struggle," namely, the "battle of the Nibelungs": "They too stood in a hall full of blazing flames, slaking their thirst with their own blood, but they fought to the very last."[128]

In view of the imminent "downfall" of what remained of the Sixth Army, Hitler promoted its commanding officer, General Friedrich Paulus, to the rank of field marshal and praised him publicly as "the heroic defender of Stalingrad."[129] He did so, of course, assuming that Paulus would then commit suicide and demonstrate to other officers what the leaders in Berlin expected from the generals of a defeated German army. As it transpired, however, the generals in Stalingrad were not at all inclined to embrace the notion of "victory or death" when their own lives were at stake. Hitler was incensed when he learned that a few hours after his promotion, Paulus and many other generals and their staff officers had allowed themselves to be taken prisoner.[130]

In a talk with Goebbels he reaffirmed his principle that no one would ever hear "the words 'yield' or 'capitulate' from 'us.'" The propaganda minister regarded the fact that the generals of Stalingrad had become prisoners of war rather than commit suicide as "a devastating blow to the prestige of the army."[131] He feared that the idea of ending the war by capitulating might now gain ground within the Wehrmacht.

In 1944–45, then, the political and military leaders of Germany could base their thinking on the test case of Stalingrad. Did they really believe that a "final victory" could be achieved? In Hitler's case, we know that he kept well informed about the relative strength of the various combatants in all phases of the war, especially about the most important economic data. In the words of the military historian Bernd Wegner, Hitler possessed "a modern and complex overview of the war as it affected entire societies."[132] After Stalingrad at the latest, he knew that Germany could no longer win.

This knowledge could not be expressed publicly in Germany, however. Those Germans who still possessed some common sense (probably including most ordinary working people) and could assemble a relatively realistic idea of the hopelessness of Germany's position from the available information—that is, those whose thinking was "normal" in the traditional sense—were treated as outright criminals. They were labeled "defeatists" and "underminers of morale" and could count on a death sentence.[133]

In an order dated February 6, 1944, General Wilhelm Keitel created a new group, known as "National Socialist guidance officers," or political officers, whose task was to see to it that no one deviated from the policy of resistance "to the last man." By the end of the year, 623 such men were serving full-time at levels ranging from the supreme commands of the various service branches down to single divisions. Most of them were members of the National Socialist Party. In addition, there were approximately 47,000 part-time "guidance officers." In the eyes of General Georg von Hengl, the job of these political officers was to instill in the troops "hatred and an implacable will to destroy."[134]

Given the obvious discrepancy between the hopeless outlook for the German forces and the radical policy of holding out to the bitter end, one must ask: Was it in fact the regime's goal to guide the nation to a "final victory"? Did it paint the consequences of defeat in such lurid colors so as to mobilize the greatest possible amount of energy for holding out? Or were the political and military leaders of the National Socialist state considering other possibilities at the same time? In his study of Georges Sorel's theory of violence, the philosopher Hans Barth explained the purpose of the "heroic myth" as that of "preparing people for catastrophe, but not in such a way that they endure it passively as victims, but rather that they bring it about themselves in battle."[135]

Seen in this light, the policy of last-ditch resistance looks different from what the propagandists of "final victory" intended. Then one grasps the ambiguous nature of German war policy from the summer of 1944 on. On the one hand, the declared goal was military victory, but on the other hand, Hitler and his henchmen were clearly prepared to have Germany "go down with the ship" in the kind of cataclysm that Admiral von Trotha and Field Marshal von Hindenburg had once envisioned. Or one might also describe their goal as

repeating the experience of Stalingrad on a vastly larger scale—
namely, to have the entire German nation go down fighting. And in
setting this policy in motion, they committed an enormous crime
against their own people.

Hitler declared to his armaments minister Albert Speer on March
19, 1945: "If the war is lost, the people will be lost also. It is not necessary to worry about what the German people will need for elemen-
tal survival. On the contrary, it is best for us to destroy even these
things. For the nation has proved to be the weaker, and the future
belongs solely to the stronger eastern nation. In any case only those
who are inferior will remain after this struggle, for the good have already been killed."[156] In other words, using the social Darwinist thesis of the survival of the fittest, Hitler developed a heroic myth
about how the defeated end.

Hitler had another, more trivial motive for the policy of resisting
to the bitter end. As the man responsible for the war and the war
crimes committed by the Germans, he knew he would not survive a
military defeat. Hitler realized this early on. On June 16, 1941, a few
days before he launched the attack on the Soviet Union, he revealed
this conviction to Goebbels: "We have so much to answer for already
that we must win, because otherwise our entire nation—with us at
its head—and all we hold dear . . . [would] be eradicated."[137] In Hitler's mind the regime faced only two alternatives: victory or death.
To this extent, every prolongation of the war meant the prolongation of his own life. Many Nazi Party leaders and senior military officers shared this view. A number of them committed suicide following the capitulation,[138] choosing the moment and form of their own
personal *Untergang*.

It is well known that the generals and officers of the general
staffs of the Wehrmacht did not attempt to block the suicidal policy

of resistance, but willingly carried it out.[139] According to the historian Heinrich Schwendemann, their orders in the final phase of the war followed a "strategy of self-annihilation."[140] What was officially presented as a "defense" of the country was in reality a preparation for its destruction. By obeying Hitler's "Nero order" of March 19, 1945, the German army took the "scorched earth" tactics it had employed in Russia and applied them within its own borders. How is this behavior to be explained? Why did the generals agree to follow the path to catastrophe?

On the one hand, one must consider that rational and professional thinking in the military had long since been replaced by a flight from social, economic, and political realities, as became especially evident in the generals' inadequate analysis of economic potentials and the overemphasis placed on strategic and tactical "genius." Evidence for this hypothesis can be found in the daily Wehrmacht report, the war log of the OKW,[141] the "News from the Supreme Command of the Wehrmacht," published to keep the troops abreast of the war situation,[142] and the "News for the Troops."[143] If the generals essentially behaved no differently from the National Socialist Party leaders, this highlights the close ties between the two "pillars" of the regime. They were in the grip of inhumane ideologies and had committed such enormous crimes in their name that even when the war was obviously lost, they were unable to find their way back to a politically rational course of action. As Wilhelm Keitel, whose motto was "Do your duty till death," reported, Generals Schörner and Wenck were still attempting in April 1945 to cheer Hitler up with hopes that the military outlook would improve.[144]

It is difficult to judge whether and to what extent the civilian population, officers below the top ranks, and the mass of enlisted men were affected by the propaganda of last-ditch resistance. The opinion polls of the security service (SD) of the SS, which continued until about the middle of 1944, reveal that after the Germans lost the battle of Stalingrad, the mood of euphoria in the population vanished. The potential for enthusiasm that could be mobilized through propaganda promoting the ideology of the "master race" and military victories was largely exhausted by then. No clear mood of opposition to the National Socialist regime and the war had arisen either, but something like an abandonment of the collective flight from reality can be observed.

Correspondence from the field reflects very different attitudes among the soldiers. The attitudes ascertained by the research of the Wehrmacht propagandists in the last six months of the war do not indicate that the Germans were motivated by any desire for collective self-immolation at this point. They suggest instead that ordinary people were thinking and acting in realistic terms. They countered the ruling elite's cultivation of a doomsday scenario with a determined will to survive.[145] Nevertheless, the extreme militarism of the Third Reich nipped in the bud any potential civilian movement to end the war.

CHAPTER FIVE

The Legend of the
Wehrmacht's "Clean Hands"

AFTER THE WAR a legend about the Wehrmacht lived on for decades: that it had "kept its hands clean." Developed and disseminated in the last phase of the war and the immediate postwar period by the Wehrmacht leaders themselves, it was to become what was perhaps their greatest victory. One joke runs that although the German army may not have done so well in the war itself, it had a really great public relations strategy for winning the postwar. Not until fifty years after the war had ended did the legend begin to crumble and scholars begin to trace and discuss the story of its amazing success.

The literature on this topic can be listed in short order. The first scholar who should be mentioned in this connection is the Israeli military historian Omer Bartov, author of a book on Hitler's Wehrmacht in which he investigated German soldiers' motives for fighting.[1] Then, in an essay published in 1995, he took up the question of how historians, and West German military historians in particular, had dealt with the history of the Wehrmacht in the preceding decades.[2] Bartov distinguishes between several phases of progress in researching the subject and points out which questions scholars had excluded either completely or in part. It must be stated at the outset, however, that the long life of the public legend of the Wehrmacht should presumably be regarded as resulting only to a small degree from the hesitancy of historians to delve into it. The career of this legend is embedded in the larger question of how Germany dealt with the history of the Third Reich and the Second World War as a whole.

Here the active "politics of amnesty" of the new Federal Republic of Germany played an important role, as Norbert Frei has demonstrated for the years up to 1955.[3] And Ulrich Herbert and Olaf Groehler have assembled a valuable collection of essays on the topic of how differently the Nazi past, especially the Holocaust, was treated by the two postwar German states.[4] From a survey of the literature by Gerd R. Ueberschär titled "The Murder of the Jews and the War in the East," it becomes clear that research on what may well be the most problematic aspect of the Wehrmacht's history, namely, its participation in the Holocaust, is still in the beginning stages.[5]

Finally, Klaus Naumann, a member of the Hamburg Institute for Social Research, has written on how the connection between the Wehrmacht and the war of annihilation was perceived in Germany in the years from 1945 to 1995.[6] He concluded that the Wehrmacht's crimes during the Second World War had rendered both the war on the eastern front and the Wehrmacht itself taboo subjects.[7] The legend is the visible sign of this taboo, so to speak. But Naumann's hypothesis can represent no more than a first approach to the subject, for the sociopolitical dimension (i.e., the question of which political and social groups had an interest in propagating a certain image of the Wehrmacht, and with what means they attempted to promote it) has hardly been investigated at all to date, although the documentary material has been available since the Nuremberg trials.

The Birth of a Legend

Getting Rid of the Evidence

Did German soldiers have general knowledge during the war of both the criminal strategy of the Wehrmacht in the East and the extermination of the Jews? In order to answer this question in any detail, it is necessary first to discuss how the Wehrmacht functioned in such areas as keeping information classified and systematically making little information available.

Within the Wehrmacht the principle reigned that individual soldiers should know only as much about the military situation as was necessary for them to perform their immediate assignments. Enlisted men were not supposed to think about the larger picture, but simply obey the orders of their superiors. To this extent the classification and withholding of information represented a means of military control. Only secondarily did it serve the purpose of increasing the efficiency of troop operations. Furthermore, if a captured soldier was not supposed to provide valuable military information to the enemy, this goal was most easily achieved by ensuring that he never had access to any. The military leaders intended for the horizons of millions of enlisted men to remain limited: the less they knew, they better.

Ordinary enlisted men, like the civilian population at home, caught glimpses of important military and political events in the way their government intended, namely, through the daily "armed forces report" on the radio and the speeches of Nazi leaders, also broadcast on the radio.[8] Soldiers received further information from direct orders, army newsletters, and a number of news sheets distributed at the front. All of them were put together according to rules laid down by the propaganda department within the OKW, which also kept a watchful eye on whatever was published. There were thus certain prospects for successfully keeping some information secret and suppressing unwelcome news.

One such piece of information was the "commissar decree" (directing that Russian political commissars were to be shot if captured), which was disseminated in writing to the commanders in chief of the various armies, who were to pass it on in oral form only. Issuing some orders in camouflaged language served a twofold purpose; first, the aim was to suggest that the extermination of certain groups was a military necessity occurring within the framework of normal combat; second, it was to leave as few traces as possible, as when Jews were falsely identified as "partisans," Gypsies as "criminals," women as "female partisans," and children as "scouts" and "lookouts."[9] No mention was made of killing Jews, but rather euphemistically of "further treatment" of Jews or of the "solution to the Jewish question." Policies such as the arrest and murder of Jews and partisans were concealed behind phrases such as "mopping-up operations" and "pacification," or "deportation" and "resettlement."[10] The supreme commands repeatedly issued orders that care should be taken to carry out executions of Russian political commissars, prisoners of war, Jews, "partisans," "vagrants," and other groups identified as undesirable "at a distance from the troops if possible" and "inconspicuously, away from the actual front lines."[11] In the logs of army units such killings were "concealed by means of careful use of language."[12]

Again and again, regular soldiers photographed shootings or hangings carried out by either SS *Einsatzkommandos*, local collaborators, or Wehrmacht units themselves. Orders were issued, and frequently repeated, that taking photographs was not permitted and represented an infraction of regulations,[13] but these were only partially successful in suppressing documentary evidence of the crimes. As defeat became more likely in 1944–45, when the danger threatened that mass graves might be discovered and offer incontrovertible evidence of war crimes to the outside world, SS units began returning to the sites, digging up the bodies, and burning them.[14]

How much did the soldiers fighting on the eastern front know about all of this? One must be aware that in addition to the official channels of information, a great deal of news circulated informally at the front and at home, and passed from the front to civilians in Germany. Soldiers spoke of their own experiences to other soldiers, and despite military censorship the letters they sent home also played an important role in spreading news. In many such letters available to us today, it becomes clear both how effective regime propaganda was in influencing soldiers' views and also how common the knowledge was that Jews were being murdered.[15] In addition, rumors flourished both at the front lines and on the home front.[16] Rumors represented a counterweight to official propaganda characteristic of a dictatorship, since they allowed information to spread that the regime would rather have kept secret. It will probably never be possible to determine precisely how much soldiers knew. There is good reason, however, to doubt that any German enlisted man serving on the eastern front could have remained unaware of the "racially" motivated murders that were being committed.

And the officers serving in the East? What did they know about the killings of Jews? We know from a report on a trip to the front filed by Major Rudolf-Christoph von Gersdorff, who in 1941 was serving as an intelligence officer (Ic) on the staff of the High Command of Army Group Center, that the officers in the East were fully informed about the murders being perpetrated by the SS Einsatzgruppen and other crimes. The following passage from his report of December 1941 leaves no room for doubt:

> In all conversations of any length with officers, I was asked about the shootings of Jews, without having made any reference to them myself. I gained the impression that the officer corps is generally opposed, one could almost say, to the shooting of Jews, prisoners, and political commissars. In the case of the commissars it is mainly because killing them increases the strength of the enemy's resistance. The shootings are regarded as bringing dishonor on the German army, and on the officer corps in particular. Officers brought up the question of responsibility for them, in stronger or less strong language depending on the individual's temperament and disposition. I was able to ascertain that the existing facts have become known in full, and that the officers at the front discuss them far more than was to be assumed.[17]

Nevertheless, for the most part one searches in vain through the war logs and other records of the Wehrmacht for any references to these "existing facts." How can this be explained? It is likely that most commanders had an awareness of wrongdoing, and thus ensured that the files remained "clean." Furthermore, the Allies announced that after their victory over the Wehrmacht they would establish tribunals to try war criminals, a threat that probably had much the same effect.

Yet keeping the official army records "clean" did not begin to remove all the traces of the crimes, for the SS reports, especially those of the Einsatzgruppen in the Soviet Union, described their activities openly. They also mentioned the willingness of Wehrmacht units to cooperate. No effort was made to cover up these activities in the SS reports; rather, their aim was to provide the bureaucracy with documentation of efficient mass killings. Their tone is often triumphant, in expressions such as "Lithuania is Jew-free!"[18] or "The Crimea is Jew-free!"[19] The discrepancy between the surviving records of the two organizations has allowed historians to reconstruct events with a great degree of accuracy.

With regard to the reputation of the Wehrmacht among the German population at home, it is interesting to note that during the final year of the war, the army was considered more reliable than National Socialist propaganda. In any event, in the summer of 1944 the regime called a halt to the propaganda activity of the SD, the security service of the SS, which had provided important "talking points" for civilian discussion groups in the preceding years. Instead the OKW was now instructed to assign this task to Wehrmacht soldiers in major German cities. Accordingly, regular soldiers played the double role of opinion pollsters and conveyers of a "no surrender" message in the last six months of the war.[20] They played their part in preventing revolutionary sentiments from spreading, as had occurred in 1918, when the population had begun pressing for a swift end to the war.

Blurred Images of the Wehrmacht in 1945

Given the existence of such disparate channels of communication, could the German public have had a clear picture of an organization as large as the Wehrmacht when the war ended in 1945? Or must one not rather assume that during the phase of military collapse, very different ideas of this institution and its role in the war existed

side by side? To some extent these ideas must still have been influenced by National Socialist propaganda. Yet they must also have
reflected the personal experience of soldiers and civilians, which
varied greatly. Anyone trying to assess how impressions of the Wehrmacht could have been formed in the war years must be aware that
in the decade between 1935 and 1945, approximately 20 million people served in its ranks. Leaving aside the political implications, one
must recognize that sheer numbers had given it the character of a
"people's army."[21] A father or son from virtually every German family had been drafted into the Wehrmacht and become a cog in its
machinery, and this fact was significant in psychological terms.

Personal experience probably dominated the picture that many
had of the Wehrmacht at war's end. This meant, however, that people in Germany saw the institution through very different lenses.
For refugees from East Prussia who had been evacuated across the
Baltic on German navy ships, the Wehrmacht represented rescue in
a time of crisis. But the experience of other refugees, who had received hardly any help from the German troops flooding back from
the East,[22] was not the same at all. Still another picture of the
Wehrmacht had probably impressed itself on the German inhabitants of towns and villages through which the battle-hardened, exhausted, and demoralized members of their own army had passed
on their retreat, sometimes looting and plundering like an enemy.[23]
In the furor of the final phase of the war, millions of enlisted men
must have hated superiors who were determined to enforce a policy
of holding out to the bitter end and summarily sentenced to death or
simply shot anyone who saw the coming capitulation as inevitable
and reacted accordingly.[24]

Most members of the military leadership refused to look reality
in the face even in the concluding phase of the conflict. They con-

tinued a war that had been lost in military terms long before—determined to "go down fighting," as the much-used phrase had it[25]—and showed little hesitation in waging war against citizens of their own country. Some of these officers, taking the consequences of their actions as the regime was foundering, committed suicide. It is well known that Hitler, Goebbels, Himmler and National Socialist Party *Gauleiter* such as Paul Giesler, Wilhelm Murr, Bernhard Rust, Gustav Simon, and Josef Terboven killed themselves, as did many less prominent leaders of the NSDAP and the SS, and government officials. What was and is less generally known is that Wehrmacht officers—thought to number in the thousands—also took their own lives.[26] Former Lieutenant General Josef Folttmann assembled a list containing the names of generals who committed suicide in 1945, with the telling title "The Generals' Self-Sacrifice."[27] Folttmann counted thirty-five army generals, six Luftwaffe generals, eight admirals, thirteen generals of the Waffen SS, and five police generals. While it is possible to interpret their suicides as an admission of guilt, this cannot be proved. The majority of the leadership followed a different path: they remained determined to go on erasing traces of their crimes.

As an institution, the Wehrmacht had come to be synonymous with the war and violence, and all those who welcomed the end of the terrible conflict shed no tears over its mandated dissolution. And certainly millions of enlisted men must have felt some satisfaction at the fact that the officers who had wielded the power of life and death over them as military commanders were now stripped of that authority. After the First World War, millions of people had joined in chants of "No more war!" Now many Germans took up a far more radical and specific slogan: "No more military!"[28]

The policy of the occupying powers played a further role. The

Allied authorities exposed the scale of the crimes that had been committed by requiring Germans in internment centers and prisoner of war camps to watch films about the mass murders in concentration camps; many civilians were forced to attend showings of them as well. One unintentional effect on the generally poorly informed German audiences, however, was to focus their attention on the SS. People tended to ignore the role of the Wehrmacht, although toward the end of the war it had provided soldiers to serve as concentration camp guards.[29] Research would be needed on the question of whether, through their policies, the Allies contributed in any way to the picture that was beginning to emerge, according to which the SS had committed the crimes and the Wehrmacht had "kept its hands clean."

It should be kept in mind, then, that at the time of the unconditional surrender in May 1945 and immediately afterward, Germans had no unified picture of the Wehrmacht but rather a large number of different points of view, depending on their personal interests and experiences. *The* picture of the Wehrmacht did not yet exist; it still had to be created.

The Legend Begins: Dönitz's Final Report

This image was created, quite officially, by high-ranking representatives of the National Socialist regime and the Wehrmacht. The actual starting point of the legend[30] must be considered the last edition of the "Wehrmacht Report," published on May 9, 1945. The man responsible for it was Grand Admiral Karl Dönitz, who by then was functioning as Hitler's successor, that is, as the new head of state as well as supreme commander of the armed forces.[31] This was the final bulletin in which the end of the war was announced. Simultaneously, Dönitz and his advisers seized the opportunity to offer an interpretation of the war and the role of the Wehrmacht that suited their interests. The relevant passages run as follows:

> Since midnight the guns have been silent on all fronts. On the orders of the Grand Admiral the Wehrmacht has called a halt to the fighting, which had no prospect of success. This marks the end of almost six years of heroic struggle. Those years brought us great victories but also grave defeats. In the end the Wehrmacht succumbed honorably to a vastly greater force.
>
> German soldiers fought bravely for their country, remaining loyal to their oath and performing acts of valor that will never be forgotten. They were supported until the end by those on the home front, who gave their all and made enormous sacrifices.
>
> The unparalleled achievement of those at the front and at home will be justly acknowledged by the later judgment of history.
>
> Nor will our opponents fail to show respect for the achievements and sacrifices of German fighting men on land, at sea, and in the air. Every soldier can thus stand proud and tall as he lays down his arms and can set to work with courage and confidence, in the darkest hours of our history, for the everlasting life of our people.
>
> The Wehrmacht pays homage in this dark hour to its comrades felled by the enemy. The fallen demand our unconditional loyalty, devotion, and discipline toward the fatherland, now bleeding from countless wounds.[32]

The core message conveyed was that while the war had been lost to the superior force of the enemy, the German armed forces had waged it heroically and honorably, and given their all; soldiers had fought valiantly and efficiently, making great sacrifices and always remaining true to their oath. The Wehrmacht's achievements would be judged favorably by both its opponents and history, and never be forgotten.

The Generals' Memorandum of November 1945

Admiral Dönitz's report in May established the guidelines for further development of the legend. It should not be overlooked, however, that immediately after the capitulation, a few generals took steps to acknowledge the truth in their statements. Thus, as he was preparing for the Nuremberg trials, former General Hans Röttiger, who had commanded panzer troops, wrote of his recognition "that the struggle against bandits that we were waging had as its ultimate aim the exploitation of the military for the purpose of ruthlessly exterminating Jewry and other unwanted elements."[35] He later withdrew this document, probably on the advice of his lawyer, and it was replaced by a sanitized version. Röttiger later advanced to the position of First Inspector General of the army in the postwar German Bundeswehr.

At about the same time, in November 1945, several high-ranking former Wehrmacht generals wrote a memorandum for the International Military Tribunal in Nuremberg. The suggestion that they do so had come from the American general William J. Donovan, who was opposed to prosecuting the German general staff as a criminal organization and therefore—counter to his instructions—wanted to offer the generals an opportunity to prepare the best possible defense. This led to a vehement dispute with the American chief prosecutor, Judge Robert H. Jackson, as whose deputy General Donovan later served in the trial before the International Military Tribunal.[34] Even at this early stage the first indications of the new constellations of the Cold War were surfacing. Donovan numbered among the representatives of the United States at the trial who took the view that Americans ought to do everything in their power to win over the Germans as allies in the conflict with the Soviet Union.[35]

The generals who participated in drawing up the memorandum were Walther von Brauchitsch, commander in chief of the army from 1938 to 1941; Erich von Manstein, commander of the Eleventh Army in 1941–42 and until March 1944 commander of Army Group South; Franz Halder, chief of the army general staff from 1938 to 1942; Walter Warlimont, deputy chief of operations, Armed Forces High Command; and Siegfried Westphal, chief of staff to the Commander in Chief West.

The generals' memorandum, titled "The German Army from 1920 to 1945,"[36] was designed to counter the Allies' declared intention of assigning to the army general staff explicit responsibility for war crimes and crimes against humanity. While it was conceived from the outset as a contribution to their defense effort, the generals in fact turned it into a complete denial of guilt. One scholar has characterized the memorandum as a "document of self-deception."[37] But it was much more than that, namely, an important further step in the great cover-up that would produce the legend of the Wehrmacht's "clean hands."

Manfred Messerschmidt has analyzed the contents of the memorandum, which remained largely ignored until the 1990s. He contrasted the generals' claims of innocence with reality and reached the following conclusion: the writers saw it as their top priority "to demonstrate that the army had been against the party and the SS, had disapproved of almost all of Hitler's important decisions, and had opposed the commission of war crimes."[38] Thus, their self-defense already contained all the key elements of what would become the dominant public view of the Wehrmacht for decades, glossing over their true actions and playing down the role of the OKW and OKH in the Second World War. Messerschmidt's bitter conclusion: not one of the writers took responsibility for his own actions or failures to act.[39]

The generals' attempts to put the best face on their conduct of the war in the 1945 memorandum would be adopted as the main theme of the defense in the subsequent war crimes trials. The chief counsel for their defense, Dr. Hans Laternser, based his pleadings throughout on a picture of the Wehrmacht as outlined in Admiral Dönitz's last report and the generals' memorandum. The latter document was passed from hand to hand among former officers, not just those on trial in Nuremberg. Because of the signers' prominence and their high military rank, their self-exculpatory claims appear to have been taken at face value in those circles and "elevated to the status of historical truth."[40]

The War Crimes Trials

The International Military Tribunal (IMT) found twenty defendants guilty in the main war crimes trial. Several of them were military leaders, including:

> Hermann Goering, who like Hitler held both military and political offices, was Reich minister for aviation and simultaneously commander in chief of the Luftwaffe with the special rank of *Reichsmarschall*, which had been created

expressly for him. Goering was sentenced to death and committed suicide on the eve of his execution.

Wilhelm Keitel, field marshal and chief of staff of the OKW, received the death sentence and was executed.

Alfred Jodl, a general and chief of operations of the OKW, was Hitler's most trusted adviser on operational matters. He was also sentenced to death and executed.

Erich Raeder, grand admiral and commander in chief of the navy up to 1943, was sentenced to life imprisonment.

Karl Dönitz, grand admiral, Raeder's successor as commander in chief of the navy, and briefly Hitler's successor as president of the Reich, was sentenced to ten years in prison.[41]

Fourteen of the defendants found guilty had played a generally non-military role in events that were deemed war crimes by the Allied judges.

The notion that German elites shared responsibility for the crimes was also reflected in the disposition of the twelve follow-on trials, known as the NMT trials, since they were conducted by the United States Nuremberg Military Tribunal. Military officers numbered among the defendants in three of them: the Milch Case (NMT 2), the Hostage Case (NMT 7), and the High Command Case (NMT 12). Whereas Case 7 concentrated on a particular theater of war, namely, the Balkans (and Greece), in Case 12 the defendants were representative members of the Wehrmacht leadership. It was the intention of the American occupation forces, under whose supervision the trials took place, to use Case 12 to expose the role that the

German military elite played in the war crimes of the National Socialist regime and to see that the guilty parties paid the penalty.

Already in the earlier IMT trial not only top regime leaders had been prosecuted but also "criminal organizations" deemed to have carried out important functions within the system, such as the leadership corps of the National Socialist Party, the Gestapo and Security Service (SD), the SS, the SA (Sturm Abteilung, the "storm troopers"), and the cabinet of the Reich. The "General Staff and High Command of the German Armed Forces" were originally intended for inclusion as one such organization.[42] Under this last heading the prosecutors of the International Military Tribunal grouped the highest-ranking military leaders of the Wehrmacht, that is, about 130 officers who had served in the OKW at any point between February 1938 and the end of the war; in the High Commands of the army, navy, and Luftwaffe; or as field commanders.[43]

During preparations for the trial, however, it became apparent that the idea of indicting the "General Staff and High Command" —as opposed to, say, the Wehrmacht in its entirety—lacked a compelling rationale and as a result could not be carried out.[44] The tribunal ultimately determined that neither the general staff nor the OKW could be considered an "organization" or a "group" under the terms of Article 9 of its constitution.[45] For this formal legal reason, therefore, the "General Staff and High Command of the German Armed Forces" could not be declared a "criminal organization." After this judgment of the IMT was handed down, only trials against individual defendants could take place. Such trials would serve the desired purpose better than trying to declare the general staff as a whole to be a criminal organization.[46]

Nevertheless, the judgment was by no stretch of the imagination an acquittal. Its concluding passage, which was read out by the presiding judge, Sir Geoffrey Lawrence, ran as follows:

They have been responsible in large measure for the miseries and suffering that have fallen on millions of men, women and children. They have been a disgrace to the honourable profession of arms. Without their military guidance the aggressive ambitions of Hitler and his fellow Nazis would have been academic and sterile. Although they were not a group falling within the words of the Charter they were certainly a ruthless military caste. The contemporary German militarism flourished briefly with its recent ally, National Socialism, as well as or better than it had in the generations of the past.

Many of these men have made a mockery of the soldier's oath of obedience to military orders. When it suits their defence they say they had to obey; when confronted with Hitler's brutal crimes, which are shown to have been within their general knowledge, they say they disobeyed. The truth is they actively participated in all these crimes, or sat silent and acquiescent, witnessing the commission of crimes on a scale larger and more shocking than the world has ever had the misfortune to know. This must be said.

Where the facts warrant it, these men should be brought to trial so that those among them who are guilty of these crimes should not escape punishment.[47]

Despite this moral condemnation of the Wehrmacht elite, the former professional soldiers of the Wehrmacht immediately set about reinterpreting the failure to convict the group "General Staff and High Command" on formal grounds into a full acquittal and presented this false conclusion to the public. To the present day the claim is repeated in certain circles that the leadership of the Wehrmacht was acquitted in the Nuremberg war crimes trials, even by the standards of what they refer to disparagingly as "victor's justice." This represents one of the fateful postwar legends.

Case 12: The Nuremberg "High Command" Trial of 1948–49

In the Potsdam Declaration of August 2, 1945, the Allies recalled what their central purpose had been in waging war against Germany: "German militarism and nazism will be extirpated and the Allies will take in agreement together, now and in the future, the other measures necessary to assure that Germany never again will threaten her neighbors or the peace of the world."[48] The declaration assigned the task of carrying out the demolition of militarism and Nazism in practical terms to the Allied Control Council and attached a catalogue of primary objectives: the complete disarmament and demilitarization of Germany, the abolition of all military and National Socialist organizations, the reorganization of the entire educational system on democratic and peaceful principles, and finally, the aim of arresting war criminals and bringing them to judgment.

This was a goal that the victorious powers had failed to achieve after the First World War, when they wanted to have German war criminals extradited and placed on trial. Now the Allies established an International Military Tribunal and other courts that prosecuted and convicted German war criminals in the years between 1946 and 1949—the goal that the victorious powers had failed to realize after the First World War. They did not, however, commit the obvious mistake of equating or confusing militarism with the military; they did not aim solely to break up the Wehrmacht of the National Socialist state. Rather they recognized that the militarism that had taken hold in Germany between 1933 and 1945 had eventually infused all other spheres of life in Germany—political, economic, social, and intellectual. One symptomatic indicator was the fact that even civilian representatives of the government regularly appeared in public in military or military-style uniforms and adopted a corresponding manner. Far more significant in terms of actual political power was Hitler's joining of political and military leadership in his double role of "Fuehrer and Supreme Commander of the Armed Forces."

This structure of the National Socialist form of militarism explains why the accused at the Nuremberg war crimes trials were not only soldiers but also leading representatives of all the groups that had provided essential support to the whole system. The Wehrmacht, or more precisely the military leadership of the Wehrmacht, represented just one of these elites that were responsible for war crimes, along with economic leaders, top bureaucrats, scientists, and high-ranking members of the criminal justice system. The political importance of the Wehrmacht could hardly be overstated, since it did indeed represent, especially during the war years, the "second pillar" of the regime (alongside the Nazi Party itself) of which Hitler had spoken in 1933.

In the follow-on "High Command trial" of 1947–48 conducted by the American authorities, the fourteen accused men were members of the military leadership. They included several field marshals along with other high-ranking officers, such as prominent troop commanders whose achievements had been repeatedly emphasized by National Socialist propagandists in attempts to bolster the waning legitimization for continuing the war. There were relatively few generals among the men, who had been selected from the previously mentioned list of 130 drawn up by the IMT. Most of the defendants belonged instead to the second tier of the hierarchy and could thus be seen, in a manner of speaking, as representative of the entire military elite—or at least that was the reasoning of the authority issuing the indictments.

The accused[49] were:

Wilhelm von Leeb, born in Landsberg on the Lech in 1876, career soldier after graduating from a classical *Gymnasium,* promoted to rank of field marshal in July 1940. From the summer of 1941 to January 1942 commander in chief of Army Group North in the campaign against the Soviet Union, with General Ernst Busch (Sixteenth Army), General Hoepner (Panzer Group 4), and Field Marshal von Küchler (another defendant in the same trial) serving under him.

Hugo Sperrle, born in Ludwigsburg in 1885, the son of a brewery owner, completed high school. Career soldier, officer in the Luftwaffe, commander of "Legion Condor," the German force that participated in the Spanish Civil War. Promoted to general in July 1940, appointed commander in chief of Air Fleet 3 in 1941.

Georg von Küchler, born near Hanau in 1881, joined the army after receiving his *Abitur.* In the campaign against the Soviet Union was commander in chief of the Eighteenth Army in Army Group North (under Leeb), which advanced through the Baltic region to Leningrad. Promoted to field marshal in June 1942, succeeded Leeb as commander in chief of Army Group North and retained that command until January 1944.

Johannes Blaskowitz, born in East Prussia in 1883, son of a Protestant pastor, joined the army after high school. In the 1939 campaign against Poland he was a colonel-general and commander in chief of the Eighth Army, and protested at this point against the killings of Jews in Poland. He was named commander in chief of the First Army on the western front, but Hitler never promoted him again because of the critical memoranda he submitted during the Polish campaign.

Hermann Hoth, born in Neuruppin in 1885, son of an army staff physician. Became a soldier after his *Abitur*. Promoted to colonel-general in 1940, named commander of Panzer Group 3 belonging to Army Group Center on the eastern front. Appointed commander in chief of the Seventeenth Army (Army Group South) in October 1941, then commander in chief of the Fourth Panzer Army in 1942–43.

Hans Reinhardt, born in Bautzen in 1887, attended a classical *Gymnasium*, then entered the army. In 1941 he commanded a panzer corps (Army Group North) that saw action at Leningrad. Promoted to colonel-general in 1942, commanded the Third Panzer Army, also on the eastern front, until he was assigned to lead Army Group North in August 1944.

Hans von Salmuth, born in Metz in 1888, son of an officer. Attended a classical *Gymnasium*, then joined the army. Commanding general of an army corps on the eastern front, named commander in chief of the Second Army in July 1942, promoted to colonel-general in 1943.

Karl Hollidt, born in Speyer in 1891, son of a *Gymnasium* professor. After classical *Gymnasium* became a career soldier, became commanding general of an infantry corps in the Sixth Army (Army Group South) in 1942, promoted to colonel-general in 1943.

Otto Schniewind, born in Saarlouis in 1887, son of an attorney and notary, attended classical *Gymnasium*, joined the Imperial Navy. Promoted to admiral in 1940, chief of staff of the Naval War Staff from 1939 to 1941 under Raeder, commander of the fleet from 1941 to July 1944, named general-admiral in 1944.

Karl von Roques, born in Frankfurt on the Main in 1880, joined the army after his *Abitur*, commander Rear Area (Army Group South) as an infantry general in 1941–42.

Hermann Reinecke, born in Wittenberg in 1888, son of an officer, joined the army after his *Abitur*. Named an infantry general in 1942, chief of the Armed Forces General Affairs department in the OKW, from 1943 simultaneously chief of the National Socialist Guidance Staff of the OKW, from 1938 to 1945 responsible for prisoners of war under Keitel.

Walter Warlimont, born in Osnabrück in 1894, attended classical *Gymnasium*. Career soldier, spent some time at university after 1918, chief of the National Defense department in the OKW, named deputy chief of operations in the OKW in 1942, promoted to lieutenant-general, and to artillery general in 1944.

Otto Wöhler, born near Hannover in 1894, attended high school, joined the army, named chief of the general staff of Army Group Center in March 1942. Became an infantry general and commanding general of the First Army Corps in 1943, commander in chief of the Eighth Army in 1944 and, at the end of 1944, commander in chief of Army Group South until virtually the end of the war.

Dr. Rudolf Lehmann, born in Posen in 1890, son of a professor of law. Studied law, received his doctor of laws degree from the University of Marburg in 1920. Named presiding judge of an appeals panel at the Reich court-martial *(Reichkriegsgericht)* in 1937, chief of the legal division of the OKW in 1938, promoted to judge advocate general of the OKW in 1944.

It is not entirely clear how the term "High Command trial" became accepted, first in Allied usage and then in general German usage. If one takes the service ranks of the accused as a basis, the term is in fact misleading. Only three of the fourteen defendants actually belonged to the OKW, namely:

General Hermann Reinecke, who was responsible for the supervision of prisoners of war as chief of the Armed Forces General Affairs department;

Judge Advocate General Rudolf Lehmann, chief of the Legal Division of the OKW; and

General Walter Warlimont, deputy chief of operations in the OKW, that is to say, the deputy of Alfred Jodl.

The other defendants in the trial were former troop leaders, that is, commanders in chief *(Oberbefehlshaber)* of various armies and army groups. And indeed the official name of the trial was not the "High Command trial" but rather *United States of America v. Wilhelm von Leeb, et al.* (Case 12).[50]

Although "High Command trial" became the accepted name, it appears to have had little to do with the terminology used by the In-

ternational Military Tribunal. Even though the tribunal had rejected the hypothesis that the "General Staff and High Command
of the Armed Forces" constituted a "criminal organization," the
American prosecutor Telford Taylor and his colleagues prepared
Case 12 so as to give the impression that the fourteen defendants
were once again being placed on trial as a group representing the
Wehrmacht leadership. Perhaps this should be regarded as an attempt by the Americans to achieve the collective prosecution of the
OKW that had failed in the IMT trial.[51]

The High Command trial ran from December 30, 1947, to October 29, 1948. The indictment had been presented on November 28,
1947. The defendants appeared in court at the end of December,
but the actual proceedings did not get under way until February 5,
1948. On the very same day, one of the accused, General Johannes
Blaskowitz, committed suicide, so only thirteen defendants remained
on trial before American Military Tribunal 5-A.

The court held 233 sessions in the Nuremberg Palace of Justice.[52]
The panel consisted of Presiding Judge John C. Young, former chief
justice of the Supreme Court of Colorado; Judge Winfield Hale, a
judge of the Appellate Court of Tennessee; and Judge Justin W.
Harding, who had already served as a judge in the "Justice Trial"
(Case 3).[53] Hans Laternser served as one of the German defense attorneys and represented the main defendant, Field Marshal von
Leeb.[54] He also coordinated the general defense for all the accused.
The judgment was announced on October 28, 1948, making it the
next to last. (The trial of Ernst von Weizsäcker went on until April
1949.)

It was characteristic of the proceedings that the prosecution could
base its accusations on a large number of documents containing
valuable evidence, which its competent and efficient staff had begun

to assemble even before the main war crimes trial before the International Military Tribunal (1945–46).

Just as in the IMT trial, the High Command trial turned on charges of crimes against peace (preparation for wars of aggressions), war crimes, and crimes against humanity, with the last two predominating. The court considered in particular the criminal orders drawn up by the Wehrmacht leadership, the issuance of these orders to the troops, and the multitude of appalling war crimes that resulted from them. It focused on the "commissar decree" of 1941 and the murder of political commissars in the Red Army to which it led, as well as on the "commando order" of 1942. This latter order served as the basis for the murders of Allied soldiers who had fought as commandos, mainly on the coasts of western Europe and Greece, and been taken prisoner by the Germans. The court also dealt with the crimes against other prisoners of war, chiefly soldiers of the Red Army, whose deaths after being taken captive numbered in the millions. A further charge involved the defendants' share in the responsibility for the Wehrmacht's criminal measures against civilians in occupied areas. Untold numbers of them had been killed by Germans or deported to Germany to perform forced labor.

In their defense, the generals on trial typically denied all personal guilt, citing orders from above, or alleging that they had not known of the crimes or could not remember details clearly. Not one of the high-ranking officers showed any sign of remorse or acknowledged that he had borne any responsibility for war crimes; only General Blaskowitz's suicide points in this direction.

On the charge of having planned wars of aggression and thereby committed "crimes against peace," all the defendants were acquitted. The military tribunal did succeed in showing that many of them had been present at the sessions in which Hitler laid out his

plans to attack other countries. And some of them had even participated in planning the campaigns for those attacks. The IMT had
previously found Keitel and Raeder guilty of crimes against peace.
Surprisingly, however, the tribunal now found that

> the acts of Commanders and Staff Officers below the policy
> level, in planning campaigns, preparing means for carry-
> ing them out, moving against a country on orders and fight-
> ing a war after it has been instituted, do not constitute the
> planning, preparation, initiation and waging of war or the
> initiation of invasion that International Law denounces as
> criminal.
>
> Under the record we find the defendants were not on the
> policy level, and are not guilty under Count I of the Indict-
> ment.[55]

On the charges of having committed war crimes and crimes
against humanity under counts two and three, eleven of the defendants were found guilty. Generals Warlimont and Reinecke, who
had served on the staff of Hitler's closest military advisers, received
life sentences. Field Marshal von Küchler and Generals von Salmuth
and von Rocques were sentenced to twenty years in prison, while
Generals Reinhardt and Hoth were given sentences of fifteen years.
Judge Advocate General Lehmann and Generals Wöhler and Hollidt received sentences of five to eight years, and the man after
whom the trial was officially named, General von Leeb, was given
the light sentence of three years, which was considered as served
by the end of the trial itself. Both Field Marshal Sperrle of the
Luftwaffe and Admiral Schniewind were acquitted.

The convictions resulted, as the proofs of individual guilt submitted to the tribunal showed, because the defendants had participated in drawing up criminal orders such as those authorizing the shootings of commissars and commandos, in committing crimes against prisoners of war and civilians, in deporting civilians from occupied countries to perform forced labor, and either participating in or providing support for the murders of Jews in the East.

The Allies' Concern about Possible Legends

One of the reasons for conducting the twelve follow-on trials in general and the High Command case in particular was the Americans' well-founded concern that, after the conclusion of the trial against the major war criminals, dangerous myths might be created and spread in Germany. Thus the American prosecutor Walter H. Rapp explained during a radio interview in 1948 that the most important effect that the High Command case was intended to produce was "the prevention of legends." Without the prosecution of "two or three field marshals and a dozen or more generals," Rapp believed, the impression could spread in the general public, "as it appears to have done after the First World War," that "the generals were or are kind, highly educated old gentlemen who would never have considered doing the kinds of things of which they were accused." He continued, "I believe the fact that the generals' true faces have now been exposed and that they have been shown for what they really are must be a great help in ensuring that in future the population will never place blind trust in a general or expect him to bring about the reconstruction or rebirth of Germany."[56]

In fact, some circles in Germany began making efforts early on to limit the responsibility for undeniable war crimes to the men who had already been convicted. The war criminals who had not yet been charged, some high-ranking officers among them, now saw an opportunity to present themselves to the public as in effect exonerated and morally rehabilitated. In retrospect one can say that fears with respect to the creation of legends were all too justified, especially the legend of the Wehrmacht's "clean hands." By the end of the 1940s, the political winds had begun to shift in the western zones of Germany to the extent that growing numbers of citizens rejected the legitimacy of the war crimes trials, and a process of rehabilitating old National Socialists and integrating them into West German society began on a large scale, supported by a policy of cover-ups and denial.[57] In other words, the war crimes trials did not succeed in creating a psychological distance between the German public and the Wehrmacht.

Keeping the Memory of War Crimes Alive

In 1948—that is to say, while the follow-on trials were still under way—the International Military Tribunal issued instructions for a German edition of the proceedings against the major war criminals to be published in forty-two volumes, alongside the English, Russian, and French editions. No such procedure was instituted for the subsequent trials conducted by the American military tribunal, including the High Command case. The United States government published a fifteen-volume edition in English between 1949 and 1953, known as the "Green Series,"[58] which included key excerpts from all twelve cases,[59] including those involving Wehrmacht generals.[60] Nevertheless, this collection remained largely unknown in Germany.

In general it can be said that virtually no one was interested in publishing materials from the follow-on trials in West Germany in the 1950s. Only one of the tribunal's documents—the judgment against Ernst von Weizsäcker in Case 11, the "Ministries" or "Wilhelmstrasse" trial—was published in German in 1950.[61] As far as the High Command case is concerned, it is significant that in the period after the war the sole book to appear was a collection of the speeches for the defense by attorney Hans Laternser.[62] Overall the lack of attention to the Nuremberg follow-on trials was characteristic of the "move on" mentality of the 1950s. The "scrupulous forgetting"[63] was an essential component of the great collective repression that Ralph Giordano has called "the Germans' second crime."[64]

The West German government's policy of taking no notice of the judgments handed down in the war crimes trials of the 1940s played a not insignificant role in advancing this attitude.[65] Probably in reaction, and to make a political point, the East Berlin publishers Rütten and Loenig, which had already brought out the judgment of the IMT trial,[66] began publishing all of the judgments of the follow-on trials, beginning with Case 12 against the High Command in 1960.[67] The polemical tone of its foreword owed a great deal to the Cold War climate of that era.[68] After this the High Command trial fell into oblivion until journalist Jörg Friedrich published his massive *Das Gesetz des Krieges* (The Law of War) in 1993.[69] This book, whose subtitle reads *The Trial against the High Command of the Wehrmacht*, is not so much a historical study of the trial as a long essay that uses material from it to support and illustrate certain general hypotheses about problems of modern warfare. Thus there is still no German edition of the case. Generally speaking, one can say that the High Command case needs to be rediscovered by Germans with an interest in recent history.

The Kesselring and Manstein Trials

Just like the men indicted in Nuremberg, German generals put on trial in other countries denied that the Wehrmacht had participated in any war crimes. They included the former commander in chief Southwest, Field Marshal Albert Kesselring, whom the British tried before a military court in Venice in 1946–47. Although the Wehrmacht committed numberless war crimes in Italy under Kesselring's command, the general disputed this with "unimaginable brazenness" and "audacity," claiming "that despite the gory nature of war, German soldiers' actions were based on humane, cultural, and economic criteria to a degree very rarely seen in wars on this scale."[70] Kesselring even expected that the Italians would erect a monument to him.

Kesselring's successor as commander in chief Southwest, General Heinrich von Vietinghoff-Scheel, also painted a falsely rosy picture when he claimed, "Here both sides fought decently from the first day to the last, just like in old times . . . The war in Italy ended as it had begun and run its course: 'fairly.'"[71] Here again the claim was raised, in a distortion of the historical record, that the Wehrmacht had fought fairly in Italy from 1943 to 1945 despite 46,000 Italian military internees and prisoners of war, 37,000 political deportees, and the loss of 7,400 Jewish lives and the lives of another 16,000 Italian civilians.[72]

The trial of Field Marshal Erich von Manstein before a British military court in 1949 showed—even more clearly than the High Command case—to what extent historical truth had had to be sacrificed in the meantime to the demands of the Cold War. In the politically conservative portion of the British public, but also at the liberal and left-wing end of the spectrum, more and more voices were being raised in favor of sparing the West Germans in view of the threatening international situation. Their wish was to go easy on them, in the person of the prominent former field marshal, in order to win them over to an Atlantic defensive alliance. With this political goal in view, many Britons were willing to draw a positive picture of the Wehrmacht against their better knowledge. Prominent British politicians and jurists thought it appropriate to present the Wehrmacht as an army that had fought a purely military war just like others.[73] Former prime minister Winston Churchill went so far as to contribute to a fund so that Manstein would be able to pay two British defense attorneys.

Ultimately two men were found to play this role who represented what must certainly have been an optimal combination: Reginald D. Paget, a Labor M.P. and former naval officer, and Samuel C. Silkin, another Labor M.P. and son of the minister of agriculture, who was also Jewish.[74] With the support of the German attorneys Laternser and Leverkuehn, who had gained experience in defending Wehrmacht generals, Paget and Silkin shaped their pleadings along the lines of the generals' memorandum of 1945. The defense turned into a "crusade" against the Allies' humiliation of the German general and for the cause of "saving the honor of the German Armed Forces." The specific features of the German war of annihilation in eastern Europe, the aims to conquer territory, the racism and extermination of Jews were played down, and the Wehrmacht's participation in the planning and execution of this campaign was passed over. Paget described the documents submitted to the court as showing that, in his opinion, "the Wehrmacht displayed a large degree of restraint and discipline in circumstances of unimaginable cruelty." On the subject of the planned rearmament of West Germany, he added: "For Germany Manstein will never be a war criminal. He is a hero of his people and will remain one."[75]

Nevertheless, the prosecution was able to demonstrate that Manstein agreed with the goals of the war of annihilation, and furthermore that he was informed about both the shootings of Jews and political commissars and Wehrmacht assistance in the killings carried out by Einsatzgruppe C. The British military court, presided over by Lieutenant General Frank Simpson, sentenced Manstein to eighteen years in prison. With the cooperation of the noted British military historian Sir Basil Liddell Hart, the defense team appealed to the British public to support a general amnesty for war crimes. Manstein's sentence was reduced to twelve years in 1950, and in May 1953 he was released.[76]

Paget published a sympathetic account of Manstein's military career and trial in 1952 in a book that was also translated into German.[77] It probably helped, in both Great Britain and Germany, to solidify the legend that the Wehrmacht had remained "clean."

Finally, it should be mentioned that even the Briton perhaps best known for his pacifism, the philosopher Bertrand Russell, struck the same note as these politicians and jurists when he declared publicly in Germany in 1949 that Manstein presumably deserved to be punished, but that in the existing political situation the trial was wrong. One had to keep in mind, Russell wrote, that the victors' war crimes had not been punished. If Europe—meaning an anti-Soviet western Europe—wished to regain its vigor, it would have to cooperate with Germany. In politics it was necessary to concentrate on the future rather than the past.[78]

As such comments show, the legend of the Wehrmacht's "clean record" was spread not just by German generals; vocal proponents of this view came forward even in the Allied countries once the Cold War had begun.

The Missing Debate on the Wehrmacht and the Holocaust

A topic raised explicitly neither in the IMT trial of major war criminals nor in the High Command case was the possible connection between the Wehrmacht and the Holocaust, that is, collusion or complicity in the systematic murder of some 6 million Jews in the territory conquered by the German armed forces.[79] The mass extermination was investigated in Case 9 of the NMT follow-on trials (the "Einsatzgruppen case"), but not in the trials of the military elite.[80] How can that be explained? What prompted the Allies to hang back so noticeably in facing the question of the systematic destruction of the European Jews? Were they unaware of the scope of the problem? Did they just not want to know, as the English historian Walter Laqueur speculates?[81] Did this make them react with suspicion even to firsthand information from witnesses such as Jan Karski?

Karski was a Polish cavalry officer to whom the Polish government in exile in London assigned the task of obtaining information on Hitler's plans to exterminate the Jews of Europe. Disguising himself as a Ukrainian guard, he gained entry into the Warsaw ghetto and Isbica Lubelska, a holding camp for the Belzec death camp. He was an eyewitness to the misery of the starving inhabitants of the ghetto and the shooting of Jews. He was later able to pass on what he knew to both the British foreign minister Anthony Eden and President Franklin D. Roosevelt in person, but his information did not prompt any discernible political or military reaction.[82]

As we know today, the British were soon able to decipher the reports being transmitted via radio from the Einsatzgruppen of the SS to the Reich Security Main Office. In other words, they were well informed about these groups' murderous activities in Poland and the Soviet Union.[83] The reason why this information was kept secret remains unexplained. Some commentators have suggested military grounds, for if the Germans had learned that their code had been broken, it would have been impossible to go on intercept-

ing the enemy's messages. Others suggest that the British government may have been secretly in sympathy with the elimination of
Jews and Bolshevist functionaries. One question raised repeatedly in
this context is why the Western powers did not bomb the access
routes to Auschwitz. In any case, the Allies knew more than they
were prepared to admit.[84] The same holds true for the Catholic
Church, which admitted its failures in this regard for the first time
in 1997.

What were the reasons why the Holocaust was to a large extent
excluded from the Nuremberg war crimes trials? Should they be
sought in American domestic politics, as Raul Hilberg conjectures?
Was the aim to prevent the still widespread discrimination against
African Americans in the United States from being connected in any
way with the Germans' murders of Jews? Or was it to prevent the
fact from becoming known that the Allies knew about the killings
early in the war? Was it that the Allied prosecutors and judges could
not conceive that the conduct of the war and the killings of Jews
were closely connected, or that the murders could not have occurred
without the cooperation of the Wehrmacht? Or were they themselves taken in by the legend that, while the Wehrmacht may have
committed some war crimes, it neither knew of nor cooperated in
the specific crime against humanity that the mass murder of Jews
represented?

These questions still await investigation. For now we can only
point to the fact that while the Nuremberg trials dealt with war
crimes and crimes against civilians, the Holocaust as such was passed
over. As a result, the former Wehrmacht generals were largely
spared the task of defending themselves on the "front" of public
opinion.

Writing History from the Wehrmacht's Point of View

General Franz Halder and the "Historical Division"

In addition to writing briefs for the defense for the Nuremberg military tribunal, former Wehrmacht officers had another outlet for preserving their personal view of the war for posterity: they could write history on commission for the Allies. The military historian Bernd Wegner sheds light on the key point of this truly astonishing practice when he notes that the old saw that history is written by victors was not borne out after 1945: "The writing of (West) German history on the Second World War, and in particular on the Russian front, was for over two decades, and in part up to the present day—and to a far greater extent than most people realize—the work of the defeated."[85]

The opportunity to depict their own military achievements in the conflict was offered to German prisoners of war who had served as officers by the Historical Division of the United States Army.[86] Senior and top officers who appeared suitable on the basis of their education and experience were recruited to participate in a project to write the history of military events during the Second World War. None of them were trained historians except for General Waldemar Erfurth, who had earned a doctorate in the field. In June 1946 no fewer than 328 German officers, all prisoners of war, were writing for the history program; most of them held the rank of general. By March 1948 they had produced more than one thousand separate manuscripts totaling about 34,000 pages.[87] American military officials were able to persuade General Franz Halder, former chief of the army general staff, to take on overall leadership of the project. Halder was held in great esteem by the German officer corps. He

was widely believed—erroneously—to have been an opponent of
Hitler, but he embodied more than any of his peers the spirit of the
Prussian and later German general staff. The reason he gave for his
willingness to cooperate with the Americans on the history program
was revealing: it was important, Halder declared, "to continue the
battle against Bolshevism."[88] Arguments in the same vein were put
forward by Admiral Dönitz, who had for a brief time succeeded Hitler, and General Reinhard Gehlen, the later head of the West German intelligence service. Serving as Halder's deputy was General
Adolf Heusinger, who was simultaneously working in the "Gehlen
Organization,"[89] and later became the first inspector general of the
Bundeswehr. Like Gehlen, Heusinger represents a strand of continuity between the Wehrmacht and the Bundeswehr. Beginning in
about 1947, the Americans running the Operational History (German) Section and its counterpart, the Naval Historical Team, shifted
its focus from accounts of German operations during the war to
studies of the Soviet Union, a development clearly connected with
the growing tension between East and West.[90]

An essential component of the picture of the Wehrmacht assembled by the former officers had to do with the allegedly outstanding
professional skills of the leadership and the unusual courage and en-
durance of German soldiers. In fact there was—and probably still
is—a degree of "admiration for the professionalism of the German
military among British and American forces, based on their battlefield experience"[91] (in addition to revulsion at the war crimes
committed by members of the Wehrmacht leadership). This may
well represent something like professional solidarity among career
soldiers. Such admiration continued to be expressed in books by Sir
Basil Liddell Hart and a number of memoirs by British and American officers; it still crops up in radical right-wing circles and the

work of apologists for the Wehrmacht when they wish to defend the fiction of a war fought fiercely but "fairly," against all the evidence amassed by more critical military historians.

During his fifteen-year association with the Historical Division, Halder expressed a preference for being addressed as "General" by his fellow officers and acted as if he were their commanding officer in dealing with their manuscripts. Furthermore, he laid down a version of the political context in which the Wehrmacht had acted and insisted that all the German officers writing for the program abide by it:

> According to [Halder's version of events], the Wehrmacht in general and the army leadership in particular were in effect victims of Hitler on a historic scale, or at the very least abused instruments of his criminal policies, which they sought to oppose in every possible way up to and including tyrannicide (viz. the plot of the Twentieth of July). From this perspective the military strategy for which they were responsible appears somehow almost miraculously detached from the political goals of the regime. When the war was not described simply in terms of "fate" or as a necessary preventive strike, it was interpreted basically ahistorically as the work of a demonic personality—it was "Hitler's war." The writers then attempted to distance themselves from it in two different ways: first of all on a moral level, by sharply distinguishing the uncompromising but essentially "decent" form of war conducted by the regular troops from the dirty and criminal operations of the SS; and second on a technical or professional level, by blaming all the tactical and strategic defeats not on their own mistakes, but rather on a combina-

tion of difficult terrain and climatic conditions on the one hand, and Hitler's dilettantism and stubbornness on the other.[92]

This was admittedly a cleverly conceived global defense offered by men who were personally involved and partially responsible, and who, thanks to the support of the Allied military forces, had access to source materials that did not become available to professional historians until the early 1960s or even later. Halder and his ex-Wehrmacht officers enjoyed a privileged position, although they were themselves dilettantes in the matter of history, and the few historians who were working on the history of the Second World War in the 1950s were obliged to seek information from the general and his colleagues.[93] Halder, as head of the German section of the Historical Division in Karlsruhe, could acquire "the role of a doyen in the field of the history of the Second World War."[94] His influence not only on authors of memoirs and historians but also on newspaper editors and writers of military stories was considerable.

In the work of the Historical Division the traces of the war of annihilation for which the Wehrmacht leadership was responsible were covered up once again. The set of instructions sent by former Field Marshal von Küchler to his military colleagues working for the division at the POW camp in Garmisch-Partenkirchen typifies the way in which former high-ranking officers were allowed to shape legends about their own institution. He directed them to obey the following guidelines: "It is *German* deeds, seen from the German standpoint, that are to be recorded; this will constitute a memorial to our troops." Thus, "no criticism of measures ordered by the leadership" was permitted; no one could be "incriminated in any way," and the achievements of the Wehrmacht were to be appropriately highlighted.[95] Censorship disguised as a "scholarly commission" ensured that no deviations from the guidelines occurred. The former officers—schooled in esprit de corps, obedience, and personal loyalty—probably saw few difficulties in following their instructions, particularly since the guidelines reflected their own views and furthered their own interests.

One of the officers who worked in the Historical Division, former General Geyr von Schweppenburg, confirmed that it was definitely possible there "to allow one or the other piece of incriminating evidence that could have been used at the Nuremberg trial to disappear. The Americans even helped out."[96]

Generals' Memoirs and Adventure Stories

The decade of the 1950s in Germany was a time of rebuilding, growing prosperity, and political stability dominated by the Cold War and the ideology of anti-Communism, but also by the attempt of many Germans to avoid dealing with politics and history at all. Under these circumstances it was naturally impossible for any self-critical review of recent history to thrive. Instead, the view of the National Socialist era fluctuated between extremes, with a tendency either to demonize the regime or to play down its negative side. Although many Germans recognized and accepted some degree of guilt and responsibility, denial of guilt and self-exoneration were rife.[97]

A number of German officers who had occupied positions of leadership during the Second World War and who afterwards worked for one of the various historical projects sponsored by the Allies left the preserve where they had quietly written classified studies in the spirit of the general staff and published their own memoirs in the 1950s. They included General Franz Halder,[98] Grand Admiral Karl

Dönitz (who had been found guilty of war crimes),[99] the once prominent panzer commander General Heinz Guderian,[100] and Field Marshals Albert Kesselring[101] and Erich von Manstein[102] (both convicted
as war criminals by a British military court in Venice). Manstein was
still held in high esteem as a military strategist in West Germany in
the 1950s.

Other authors were General Siegfried Westphal,[103] one of the
authors of the generals' memorandum of 1945; Erwin Rommel,
commander of the German troops in Africa[104]; Adolf Heusinger,[105]
Halder's deputy in the Historical Division and later inspector general of the Bundeswehr; and Generals Warlimont and Greiner. Still
other Wehrmacht officers—such as Tippelskirch, Philippi, Heim,
Mellenthin, Doerr, Erfurth, and Middeldorf—became known as the
authors of uncritical studies on particular aspects of the war.[106]

Despite all the differences in detail, these books tend to depict
Hitler as a little corporal who interfered with the professional military's handling of the war.[107] The title Erich von Manstein chose,
Lost Victories,[108] sums it up. Given their general apologetic tone, one
is not surprised to find no mention in them at all of war crimes or
the Wehrmacht's participation in the killings of Jews.

Bernd Wegner and others have pointed out correctly that the generals' memoirs shaped perceptions of the Wehrmacht not just in the
decade in which they appeared; their influence has been far greater,
as a number of internationally renowned historians and journalists
adopted this favorable picture of an efficiently run force that participated in war crimes to no greater degree than other armies. In this
group Basil H. Liddell Hart, the influential British writer on military affairs, stands out. He edited the English editions of Rommel's
papers and Guderian's memoirs and enthused about the professional

abilities of Wehrmacht officers in his own publications.[109] Authors like Albert Seaton and Earl F. Ziemke, whose approach highlighted strategy and operations, also expressed admiration for their skill and leadership. David Irving's work, with its more politically accentuated interpretations of the Wehrmacht and National Socialism, has also proved influential.

Omer Bartov has summed up this development by pointing out that as a result, a number of legends have become accepted in much of the world and among more than a few military historians in Great Britain and the United States: that the Wehrmacht kept its distance from the regime; that officers served their country, not the Fuehrer, with devotion; that the generals were horrified by the crimes of the SS and offered resistance to them; that they strictly adhered to moral standards and the code of professional soldiers.[110]

The general tendency to repress and deny guilt also found expression in the pictorial images of the 1950s, in memoirs of the war years, popular magazines and newspapers, youth literature, and other books and films. Their common thread was a romantic depiction of war as a great adventure for idealists and daredevils,[111] evoking the experience of comradeship and stressing the abuse of millions of decent soldiers by a criminal regime.[112] Thus they present a guilty Nazi leadership on one side and on the other a misled population, including the men in the Wehrmacht. This perspective dominated West German recollections of the Second World War for decades. The argument of these authors offered an apology for the Wehrmacht in the sense that the military defeat at Stalingrad in 1942–43 was declared to be the responsibility of the "demon" Hitler or else "fated,"[113] so that the armed forces were let off the hook and declared to have "kept their hands clean."

The Cold War Begins

Eisenhower's and Adenauer's Declarations of Honor

As it turns out, two documents were more important for the self-respect of the Wehrmacht elite and the perceptions of the German public than the semi-acquittal by the International Military Tribunal at Nuremberg—namely, the two public declarations made by the commander in chief of NATO forces in Europe, General Dwight D. Eisenhower, on January 23, 1951, and Federal Chancellor Konrad Adenauer on April 5, 1951. They occurred as the result of a politically tense situation in which the governments of both the United States and the Federal Republic of Germany knew that a West German army would have to be built up in the foreseeable future, and that the expertise of the former Wehrmacht elite would be indispensable in creating it.

The immediate background of the declarations was the "Himmerode Memorandum" of 1950.[114] Its authors were a group of former Wehrmacht officers whom Chancellor Adenauer had invited to a conference on military affairs held at the monastery of Himmerode in the Eiffel. Included in their number was former General Hermann Foertsch, who had served in the 1930s under General Walter von Reichenau as one of the leaders responsible for indoctrinating the troops with National Socialist ideas. Former generals Adolf Heusinger and Hans Speidel had proposed him as an adviser for Adenauer. At the conference Foertsch—brother of Friedrich Foertsch, later inspector general of the Bundeswehr—was elected to chair the "internal structure" working group.[115] The officers assembled for the conference made it clear to the chancellor that in their view a German army could be called into existence only after representatives of the Western powers had issued a formal declaration rehabilitating the soldiers of the Wehrmacht. They demanded that the men who had been convicted as war criminals be released "if they had acted only on orders and were not guilty of any offense under the old German laws."

General Eisenhower had previously spoken of the Wehrmacht in very negative terms and identified it with National Socialism. A planned stop in Germany as part of the general's trip to Europe in January 1951 offered an opportunity to try to win him over to a more favorable view. Speidel and Heusinger met with Eisenhower in Bad Homburg and persuaded him to sign a document they had prepared, in which he declared that his earlier assessment of the Wehrmacht had been an error. The public learned of this when Eisenhower told reporters before boarding his return flight in Frankfurt that in his opinion, the fact that certain individuals had committed dishonorable and despicable acts during the war did not affect the honor of the great majority of German soldiers and officers. As he had told the chancellor and the other gentlemen with whom he had spoken the evening before, Eisenhower continued, he had become convinced that a real difference existed between German soldiers and officers as such and Hitler and his criminal gang.[116]

Shortly thereafter, on April 5, 1951, Chancellor Adenauer made a similar declaration on the occasion of a debate in the Bundestag on Article 131 of the Basic Law (the provisional West German constitution). While his statement did not rehabilitate the Wehrmacht as a whole, it officially restored the honor of those soldiers "who had not been guilty of any offense."[117]

These official statements may be regarded as marking the end of the postwar period as a time of humiliation, impotence, and a lack of professional opportunities for the former Wehrmacht elite. Now the highest political representative of the Federal Republic and the highest military representative of the Western alliance had made their peace with the very same generals whose influence the victors of the Second World War had wanted to destroy permanently—or so it must have appeared to the generals themselves. It was not so much the publicly heralded normalization of political and economic conditions—the currency reform of 1948, the founding of the Federal Republic in 1949, or the beginning of the "economic miracle"— that signaled the end of the postwar period for the military, but rather the rehabilitation of their profession. This step, in turn, created the foundations for West German rearmament. Simultaneously, and on a parallel track, Article 131 was inserted into the Basic Law, which ensured that former career soldiers were entitled to pensions and benefits like civil servants of the old regime.[118]

Adenauer's Policy on Dealing with the Past

The contemporary historian Norbert Frei has described with considerable precision how the legend of the Wehrmacht's "clean hands" was created in the 1950s.[119] In a 1997 article for the news magazine *Der Spiegel* titled "Everyday Horror," he investigated the particular question of how the Wehrmacht was depicted in the Adenauer era not in the memoirs of those involved or in publications for mass audiences, but in official policy.[120]

The following scene which Frei describes can be considered characteristic of the political atmosphere in West Germany in the early 1950s. In the fall of 1952 two convicted German war criminals managed to escape from the Werl penitentiary. One of them, Wilhelm Kappe, had been sentenced to life imprisonment by the British for shooting a Russian prisoner of war. When Kappe turned up at the house of relatives in the north German town of Aurich, the local party chairman of the Social Democrats, a fish merchant by the name of Wilhelm Heidepeter, notified the police. The fugitive was able to escape again, confident of support from the population and the press. Heidepeter, however, received threats in the wake of his "denunciation." Residents of the town gathered in front of his house armed with clubs and carrying a banner declaring, "This is where the traitor lives," and shattered the front window of his shop. Fortunately Heidepeter had already fled, so he was not present when his fellow Social Democrats stripped him of his party offices and initiated proceedings to expel him. Not one voice was raised in the press in his defense. In other words, the vast majority of the population retained the nationalistic attitudes inculcated in them earlier. Not only did they not accept the verdict that war crimes had been committed, but also they expressed solidarity with those who had been convicted, protected them, and demanded their release, preferably in the form of a general amnesty. The press and politicians joined in the chorus for the most part, with few deviations.

Representatives of the powers occupying Germany were forced from time to time to remind the German public that there had after all been some reason why people had been convicted and imprisoned as war criminals; the procedure had not been entirely random. In this case the British High Commissioner Sir Ivone Kirkpatrick felt compelled to remind them that almost all the men and women in question had been found guilty of participating in the murder or torture of Allied citizens in slave labor camps or concentration camps.

Germans apparently lacked the awareness that wrongs had been committed, however, having long since become accustomed to speaking of "so-called war criminals" and demanding their release. Already by the end of 1950 the American High Commissioner John McCloy had received death threats because he refused to pardon the war criminals in the Landsberg penitentiary (the prison where convicted war criminals were held) who had been sentenced to death. McCloy was appalled that the Germans would not recognize the enormity of what had taken place.

In fact, there existed a broad consensus across party lines in West Germany about how the past should be dealt with, for now and in the future. The demand, expressed in a threatening tone, was that it was "time to close the chapter." It is amazing to see how much energy and determination were invested in the founding years of our republic in nipping the investigation of Nazi crimes and war crimes in the bud. And it is fascinating and frightening to see how the war generation virtually cemented over its past and made outraged claims of innocence the norm. The most disturbing aspect of this process is the solidarity that developed between those who had merely gone along or not protested and the true war criminals, for in the case of the great majority this cannot be explained by self-interest. Norbert Frei concludes that it must represent "an indirect admission of the entire society's enmeshment in National Socialism." The West German hysteria over the war criminals in the early 1950s amounted to a "secondary confirmation" of the fascist social community.

Between 1949 and 1954 a number of groups represented the interests of Germans with ties to the crimes of the National Socialist past in domestic policy debates; they included influential veterans' and soldiers' organizations and also the churches. The political parties then took up the issue, followed by the federal government, including the "notorious civilian" Konrad Adenauer, and the national print media. Among the important steps in the process of exonerating the perpetrators were the "Federal Amnesty" of 1949, the recommendations of the Bundestag on ending the de-Nazification program in 1950, the "paragraph 131 law" of 1951, and the second "exemption from punishment" law of 1954. All these measures and administrative decisions connected with them were directed at the same goals, namely, commutation of prison sentences and the full reintegration of millions of former Nazi Party members into society.

With regard to the efforts to rehabilitate members of the Wehrmacht leadership, it should be noted that German politicians entered into a virtual competition for veterans' votes in 1950–51. These voters were courted in the run-up to rearmament. During the campaign, in the summer of 1953, Chancellor Adenauer made a highly publicized visit to the British prison for war criminals at Werl. This gesture contributed to the victory of the coalition parties of the Adenauer government, which emerged from the election with a two-thirds majority in the Bundestag.

Between 1950 and 1955 the drive to limit responsibility for the war and the crimes of the National Socialist regime to Hitler and a small clique of "major war criminals" had considerable success. Other Germans considered themselves to have been "seduced" by their political machinations, a status that, if looked at in the proper light, included them among the "victims." This denial of reality made possible the reintegration of the old National Socialist elite into German society. By the end of the 1950s, the idea of the generals' innocence was firmly established in people's minds. As Norbert Frei put it: "When the Americans closed Landsberg in 1958, the majority of Germans, who had never accepted the fact of the Wehrmacht's participation in the war of annihilation, had long since moved on. What was alive was the legend that it had been an 'ordinary war'—an epic tale of honor regarding the Wehrmacht's 'clean hands,' which permitted millions of German veterans to honor the memory of their fallen comrades and to find meaning in the hardships and personal sacrifice of their own military service."[121]

Wehrmacht Crimes, the Justice System, and the Statute of Limitations

The German justice system did not make any particular effort to bring criminals from the National Socialist era to trial either. As far as Wehrmacht officers are concerned, the record could not be clearer: "From 1952 to 1959 there were almost no investigations of members of the Wehrmacht, let alone trials and convictions. The few cases pending were disposed of by invoking the law of July 17, 1954, guaranteeing 'exemption from punishment.'"[122]

A new impulse to prosecute Nazi crimes actively came from the "Einsatzgruppen trial" that took place in the city of Ulm in 1958.[123] It brought to light the fact that "many terrible National Socialist crimes, especially those committed in the East, had not been dealt with by the courts at all."[124] Alarmed by this information, the ministers of justice in the German federal states decided in October 1958 to create a Central Bureau for the Prosecution of National Socialist Crimes in the city of Ludwigsburg. In the succeeding decades the prosecutors working for this bureau succeeded in assembling a valuable body of documentation that historians have consulted in growing numbers. Whether their work was successful in legal terms is another question.

In any event, to my knowledge the German justice system did not convict a single Wehrmacht officer of war crimes or crimes connected with the National Socialist regime. How is this fact, which reflects little credit on the system, to be explained? One could assume that the authorities in Ludwigsburg held back because the image of the "Wehrmacht with clean hands" was already firmly established in the minds of the West Germans; in this view, the prosecutors were unwilling to challenge the prevailing mood—that a line had been drawn under the past and people had moved on. Overall such a suspicion is not justified, however. The prosecutors from the Ludwigsburg bureau conducted solid investigations and pursued their task of picking up where the Nuremberg trials had left off and exposing National Socialist crimes with diligence.[125]

They did so under very particular conditions established by the politicians, however. The agreement concluded by the ministers of justice authorized the Central Bureau to investigate National Socialist crimes but not war crimes. This terminology drew a distinction between types of offenses that led to many problems as time passed, with political implications that have not been entirely clarified up to the present day. In any event, the specific assignment given to the Central Bureau was to investigate killings of civilians committed during the Second World War outside actual combat operations. The former head of the bureau, Adalbert Rückerl, interpreted the wording to mean that "the primary focus was to be on concentration camps, forced labor camps, and ghettos, as well as on the acts committed by special commandos and Einsatzgruppen of the Security Police and SD that qualified as murder or manslaughter." As for the investigation of genuine war crimes committed by members of the armed forces, the Ludwigsburg prosecutors were authorized to proceed only if they were "inseparably connected with crimes committed on the basis of National Socialist ideology."[126] In 1965, seven years after the founding of the bureau, new guidelines were agreed upon. Once again they contained an explicit statement that the bureau's competency did not extend to investigating war crimes.[127]

In distinguishing between "National Socialist crimes" and "war crimes," the intention was apparently to identify and charge those associated with the extermination programs aimed at European Jews as well as the Sinti and Roma Gypsy groups, which were based on ideology and essentially carried out by the SS, but not to pursue the members of the Wehrmacht who were responsible, for example, for allowing more than 3 million Soviet prisoners of war to starve to death. The underlying assumption or claim was that as a rule, no inseparable connection existed between the war crimes of Wehrmacht soldiers and their political convictions. At the time, politicians clearly considered it possible—or at least politically desirable—to draw a clear line between the two types of crimes and the two organizations, since a set of beliefs about the differing moral qualifications of the SS and Wehrmacht had long since established itself in the public consciousness.

Rückerl's successor was Alfred Streim, a senior prosecutor who died in 1996. Streim reported that the Central Bureau did in fact look into the actions of Wehrmacht soldiers, based on the legal principle that all known crimes had to be investigated. They opened "more than one thousand investigations on a large number of members of the former Wehrmacht, particularly the army," and passed the results on to the appropriate criminal authorities. "In no case" did this lead to an indictment. "The cases were closed because of a lack of evidence or the expiration of the statute of limitations, or because the defendant had died."[128] Streim noted, in very circumspect language, that "the reasons were not necessarily always ones with which we would have concurred," and further that "the reasons given for closing cases or not issuing an indictment were sometimes unconvincing and in a few cases grounds for considerable concern." He concluded that crimes by members of the regular armed forces had not been pursued further "largely for political reasons."[129] Streim thus reported more openly than his predecessor Rückerl that in this area political considerations and influences played a particular role—the details of which remain unknown to us today.

Presumably, as Rückerl hinted, an influential network of people operated behind the scenes, with great determination and success, to achieve the goal of amnesty for members of the Wehrmacht.[130] The historian Ulrich Herbert discusses the subject in his biography of a presumed key figure, Werner Best.[131] When many efforts began in the early 1960s to bring Nazi perpetrators to trial, Herbert reports, a central question arose: Who was responsible for the mass crimes of the regime in a legal sense? An important decision on this point was handed down in 1963 by the Federal Supreme Court in Germany in the case of a KGB agent named Bogdan Stashinsky, who was convicted of having assassinated two Ukrainian nationalists in Munich in 1956. The court found that Stashinsky was not guilty of murder, however; rather he had acted as an accomplice of the man who had given the orders to kill the two men, namely, the chief of the KGB in Moscow, and had thus acted merely as an abettor. In a parallel development, it became standard practice in the prosecution of crimes committed during the Third Reich to regard only Hitler, Himmler, and Heydrich as "chief National Socialist perpetrators" and the members of the SS, the Waffen SS, and the police who had carried out the mass murders in the East as "abettors." This juristic construction enabled courts to classify the actual perpetrators as "accessories to murder," and instead of being condemned to life in prison the defendants received far milder sentences.

Since the Nazi era perpetrators who had not yet been brought to trial were now likely to be charged and convicted, they continued to use their considerable influence to try to make the existing laws more favorable. Their demand for a general amnesty had to be dropped in view of the negative international reaction. Instead they sought solutions that would provide the widest possible amnesty without the effect becoming immediately apparent to the outside world. The main figures in developing this strategy were an attorney from Bonn named Lohmann, who had already acted as a defense attorney in several trials, and Werner Best, Heydrich's former deputy at the Reich Security Main Office, who in the 1960s was coordinating the defense strategy of the men who had already been charged. At the beginning of January 1963 Lohmann wrote to Best, setting forth a plan that he had clearly been working on for some time:

> Lohmann began by pointing out the judgment that the Federal Supreme Court had just handed down in the Stashinsky case, which deviated from prior verdicts of German criminal courts in recent years in suggesting that even so-called "National Socialist perpetrators" could be charged only as accessories if they had not acted on their own initiative. It would be a smart move politically, Lohmann noted, if the responsible bodies would issue a partial amnesty for all such perpetrators who had acted on orders from above and would thus now have to be legally characterized as "accessories" . . . At the same time it would be feasible to block any possible outcry from abroad about not dealing with the past by noting that the amnesty was only partial.[132]

Lohmann's calculation was that such a partial amnesty for those who had been "accessories to murder" actually amounted to a general amnesty in disguise.

In his letter to Best, Lohmann also mentioned the Wehrmacht, observing that recent trials had revealed the extent to which the armed forces had participated in the National Socialist extermination campaigns. That is, the documents collected by the defense attorneys in the trials up to the present time showed "that the orders regarding the extermination of Jews and partisans were issued through Wehrmacht channels. If one were to apply the standards of the Ludwigsburg Central Bureau to the former members of the Wehrmacht and current members of the Bundeswehr, it would be necessary to indict a huge number of people, and the Bundeswehr would be gravely discredited both at home and abroad."[135] Lohmann saw in this a way to exert pressure on the German government. If the government were prepared to accept a "partial amnesty," then it could help avoid a future "avalanche of trials" against members of the Bundeswehr. Lohman noted that some influential people in political circles took the same view: "Gehlen's office regarded the orders collected [by the defense attorneys] as a potential bombshell. I'm told Gehlen himself intends to take the matter up with the chancellor and propose that the Ludwigsburg project be shut down." Lohmann also reported that Franz Josef Strauss, the former defense minister, had criticized the National Socialist trials very outspokenly—off the record. More support could be counted on. He ended his letter by asking Best to take over "strategic leadership" in the matter, something that would naturally have to be done behind the scenes.

It is obvious that this political strategy was designed to frustrate the activities of the Central Bureau in Ludwigsburg. The document discovered by Ulrich Herbert was extremely sensitive politically, for at least three reasons:

1. We learn from lawyers who had specialized in defending war

criminals that Wehrmacht officers who had been taken on by the Bundeswehr were implicated in National Socialist crimes during the Second World War.

2. We learn further that the prosecutors of the Central Bureau in Ludwigsburg were clearly in the process of investigating such crimes committed by Wehrmacht officers and that an influential group of politicians, civil servants at the German intelligence agency, and attorneys were discussing how to prevent the disclosure of such offenses. The document informs us that Reinhard Gehlen, a former general in the Wehrmacht and at that time head of the Federal Intelligence Service, intended to talk with Chancellor Adenauer and propose that he put a stop to the Ludwigsburg investigations.

3. The consistently defensive behavior of the German justice system, after the founding of the Ludwigsburg bureau, with regard to the war crimes of Wehrmacht officers appears in a new light. References to the fact that the general public was firmly convinced of the Wehrmacht's innocence at the time do not provide a sufficient answer to the question of why the judiciary, both up to the Central Bureau's creation in 1958 and afterwards, convicted not one officer of the Wehrmacht.[134] The prosecutors in Ludwigsburg were by no means guided by the widespread attitude that it was time to draw a line under the past and move on. But on the other side was an influential network of people pursuing the goal of obtaining passage of a law that would grant amnesty to members of the armed forces.

The details of Best's efforts remain unknown.[135] But in the years that followed it became evident that a statute of limitations for murder was not achievable politically and that no majority would be found in the German Bundestag in favor of an amnesty for National Socialist perpetrators, particularly after the Social Democrats joined the governing "grand coalition" in 1966. From the perspective of the perpetrators' defense counsel, the situation now presented the following challenge: "If the desired aim was to shut down a large number of the investigations and proceedings against National Socialist perpetrators, then a legal construction would have to be found of a kind that would prevent both the majority in the Bundestag and the Social Democratic leadership at the Federal Ministry of Justice from realizing what was actually at stake."[136]

Pushing through such a measure was of course possible, it must be said by way of explaining this political detective story, only because the group of defense attorneys had contacts among top officials at the Ministry of Justice who shared their views and were thus prepared to work toward the same goal under the political radar. Apparently it was Dr. Eduard Dreher, a high-level civil servant at the ministry, who hit upon the trick that would enable them to achieve it without causing an uproar. In 1968 a prefatory bill to the Misdemeanors Bill was introduced in the Bundestag for no discernable reason. Essentially it had to do with traffic misdemeanors, but under a misleading heading it contained a substantial revision of the article of the German criminal code that dealt with the offense of acting as an accessory to murder.

Neither the top political appointees at the Ministry of Justice nor the elected members of the Bundestag spotted the legal bombshell lurking within the new version, namely, that it established a statute of limitations of fifteen years for this offense. In one stroke it removed the possibility of prosecuting all crimes committed during the Third Reich that fell into this category, since under the new law the statute of limitations for them had expired.[137] The news magazine *Der Spiegel* was the first to expose the disaster, in an article published in January 1969. In Rückerl's view irreparable harm had been done. One newspaper estimated that as a result nearly 90 percent of all National Socialist murders would go unpunished.[138] It also meant that former Wehrmacht officers who had been approved by a board of review in the mid-1950s and had taken up leading positions in the newly founded Bundeswehr were protected from prosecution. They included Hans Poeppel, the three-star general who was the subject of a 1983 article by the American historian Christopher R. Browning that connected him with the German war crimes perpetrated in Serbia in 1941.[139]

CHAPTER SIX

A Taboo Shatters

Historical Research

Critical Military Historians and Their Work

IN THE 1950s historians in West Germany, especially those at universities, paid very little attention to the Second World War, and even less to the Wehrmacht. It was for this reason that the former German generals who wrote down their version of its history under the roof of the American Historical Division could exercise a decisive influence on the subject. Some of them also published memoirs characterized by a desire to justify themselves and whitewash the Wehrmacht. In their accounts for the United States military—which was particularly interested in the Germans' experience of the Soviet Red Army's tactics—the Wehrmacht officers drew mainly on their personal recollections. Sometimes the Americans made original sources, that is, the Wehrmacht's own records, available to them, thereby placing them at a considerable advantage over other researchers.

When the Wehrmacht files were returned to Germany by the Americans and British in the early 1960s and placed in the German

Federal Archives–Military Archives, conditions were created that enabled scholars to probe the history of the Wehrmacht. Works published during the 1960s—such as Andreas Hillgruber's book *Hitlers Strategie* (Hitler's Strategy), the reports by Helmut Krausnick and Hans-Adolf Jacobsen on the commissar decree and the concentration camp system, and the books on the Wehrmacht by Manfred Messerschmidt and Klaus-Jürgen Müller published in 1969—brought important advances in our knowledge of the field.[1] The 1970s and 1980s saw publication of the studies by Christian Streit and Alfred Streim on the fate of Soviet prisoners of war in German custody and a series of monographs by the historians of the Military History Research Institute, which is funded by the German Federal Ministry of Defense. They covered the war of extermination in the East, and German war crimes in Yugoslavia, Greece, and Italy. The research of the Austrian historian Walter Manoschek uncovered the crimes of the Wehrmacht in Serbia.[2]

In the early 1980s Manfred Messerschmidt, chief historian of the institute, summarized research on the Wehrmacht up to that time and discussed the problems of creating a military tradition given the current state of knowledge.[3] His conclusion: "The campaign against the Soviet Union, like all other German military undertakings after 1939, had the character of a war of aggression, with all the wrongfulness that suggests. But beyond that it must be regarded as a criminal event planned with the cooperation of the army, Luftwaffe, navy, and Wehrmacht leaders; it represents the absolute nadir of German military history."[4] The criminal orders of the Wehrmacht leadership and the anti-Semitic statements of high-ranking soldiers acquired crucial significance, Messerschmidt found, in the context of questions about the connections between the Wehrmacht and the Bundeswehr: "They reflect the zenith of a development undergone by the German national state when the conservative and nationalistic traditions of a military state were combined with components of racial ideology and ethnicity."[5]

These findings painted a picture of the Wehrmacht based on scholarly research that utterly contradicted the existing legend. Was it possible, in the light of these new insights, to cling to the old sugarcoated version, or did they call for a critical revision? In Messerschmidt's own view (which had political consequences at the time) the answer was: "Possibilities for identification with the attitudes, existence, and campaigns of the Wehrmacht should be inconceivable for the Bundeswehr. The primacy of politics in the parliamentary democracy cannot be compared with the Wehrmacht's position within the 'ethnic community.' Any links to soldierly virtues of the Wehrmacht or individual members of it cannot ignore the question of whether such virtues were consciously exercised or blindly devoted to serving National Socialism and Hitler."[6]

Research on the Holocaust and Military History

Scholarly research on the Holocaust has not come to an end yet—far from it. Among other things, the Goldhagen debate in 1996 over the motives of the perpetrators[7] revealed that crucial questions have not been answered satisfactorily. Maybe they have not even been asked yet. Goldhagen's thesis—that a widespread "eliminationist anti-Semitism" allowed the Holocaust to become a "national project"— was received critically for the most part by German historians. The general public's reception of his ideas, however, showed that he had clearly been able to fill an existing vacuum. Perhaps the rejection of his thesis also needs to be considered and interpreted in the larger context of a discussion of our current political culture, which has remained unsettled since the historians' debate of 1986.[8]

In other words, "research on the National Socialist persecution of Jews still presents one of the great challenges of contemporary historiography."[9] It can hardly be said that German historians were out in front on this topic in the first few decades after the Second World War;[10] rather the Americans and Israelis took the lead, and West German scholars did not enter the international debate until the end of the 1970s.[11] And then it is noticeable that they have tended to exclude the role of the Wehrmacht. Christian Streit and Alfred Streim were the first to discuss the treatment of Soviet prisoners of war in their books, and Helmut Krausnick and Hans-Heinrich Wilhelm opened up the subject of the Einsatzgruppen—two particular aspects of the history of the Wehrmacht that historians had avoided up to that time. Nevertheless, they did not deal with the question of whether the Wehrmacht was involved in the murder of the European Jews in certain cases, and if so, what form that involvement took. Dieter Pohl notes that "the separation of the subject of the persecution of the Jews from other areas of policy" was characteristic of Holocaust research until the 1980s, and this observation is particularly true with regard to the Wehrmacht. Only gradually was the Wehrmacht's share in the Holocaust exposed, Pohl writes, citing Manoschek's work on Serbia and the volume edited by the Hamburg Institute for Social Research, *The German Army and Genocide*.[12]

In a recent research article on the Holocaust, Gerd R. Ueberschär notes that the "criminal orders" given to regular soldiers "reveal a high degree of responsibility, involvement, and participation of the military leadership in this extermination campaign.[13] He further emphasizes, with reference to the work of Manfred Messerschmidt and Omer Bartov, "that the Wehrmacht was permeated with National Socialist ideology and propaganda about the total annihilation of 'Jewish Bolshevism' by so-called 'Aryans' and the 'master race,'

and that Wehrmacht commanders had no scruples about cooperating with the criminal extermination campaign of the National Socialist regime."[14] And finally, the armed forces themselves played an
active role in this campaign, as Ilya Ehrenburg and Vasily Grossman's *Black Book* has shown.[15]

The Israeli historian Omer Bartov, who now teaches in the United
States, has recognized the undeniable achievements of the critical
wing of West German military historians, but he also reproaches
them for their omissions: "Even in confronting sensitive political,
ideological, and conceptual issues, they have . . . failed seriously to
address some of the most difficult and potentially explosive questions, such as . . . the involvement of the army in the Holocaust."[16]
His criticism is directed in particular at the series *Germany and the
Second World War* by the members of the Military History Research
Institute. It also takes up the warning issued by the well-known German historian Andreas Hillgruber in 1985.[17] He pointed out during a
conference on the build-up to the decision to murder the European
Jews that the campaign against the Jews had to be regarded as a genuine part of the Second World War and could not be described as a
separate event. In the eyes of a large number of National Socialist
leaders, the war served as a means of altering the racial balance of
Europe. The physical extermination of the Jews in Europe was intended to bring about a decisive advance in the "racial revolution"
and give permanence to the goal of German world power.[18]

Those familiar with research developments in the field will have
to admit that such criticism is justified, at least in part. Military historians have in fact devoted far too little attention to the forms of
participation (which no doubt varied from region to region) in the
murder of the Jews. They did, however, make one contribution that
should not be overlooked, namely, to investigate and document the

origins of the orders later characterized as "criminal" and through them the Wehrmacht leadership's undeniable responsibility for a war that became a criminal undertaking. When the generals referred in their orders to "Bolsheviks, Jews, commissars, and inferior races," they also spoke of the necessity of exterminating them, sending soldiers down the fateful path that made the Holocaust possible.

Too little research has been done to date on the practical aspects of the extermination campaign. A generation of younger historians has taken up this subject in recent years and begun to produce a number of studies showing how this campaign proceeded in various regions, based on empirical evidence and with little emphasis on moral judgments. Some of their results were presented in a lecture series at the University of Freiburg in the winter of 1996–97.[19] Walter Manoschek reported on the persecution and murder of Jews in Serbia; Christoph Dieckmann and Thomas Sandkühler covered Lithuania and Galicia, respectively,[20] while Dieter Pohl spoke on Poland under the "General Government," and Christian Gerlach on White Russia.[21] The framework was the same for all of these cases, in that each region had first been conquered by the Wehrmacht, and then placed under an administration run by the occupiers.

With the exception of Manoschek's work on Serbia and Gerlach's on White Russia, none of these studies focuses on the Wehrmacht and its share in the mass executions. Nevertheless, the Wehrmacht is always present, for as the regional studies make clear, to a far greater extent than had previously been realized, there was close cooperation in the occupied countries between the various German organizations and authorities, that is, the civil administration, labor offices, regional SS and police forces, economic administrators, and also the Wehrmacht.[22] Despite all the regional differences, it can be established that in each place the killings of Jews acquired their own dynamic[23]; there were no precise orders from above on how to proceed, but only general instructions that left a great deal open to interpretation by troops "on the ground."[24] Nowhere did the Wehrmacht act as a brake, but on the contrary, it developed significant drives of its own, as in Serbia and White Russia.

Until recently, military historians who worked on the Wehrmacht in the Second World War and historians of the Holocaust pursued their topics independently of each other. The reasons why this was so, and the degree to which specific interests and happenstance played a role, are still worthy of consideration today. In any event, the separation of these two tracks once more reinforced the impression that the military pursued its own war, and the murder of Jews was the "dirty business" of the SS and its Einsatzgruppen. The new approaches I have described, which shed light on the cooperation of German occupying authorities in a given region, are guided by the desire not to repeat this mistake.

Perceptions of the Wehrmacht in the Bundeswehr

The Significance of History in Legitimizing the Military

The question of how officers of the Bundeswehr (founded in 1955) perceived the Wehrmacht is naturally of particular interest, since— if we follow chronology and leave aside all political implications— the latter was its direct predecessor as an institution. No other federal institution in West Germany was as intimately connected with its history. No one could overlook the fact that both were staffed to a considerable extent by the same people: the officers approved by the commission to build up the new force had all served in the Wehrmacht.[25] Such continuity in personnel and the simultaneous wish of politicians to distance themselves from the Wehrmacht as an institution gave rise to an ongoing disagreement for decades about the kinds of tradition the Bundeswehr ought to recognize.[26] For the generation of officers who founded the Bundeswehr, the Wehrmacht was not merely another topic on which reasonable people could disagree; it was a piece of their own biography and outlook.

The desire to cling to perceptions of a "clean" Wehrmacht that had fought bravely and effectively was connected directly with German career soldiers' self-image, since the military, far more than other professions, tends to derive its legitimacy—its right to exist—from history. Soldiers see the necessity of their profession as based on historical experience, on the fact that there have "always" been wars, and for that reason no country can do without soldiers and organized preparations for war. In their view, an orientation based on the past and derived from a country's military traditions can furthermore build a sense of personal confidence and a knowledge of how to behave in challenging situations.[27]

This was the thinking of German generals not just in the Kaiser's time and the National Socialist era;[28] some hold that belief even today. During the Persian Gulf war of 1991, for example, one major general in the Bundeswehr complained that German society had a generally bad attitude toward war. He informed his readers that "the real thing" was not peace, "no matter how convincing and also appealing that may seem at first glance. The real thing is war, and the Basic Law is quite definite on that point. The task assigned to the Bundeswehr by the [German] constitution is defense, pure and simple, not peace." The author, Johann Adolf, Count Kilmansegg, supported this view with a general justification of war based on history. Wars occurred, he wrote, "because this world is as it is, good and bad, peaceful and violent, just and unjust." And this would remain so for all time, "since war, violence, death, and injustice cannot be abolished forever through a single great moral and political effort."[29]

In such a context the enormous sensitivity of the topic of history for the German military, in both emotional and intellectual terms, becomes understandable. Or to put it the other way around: anyone threatening to take their history away from German career soldiers—for instance, by destroying the retouched legends of the Wehrmacht—is pulling the rug out from under them, so to speak. The persistence of most West German military professionals in clinging to perceptions of the Wehrmacht that are at least not fundamentally negative can be explained to a considerable extent by these circumstances.

Since the 1960s the proponents of top officers in the Bundeswehr who subscribe to these views and hence to the Wehrmacht as a form of role model have been known as "traditionalists."[30] They have constituted a majority opposed by a small group of "reformers" led by Wolf Count von Baudissin, whose goal was to make a fresh start.

Favorable Perceptions in the Early Years of the Bundeswehr

When the Bundeswehr was founded in 1955, the West German public had already embraced a largely favorable image of the Wehrmacht, in developments I have already described.[31] People wanted to put the past and its burdens behind them and enjoy the material blessings emerging from the "Economic Miracle." It was in such an atmosphere that the Bundeswehr was built up. The soldiers had a few central points of historical and political orientation that, in a manner of speaking, provided an ideological foundation for the organization in its formative years.[32] They included the traditional perception of the Soviet Union (or Communism) as an enemy and a positive—or at least not totally negative—perception of the Wehr-macht. The "traditionalists" among the officers who had served in the Wehrmacht themselves passed on these favorable associations to succeeding generations. Their belief that the two armies should be linked by an unbroken tradition led to a certain number of deci-sions with consequences that still occupy the Bundeswehr today. The names given to army bases are a case in point. In the build-up phase, the leaders of the Bundeswehr chose them from a list assembled by the Wehrmacht on instructions from Hitler in 1937–38. At that time Hitler was conducting his campaign to rename bases,[33] which in ret-rospect must be interpreted as part of the ideological campaign to prepare for the coming war; some two hundred new military bases were built and named after battles and heroes of the "Great War" of 1914–1918. These same names were now adopted by the Bundes-wehr.[34]

While the connection to the Wehrmacht was somewhat indirect in this instance, there were other cases in which the troop com-manders of the early years did not hesitate to name a rather large number of army bases after generals of the Wehrmacht. It should be noted that the creation of such links to the Wehrmacht stemmed not from instructions issued by the federal minister of defense but rather from initiatives within the army; at the outset the ministry had given the army leaders a free hand on such questions, and they proceeded to demonstrate how they felt about the Wehrmacht. Among the officers who had served Hitler loyally and were now sig-nally honored by the Bundeswehr one finds General Werner von Fritsch, Colonel Werner Mölders, Field Marshal Erwin Rommel, Major General Adalbert Schulz, General Hasso von Manteuffel, General Eduard Dietl, and General Ludwig Kübler.[35]

The fact that this list includes anti-Semites, men who had been committed Nazis from day one, and war criminals either was apparently unknown to the responsible troop commanders or—as is more likely—carried no particular weight with them. The determination to retain their names even decades later, when information on their ideology and actions had long since become available, reveals the enormous influence of the traditionalists within the Bundeswehr. (One need only think of the battle over Camp Dietl in Füssen, locally dubbed the "Seven Years' War.")[36] Occasionally the military leaders attempted to make local politicians—who apparently knew little history except the military variety—responsible for the choices; this merely shows that the necessary sensitivity to the past was lacking in those circles as well.

The Reformers

For the circle of reformers around Wolf Count von Baudissin, the goal was to risk a genuinely new beginning with the Bundeswehr and set up a military force that would identify itself with parliamentary democracy.[37] In their view, German military history from the founding of the empire in 1871 in general, and the history of the Wehrmacht in particular, offered very little material as a starting point. Baudissin took the stance that the Bundeswehr should not follow in the footsteps of either the Reichswehr or the Wehrmacht but instead "create something fundamentally new today without borrowing from either of the old armed forces."[38] Baudissin was convinced that the Wehrmacht had to be regarded as an organization that had served a criminal regime, issued criminal orders itself, and committed crimes—all of which rendered it guilty.[39] First at the "Blank Office"[40] and then at the federal Ministry of Defense, the contrast between Baudissin and his associates and the "traditionalists" could hardly have been clearer.

It should be stressed, however, that the reformers were in good company intellectually speaking when they placed the Wehrmacht in the context of Germany's militaristic and authoritarian traditions and the National Socialist dictatorship. This was exactly the view taken by foreign and German historians. In the 1950s the former found themselves in rare unanimity in support of the conservative historian Gerhard Ritter's observation that the Wehrmacht embodied the "most extreme militarism" in German history.[41] Only with the onset of the Cold War, when the concept of militarism was adapted for the propaganda battles of the time, did that consensus break down.[42]

Furthermore the reformers opposed the traditionalists on the question of how the participants in the plot to assassinate Hitler on July 20, 1944, should be viewed. They insisted that this small group of officers ought to be considered a primary model for the Bundeswehr and hence a new source of tradition, a highly sensitive issue for their opponents, who would not have been able to combine it with the legend of the "clean" Wehrmacht.

Most of the former Wehrmacht officers thus rejected the idea out of hand. The traditionalists regarded the men who had plotted against Hitler as officers who had broken their oath of loyalty, in violation of the long Prussian and German tradition of obedience to authority. As a rule such officers were considered despicable. On this subject the former Wehrmacht general Erich von Manstein, who had regained political influence in the 1950s, uttered the memorable statement that the plot of July 20 was "unworthy of an officer."[43] Hence it is not surprising that the reformers' positive view of military resistance in the Wehrmacht could not prevail until discussions had gone on for decades and a new generation had grown up. It took a long time, too, until this view was symbolically expressed by naming several Bundeswehr barracks after Wehrmacht officers such as

Beck, Fellgiebel, Kranzfelder, Stauffenberg, and Tresckow—all of them members of the resistance who gave their lives fighting the unjust regime of the National Socialists.[44]

The traditionalists, for their part, defended their positive view of the Wehrmacht by pointing to its high degree of military professionalism and effectiveness, which they noted had also been praised by its opponents.[45] In addition, they cited the oath they had sworn as officers, the principle of obedience to orders, the legal practice that had arisen in Germany of holding only the issuers of criminal orders as guilty (not those who followed them), and the brave sacrifices made by the soldiers of the Wehrmacht. These were the arguments of the Wehrmacht legend, already present as such in Admiral Dönitz's last report of May 9, 1945. The reformers countered with the argument that technical and operational successes of the military could not be separated from the criminal regime on whose behalf they had been achieved.

The First "Traditions Decree" of 1965

Can one say that in the first years of the Bundeswehr's existence two opposing views of the Wehrmacht were in competition? Certainly different assessments of it existed. The more critical of the two, however, never really had a chance of prevailing against the stronger group of military traditionalists. The literature on the Bundeswehr's first decade occasionally mentions a situation in which the enlisted men were taking over traditions from the Wehrmacht in an unexamined and uncritical manner that was also not authorized from above. This kind of "wild growth"[46] represented not so much a general lack of orientation that called for guidance from the leadership as a general reactionary outlook favoring the Wehrmacht as a model.

The Ministry of Defense realized early on that it would have to find practical ways of creating a tradition that would be acceptable both to the West German public and to the country's allies in the West. The real bone of contention, it emerged repeatedly, was the Wehrmacht and the perpetuation of symbolic links to it. Thus a full ten years went by before the minister of defense, then the Christian Democrat Kai-Uwe von Hassel, could issue a first decree concerning the cultivation of traditions in the Bundeswehr on July 1, 1965.[47]

What perceptions of the Wehrmacht did it endorse? The answer is, in fact, none, for the term "Wehrmacht" did not appear in it. The wording of the decree reflected the ongoing controversies between the traditionalists and the reformers in so far as it fell back on vague and wordy generalities such as, "In history everyone shares good fortune and merit as well as catastrophic destiny and guilt" (paragraph 6). Following the "qualified" declarations on the Wehrmacht soldier's honor issued by Adenauer and Eisenhower in 1951, the authors used quite general language to suggest that those few soldiers who committed crimes should be distinguished from the many soldiers who fought bravely and behaved well, even heroically. They avoided making any statement about the Wehrmacht as an institution. The decree did, however, praise the members of the resistance who participated in the plot of July 20, 1944, a statement to which the majority of Wehrmacht veterans were by no means receptive: "Ultimately responsible only to their own consciences, soldiers proved themselves by offering resistance to the injustice and crimes of the National Socialist dictatorship, up to and including the ultimate sacrifice of their own lives" (paragraph 14).

When the reformers considered the question of whether their ideas (and critical assessment of the Wehrmacht) had prevailed not only in government legislation and military textbooks but also in the everyday activities of the Bundeswehr, they were forced to concede that the reform efforts had failed, and that the restoration of the military on the model of the old Wehrmacht had succeeded to a considerable degree.[48] Not only was the Wehrmacht increasingly viewed in positive terms, but it was even seen through rose-colored glasses. One symptom of these developments was a public statement by a commander of the Leadership Academy of the Bundeswehr, who in 1965 summed up his own achievements as having "realized the Wehrmacht model of 1939."[49]

The Second "Traditions Decree" of 1982

In the early 1980s a public debate over whether Germany should upgrade its weapons systems resulted in a broad wave of criticism of the Bundeswehr's still unresolved relationship to symbols and traditions of the Wehrmacht. Part of that discontent took the form of protests against military ceremonies when public officials were sworn in. In this situation the minister of defense, the Social Democrat Hans Apel, took an important step when—only a few weeks before the expected collapse of the government majority—he issued a second decree that for the first time contained an explicit rejection of all symbolic links to Wehrmacht traditions.[50] Reflecting the documentation of the role of the Wehrmacht in the Second World War, the new guidelines stated: "Military forces were in part enmeshed in National Socialism and its guilt, and in part misused. No guilt results from the latter. An unjust regime such as the Third Reich cannot be a source of tradition" (paragraph 6). Like its predecessor, the decree avoided any mention of the Wehrmacht, probably for tactical reasons. Nevertheless, no one could be in doubt any longer about the matter itself.

Manfred Wörner, a Christian Democrat and Apel's successor as minister of defense, announced in his very first speech on taking office that he intended to throw out the traditions decree as soon as possible, but nothing of the kind occurred. This was hardly due to a reduction of the pressure being exerted by veterans' organizations. Rather it is likely that the new defense minister, who was quite prepared to work with the traditionalists, found that he had little room to maneuver. Recent findings, to which the scholars of the Military History Research Institute had made a not insignificant contribution, left him little choice. The staff at the ministry had probably realized that the image of the supposedly "clean" Wehrmacht could not be maintained, given the growing number of scholarly publications proving the contrary. Thus the decree of 1982 remains in force and continues to constitute the official guidelines for acceptable traditions in the Bundeswehr.

The Veterans' Organizations Protest

While the traditionalists among the active military leadership were obliged to follow the new guidelines, veterans' organizations mounted vehement protests.[51] They feared that the positive image of the Wehrmacht which they had kept alive for decades would begin to crumble in earnest. They challenged the politically unwelcome findings of academic military historians and were not above attacking their reputations, even demanding the dismissal of Manfred Messerschmidt, then the chief historian at the Military History Research Institute,[52] who had taken a very clear stand on several occasions.[53] The veterans' objections included claims that the historians had "defamed the German military" and "maliciously and in a defamatory manner attacked the reputation of German soldiers."[54] Millions of Wehrmacht soldiers and "the military service of Germans" had been slandered, they protested.[55] The extreme right-wing *Deutsche Wochen-Zeitung* informed its readers that German history was being "officially falsified" at the institute, at taxpayers' expense.[56]

General Secretary Körber of the Federation of German Veterans' Organizations went public with a characteristic type of argument. Denying that an extermination campaign had ever taken place, he declared that criminal behavior had occurred only in isolated instances: "No one disputes that during the Second World War soldiers of the Wehrmacht committed crimes, too. When such acts became known they usually led to sentencing of the offender by a court. If such regrettable instances are generalized and ascribed to the Wehrmacht as a whole, as Dr. Messerschmidt has done, it amounts to discrimination . . . Defaming German soldiers in general means the defamation of more than 11 million German men, many of whom sacrificed their lives or their health for our fatherland."[57]

General Heinz Karst, a member of the traditionalist faction and at one time head of educational programs for the Bundeswehr, who had earlier published an influential book, *Das Bild des Soldaten* (The Soldier's Image), now speculated in the rightist journal *Criticon* that the military historians publishing critical assessments of the Wehrmacht clearly wanted a "second wave of 'demilitarization.'" First, there had been a peace movement protesting the upgrading of the German army's weapons systems; now Karst thought he saw a parallel movement, an "attack on the Wehrmacht and the war generation that built up the new German democracy. Almost all the politicians of the founding generation, with the exception of Adenauer and Ollenhauer, served as soldiers in the Wehrmacht. Most of them were officers, like Karl Carstens, Alfred Dregger, F. J. Strauss, Helmut Schmidt, Wilhelm Berkhan, and "Ben Wisch";[58] others, like Carlo Schmid, served in the role of legal advisers. The Bundeswehr was built up almost entirely by officers and noncommissioned officers of the Wehrmacht." Karst mentioned a "press campaign" against the Wehrmacht, the German need to deal with the past, and, quoting Theodor Heuss, a recent "tendency toward self-destructiveness" on the part of Germans. He then went on to describe the career to date of the Wehrmacht legend in the manner characteristic of traditionalists: "Up to a few years ago the Wehrmacht was seen as a fighting force that deserved respect on the whole, although it was not disputed that instances of wrongdoing had occurred: ideological adjustments to Hitler's ideas, crimes, and toleration of crimes at the fringes. Now, however, some perceive the Wehrmacht as the enemy and have begun eagerly searching for evidence that it committed outrages. No other nation on earth," Karst continued, politicizing the critical historians, "would permit this kind of 'research' to be visited upon the millions of their dead from the front and the POW camps."[59] Whereas abroad the outstanding military feats of the Wehrmacht were admired, in their own country the soldiers—who were after all subject to the authority of political leaders—were being "vilified again in a second wave that has been rolling through the media and 'scholarship' since 1979."[60] Thus it was only logical that former General Karst would call Apel's decree of 1982 "disastrous." In May 1988 *Deutschland Magazin*, another right-leaning publication, ran a cover story on the subject of "How leading scholars of the Military History Research Institute defame soldiers and falsify history," in which Heinz Karst once again had his say.[61]

After Fifty Years a Taboo Is Broken

As is well known, it is one thing to present the results of years of research in scholarly tomes and quite another to acquaint a larger public with the upshot of what they contain. In fact, for a long time the public took little or no notice of the findings concerning the Wehrmacht, so that the touched-up picture created in the postwar years remained surprisingly intact. It seems likely that this was due primarily to the influence of the war generation, but with the passage of time its spokesmen, who, like Hans Filbinger, saw themselves as belonging to a cohort that had been unfairly denigrated and "reviled,"[62] had increasing difficulty prevailing against other views.

The "historians' quarrel" of 1986–87 revived the discussions of recent German history and raised the historical and political consciousness of the younger generations. They persisted in asking questions about what was known of the role of the Werhmacht in the National Socialist state, particularly with regard to the war on the eastern front. Television programs, important weekly newspapers, and a few publishers (such as Fischer, which brought out a series on the era), did their part by making the information more widely available.[63]

The Wehrmacht Exhibition, 1995–1999

Fifty years after the end of the Second World War the time was then ripe for a far-reaching revision of the notion, still widely held by the general public, that the Wehrmacht had fought a war like any other army and was not guilty of particular crimes. The touring exhibition mounted by the Hamburg Institute for Social Research provided the catalyst.

The public debate that ensued on the history of the Wehrmacht can be called unparalleled in terms of both length and the degree of participation. The interest in Daniel Jonah Goldhagen's theses on the character of anti-Semitism in Germany was equally great, but of shorter duration, while Victor Klemperer's diaries were much read and well received, but gave rise to no fundamental controversies. The historians' quarrel of 1986–87 had essentially taken place among professionals, and the public served merely as an audience.

The Wehrmacht, by contrast, became a focus of historical and political interest for hundreds of thousands if not millions of citizens. Often they were members of the younger generations, and their goal was to gain information. They simply wanted to know what had really happened and what had previously been withheld from them. Among those who became involved, however, there were also many prominent figures, as the impressive list of speakers who opened the exhibition in different cities attests. They included Klaus von Bismarck (at the opening in Hamburg), Iring Fetscher in Potsdam, Erhard Eppler in Stuttgart, Johannes Mario Simmel in Vienna, Diether Posser in Essen, Jutta Limbach in Karlsruhe, Christian Ude in Munich, Hans Eichel and Ignaz Bubis in Frankfurt, Hans-Jochen Vogel in Marburg, and Johannes Rau in Bonn.[64] Eighty more cities had applied to host the exhibition by November 1999, when scholarly reservations led to its being withdrawn for revision or the development of a new approach.

On an emotional level, the shattering of the taboo threatened the shelter to which the war generation had fled, in a manner of speaking, after 1945. Once they had assigned all responsibility for mass crimes to the Nazi leaders and the war criminals sentenced at Nuremberg, they constructed the pleasing picture of a "clean" Wehrmacht, which helped them to repress their dreadful memories and guilt feelings.

The breadth and intensity of the upheaval in the 1990s was connected, among other things, with the sheer size of the Wehrmacht. Roughly 20 million men had passed through this gigantic military force of the National Socialist system, making it truly an army of the people. To a far greater degree than the Bundeswehr of today, it represented and reflected the general population of the country. Thus it cannot be understood solely as an institution of the state, but must be seen as a part of society, closely bound up with the lives of the average German family. Clearly, millions of men who served in it retained a sense of connection even after the war ended. This helps to explain what is otherwise scarcely comprehensible, namely, the fact that senior generals and the many "little guys" in uniform shared a common identity, as it were, and did not differentiate between levels of responsibility or particular interests. To this extent the legend of the Wehrmacht fulfilled a social function.

When the discussions about the Wehrmacht began in 1995, their tone was muted. The social scientist Klaus Naumann has analyzed the reports in German daily and weekly newspapers of that year, the fiftieth anniversary of the war's end.[65] The enormous significance of the Third Reich, the war of extermination, and genocide for the Germans' self-image became apparent. In the anniversary year, however, what the media recalled was not primarily the Wehrmacht but the liberation of the concentration camps, the final phase of the Allied bombing campaign, the onset of streams of refugees from the East, the last days of the war in particular localities, and finally the unconditional surrender on May 8, 1945. Echoing the assessment given by Federal President Richard von Weizsäcker on the anniversary ten years earlier, the newspapers almost uniformly characterized the military defeat of the Wehrmacht and the National Socialist state as a "liberation." The pattern of interpretation centered on this one word.

Yet perceptions of the Wehrmacht itself remained diffuse. In recollections from many different places around the country, members of the Wehrmacht appeared in a variety of roles: the poor grunt, the soldier determined to do his duty, the fanatic who wanted to hold out no matter what, and the deserter trying to escape coercion to fight to the death. In accord with the newly won consensus that the surrender represented a liberation, the tenor of the reports was that the soldiers of the Wehrmacht had been "neither heroes nor criminals." Thus in the general atmosphere of the time, when the Hamburg exhibition opened in March 1995 it was definitely bucking the trend, for it challenged the aspect of the postwar consensus that had blotted out the realities of the war for the sake of harmony and pacification. And half a century after the war the generation that had fought it and lived through it no longer had the energy to steer the discussion, as it had done before.

The shattering of the taboo did not occur abruptly but was rather an unfolding process. On the first stops on the exhibition's tour (Hamburg, Berlin, Potsdam, Stuttgart, Freiburg, Mönchengladbach, Essen, Erfurt, Regensburg, Nuremberg, Karlsruhe, and the Austrian cities Vienna, Klagenfurt, Linz, and Innsbruck), the visitors tended to be people with a special interest in the subject, and the accompanying program was dominated by scholarly lectures.[66] The breakthrough to coverage by the major media did not occur until two years after the opening. It resulted in part from the greater public awareness of history and politics created during the anniversary year of 1995, but also from the altered political framework, that is, the end of tensions between East and West and German reunification. A major factor was also the younger generation in Germany, which no longer defined itself in relation to the Second World War, as did its elders.

But the decisive impetus for increasing public interest in the exhibition came from the polarization of politics in the cities of Munich and Bremen in the winter of 1996–97. The two major conservative parties, the Christian Democratic Union and Christian Social Union, along with the right-wing National Democratic Party and the veterans' organizations, mounted protest campaigns, singing the old refrain of the "clean" Wehrmacht. As a result, people by the hundreds of thousands, particularly the young, began paying attention to the subject of the Wehrmacht and the war of extermination on the eastern front—often for the first time in their lives. Once their interest had been aroused, they swarmed to see the source of the contention. A symbol for the history books might be the image of the long lines that formed daily in front of Munich's city hall of people prepared to wait several hours in order to see the exhibit and make up their own minds about this chapter of German history.

The public debates over the Wehrmacht were documented in several books, particularly the vehement and scandal-tinged disputes in Bremen[67] and Munich.[68] The proponents of the image of a "clean" Wehrmacht found a supporter in Rüdiger Proske, a World War II veteran and former television journalist. In two booklets Proske accused the critical historians of having begun their "march through the institutions" in 1968 and now, as holders of senior positions, to have joined like-minded journalists, judges, and politicians in declaring "war on the Wehrmacht."[69] While some traditionalists may have appreciated Proske's confirmation of their position, the wider public took little notice of his message.

The companion volume to the exhibition, by contrast, as well as the catalogue and a booklet published by the weekly *Die Zeit* titled "Obeying Orders to Commit Murder? The Hidden War of the German Wehrmacht," became bestsellers.[70] The journalist Heribert Prantl collected the most important texts of the German controversy and published them in paperback under the title *Crimes of the Wehrmacht.*[71] The Fritz Baur Institute in Frankfurt produced a set of materials for the use of teachers whose classes saw the exhibit,[72] and a further publication presented the reactions of visitors.[73] Once again readers could encounter the familiar patterns of perception: some reported that they "had always known" about the crimes, while others did not dispute that the crimes depicted had taken place but wanted to see them presented "in a broader context."

People in the latter category encountered further challenging documentation in the film and book by the Viennese filmmaker Ruth Beckermann, who interviewed veterans at the exhibition itself in Vienna in the fall of 1995. She wanted to know, she reported, "either how these men had participated in the extermination of Slavs and Jews or what they had seen and heard." Beckermann titled her work *Jenseits des Krieges* (Beyond War), to reflect their experiences outside the bounds of normal wartime events. The writer Robert Menasse provided a notable commentary on their statements in his foreword: "Whether they speak or remain silent: it is all one. Speaking and silence betray them."[74] He proposed a new interpretation for the silence, namely, to regard it not as an indication of the incorrigibility of the perpetrators but as a reflection of the monstrousness of the events, which surpass all attempts of the mind to assimilate them.

Perceptions of the Wehrmacht in Today's Bundeswehr

In the course of the considerable public discussion over the role of the Wehrmacht in the war which was set in motion by the Hamburg exhibition, the leadership of the German armed forces naturally considered whether the interpretation of the Wehrmacht established by the guidelines of 1982 could be maintained, or whether changes would be necessary. The Ministry of Defense commissioned a study on "the Wehrmacht in the Third Reich"[75] and developments in new research, which came up with the following conclusions. The memoirs written by former generals in the 1950s stressed that National Socialist crimes had occurred without the participation of the Wehrmacht. The distinction between the Wehrmacht as a force essentially obeying international law and the SS as an instrument of Hitler's policy of extermination had dominated until about 1975 (meaning in the view of the general public). This distinction had been abandoned, however, by serious scholars in the mid-1960s. Writing in the mid-1990s, the authors of the ministry's new study reached the conclusion that although historians had not agreed on a single picture of the Wehrmacht, there was a growing tendency to depict it "as a real instrument of the National Socialist policy of extermination." The study provided an accurate list of the hypotheses (called "claims") currently being debated by the public: (1) the Wehrmacht had played a decisive role in the Holocaust; (2) its campaign against partisans had amounted to genocide; (3) it had murdered prisoners of war; (4) it had carried out criminal orders; and (5) its courts had suppressed resistance to National Socialism by convicting deserters and subjecting them to draconian sentences. Finally, the authors of the study summed up the current state of research as follows: "The Wehrmacht took part in the violent National Socialist policies, and its role increased as time went by. As the war continued, it was increasingly enmeshed in the crimes of Hitler and his regime. The scope of this participation and enmeshment remains a problem for scholars and must be clarified by further research."[76] The political conclusions the authors drew looked like this: "The connection of the Wehrmacht to the National Socialist state, the fact that the regime made it an instrument of its criminal policies, and finally the culpable enmeshment of military leaders and soldiers in all ranks in the regime's outrages mean that the Wehrmacht as a whole cannot serve as a source of traditions for the Bundeswehr."[77]

One word from this assessment that requires further discussion is
Verstrickung, "enmeshment," a term that conceals the true situation.
It has cropped up in the debates about the role of the Wehrmacht
during the Nazi era for decades, and is meant to suggest that during
the Second World War the Wehrmacht was drawn into unpleasant
events or became trapped in an unfortunate position from which it
could not extricate itself. The word carries an implication that others
were guilty, that is, that Hitler and the other Nazi criminals drew
the Wehrmacht into a criminal war. The current state of knowledge,
however, requires that we regard the Wehrmacht as having been
aware of the crimes and in fact a co-perpetrator; its share of responsibility for them must be properly emphasized.

This analysis of the state of research into the history of the
Wehrmacht confirmed Apel's 1982 guidelines on tradition once
again. In November 1995 Defense Minister Volker Rühe gave a
speech in Munich in which he made the political consequences resulting from that analysis very clear. Speaking to commanders of the
Bundeswehr, Rühe declared: "As an organization of the Third Reich,
the Wehrmacht was enmeshed in crimes of National Socialism at
the top level, with portions of its troops, and with its soldiers. As an
institution it cannot for that reason be the founder of traditions."[78]
This marked an end for the time being to decades of debate within
the Bundeswehr—to the degree that ministers have any control
over the matter. It would be even more important, however, for the
Bundeswehr to discuss the facts of the Wehrmacht's history and
make them known, so that the old legend cannot flourish underground.

An Unwelcome Memory

Raul Hilberg, a scholar of the Holocaust who since the end of the
war has studied and analyzed the murder of European Jews from the

perspective of the perpetrators, has experienced over and over again that the public in fact really did not want to know what happened and why it happened. He encountered skepticism, rejection, and lack of interest everywhere, even in Israel, where people were focused on stabilizing their newly founded country. The public in the United States also reacted negatively. Since West Germany had become an ally in the course of the Cold War, the Americans did not want to know too much about German crimes during the Second World War. The part of the German past that interested American leaders was instead the battles against the Soviet Union, from which they hoped to gain useful information. Thus it came about that the research being gathered on the Holocaust received very little attention. The findings were not actively suppressed; only after many attempts was a publisher found for Hilberg's book *The Destruction of the European Jews,* which first appeared in the United States in 1961. It was not until 1982 that the small Berlin publishing house Olle & Wolter brought out a German translation.[79] It finally reached a wider German public when the large publisher Fischer brought out a revised edition in paperback in 1990 in its series "The National Socialist Era."[80] But for a long period of time the history of the Holocaust was—as Hilberg put it with some bitterness—an "unwelcome memory."[81]

The same may be said of the history of the Wehrmacht, which is after all closely connected with that of the Holocaust. A broad segment of the German public welcomed neither the work of the Nuremberg military tribunals in the late 1940s in uncovering war crimes nor the work of historians from the 1960s on that revealed the Wehrmacht's crimes. The reminders of incriminating facts were unwelcome as well, and they encountered determined resistance. Critical historians were forced into the role of bearers of bad news and denounced as disloyal; they had "fouled their own nest." Members of the war generation exerted themselves to promote the policy of repression and revision that had begun in the Adenauer era and to frustrate all attempts to set the record straight; and as we have seen, their efforts enjoyed a large degree of success for decades. Not until fifty years had passed after the end of the war and the collapse of the Nazi regime did the younger German generations who had grown up in the meantime want to know what really happened. Only then did the information that had long since been uncovered on the Wehrmacht's participation in a campaign of extermination in eastern Europe reach the general public. Only then did the circles that had been concerned to uphold the legend of "clean hands" lack the numbers, energy, and influence to keep the truth from coming out.

This delayed willingness to relinquish cherished legends concerning the Second World War and European fascism can be observed in countries other than Germany, incidentally. In Italy, and also in France, Switzerland, Sweden, Denmark, and elsewhere, a process has been observable since the mid-1990s in which the truth has gradually come to the fore.[82] National myths are crumbling everywhere. The younger generations no longer feel compelled to evade unpleasant truths and are beginning to see the history of their countries with new eyes.

A Man Who Rescued Jews as a Role Model: A Political Watershed?

On May 8, 2000, an army base was for the first time named after a Wehrmacht soldier who saved the lives of some three hundred Jews, actions for which he had been sentenced to death by a military court and shot. This man was Sergeant Anton Schmid from Austria, and the base in the town of Rendsburg in Schleswig-Holstein now bears his name.[83] Until that time the base had borne the name of General

Günther Rüdel, a member of the top leadership of the Wehrmacht that as a whole represented a crucial pillar of support for the National Socialist regime. Rüdel, however, did not condemn prisoners at the Volksgerichtshof, the "People's Court," as has been claimed;[84] rather he participated in one case on a voluntary basis and succeeded in winning an acquittal. Both President Johannes Rau of Germany and Defense Minister Rudolf Schärping attended the official renaming ceremony. The German American historian Fritz Stern, who had been awarded the German Book Dealers' Peace Prize in 1999, delivered an address on the occasion,[85] which can be considered a milestone in the controversy over traditions in the Bundeswehr.

Reporting from the trial of Adolf Eichmann in Jerusalem in 1961, Hannah Arendt summed up the story of Sergeant Anton Schmid of the Wehrmacht. He "was in charge of a patrol in Poland that collected stray German soldiers who were cut off from their units. In the course of doing this, he had run into members of the Jewish underground, including Mr. [Abba] Kovner, a prominent member, and he had helped the Jewish partisans by supplying them with forged papers and military trucks. Most important of all: 'He did not do it for money.' This had gone on for five months, from October, 1941, to March, 1942, when Anton Schmidt [sic] was arrested and executed."[86]

Arendt continued:

> During the few minutes it took Kovner to tell of the help that had come from a German sergeant, a hush settled over the courtroom; it was as though the crowd had spontaneously decided to observe the usual two minutes of silence in honor of the man named Anton Schmidt [sic]. And in those two minutes, which were like a sudden burst of light in the

midst of impenetrable, unfathomable darkness, a single thought stood out clearly, irrefutably, beyond question—how utterly different everything would be today in this court-room, in Israel, in Germany, in all of Europe, and perhaps in all countries of the world, if only more such stories could have been told.[87]

Who was the man from the Jewish underground resistance who provided such powerful testimony about an unknown sergeant in the Wehrmacht? Abba Kovner emerged as a partisan commander in German-occupied Lithuania at the age of twenty-three. Born in Sevastopol, he had attended a Hebrew secondary school in Vilna, then a center of Jewish culture known as the "Jerusalem of Lithua-nia." When the Wehrmacht seized the city in late June 1941, he fled with a group of friends to a Dominican convent on the edge of town. On learning that the Germans were murdering Lithuanian Jews, he formed a group of Jewish partisans. Kovner recognized earlier than others that the massacres by the SS Einsatzgruppen were part of a systematic plan, and he was the first to call for armed resistance.

On December 31, 1941, a manifesto by Kovner was read aloud in a partisan camp, in which he stated: "Hitler plans to kill all the Jews of Europe ... [T]he Jews of Lithuania are the first in line. *Let us not go like sheep to the slaughter.* We may be weak and defenseless, but the only possible answer to the enemy is resistance!"[88] During the winter of 1941–42, the young partisan commander Abba Kovner came into contact with Sergeant Schmid directly or indirectly. He at once registered the extraordinary aspect of the situation—that a member of the Wehrmacht was helping Jews in Vilna who were threatened with extermination.

After the end of the Second World War, Kovner emigrated to Palestine. He later became an influential poet and writer in Israel, where he chaired the Hebrew Writers Association. His testimony at the Eichmann trial made a deep impression on those present. We do not know whether it registered in West Germany, but the general commitment to repression at the time makes it unlikely.

The Jewish writer Hermann Adler was the first to refer to Schmid's rescue work in print, in his volume of poetry *Gesänge aus der Stadt des Todes* (Songs from the City of Death), published in 1945. In a preface Adler wrote, "I remember also an obscure sergeant from Vienna, Anton Schmid, who was sentenced to death by firing squad by a German military court because he saved those who were being persecuted, and who now rests under a simple wooden cross at the edge of the German soldiers' cemetery in Vilna."[89]

Sergeant Schmid had hidden Hermann Adler and his wife, Anita, in the Wehrmacht building where he worked in occupied Lithuania and befriended them. With the Adlers acting as go-betweens, Schmid was able to work together with the Jewish underground resistance.[90] Adler was thus a direct eyewitness to Schmid's rescue operations. Even though Hermann Adler's poems, written mostly in the Vilna ghetto, received a prize from the literature commission of the city of Zurich, the information about Anton Schmid did not enter the public consciousness in Germany.

The same holds true of another book of poems by Adler titled *Ostra Brama* (the name of a church in Vilna), in the eighth section of which Adler commemorated the extraordinary Anton Schmid under the title "A Friend's Sure Hand."[91] In the 1960s Adler was then commissioned to write scripts about Schmid for a television documentary and a radio broadcast in Germany.[92]

The state of Israel honored Anton Schmid in 1967 as one of the "Righteous among the Nations" for risking his life to save Jews during the Holocaust.[93] On the grounds of the Yad Vashem memorial in Israel a tree was planted in his name, accompanied by an inconspicuous stone tablet inscribed "Anton Schmid—Austria." Austria, the country of his birth, is named there, not Germany, in whose army he was forced to serve, and little notice was taken in Germany of even this honor. Not until 2000, nearly sixty years after Anton Schmidt's actions and nearly forty years after Eichmann's trial in Jerusalem, did this extraordinary soldier receive official recognition in Germany, on an occasion that offered an opportunity to learn more about his virtually unique case.

The facts had been collected long before, to the extent that it was possible. Several of the people whose lives Anton Schmid had saved in Vilna testified later to his remarkable acts. The *Encyclopedia of the Holocaust* provides this summary:

A sergeant in the Wehrmacht, stationed in Vilna, Schmid was responsible for collecting straggling German soldiers near the railway station and reassigning them to new units. A large group of Jews from the Vilna ghetto were assigned to different labor duties in Schmid's outfit: upholstering, tailoring, lock-smithing, and shoe mending. He gained their affection and confidence. Shocked by the brutalities of the mass killings at Ponary, Schmid decided in late 1941 to do whatever he could to help Jews survive. He managed to release Jews incarcerated in the notorious Lakishki jail, rescued Jews in various ways, and surreptitiously supplied food and provisions to Jews inside the ghetto. In three houses in Vilna under his supervision, Jews were hidden in the cellars during Nazi-staged *Aktionen* (i.e., massacres). Schmid also became personally involved with leading figures in the Jewish un-

derground such as Mordecai Tenenbaum (Tamaroff), and cooperated with them. He helped some of them reach Warsaw
and Bialystok (to report on the mass killings at Ponary) by
transporting them over long distances in his truck. Some of
these underground operatives met, planned activities, and
slept in his home. He sent other Jews to ghettos that were
relatively more secure at that time, those of Voronovo, Lida,
and Grodno.[94]

After the war Simon Wiesenthal not only hunted down Adolf
Eichmann and other Nazi criminals, but also collected information
on Anton Schmid for his documentation center in Vienna, preparing
the way for Schmid's recognition at Yad Vashem. Wiesenthal, who
spoke with several survivors of the Vilna ghetto, provided even more
details about Schmid's activities: "He would slip into the ghetto, at
great personal risk, bringing food to starving Jews. He would carry
milk bottles in his pockets and deliver them for babies. He knew that
thousands of Jews were hiding elsewhere in Wilna, and he acted as a
courier between them and their friends in the ghetto. He carried
messages, bread, drugs. He even dared to steal *Wehrmacht* guns,
which he gave to Jewish resistance fighters." From his informants
Wiesenthal gained the impression that Anton Schmid became "a secret one-man relief organization."[95]

Hermann Adler mentions that Schmid had fellow soldiers he
could depend on, who made it possible for Schmid often to keep
more than twenty people in his quarters overnight and then drive
them to Warsaw, where he was supposed to deliver German soldiers
who had become separated from their units.[96] This reference claims
our particular interest, since it sheds a little light on Schmid's immediate surroundings. Without buddies who would at least cover for

him (if not actively provide support), it is unlikely that Schmid could have continued to carry out such risky operations over a period of several months.

We know from other sources that many enlisted men were not yet so affected by radical propaganda at the time in question, the autumn of 1941, that they would have approved of the extermination campaigns of the SS. One important indication of this stems from the order issued by Walter von Reichenau, commander of the Sixth Army, dated October 10, 1941, cited previously. Reichenau reached the conclusion that many soldiers still had "unclear ideas" about how to behave when confronted with the "Jewish-Bolshevist system": "Here in the East our soldiers must not only engage in battle according to the rules of war, but also be the bearers of a relentless ethnic message." Hence they would have to "accept the necessity for the harsh but just expiation exacted from Jewish *Untermenschen*."[97] In sum, then, Reichenau was not content with the degree of zeal displayed by the soldiers and demanded, in the form of an order, that they ruthlessly "eliminate the treachery and brutality of non-German individuals," meaning that they should support the murders being committed by the SS Einsatzgruppen.

In Lithuania, and in Vilna in particular, where Anton Schmid was assigned to pick up stray German soldiers, the terror against Jews had already escalated by October 1941.[98] Several thousand Jews had been murdered. On September 6, 1941, the remaining Jewish population of Vilna had been moved to two ghettos. Those deemed capable of work or possessed of useful skills had been sent to one and the rest to the other, and the two groups had received different identity cards. Then a series of "selections" had taken place in the second ghetto, and the victims were transported by truck or railroad to the village of Ponary eight kilometers south of Vilna, where they were shot.[99] The site was a wooded area next to the railroad tracks, where Soviet firms had made excavations in 1940–41 in preparation for the installation of underground oil tanks.[100] Everyone in the vicinity knew of the mass shootings.

The Polish writer Józef Mackiewicz, who at that time lived in Vilna, only a few kilometers from Ponary, heard "repeated short bursts of gunshots, many of them; sometimes they would go on for hours, or sometimes it would be rounds of machine-gun fire. This happened on different days, almost always in broad daylight. Sometimes on several days in a row, usually near dusk or morning." He knew that "mass slaughter" was occurring, that Ponary was "one of the biggest Jewish slaughterhouses in Europe": "In this war Ponary came to stand for horror of a kind we had not known before. The sound of these letters with a *y* at the end made people's blood run cold. Their dark notoriety seeped slowly through the country after 1941, further and further, like sticky, congealing human blood."[101]

The group responsible for the killings in Lithuania from July 2, 1941, on was Einsatzkommando 3 under SS Colonel Karl Jäger. The figures in his report—officially titled "Complete List of Executions of Jews Carried Out before December 1, 1941, in the Area of EK 3"—and other sources indicate that of the 55,000 Jews in the population of Vilna, only 16,500 were alive at the beginning of December.[102] That means that in about six months some 38,000 Jews had been murdered. Another 5,000 were thought to have fled into the forests.[103]

This was the situation in which Sergeant Anton Schmid decided to strike out on his own and help as many Jews as he could. A writer named Purpur, whom Schmid hid in his living quarters, asked him once, "Isn't it reckless, risking your life like this?" "We're all going to croak sometime," Schmid told him. "But if I get to choose between croaking as someone who killed people or someone who helped them, then I'd rather go out as a helper."[104] Where did Anton Schmid find the courage to swim against the murderous tide sweeping past him and act in violation of the tenor of military orders, although he was fully aware that by providing practical help he was endangering his own life?

In general it is a difficult task to gather enough biographical material on an enlisted man to be able to comment on his socialization and his motives for saving lives. In Schmid's case we know this much. He was born in modest circumstances on January 9, 1900, in Vienna, where his father worked for the post office. He trained as an electrician. In July 1918, in the last year of the First World War, he was drafted, but given permanent leave a few months later. He married and had a daughter. In 1928 he opened an electrical appliance store in Vienna. After the German annexation of Austria in 1938, he helped several Viennese Jews escape to Czechoslovakia. Although Schmid was nearly forty, he received another draft notice in 1939, this time from the German Wehrmacht.[105] Because of his age he was not sent to the front but assigned to support units in rear areas, first in Poland, then in the campaign against the Soviet Union. In the Lithuanian city of Vilna he belonged to Company 2 of Landesschützen-Bataillon 898 and was appointed leader of the local group that collected soldiers separated from their units.[106]

His activities helping Jews lasted for a period of several months, as far as we know, from October 1941 to February 1942. He saved the lives of about 350 people by giving them the yellow identity cards that indicated they were skilled in trades useful to the Germans. In addition, he maintained contacts with members of the Jewish underground that was preparing for the uprising in the Warsaw ghetto.[107] At some point his superiors learned of his activities, for members of the Gestapo became aware of the presence of many Jews from Vilna in the Lida ghetto. When some of them were arrested and tortured, they revealed that they had arrived there with Schmid's assistance.[108] In any event, Schmid was tried by the war court of the office of Field Commander (V) 814/Vilna, which sentenced him to death on February 25, 1942. Unfortunately, the files of the court, including the judgment, have not survived, so we cannot learn how the court redefined the act of assisting Jews, which did not break any military law, into a crime for which Schmid could be condemned. Apparently the formal charge was accepting bribes, but it could also have been providing aid and comfort to the enemy, collaboration, or something of a similar nature.[109] Stephanie Schmid received notification of the death sentence and demanded information from the court, which fended her off with formalities.[110] It is known only that Schmid was executed on April 13, 1942, and buried at the military cemetery in the Anatol district of Vilna.[111]

Simon Wiesenthal, who talked with people Schmid had rescued, had this to say about the personality of the forty-two-year-old sergeant: "Schmid was not the drill-sergeant type. He was a quiet man who did a lot of thinking and said very little; he had few friends among his army buddies." Wiesenthal describes the only known portrait of him[112] as follows: "It shows a thoughtful face, with soft, sad eyes, dark hair, and a small mustache." He was "a devout Catholic who suffered deeply when he saw other people suffer. He was also a man of exceptional courage . . . Schmid decided it was his Christian duty to help the oppressed Jews." One of the survivors told Wiesenthal: "He did it out of the goodness of his heart. To us in the ghetto the frail, quiet man in his *Feldwebel's* uniform was a sort of saint."[113]

After the war court had sentenced him to death, Anton Schmid wrote a farewell letter to his wife in Vienna, which may bring us closer to the personality and motives of this extraordinary man:

I must tell you what fate awaits me, but please, be strong when you read on . . . I have just been sentenced to death by a court-martial. There is nothing one can do except appeal for mercy, which I've done. It won't be decided until noon, but I believe it will be turned down. All similar appeals have been turned down. But my dears, cheer up. I am resigned to my fate. It has been decided from Above—by our dear Lord—and nothing can be done about it. I am so quiet that I can hardly believe it myself. Our dear God willed it that way, and He made me strong. I hope He will give you strength, too.

I must tell you how it happened. There were so many Jews here who were driven together by the Lithuanian soldiers and were shot on a meadow outside the city—from 2,000 to 3,000 people at one time. They always picked up the small children and smashed their heads against trees—can you imagine that? I had orders (though I didn't like it) to take over the [soldiers' retrieval unit] . . . where 140 Jews worked.[114] They asked me to get them away from here. I let myself be persuaded—you know I have a soft heart. I couldn't think it over. I helped them, which was very bad, according to my judges. It will be hard for you . . . but forgive me: I acted as a human being, and didn't want to hurt anyone.

When you read this letter, I will no longer be on this

earth. I won't be able to write you anymore. But be sure that we shall still meet again in a better world with our Lord.[115]

On April 13, 1942, the day of his execution, Schmid was able to write one more letter to his wife:

> My dear Steffi . . . I could not change anything, otherwise I would have spared you and Grete all this. All I did was to save people, who were admittedly Jews, from the fate that now awaits me, and that was my death. Just as in life I gave up everything for others . . . Now I close my last lines, the last I can write to you, and send you my love. I kiss you both, and another kiss to you, Steffi, you are everything to me in this world and the next, where soon I will be in God's hand, many kisses, love forever from your Toni.[116]

In the early 1960s, during Adolf Eichmann's trial in Jerusalem, Simon Wiesenthal was able to learn the address of Anton Schmid's widow. He visited her and found a woman who had grown old and tired running a small shop to make a bare living. Her married daughter, Grete, now lived with her, and they told Wiesenthal "that life had not been easy for them in 1942, when it became known in their district that *Feldwebel* Schmid had been executed because he'd tried to save some Jews. Some neighbors even threatened Frau Schmid, the widow of a 'traitor,' and told her to go elsewhere. A few people broke the windows in her home."[117] Simon Wiesenthal made it possible for Stephanie Schmid and her daughter to travel to Vilna in October 1965 to visit Anton Schmid's grave.

In her book on Eichmann's trial, Hannah Arendt noted how different the world would be "if only more such stories could have been told." It should be said that even within the German Wehrmacht there were more soldiers willing to save lives as Anton Schmid did[118]—but until recently the German public took very little interest in them. In the past that may have been because the great majority of perpetrators and the people who went along with them, the witnesses and those with knowledge of crimes, did not want to be confronted with the shaming evidence that even in the Wehrmacht there were men who helped Jews and saved lives.

They were not members of a resistance group like the officers who tried to assassinate Hitler on July 20, 1944. They wrote no reports or memoranda, nor did they strive to change existing orders or power structures. Rather than taking on the institution—which they believed they had no chance of influencing—they provided practical help to those who were worst off. In this they acted differently than the officers of the general staff, most of them aristocrats, who were behind the plot to kill Hitler. Nevertheless, the attempts to save lives and help victims were without doubt an expression of resistance against the despotic National Socialist regime, and so it is appropriate to call them resisters.

Anton Schmid was not a career soldier but a "civilian in uniform," a Viennese shopkeeper who had been drafted and forced to go to war. He was able to preserve the humane orientation he had acquired before his induction into the Wehrmacht, and act on it. They were not many others like him, perhaps a dozen or so out of a total of about 18 million.

Why did it take until the year 2000 for an army base to be named after so deserving a man? Anton Schmid was honored at the Israeli Yad Vashem memorial site in Jerusalem in 1967 as one of the

"Righteous among the Nations." No one in Germany or in the Bundeswehr took advantage of this opportunity to honor him here as well. In the 1990s two different ministers of defense, Rupert Scholz and Volker Rühe, both members of the CDU, received proposals to name a base after Schmid but showed no interest.

Rühe was fully occupied in a struggle to preserve the names of two army bases commemorating Dietl and Kübler, two seriously incriminated Wehrmacht generals. Given the newly awakened interest of the public in such matters, it was a lost cause, but not until several years had gone by. Rühe's successor, Rudolf Schärping, then began carrying out an intention he had announced in 1994 to make changes in the sensitive question of names of army bases "where the valid law on military tradition is being flouted."[119]

Choosing an appropriate base would pose an unforeseen problem, as it happened, since the leaders at the Noncommissioned Officers School II in Weiden (Oberpfalz) refused to accept renaming, even though their institution retains the problematic name Ostmark-Kaserne to this day.[120] Nor, apparently, could the commanders of Camp Boldt in Delitzsch and Camp Lützow in Münster be persuaded to accept the name of Anton Schmid, for the *Schleswig-Holsteinische Landeszeitung* reported that the Rudel-Kaserne in Rendsburg was the "fourth choice."[121] This may be the reason why a majority of the soldiers and civilians working there protested against the change in name imposed on them "from above."

It is precisely because the number of people prepared to assist and save lives was so tiny that we should honor their memories today. The renaming of a Bundeswehr base after one of them could mark the beginning of a new tradition. The outlook for such a shift has improved.

CHAPTER SEVEN

Conclusion

THE GERMAN WEHRMACHT bears the onus of having waged a war of extermination in eastern Europe between 1941 and 1944 in violation of international law. The essential outlines of what happened, known since the Nuremberg war crimes trials, have now been confirmed by German and international historians, with the addition of much specific detail. The facts are thus known, including the Wehrmacht's murderous treatment of Soviet prisoners of war. There is still a need for more research on the extent of the German army's participation in the killings of Jews.[1]

In the meantime, a younger generation of German historians has taken up the subject, which was ignored and repressed for decades.[2] They are in the process of examining and evaluating new source materials that will not only enable us to understand better what regional differences existed in carrying out extermination policy, but also provide more insight into how the process of killing proceeded as a whole. As we now have grounds to believe, it was not set in motion as the result of a single central order issued by Hitler, but rather gained momentum from impulses on the ground in many different places.

Proof has been furnished long since that commanders of the Wehrmacht and the German army prepared the war of extermination in the form of fundamental written orders, and that they inculcated racist ideology in soldiers during the war through a propaganda campaign. What still requires an explanation is the causes of this development; in particular, we need an answer to the question of why the generals of the Wehrmacht followed the dictator Hitler on the path to a racial war. As this book has been able to demonstrate, one date stands out in the immediate run-up to the attack on Russia, namely, March 30, 1941. On that day Hitler delivered a speech to about 250 generals on the approaching war against the Soviet Union. Afterwards the military elite were prepared to stand "shoulder to shoulder" with the Fuehrer of the National Socialist state, who at the same time was supreme commander of the Wehrmacht. The generals offered no protest against Hitler's plans for conquest and extermination; rather they prepared to go down this path with him.

The underlying causes for this agreement cannot be sufficiently explained by examining the immediate period before "Operation Barbarossa" began. They must be traced back to the era between the two world wars, and even before World War I. As far back as that there existed in some segments of German society, especially the military, perceptions of Russians and Jews as enemies, which were later combined with anti-Bolshevist slogans. Traditional patterns of thought are evident first in the Prussian and later in the German military that must be regarded as a significant part of the ideological background of the Second World War.

Historical research in Germany has made a detour around anti-Semitism in the military of the empire and the Weimar and National Socialist eras. Historians have tended to deny the continuity of such negative perceptions and assigned responsibility for their undeniable existence during the Second World War to National Socialism alone. Yet the connections to be made seem obvious: between the Jewish "head count" of 1916, the assassinations of Jewish politicians of the Weimar Republic that were committed by German officers both on active duty and retired, the "Aryan clause" of the Stahlhelm veterans' organization in the 1920s, the introduction of a similar clause in the Reichswehr in 1934, and the later extermination policy. Under National Socialist rule, anti-Semitism was propagated by the state for the first time, including in the armed forces. It was Hitler who then took the traditional right-wing perceptions of who was an enemy of Germany and connected them with "Jewish Bolshevism," adding the traditional element of anti-Slavic feeling and turning the combined image into the ideological core of the campaign against Russia. The background of these ideological currents makes it possible to explain why in March 1941 Hitler encountered no serious resistance from the German military elite.

Furthermore, no perceptible disagreement existed between the leaders of the Nazi Party and the Wehrmacht on the question of whether "great matters" could be solved by other means than warfare. They shared the conviction that there was no alternative. The way of thinking had a long tradition first in the Prussian and then in the German military, as did the idea that in case of doubt the so-called "necessities of war"[3] overrode any limits imposed on the conduct of warfare by international law. This led to a generally dismissive attitude toward international legal restrictions regarding warfare among the officers of the Wehrmacht.

Contemporary and military historians, drawing heavily on primary sources, have described the form that the Wehrmacht's campaign against "Jewish Bolshevism" took in practice in such places as Poland, Serbia, and Russia.[4] They have also debated whether the campaigns in the West—in Greece, Italy, and France, for example—in fact differed so fundamentally from the war on the eastern front, as has often been assumed on the basis of a lack of racist motives for extermination. These questions have been discussed elsewhere, with comparisons of different theaters of war.[5]

In recent years we have gained greater insight into the experience of the "average Joe" in uniform, meaning the many millions of enlisted men and noncommissioned officers who participated in the exterminationist campaign on the eastern front. Many of them followed the generals' ideological guidelines reluctantly, while others supported the campaign on the basis of their own convictions. Recent research has revealed a considerable amount of agreement with and support for the regime's goals at the bottom of the military hierarchy.[6] Very few summoned the courage to resist this war—to the extent that it was possible at all.

While the Wehrmacht was officially dissolved after the capitulation of May 8, 1945, that did not put an end to its history. Some believe that only after that date did the Wehrmacht achieve its ultimate victory, namely, in its struggle to preserve its image as an army with "clean hands" in the eyes of the public both at home and abroad. The myth of the Wehrmacht lived on.[7] The policy of apology evident in the memoirs of former generals—in concert with many like-minded people in West Germany—worked successfully for decades. Within the Bundeswehr, the Wehrmacht continued to provide a central point of historical reference and to serve as a model, even though official decrees in fact did not permit such a connection.[8]

Not until the last quarter of the twentieth century did the results of research by critical historians reach the general public in Germany. A highly controversial exhibition on the crimes of the Wehrmacht in the war of extermination, mounted in the late 1990s, contributed decisively to the shattering of the old taboo and a new willingness to face the particularly grim topic of the Wehrmacht's connection with the Holocaust.

In the year 2000 the time was finally ripe for a symbolic political act: the naming of a Bundeswehr base after a Wehrmacht sergeant who had saved the lives of Jews, in place of a World War II general. It appears to suggest the gradual emergence of the Bundeswehr from the shadow of the Wehrmacht.[9] We must wait and see, however, whether a living tradition will develop from this one symbolic act.

As the war generation departs the scene, German society finds itself at the beginning of the twenty-first century in the midst of a major process of reorientation. The myth of the Wehrmacht has paled. From today's perspective it appears to us a giant machinery of extermination that spread suffering and misery across the entire continent of Europe and paid little heed to humanity and international law in its campaigns. Measured by the standards of civilian society, which contrast markedly from those of the earlier martial culture,[10] only those few resistance fighters in the Wehrmacht who protested against extermination in one way or another deserve our respect.

For a long time now the officers involved in the conspiracy of July

20, 1944, have been celebrated for opposing the dictator—although only at a very late date—and for supporting the true interests of Germany. Recently, however, their reputation has been somewhat tarnished by revelations that they were not only anti-democratic in their attitudes but also personally "enmeshed" in the extermination campaign before they courageously began conspiring to assassinate Hitler.

At the same time, most German citizens now feel respect for soldiers who deserted from the Wehrmacht, and those "defeatists" and "underminers of morale" who refused at some point to follow their leaders during the war. There is growing interest for those few who provided assistance and saved lives while wearing the uniform of the Wehrmacht, thereby proving that courageous acts in violation of orders and the expectations of their superior officers were possible even in an organization perceived to have been totalitarian. The legend of the Wehrmacht's "clean hands" now belongs to the past.

Notes

Preface

1. The contrast between millions and hundreds of thousands comes from Michael Geyer's foreword to Hamburg Institute for Social Research, *The German Army and Genocide: Crimes against War Prisoners, Jews, and Other Civilians, 1939–1944* (New York: New Press, 1999), p. 7.

2. Ibid.

3. On this series taken in Serbia sometime in 1942, see Peter Fritzsche, "The Holocaust," in Charles Stewart and Peter Fritzsche, eds., *Imagining the Twentieth Century* (Urbana: University of Illinois Press, 1997), p. 66.

4. Bernd Boll and Hans Safrian, "On the Way to Stalingrad: The Sixth Army in 1941–42," in Hannes Heer and Klaus Naumann, eds., *War of Extermination: The German Military in World War II, 1941–1944* (New York: Berghahn Books, 2000), pp. 237–271.

5. Rhein-Sieg-Anzeiger, September 23, 1998, reproduced in Bonner Geschichtswerkstatt, *Die Austellung "Vernichtungskrieg. Verbrechen der Wehrmacht 1941 bis 1944" in Bonn vom 29.9.–1.11.1998* (Bonn, 1999), p. 17.

Foreword

1. This term, meaning "Imperial Defense (Force)," was the name of the German armed forces until 1926, when it was replaced by Wehrmacht, "Defense Force."—Trans.

2. The name of the present-day German army, the "Federal Defense (Force)."—Trans.

1. Perceptions of Russia, the Soviet Union, and Bolshevism as Enemies

1. *West-östliche Spiegelungen: Russen und Russland aus deutscher Sicht und Deutsche und Deutschland aus russischer Sicht von den Anfängen bis zum 20. Jahrhundert*, Wuppertal Research Project on the History of German-Russian Perceptions, Lev Kopelev, director.

2. Lev Kopelev, "Fremdenbilder in Geschichte und Gegenwart," introduc-

tion to Mechthild Keller, ed., *Russen und Russland aus deutscher Sicht: 9.-17. Jahrhundert,* series A, vol. 1 of *West-östliche Spiegelungen* (Munich: Fink, 1985), pp. 11–34; quotation, p. 13.

3. See Gottfried Niedhart, ed., *Der Westen und die Sowjetunion: Einstellungen und Politik gegenüber der UdSSR in Europa und in den USA seit 1917* (Paderborn: F. Schöningh, 1983).

4. See, for example, Hans-Erich Volkmann, ed., *Das Russlandbild im Dritten Reich* (Cologne: Böhlau, 1994).

5. Arnold Sywottek, "Russen und 'Sowjets'—Bilder und Feindbilder," *Begegnungen und Versöhnung mit den Völkern der Sowjetunion als Schritt im konziliaren Prozess,* Dokumentation des Evangelischen Pressedienstes 5 (1988), 16–17.

6. See Robert C. Williams, "The Russian Soul: A Study of European Thought and Non-European Nationalism," *Journal of the History of Ideas* 31 (1970), 573–588; and Arvid Broderson, "Der russische Volkscharakter: Neuere englisch-amerikanische Forschungen," *Kölner Zeitschrift für Soziologie und Sozialpsychologie* 8 (1956), 477–509.

7. See the heading "Russisches Reich" in Hermann J. Meyer, ed. *Neues Konversations-Lexikon: Ein Wörterbuch des allgemeinen Wissens,* 2nd ed., vol. 13 (Hildburghausen, 1866), p. 894.

8. See the heading "Russen" in *Meyers Großes Konversations-Lexikon,* 6th ed., vol. 17 (Leipzig and Vienna, 1907), pp. 276–277. Compare also the illustrations in Wilhelm Stöckle, *Deutsche Ansichten: 100 Jahre Zeitgeschichte auf Postkarten* (Munich: Deutscher Taschenbuch-Verlag, 1982).

9. Mechthild Keller, ed., *Russen und Russland aus deutscher Sicht: 19. Jahrhundert, von der Jahrhundertwende bis zur Reichsgründung (1800–1871),* series A, vol. 3 of *West-östliche Spiegelungen* (Munich: Fink, 1992).

10. For more on cultural relations between Germany and Russia, see Ingeborg Fleischhauer, *Die Deutschen im Zarenreich* (Stuttgart: Deutsche Verlags-Anstalt, 1986).

11. Kopelev, "Fremdenbilder in Geschichte und Gegenwart," pp. 23–24. See also Mechthild Keller, "Wegbereiter der Aufklärung: Gottfried Wilhelm Leibniz' Wirken für Peter den Großen und sein Reich," in *West-östliche Spiegelungen,* 1:391–413.

12. Fritz Fischer, "Deutschland—Russland—Polen vom Wiener Kongress bis zur Gegenwart," in *Hitler war kein Betriebsunfall: Aufsätze* (Munich: Beck, 1992), pp. 215–256; quotation p. 224.

13. The rich scholarly and cultural contacts between the two countries were discussed by Karl Schlögel in a talk titled "Die schwierige Rückkehr zur Normalität: Veränderungen im Bild der Deutschen von der Sowjetunion," given in Kiev on May 19, 1995; see p. 12.

14. For Max Planck's speech, see ibid., pp. 15–16. For a more general treatment of cultural relations in the 1920s, see Günter Rosenfeld, *Sowjetunion und Deutschland 1922–1933* (East Berlin: Akademie-Verlag, 1983).

15. Karl-Heinz Ruffmann has studied the concrete significance of this process; see his article "Schlüsseljahre im Verhältnis zwischen dem deutschen Reich und der Sowjetunion," *Aus Politik und Zeitgeschichte: Beilage zur Wochenzeitung Das Parlament* 24 (1991), 3–10.

16. The fundamental study in this area is Peter Lösche, *Der Bolschewismus im Urteil der deutschen Sozialdemokratie 1903–1920*, vol. 29 of *Veröffentlichungen der Historischen Kommission zu Berlin* (Berlin: Colloquium Verlag, 1967).

17. See the detailed study by Jürgen Zarusky, *Die deutschen Sozialdemokraten und das sowjetische Modell: Ideologische Auseinandersetzung und aussenpolitische Konzeptionen 1917–1933*, vol. 39 of *Studien zur Zeitgeschichte* (Munich: Oldenbourg, 1992).

18. Bebel's remark became well known; Gustav Noske quoted it in his speech in the Reichstag in 1907. Stenographic reports on the debates of the Reichstag, vol. 228, session of April 24, 1907, p. 110.

19. Rosa Luxemburg, *Die Krise der Sozialdemokratie* (Junius-Broschüre, 1916), in *Politische Schriften*, ed. Ossip K. Flechtheim, vol. 2 (Frankfurt: Europäische Verlags-Anstalt, 1966), p. 151.

20. Gustav Noske in the Chemnitz *Volksstimme* of August 1, 1914; quoted from Wolfram Wette, *Gustav Noske: Eine politische Biographie*, 2nd ed. (Düsseldorf: Droste, 1987), p. 139.

21. Arnold Sywottek takes a different view, however, arguing that in Germany the First World War was still regarded in nineteenth-century terms as a "war for hegemony" and hence not yet a modern war in which an entire nation was seen as the enemy. Sywottek, "Russen und 'Sowjets'—Bilder und Feindbilder," p. 17.

22. See Günter Gorski et al., *Deutsch-sowjetische Freundschaft: Ein historischer Abriss von 1917 bis zur Gegenwart* (East Berlin, 1975).

23. Fischer, *Hitler war kein Betriebsunfall*, pp. 177–178.

24. Fritz Fischer, *Bündnis der Eliten: Zur Kontinuität der Machtstrukturen in Deutschland 1871–1945* (Düsseldorf: Droste, 1979), p. 24.

25. The card is reproduced in Stöckle, *Deutsche Ansichten: 100 Jahre Zeitgeschichte auf Postkarten*, p. 54.

26. The text is included in Klaus Böhme, ed., *Aufrufe und Reden deutscher Professoren im Ersten Weltkrieg* (Stuttgart: Reclam, 1975), pp. 47–49.

27. See Rolf-Dieter Müller, "Von Brest-Litowsk bis zum 'Unternehmen Barbarossa': Wandlungen und Kontinuität des deutschen 'Drangs nach Osten,'" in Dietrich Goldschmidt et al., eds., *Frieden mit der Sowjetunion:*

Eine unerledigte Aufgabe (Gütersloh: G. Mohn, 1989), pp. 70–86; and, for a more extended treatment of the subject, R.-D. Müller, *Das Tor zur Weltmacht: Die Bedeutung der Sowjetunion für die deutsche Wirtschafts- und Rüstungspolitik zwischen den Weltkriegen* (Boppard: H. Boldt, 1984).

28. See Rolf-Dieter Müller, "Rapallo: Karriere eines Reizwortes," *Die Zeit*, no. 16 (April 10, 1992), 60. For a more comprehensive treatment, see F. A. Krummacher and Helmut Lange, *Krieg und Frieden: Geschichte der deutsch-sowjetischen Beziehungen von Brest-Litowsk zum Unternehmen Barbarossa* (Munich: Bechtle, 1970), pp. 103–254.

29. See Manfred Zeidler, *Reichswehr und Rote Armee 1920–1933: Wege und Stationen einer ungewöhnlichen Zusammenarbeit*, vol. 36 of *Beiträge zur Militärgeschichte* (Munich: R. Oldenbourg, 1993).

30. See Andreas Hillgruber, "Das Russlandbild der führenden deutschen Militärs vor Beginn des Angriffs auf die Sowjetunion," in Alexander Fischer et al., *Russland—Deutschland—Amerika: Festschrift für Fritz T. Epstein zum 80. Geburtstag* (Wiesbaden: Steiner, 1978), pp. 296–310; reprinted in Hans-Erich Volkmann, ed., *Das Russlandbild im Dritten Reich* (Cologne: Böhlau, 1994), pp. 125–140.

31. Compare the broad spectrum of analyses in the collection edited by Werner Röhr et al., *Faschismus und Rassismus: Kontroversen um Ideologie und Opfer* (Berlin: Akademie Verlag, 1992). The question of the extent to which racism was a component of National Socialist propaganda, however, is not discussed there explicitly.

32. Gerd R. Ueberschär and Wolfram Wette, eds., *"Unternehmen Barbarossa": Der deutsche Überfall auf die Sowjetunion 1941* (Paderborn: F. Schöningh, 1984).

33. For a detailed discussion, see Wolfram Wette, "Das Russlandbild in der NS-Propaganda: Ein Problemaufriss," in Volkmann, *Das Russlandbild im Dritten Reich*, pp. 55–78.

34. See the illustrated brochure *Der Untermensch*, prepared by the SS-Hauptamt-Schulungsamt (Berlin, [1942]).

35. See Rolf-Dietrich Müller, "Raub, Vernichtung, Kolonisierung: Die deutsche Wirtschaftspolitik in den besetzten sowjetischen Gebieten 1941–1944," in Hans Schafranek and Robert Streibel, eds., *22. Juni 1941: Der Überfall auf die Sowjetunion* (Vienna: Picus, 1991), pp. 99–111; and R.-D. Müller, *Hitlers Ostkrieg und die deutsche Siedlungspolitik: Die Zusammenarbeit von Wehrmacht, Wirtschaft und SS* (Frankfurt: Fischer Taschenbuch-Verlag, 1991).

36. For more on this subject, see Wolfram Wette, "Die propagandistische

Begleitmusik zum deutschen Überfall auf die Sowjetunion am 22. Juni 1941," in Überschär and Wette, *"Unternehmen Barbarossa,"* pp. 45–65.

37. See Hans-Heinrich Wilhelm, *Rassenpolitik und Kriegsführung: Sicherheitspolizei und Wehrmacht in Polen und der Sowjetunion* (Passau: R. Rothe, 1991); Klaus Meyer and Wolfgang Wippermann, eds., *Gegen das Vergessen: Der Vernichtungskrieg gegen die Sowjetunion* (Frankfurt: Haag & Herchen, 1992); Hans-Heinrich Nolte, *Der deutsche Überfall auf die Sowjetunion 1941* (Hannover: Niedersächsische Landeszentrale für Politische Bildung, 1991); Ernst Klee and Willi Dreßen, eds., *"Gott mit uns": Der deutsche Vernichtungskrieg 1941–1945* (Frankfurt: S. Fischer, 1989); Paul Kohl, *"Ich wundere mich, dass ich noch lebe": Sowjetische Augenzeugen berichten* (Gütersloh: G. Mohn, 1990).

38. Andreas Hillgruber, "Die 'Endlösung' und das deutsche Ostimperium als Kernstück des rassenideologischen Programms des Nationalsozialismus," *Vierteljahrshefte für Zeitgeschichte* 20 (1972), 133–153.

39. Fischer, *Hitler war kein Betriebsunfall,* p. 178.

40. See the collection of propaganda posters in Reiner Diederich, Richard Grübling, and Max Bartholl, *Die rote Gefahr: Antisozialistische Bildagitation 1918–1976* (West Berlin: VSA, 1976).

41. Arnold Zywottek, "Die Sowjetunion aus westdeutscher Sicht seit 1945," in Niedhart, *Der Westen und die Sowjetunion,* pp. 289–362.

42. Zeidler, *Reichswehr und Rote Armee 1920–1933.*

43. See Olaf Groehler, *Selbstmörderische Allianz: Deutsch-russische Militärbeziehungen 1920–1941* (Berlin: Vision Verlag, 1992).

44. Manfred Zeidler has written an essay on this particular topic, "Das Bild der Wehrmacht von Russland und der roten Armee zwischen 1933 und 1939," in Volkmann, *Das Russlandbild im Dritten Reich,* pp. 105–123.

45. Lecture given by Joachim von Stülpnagel in February 1924, "Gedanken über den Krieg der Zukunft," in the German Federal Military Archives, Freiburg i. Br., RH 2/417, Bl. 3–46, fols. 4 and 11–13. For the context in which the plans for mobilization took place, see Carl Dirks and Karl-Heinz Janßen, *Der Krieg der Generäle: Hitler als Werkzeug der Wehrmacht* (Berlin: Propyläen, 1999), pp. 11–33.

46. Zeidler, *Reichswehr und Rote Armee 1920–1933,* pp. 106 and 109–110.

47. Wilhelm Keitel (1882–1946) was named chief of staff of the Armed Forces High Command (Oberkommando der Wehrmacht, OKW) in 1938 and as such played a major role in all planning for the war; he was promoted to the rank of field marshal in 1940, and signed the "commissar decree" directing that Russian political commissars were to be shot if captured, and others in violation of international law, including the

"Kugelerlass" (ordering that prisoners of war who tried to escape be handed over to the Gestapo) and the "night and fog" decree (which ordered the clandestine arrest of persons considered dangerous to the state, who were then incarcerated in concentration camps or shot). For the context of Keitel's remarks, see ibid., pp. 109–110.

48. Ibid., p. 110.

49. Cited according to ibid., p. 111, with n. 24.

50. On May 5, 1941, Krebs reported to General Franz Halder, the army chief of staff, that the Russian military leadership was "decidedly bad." Colonel General Halder, "Kriegstagebuch" (war diary), vol. 2, cited in Groehler, *Selbstmörderische Allianz*, pp. 177–178.

51. Ibid., p. 114.

52. See Bernd Boll and Hans Safrian, "On the Way to Stalingrad: The Sixth Army in 1941–42," in Hannes Heer and Klaus Naumann, eds., *War of Extermination: The German Military in World War II, 1941–1944* (New York: Berghahn Books, 2000), pp. 251–253.

53. See the picture in Zeidler, *Reichswehr und Rote Armee 1920–1933*, p. 119; and Groehler, *Selbstmörderische Allianz*, p. 100.

54. Yuri Y. Kirshin, *Die sowjetische Militärdoktrin der Vorkriegszeit* (Moscow, 1990), p. 92. Further information on the condition of the Red Army in this period is provided in two essays, Yuri Y. Kirshin, "The Soviet Armed Forces on the Eve of the Great Patriotic War," and Bernd Bonwetsch, "The Purge of the Military and the Red Army's Operational Capability during the 'Great Patriotic War,'" both in Bernd Wegner, ed., *From Peace to War: Germany, Soviet Russia and the World, 1939–1941* (Providence, R.I.: Berghahn Books, 1997), pp. 381–394 and 395–414.

55. Zeidler, *Reichswehr und Rote Armee 1920–1933*, pp. 119, 123.

56. Hillgruber, "Das Russlandbild der führenden deutschen Militärs," p. 126.

57. Ibid., p. 127.

58. Ibid., pp. 136–140.

59. Ibid., p. 140.

60. Jürgen Förster, "Operation Barbarossa as a War of Conquest and Annihiliation," trans. Ewald Osers, in Horst Boog et al., eds., *The Attack on the Soviet Union*, vol. 4 of *Germany and the Second World War* (Oxford: Clarendon Press, 1998), pp. 481–521.

61. See Groehler, *Selbstmörderische Allianz*, pp. 189–190.

62. Gerd R. Ueberschär, "Die Haltung deutscher Widerstandskreise zu Hitlers Russlandpolitik und Ostkrieg," in Goldschmidt et al., *Frieden mit der Sowjetunion*, pp. 117–134.

63. Ibid., p. 133.

64. Ibid., p. 125.

2. Anti-Semitism in the German Military

1. Daniel Jonah Goldhagen, *Hitler's Willing Executioners: Ordinary Germans and the Holocaust* (New York: Vintage, 1997), chap. 16, "Eliminationist Antisemitism as Genocidal Motivation," pp. 416–454.

2. At this time the Armed Forces High Command, *Oberkommando der Wehrmacht*, abbreviated OKW, was composed of the High Command of the army, *Oberkommando des Heeres* (OKH), of the navy, *Oberkommando der Marine* (OKM), and of the air force, *Oberkommando der Luftwaffe* (OKL).—Trans.

3. See Helmut Berding, *Moderner Antisemitismus in Deutschland* (Frankfurt: Suhrkamp, 1988), and the included bibliography; Shulamit Volkov, *Die Juden in Deutschland 1780–1918* (Munich: Oldenbourg, 1994), vol. 16 of the *Enzyklopädie deutscher Geschichte;* and Moshe Zimmermann, *Die deutschen Juden 1914–1945,* trans. Matthias Schmidt (Munich: Oldenbourg, 1997), vol. 43 of the *Enzyklopädie deutscher Geschichte.*

4. Manfred Messerschmidt, "Juden im preußisch-deutschen Heer," in *Deutsche jüdische Soldaten: von der Epoche der Emanzipation bis zum Zeitalter der Weltkriege* (Hamburg: E. S. Mittler, 1996), pp. 39–62. This is the revised catalogue for the exhibition of the same name, prepared by the Military History Research Office, Potsdam, in cooperation with the Moses Mendelssohn Zentrum, Potsdam, and the Centrum Judaicum, Berlin. The article deals in part with the subject of anti-Semitism in first the Prussian and then the German armies.

5. Rainer Wohlfeil, "Heer und Republik," in Hans Meier-Welcker et al., eds., *Reichswehr und Republik 1918–1933* (Frankfurt: Bernard & Graefe, 1970), vol. 6 of *Handbuch zur deutschen Militärgeschichte 1648–1939.*

6. F. L. Carsten, *The Reichswehr and Politics, 1918–1933* (Oxford: Clarendon Press, 1966), for example, pp. 131–132, 200, 203, and 240–241.

7. Horst Fischer, *Judentum, Staat und Heer in Preußen im frühen 19. Jahrhundert: Zur Geschichte der staatlichen Judenpolitik* (Tübingen: Mohr, 1968).

8. See, for example, Max J. Loewenthal, *Jüdische Reserveoffiziere* (Berlin: R. Boll, 1914), and Verein zur Abwehr des Antisemitismus, ed., *Die Juden im Heere* (Berlin, 1910).

9. See, for example, der Reichsbund jüdischer Frontsoldaten, ed., *Die jüdischen Gefallenen des deutschen Heeres, der deutschen Marine und der*

deutschen Schutztruppen 1914–1918: Ein Gedenkbuch (Berlin: Reichsbund jüdischer Frontsoldaten, 1932).

10. See Clemens Picht, "Zwischen Vaterland und Volk: Das deutsche Judentum im Ersten Weltkrieg," in Wolfgang Michalka, ed., *Der Erste Weltkrieg: Wirkung, Wahrnehmung, Analyse* (Munich: Piper, 1994), pp. 736–755.

11. Ulrich Dunker, *Der Reichsbund jüdischer Frontsoldaten 1919–1938* (Düsseldorf: Droste, 1977).

12. This work was first published by the Reichsbund jüdischer Frontsoldaten under the title *Kriegsbriefe gefallener deutscher Juden* (Berlin: Vortrupp Verlag, 1935), and again the same year, under a new title required by the Nazi authorities, as *Gefallene deutsche Juden: Frontbriefe 1914–1918*. The new edition, under the original title with an introduction by Franz Josef Strauß, appeared in 1961.

13. *Kriegsbriefe gefallener deutscher Juden*, with a commentary by Franz Josef Strauss (Stuttgart-Degerloch: Seewald, 1961), pp. 12–13 and 5–6.

14. *Deutsche jüdische Soldaten 1914–1945*, exhibition catalogue prepared by the Military History Research Office for the Federal Ministry of Defense (Freiburg: Militärgeschichtliches Forschungsamt, 1982). This is a forerunner of the catalogue by Manfred Messerschmidt cited in note 3.

15. Ibid., p. 5.

16. Colonel Othmar Hackl, ibid., p. 10.

17. The *Freikorps* (free corps) were irregular military units and private militias, usually composed of First World War veterans, who actively opposed the Weimar Republic and the establishment of left-wing governments in various places. They were responsible for hundreds of assassinations and armed interventions.—Trans.

18. Rolf Vogel, "Wie deutsche Offiziere Juden und 'Halbjuden' geholfen haben," in the 1982 exhibition catalogue *Deutsche jüdische Soldaten 1914–1945*.

19. "Widmet Eure Kräfte dem Vaterlande! Dokumente zum Patriotismus deutscher Juden," pt. 8 of *Deutsche National-Zeitung*, no. 28, (July 4, 1997), 10.

20. For more on this subject, see the excellent surveys by Yaacov Ben-Chanan, *Juden und Deutsche: Der lange Weg nach Auschwitz* (Kassel: Jenior & Pressler, 1993); and John Weiss, *Ideology of Death: Why the Holocaust Happened in Germany* (Chicago: I. R. Dee, 1996).

21. Karl Demeter, *Das deutsche Offizierkorps in Gesellschaft und Staat 1650–1925*, 4th ed. (Frankfurt: Bernard & Graefe, 1965), p. 217. The "Jewish question" is discussed on pp. 217–224.

22. The fundamental source on this topic is Werner T. Angress, "Prussia's Army and the Jewish Reserve Officer Controversy before World War I," in *Yearbook of the Leo Baeck Institute* (London: Secker & Warburg, 1972), pp. 19–41; Demeter, *Das deutsche Offizierkorps*, names two exceptions from the period of the "Vormärz," p. 217.

23. For more on the principle of recruiting from "desirable groups," see Detlef Bald, *Der deutsche Offizier: Sozial- und Bildungsgeschichte des deutschen Offizierkorps im 20. Jahrhundert* (Munich: Bernard & Graefe, 1982), pp. 39–43; and Manfred Messerschmidt, "Das preußische Militärwesen," in Wolfgang Neugebauer, ed., *Handbuch der preußischen Geschichte*, vol. 3 (Berlin: de Gruyter, 2001), pp. 433–434.

24. This order is reprinted in Manfred Messerschmidt and Ursula von Gersdorff, *Offiziere im Bild von Dokumenten aus drei Jahrhunderten* (Stuttgart: Deutsche Verlags-Anstalt, 1964), p. 197; and also in Bald, *Der deutsche Offizier*, p. 39. This principle regarding the Kaiser's personnel policy for the military was repeated in more or less the same terms in the cabinet order of March 29, 1902.

25. The German phrase *vaterlandslose Gesellen*, "fellows without a fatherland," became famous after Kaiser Wilhelm II used it to describe socialists in a speech shortly before the turn of the century; he was alluding to the international character of the socialist movement.—Trans.

26. See Reinhard Höhn, *Der Kampf des Heeres gegen die Sozialdemokratie* (Bad Homburg vor der Höhe: M. Gehlen, 1969), pp. 29–61 and 107–209, vol. 3 of *Sozialismus und Heer*.

27. Werner T. Angress, "Das deutsche Militär und die Juden im Ersten Weltkrieg," *Militärgeschichtliche Mitteilungen* 19 (1976), 77.

28. Heinrich Walle, "Deutsche jüdische Soldaten 1914–1918," in the exhibition catalogue *Deutsche jüdische Soldaten 1914–1945*, p. 21.

29. Ibid., pp. 21–22.

30. Cited according to Demeter, *Das deutsche Offizierkorps*, p. 20.

31. Ibid., p. 20. Compare the brochure commissioned by the Association of German Jews and written by Max J. Loewenthal, *Jüdische Reserveoffiziere* (Berlin: [R. Boll], 1914).

32. Walle, "Deutsche jüdische Soldaten 1914–1918," p. 14.

33. Demeter, *Das deutsche Offizierkorps*, p. 220. Demeter cites the study by Jakob Segall, *Die deutschen Juden als Soldaten im Kriege 1914–1918: Eine statistische Studie* (Berlin: Philo-Verlag, 1921).

34. These aims are confirmed by the wartime letters referred to earlier in the collection *Kriegsbriefe gefallener deutscher Juden*.

35. Cited according to Walle, "Deutsche jüdische Soldaten 1914–1918," p. 18.

36. Ibid., pp. 16–17 and 29.

37. For the Reichshammerbund, see Werner Jochmann, "Die Ausbreitung des Antisemitismus," in W. E. Mosse and A. Paucker, eds., *Deutsches Judentum in Krieg und Revolution 1916–1923* (Tübingen: Mohr, 1971), p. 411.

38. Angress, "Das deutsche Militär und die Juden im Ersten Weltkrieg," p. 79.

39. Walle, "Deutsche jüdische Soldaten 1914–1918," p. 49. The author refers to this situation as a "deficiency that could not be remedied before the war ended" but consistently fails to address the question of who was responsible for it.

40. For more on the topic, see Angress, "Das deutsche Militär und die Juden im Ersten Weltkrieg," pp. 77–146; and Werner T. Angress, "The German Army's 'Judenzählung' of 1916," in *Yearbook of the Leo Baeck Institute*, vol. 23 (London: Secker & Warburg, published for the Leo Baeck Institute, 1978), pp. 117–135.

41. *Israelitisches Familienblatt*, November 9, 1916, cited according to Walle, "Deutsche jüdische Soldaten 1914–1918," p. 57.

42. Franz Oppenheimer, *Die Judenstatistik im preußischen Kriegsministerium* (Munich: Verlag für Kulturpolitik, 1922).

43. Cited from document 464, "Aufzeichnung des Oberstleutnants Max Bauer," in Wilhelm Deist, ed., *Militär und Innenpolitik im Weltkrieg 1914–1918* (Düsseldorf: Droste, 1970), vol. 1 of *Quellen zur Geschichte des Parlamentarismus und der politischen Parteien. Zweite Reihe: Militär und Politik*, pt. 2, p. 1243.

44. "Denkschrift des Oberstleutnants Max Bauer über den Reichskanzler Bethmann-Hollweg," ibid., pt. 1, p. 574. Similar opinions can be found in pt. 2, pp. 673 and 717.

45. Letter of October 2, 1917, document 395, ibid., p. 1067.

46. Notes by Max Bauer on the domestic political situation from April 23, 1918, document 452, ibid., p. 1214.

47. Fritz Fischer, *From Kaiserreich to Third Reich: Elements of Continuity in German History, 1871–1945*, trans. Roger Fletcher (London: Allen & Unwin, 1986), p. 72.

48. From an anti-Semitic flyer of 1918, cited according to Angress, "Das deutsche Militär und die Juden im Ersten Weltkrieg," p. 77 and n. 2.

49. Weiss, *Ideology of Death*, pp. 211–212.

50. Ibid., p. 212.

51. Erich Ludendorff, *Kriegführung und Politik*, 3rd ed. (Berlin: Mittler & Sohn, 1923), pp. 141, 322, 339.

52. One exception was General Ludwig Beck, who did not accept these notions.

53. Heinz Hagenlücke, *Deutsche Vaterlandspartei: Die nationale Rechte am Ende des Kaiserreiches* (Düsseldorf: Droste, 1997), vol. 108 of *Beiträge zur Geschichte des Parlamentarismus und der politischen Parteien*, pp. 16–17.

54. Ibid., pp. 136–137; for more on Tirpitz, see pp. 123–123, 219, and 280.

55. Hagenlücke makes this claim for Tirpitz at least, but without discussing the subject in detail or providing any sources; ibid., p. 407.

56. From the minutes of the executive committee meeting of the Pan-German League on October 19–20, 1918, cited according to ibid., p. 410.

57. Michael Epkenhans, "'Wir als deutsches Volk sind doch nicht klein zu kriegen': Aus den Tagebüchern des Fregattenkapitäns Bogislav von Selchow 1918/19," *Militärgeschichtliche Mitteilungen* 55 (1996), 165–224.

58. Ibid., p. 199.

59. See Wolfram Wette, "Die propagandistische Begleitmusik zum deutschen Überfall auf die Sowjetunion am 22. Juni 1941," in Gerd R. Ueberschär and Wolfram Wette, eds., *"Unternehmen Barbarossa": Der Deutsche Überfall auf die Sowjetunion 1941* (Paderborn: F. Schöningh, 1984), esp. pp. 120–121.

60. Epkenhans, "Aus den Tagebüchern des Fregattenkapitäns von Selchow," p. 200.

61. See Wolfram Wette, *Gustav Noske: Eine politische Biographie*, 2nd ed. (Düsseldorf: Droste, 1987), pp. 308–315; and Klaus Gietinger, *Eine Leiche im Landwehrkanal: Die Ermordung der Rosa L.* (Berlin: Verlag 1900, 1995), pp. 112–113 and the appendix "Die Beteiligten des Mordkomplotts" (participants in the assassination plot), pp. 127–133.

62. Gustav Strübel, "'Ich habe sie richten lassen': Vor 70 Jahren: Offiziere morden, Richter versagen, die SPD zahlt den Preis," in Sebastian Haffner et al., *Zwecklegenden: Die SPD und das Scheitern der Arbeiterbewegung* (Berlin: Verlag 1900, 1996), pp. 109–122.

63. Weiss, *Ideology of Death*, p. 217.

64. Wette, *Gustav Noske*, pp. 251ff.

65. Gietinger, *Eine Leiche im Landwehrkanal*, pp. 48–49.

66. The victims are listed by name by Emil Julius Gumbel in *Vier Jahre politischer Mord* (1922; rpt. Heidelberg: Verlag Das Wunderhorn, 1980), pp. 43–49.

67. Weiss, *Ideology of Death*, p. 215.

68. Cited from a letter to his wife, dated November 3, 1918, in Fritz Ernst, "Aus dem Nachlass des Generals Walther Reinhardt," *Die Welt als Ge-*

schichte 18 (1958), 39–65 and 67–121. Sonderdruck (Stuttgart, 1958), p. 5.

69. Carsten, *The Reichswehr and Politics,* p. 136.

70. Ibid. p. 220.

71. Wohlfeil, "Heer und Republik," pp. 138–139. *Pleitegeier* translates literally as "bankruptcy vulture"; its presence is invoked in impending financial catastrophes, associated with Jewish moneylenders by anti-Semites.—Trans.

72. "Die schwarz-rot-goldene Judenfahne," in the supplement to *Vorwärts* 440 of August 29, 1919 (morning edition).

73. Session of July 26, 1919; *Verhandlungen der Nationalversammlung* [Debates of the National Assembly], 328:1970; see also Wette, *Gustav Noske,* p. 583.

74. See Wette, *Gustav Noske,* p. 583.

75. The text of Scheidemann's speech on September 11 was printed in his party's newspaper, *Vorwärts* 446 of September 12, 1919 (morning edition), p. 1. For the context, see Wette, *Gustav Noske,* pp. 584–589.

76. Session of October 7, 1919; *Verhandlungen der Nationalversammlung,* 330:2888; see also Scheidemann's editorial in *Vorwärts* 586 of November 15, 1919, titled "Der Feind steht rechts!"

77. This is discussed in detail later in this chapter.

78. See the statistics assembled by Emil Julius Gumbel, a pacifist and mathematician, in *Vier Jahre politischer Mord* (1922; rpt. Heidelberg: Verlag Das Wunderhorn, 1980). For information on Gumbel himself, see Christian Jansen, *Emil Julius Gumbel: Portrait eines Zivilisten* (Heidelberg: Verlag Wunderhorn, 1991).

79. Emil Julius Gumbel, with the assistance of Bertold Jacob and Ernst Falck, *"Verschwörer verfallen der Feme": Opfer/Mörder/Richter 1919–1929* (Berlin: Malik-Verlag, 1929), p. 114. See also Irmela Nagel, "Fememorde und Fememordprozesse in der Weimarer Republik" (Ph.D. diss., University of Cologne, 1991).

80. Martin Sabrow, *Der Rathenaumord: Rekonstruktion einer Verschwörung gegen die Republik von Weimar* (Munich: Oldenbourg, 1994), vol. 69 of *Schriftenreihe der Vierteljahrshefte für Zeitgeschichte* (Munich: Oldenbourg, 1994), p. 17; reviewed by Armin Wagner, *Militärgeschichtliche Mitteilungen* 55 (1996), 503–505. See also the special study by Gabriele Krüger, *Die Brigade Ehrhardt,* vol. 7 of *Hamburger Beiträge zur Zeitgeschichte* (Hamburg: Leibniz-Verlag, 1971).

81. Ernst von Salomon, *Der Fragebogen* (Hamburg: Rowohlt, 1951), p. 394.

82. Sabrow, *Der Rathenaumord,* p. 150.

83. Ibid., pp. 33–34.

84. See Susanne Meinl, *Nationalsozialisten gegen Hitler: Die national-revolutionäre Opposition um Friedrich Wilhelm Heinz* (Berlin: Siedler, 2000). Meinl also traces the lines of continuity from the Ehrhardt naval brigade to the SS.

85. *Die Freiheit* (presumably the issue of October 9, 1919), cited according to Gustav Noske, *Erlebtes aus Aufstieg und Niedergang einer Demokratie* (Offenbach: Bollwerk-Verlag K. Drott, 1947), pp. 146 and 148.

86. Noske, *Erlebtes aus Aufstieg und Niedergang einer Demokratie*, pp. 146 and 148.

87. Ibid., pp. 147–148; in this context Noske mentions Richard Fischer, the managing director of the party newspaper, *Vorwärts*, who expressed his anti-Semitic sentiments quite frequently in no uncertain terms.

88. Details can be found in Hans Langemann, *Das Attentat: Eine kriminal-wissenschaftliche Studie zum politischen Kapitalverbrechen* (Hamburg: Kriminalistik, 1956), pp. 128ff.

89. Wilhelm Hoegner, *Die verratene Republik: Deutsche Geschichte 1919–1933* (Munich: Isar, 1979), p. 83.

90. Karl Hellferich, *Fort mit Erzberger* (Berlin, 1919). For more on the context of this leaflet's publication and the campaign against Erzberger, see Sabrow, *Der Rathenaumord*, pp. 17–18.

91. Weiss, *Ideology of Death*, p. 227.

92. For a biographical sketch of Killinger, see Christian Zentner and Friedemann Bedürftig, eds., *The Encyclopedia of the Third Reich* (New York: Da Capo Press, 1997). The fact that von Killinger had given the assassination order emerged in a trial held in 1947; Sabrow, *Der Rathenaumord*, p. 27.

93. Sabrow, *Der Rathenaumord*, p. 29.

94. Ibid., pp. 45–46.

95. This is discussed in detail later in this chapter.

96. For more details, see Sabrow, *Der Rathenaumord*, pp. 76–77.

97. Ibid., pp. 56–57.

98. From contemporary press reports, cited according to ibid., p. 72.

99. Arnold Brecht, *Rathenau und das deutsche Volk* (Munich: Nymphenburger Verlagshandlung, 1950), p. 7. From 1921 to 1927 Brecht was a senior official in the German Ministry of the Interior; he emigrated to the United States in 1933.

100. For more details, see Sabrow, *Der Rathenaumord*, pp. 74–75.

101. Ibid., pp. 76–77.

102. Walther Rathenau, *Hauptwerke und Gespräche*, ed. Ernst Schulin (Munich: G. Müller, 1977), p. 854.

103. Weiss, *Ideology of Death*, pp. 227–228.

104. Sabrow, *Der Rathenaumord*, pp. 70–71. Rathenau's attitudes toward the military were studied by Gerhard Hecker in *Walther Rathenau und sein Verhältnis zu Militär und Krieg* (Boppard am Rhein: H. Boldt, 1983).

105. Rathenau, *Hauptwerke und Gespräche*, p. 841; Weiss, *Ideology of Death*, p. 228.

106. Cited according to Sabrow, *Der Rathenaumord*, p. 115, n. 6.

107. Unsigned article in *Der Wiking* of February 15, 1922, according to ibid., p. 116.

108. Ibid., pp. 87 and 90.

109. More information on the biographies of Kern, Fischer, and Karl Tillessen can be found ibid., pp. 96, 118–119, and 134.

110. Ibid., p. 150.

111. An excerpt from Kern's sentencing at his trial, according to ibid., p. 114.

112. Cited according to ibid., p. 122.

113. Noske, *Erlebtes aus Aufstieg und Niedergang einer Demokratie*, p. 224.

114. See Sabrow, *Der Rathenaumord*, pp. 169–183.

115. Ibid., pp. 171–172.

116. Cited according to ibid., p. 176.

117. Volker R. Berghahn, *Der Stahlhelm: Bund der Frontsoldaten 1918–1935* (Düsseldorf: Droste, 1966), vol. 33 of *Beiträge zur Geschichte des Parlamentarismus und der politischen Parteien* (Düsseldorf: Droste, 1966), pp. 286–287.

118. Ibid., pp. 65–66.

119. Ibid., pp. 66–67.

120. Ibid., p. 239.

121. Ibid., pp. 240–241.

122. Ibid., pp. 241–243.

123. See Hagenlücke, *Deutsche Vaterlandspartei*, and the review by Hans-Ulrich Wehler in *Die Zeit*, "Rechte Trommler," June 6, 1997, p. 15.

124. There is a good summary of the DNVP and its milieu in Hans Mommsen, *The Rise and Fall of Weimar Democracy*, trans. Elborg Forster and Larry Eugene Jones (Chapel Hill: University of North Carolina Press, 1996), pp. 67–68.

125. Cited according to Carsten, *The Reichswehr and Politics*, p. 31.

126. Walle, "Deutsche jüdische Soldaten 1914–1918," p. 60.

127. Ibid., p. 67.

128. See ibid., p. 67, and Dunker, *Der Reichsbund jüdischer Frontsoldaten*.

129. Mommsen, *The Rise and Fall of Weimar Democracy*, pp. 303–304.

130. Klaus-Jürgen Müller, *Armee und Drittes Reich 1933–1939: Darstellung und Dokumentation*, 2nd ed. (Paderborn: F. Schöningh, 1989), p. 57.

131. *Reichsgesetzblatt* (1933), vol. 1, p. 175, reprinted in Ingo von Münch and Uwe Brodersen, eds., *Gesetze des NS-Staates: Dokumente des Unrechtssystems*, 2nd ed. (Paderborn: F. Schöningh, 1982), p. 30.

132. The text of the order can be found in Klaus-Jürgen Müller, *Das Heer und Hitler: Armee und nationalsozialistisches Regime 1933–1940* (Stuttgart: Deutsche Verlags-Anstalt, 1969), pp. 592–593.

133. Müller, *Armee und Drittes Reich*, p. 58.

134. Announcement by the Ministry of Defense, October 12, 1933, cited according to Müller, *Das Heer und Hitler*, p. 79, n. 223.

135. Official list of the soldiers affected by application of the "Aryan paragraph" to the Reichswehr (June 1934), cited according to ibid., p. 598.

136. Müller offers a sample based on correspondence collected by a Captain Lebram in *Armee und Drittes Reich*, pp. 59–60.

137. In this context Müller uses rather cautious language, writing of Fritsch that he "does not appear to have been free of the widespread and generally unexamined anti-Semitic prejudices" of the time (*Das Heer und Hitler*, p. 82).

138. Manfred Messerschmidt, "Die Wehrmacht als tragende Säule des NS-Staates (1933–1939)," in Walter Manoschek, ed., *Die Wehrmacht im Rassenkrieg: Der Vernichtungskrieg hinter der Front* (Vienna: Picus, 1996), p. 45.

139. Included as Document no. 4 in Müller, *Das Heer und Hitler*, pp. 593–598.

140. Ibid., p. 597.

141. Ibid., p. 83, n. 242.

142. See the comment by Manstein's former ordnance officer Alexander von Stahlberg, *Bounden Duty: The Memoirs of a German Officer, 1932–1945*, trans. Patricia Crampton (London: Brassey's, 1990), p. 315.

143. In an order of November 20, 1941, cited in its entirety as Document no. 22 in Gerd R. Ueberschär and Wolfram Wette, "Unternehmen Barbarossa," pp. 343–344.

144. Stahlberg, *Bounden Duty*, p. 314.

145. See ibid., pp. 286–287, 312–314. After the Eleventh Army took the Crimean peninsula, the Einsatzgruppe D murdered 23,000 Jews there. For more on the cooperation between the Eleventh Army (Manstein) and Einsatzgruppe D (under Lieutenant General Otto Ohlendorf), see Bernd Boll, "Generalfeldmarschall Erich von Lewinski, gen. von Manstein," in Gerd R. Ueberschär, ed., *Vom Kriegsbeginn zum Weltkriegsende* (Darmstadt: Primus, 1998), vol. 2 of *Hitlers Militärische Elite*, pp. 146–147.

146. Stahlberg, *Bounden Duty*, pp. 313–314.

147. Manstein criticized Hitler and defended his own actions in his autobiography, *Lost Victories*, ed. and trans. Anthony G. Powell (Chicago: H. Regnery, 1958). His remark about mutiny was reported by an officer who participated in the plot of July 1944 to assassinate Hitler; see Rudolf-Christoph Frhr. von Gersdorff, *Soldat im Untergang*, 2nd ed. (Frankfurt: Ullstein, 1977), p. 134.

148. Compare Christian Schneider, "Denkmal Manstein: Psychogramm eines Befehlshabers," in Hannes Heer and Klaus Naumann, eds., *Vernichtungskrieg: Verbrechen der Wehrmacht 1941–1944* (Hamburg: Hamburger Edition, 1995), pp. 402–417.

149. Messerschmidt, "Die Wehrmacht als tragende Säule des NS-Staates," p. 47.

150. Reichsbund jüdischer Frontsoldaten, ed., *Die jüdischen Gefallenen des deutschen Heeres, der deutschen Marine und der deutschen Schutztruppen, 1914–1918: Ein Gedenkbuch* (Berlin, 1932). For details, see Messerschmidt, "Die Wehrmacht als tragende Säule des NS-Staates," p. 44.

151. *Militär-Wochenblatt*, no. 14 (October 11, 1933), columns 448–449; no. 17 (November 4, 1933), columns 552–553; cited according to Müller, *Das Heer und Hitler*, p. 81, n. 237.

152. Messerschmidt, "Die Wehrmacht als tragende Säule des NS-Staates," p. 48.

153. The full text of the law is printed in *Reichsgesetzblatt* 1 (1935), 609–614.

154. Ibid., p. 611.

155. The full text of the decree is printed in the *Politisches Handbuch* edited by the Oberkommando der Wehrmacht, pt. 1 (Berlin, 1938), section G. It was reprinted in the edition of 1943, section G, p. 100 (in the collection of the library of the Federal Archives–Military Archives, hereafter cited as BA-MA).

156. The text is printed in the *Reichsgesetzblatt* 1 (1935), 1146; see paragraph 2, section 1.

157. *Reichsgesetzblatt* 1 (1936), 518.

158. Uwe Dietrich Adam, *Judenpolitik im Dritten Reich* (Düsseldorf: Droste, 1972), p. 331.

159. Oberkommando der Wehrmacht, Nr. 524/40 (secret), Berlin, April 8, 1940, BA-MA, Reichsheer 15/186, fols. 99–101.

160. Messerschmidt, "Juden im preußisch-deutschen Heer," p. 59.

161. Bryan Mark Rigg, *Hitler's Jewish Soldiers* (Lawrence: University Press of Kansas, 2002), p. 194.

162. Ibid., pp. 38–42, 268.

163. There is a brief biography of Milch in Zentner and Bedürftig, *Encyclopedia of the Third Reich*, p. 591.

164. Cited according to Carsten, *The Reichswehr and Politics,* p. 203.

165. Messerschmidt and Gersdorff, *Offiziere im Bild von Dokumenten,* Document no. 100, p. 259.

166. The exhibition catalogue *Deutsche jüdische Soldaten* contains a facsimile of this statement, p. 71.

167. See the facsimile of this letter published by Nicholas Reynolds, "Der Fritsch-Brief vom 11. Dezember 1938," *Vierteljahrshefte für Zeitgeschichte* 28 (1980), 370.

168. Müller, *Das Heer und Hitler,* p. 82. For more on Fritsch's political views, see also Carsten, *The Reichswehr and Politics,* pp. 200–201.

169. See Manfred Messerschmidt, *Die Wehrmacht im NS-Staat: Zeit der Indoktrination* (Hamburg: R. v. Decker, 1969), pp. 37–40.

170. Quotations taken from the introduction to *Schulungshefte für den Unterricht über nationalsozialistische Weltanschauung und national-politische Zielsetzung, Jahrgang* 1, *Heft* 1, ed. Oberkommando der Wehrmacht, J (II) (Berlin, February 14, 1939), BA-MA, Amtsdrucksachen RWD 12/9.

171. C. A. Hoberg, "Die Juden in der deutschen Geschichte," ibid., *Heft* 5, pp. 3–42.

172. See Messerschmidt, *Die Wehrmacht im NS-Staat,* p. 354 and n. 1193.

173. Hoberg, "Die Juden in der deutschen Geschichte," p. 3.

174. Ibid., p. 28.

175. Richard Grelling was a lawyer and journalist who co-founded the German Peace Society in 1892. See the brief biography in Helmut Donat and Karl Holl, eds., *Die Friedensbewegung: Organisierter Pazifismus in Deutschland, Österreich und der Schweiz* (Düsseldorf: Econ Taschenbuch, 1983), pp. 162–163.

176. Hoberg, "Die Juden in der deutschen Geschichte," p. 30.

177. Ibid., p. 31.

178. Ibid., p. 32.

179. Ibid., p. 37.

180. Ibid., p. 40.

181. Ibid., p. 42.

3. The Wehrmacht and the Murder of Jews

1. See the detailed and well-documented account by Jürgen Förster, "Operation Barbarossa as a War of Conquest and Annihilation," in Horst Boog et al., eds., *The Attack on the Soviet Union* (Oxford: Clarendon Press, 1998), vol. 4 of *Germany and the Second World War,* pp. 481–521.

2. Jürgen Förster, "Zur Rolle der Wehrmacht im Krieg gegen die Sowjet-union," *Aus Politik und Zeitgeschichte,* no. 45 (1980), 6.

3. See Christopher R. Browning, *Ordinary Men: Reserve Police Battalion 101 and the Final Solution in Poland* (New York: HarperCollins, 1992).

4. A portion of Halder's notes, from which the quotations are taken, was reproduced in the judgment in Case 12 of the Nuremberg trials; see *Trials of War Criminals before the Nuernberg Military Tribunals under Control Council Law No. 10,* vol. 11 (Washington, D.C.: U.S. Government Printing Office, 1950), p. 516. There are two recent biographies of Franz Halder: Gerd R. Ueberschär, *Generaloberst Franz Halder: Generalstabschef, Gegner und Gefangener Hitlers* (Göttingen: Muster-Schmidt, 1991); and Christian Hartmann, *Halder: Generalstabschef Hitlers 1938–1942* (Paderborn: F. Schöningh, 1991).

5. *Trials of War Criminals,* 11:516.

6. Heinrich Uhlig, "Der verbrecherische Befehl: Eine Diskussion und ihre historisch-dokumentarischen Grundlagen," in Europäische Publikation e.V., ed., *Vollmacht des Gewissens,* vol. 2 (Frankfurt: A. Metzner, 1965), pp. 293–294.

7. Gerd R. Ueberschär, "Hitlers Entschluss zum 'Lebensraum'-Krieg im Osten," in Gerd R. Ueberschär and Wolfram Wette, eds., *"Unternehmen Barbarossa": Der deutsche Überfall auf die Sowjetunion 1941* (Paderborn: F. Schöningh, 1984), p. 103, with reference to Halder's wartime diary.

8. Förster, "Zur Rolle der Wehrmacht," p. 6.

9. Förster, "Operation Barbarossa," p. 519.

10. A rank equivalent to general.—Trans.

11. Förster discusses how the regulations were worked out in "Operation Barbarossa," pp. 491–493.

12. The text of the order by Field Marshal von Brauchitsch is reproduced in Ueberschär and Wette, *"Unternehmen Barbarossa,"* pp. 303–304.

13. Ibid., p. 304, under point 3.

14. The text of the "Guidelines for the Conduct of the Troops in Russia" is reproduced ibid., p. 312.

15. See "Treatment of Political Commissars," June 6, 1941, with General Halder's supplements of June 8, 1941, ibid., pp. 313–314. For details on how Hitler's ideological intentions were translated into specific orders by the OKH, see Förster, "Operation Barbarossa," pp. 491–513.

16. See Hitler's "Decree on the Exercise of War Jurisdiction in the Barbarossa Area," May 13, 1941, and supplements, ibid., pp. 305–308.

17. Order of May 2, 1941, portions reproduced ibid., p. 305.

18. See also the section on Manstein in Chapter 2.

19. See Christian Schneider, "Denkmal Manstein: Psychogramm eines Befehlshabers," in Hannes Heer and Klaus Naumann, eds., *Vernichtungskrieg: Verbrechen der Wehrmacht 1941–1944* (Hamburg: Hamburger Edition, 1995), pp. 402–417. The author pursues the question of why Manstein "helped Hitler, a man whom he despised, to carry out his plans" (p. 407).

20. The text is reproduced in Ueberschär and Wette, *"Unternehmen Barbarossa,"* pp. 343–344; the quotations are from p. 344. For the results in practice, see Jehuda L. Wallach, "Feldmarschall Erich von Manstein und die Judenausrottung in Russland," *Jahrbuch des Instituts für deutsche Geschichte* 6 (1974), 457–472.

21. The full text can be found in Ueberschär and Wette, *"Unternehmen Barbarossa,"* pp. 339–340.

22. OKW/WFSt/WPr (IIe), *Mitteilungen für die Truppe* 112 (June 1941). There is a set of these newsletters in the library of the Military History Research Institute, Potsdam.

23. The author reviewed the issues from no. 200 (May 1942) to no. 390 (February 1945).

24. From the article "Weshalb kam es zur Judenfrage?" *Mitteilungen für die Truppe*, no. 264 (May 1943).

25. From the article "Freiwillige und Hilfswillige im Osten," ibid., no. 241 (January 1943).

26. From the article "Jeder Soldat ist draußen ein Propagandist für Deutschland," ibid., no. 232 (November 1942).

27. From the article "Herrenmenschen," ibid., no. 321 (April 1944).

28. See the section headed "Das erste große Operationsfeld im besetzten Polen, Herbst 1939" in Helmut Krausnick, *Hitlers Einsatzgruppen: Die Truppen des Weltanschauungskrieges 1938–1942* (Frankfurt: Fischer, 1985), pp. 26–88.

29. See Malgorzata and Krzyztof Ruchniewicz, "Die sowjetischen Kriegsverbrechen in Polen: Katyn 1940," in Wolfram Wette and Gerd R. Ueberschär, eds., *Kriegsverbrechen im 20. Jahrhundert* (Darmstadt: Primus, 2001), pp. 356–369.

30. Russia first took responsibility for the massacre at Katyn under President Boris Yeltsin in 1991.

31. Martin Bormann noted this information on October 2, 1940; cited according to Helmut Krausnick, *Die Truppe des Weltanschauungskrieges: Die Einsatzgruppen der Sicherheitspolizei und SD 1938–1942* (Stuttgart: Deutsche Verlags-Anstalt, 1981), p. 33.

32. Ibid., p. 36.

33. See the survey provided in Gerhard Schreiber, *Die Zerstörung Europas im Weltkrieg* (Tübingen, 1983), unit 10 of *Nationalsozialismus im Unterricht*, pp. 22–23.

34. Noted by Lieutenant General Blaskowitz on February 15, 1940; cited according to ibid., p. 112.

35. Ibid., p. 20.

36. Ibid., p. 22.

37. Ibid., p. 21.

38. See Marlis G. Steinert, *Hitler's War and the Germans: Public Mood and Attitude during the Second World War*, ed. and trans. Thomas E. J. De Witt (Athens: Ohio University Press, 1977), p. 57.

39. From Blaskowitz's report to Brauchitsch of November 27, 1939, cited according to Krausnick, *Hitlers Einsatzgruppen*, p. 79.

40. Noted by Blaskowitz on February 15, 1940; cited according to Schreiber, *Die Zerstörung Europas*, pp. 112–113. This is also the interpretation offered by Hans-Heinrich Wilhelm, *Rassenpolitik und Kriegführung: Sicherheitspolizei und Wehrmacht in Polen und in der Sowjetunion 1939–1942* (Passau: R. Rother, 1991), p. 32.

41. Marlis Steinert cites Defense Document Book 1 for Küchler from the Nuremberg trials; see *Hitler's War and the Germans*, pp. 57 and 104.

42. H. Rothfels, ed., "Ausgewählte Briefe von Generalmajor Helmuth Stieff," *Vierteljahrshefte für Zeitgeschichte* 2 (1954), 300.

43. Walter Manoschek, *"Serbien ist judenfrei": Militärische Besatzungspolitik und Judenvernichtung in Serbien 1941/42"* (Munich: Oldenbourg, 1993), vol. 38 of *Beiträge zur Militärgeschichte*. See also Manoschek's essay "'Coming Along to Shoot Some Jews?': The Destruction of the Jews in Serbia," in Hannes Heer and Klaus Naumann, eds., *War of Extermination: The German Military in World War II, 1941–1944* (New York: Berghahn Books, 2000), pp. 39–54.

44. First determined by Förster, "Operation Barbarossa," p. 492.

45. Manoschek, *"Serbien ist judenfrei,"* with citations from the files of Propaganda Department S (for Serbia), p. 33.

46. Manoschek, "Coming Along to Shoot Some Jews?" pp. 49 and 51.

47. Krausnick, *Die Truppe des Weltanschauungskrieges;* see also Krausnick, *Hitlers Einsatzgruppen*.

48. This SS rank was equivalent to brigadier general.—Trans.

49. This is a reference to Lithuanian nationalists, who regarded themselves as partisans on the basis of their opposition to the Red Army of the Soviet Union.

50. Cited according to Ernst Klee, Willi Dreßen, and Volker Rieß, eds., *"The*

Good Old Days": The Holocaust as Seen by Its Perpetrators and By-standers, trans. Deborah Burnstone (New York: Free Press, 1991).

51. Krausnick, *Hitlers Einsatzgruppen*, p. 179.

52. Klee et al., *"The Good Old Days,"* pp. 28–30, 32–35.

53. Krausnick, *Hitlers Einsatzgruppen*, p. 178. Stahlecker's report cited according to Klee et al., *"The Good Old Days,"* p. 24.

54. Krausnick, *Hitlers Einsatzgruppen*, p. 181, with reference to an entry in Leeb's diary.

55. Entry in the war journal of Army Group North, July 3, 1941, cited according to ibid., p. 182.

56. Helmuth Groscurth, *Tagebücher eines Abwehroffiziers 1938–40, mit weiteren Dokumenten zur Militäropposition gegen Hitler,* ed. Helmut Krausnick and Harold C. Deutsch, with the assistance of Hildegard von Kotze (Stuttgart: Deutsche Verlags-Anstalt, 1970), vol. 19 of *Quellen und Darstellungen zur Zeitgeschichte*. For analysis and commentary, see Jürgen Förster, "Securing 'Living Space,'" in Horst Boog et al., eds., *The Attack on the Soviet Union,* vol. 4 of *Germany and the Second World War* (Oxford: Clarendon Press, 1998), pp. 1209–10; and Krausnick, *Hitlers Einsatzgruppen,* pp. 163, 208, and 235.

57. Hamburg Institute for Social Research, ed., *The German Army and Genocide: Crimes against War Prisoners, Jews, and Other Civilians in the East, 1939–1944,* trans. Scott Abbott (New York: New Press, 1999), p. 90. This is the English translation of the exhibition catalogue mentioned in the text.

58. The account that follows is based on Bernd Boll and Hans Safrian's discussion of the events at Belaya Tserkov' in "On the Way to Stalingrad: The Sixth Army in 1941–42," in Heer and Naumann, *War of Extermination,* pp. 251–253.

59. From the report of one of the military chaplains, Dr. Reuss, to the 295th Infantry Division, dated August 20, 1941, reproduced in Groscurth, *Tagebücher,* Appendix 4, pp. 538–539.

60. Groscurth, *Tagebücher,* pp. 534ff.

61. Boll and Safrian, "On the Way to Stalingrad," p. 253.

62. For the activities of Einsatzgruppe C, see Krausnick, *Hitlers Einsatzgruppen,* pp. 162–169.

63. The report "UdSSR Nr. 132" of November 12, 1941, is cited ibid., p. 269.

64. Details are provided ibid., p. 270.

65. For more on this subject, see Omer Bartov, Cornelia Brink, Gerhard Hirschfeld, Friedrich P. Kahlenberg, Manfred Messerschmidt, Reinhard Rürup, Christian Streit, and Hans-Ulrich Thamer, "Bericht der Kom-

mission zur Überprüfung der Ausstellung 'Vernichtungskrieg: Verbrechen der Wehrmacht 1941 bis 1944" (November 2000), pp. 44–46, available as a PDF file from the Internet. The authors refute criticism of the exhibition on this point.

66. For the killings in Lutsk, Tarnopol, and Zhytomyr, see *The German Army and Genocide,* the English translation of the exhibition catalogue.

67. Letter of December 12, 1941, in Groscurth, *Tagebücher,* Appendix 3, p. 525.

68. From the introduction, ibid., p. 91.

69. Erhard Roy Wiehn, ed., *Die Schoáh von Babij Jar: Das Massaker deutscher Sonderkommandos an der jüdischen Bevölkerung von Kiew fünfzig Jahre danach zum Gedenken* (Konstanz: Hartung-Gorre, 1991).

70. See Boll and Safrian, "On the Way to Stalingrad"; Hartmut Rüß, "Wer war verantwortlich für das Massaker von Babij Jar?" *Militärgeschichtliche Mitteilungen* 57 (1998), 483–508; Klaus Jochen Arnold, "Die Eroberung und Behandlung der Stadt Kiew durch die Wehrmacht im September 1941: Zur Radikalisierung der Besatzungspolitik," *Militärgeschichtliche Mitteilungen* 58 (1999), 22–63. The last article tends to exonerate the Wehrmacht.

71. Krausnick, *Hitlers Einsatzgruppen,* p. 164.

72. Arnold provides the biographical information that is available on Eberhard; see "Die Eroberung und Behandlung der Stadt Kiew," p. 23.

73. The crimes of Einsatzgruppe C and its Sonderkommando 4a in the Ukraine are described by Krausnick, *Hitlers Einsatzgruppen,* pp. 162–169. On the killings of Jews in Lutsk, Tarnopol, and Zhytomyr, see Bernd Boll and Hans Safrian, "The Sixth Army on the Way to Stalingrad, 1941–1942," in Hamburg Institute for Social Research, *The German Army and Genocide,* pp. 80–87; and Dieter Pohl, "Die Einsatzgruppe C 1941/42," in Peter Klein, ed., *Die Einsatzgruppen in der besetzten Sowjetunion, 1941/42: Die Tätigkeits- und Lageberichte des Chefs der Sicherheitspolizei und des SD* (Berlin: Edition Hentrich, 1997), 71–75.

74. Proceedings of the Darmstadt county court against Callsen et al., with judgment of November 29, 1968, p. 474, in Federal Archives Ludwigsburg (formerly the Zentrale Stelle der Landesjustizverwaltung), 204 AR-Z 269/160, vol. 34, folio 683.

75. Hamburg Institute for Social Research, *The German Army and Genocide,* p. 90.

76. Ueberschär and Wette, *"Unternehmen Barbarossa,"* p. 374.

77. Christian Streit, *Keine Kameraden: Die Wehrmacht und die sowjetischen Kriegsgefangenen 1941–1945* (Stuttgart: Deutsche Verlags-Anstalt, 1978), vol. 13 of *Studien zur Zeitgeschichte*, pp. 110–115, with citations.

78. Dieter Pohl cites the report USSR no. 97 of September 28, 1941, "Die Einsatzgruppe C," p. 75.

79. See the report in the Soviet newspaper *Junost*, cited by Ernst Klee and Willi Dreßen, *"Gott mit uns": Der deutsche Vernichtungskrieg im Osten 1939–1945* (Frankfurt: S. Fischer, 1989), p. 119.

80. Rüß, "Wer war verantwortlich für das Massaker von Babij Jar?" p. 505.

81. Arnold, "Die Eroberung und Behandlung der Stadt Kiew," p. 53.

82. According to the testimony of Gerhard Schirmer; see Proceedings of the Darmstadt county court against Callsen et al., p. 464.

83. See the testimony of SS First Lieutenant Christian Schulte, adjutant to the head of Einsatzgruppe C, in the Callsen trial, cited in Klee and Dreßen, *"Gott mit Uns,"* p. 119.

84. See Rüß, "Wer war verantwortlich für das Massaker von Babij Jar?" pp. 498–499, and 506.

85. This piece of testimony from the Callsen trial is cited in Klee and Dreßen, *"Gott mit Uns,"* p. 127.

86. Report USSR no. 97 of September 28, 1941, cited according to ibid., p. 118.

87. Proceedings of the Darmstadt county court against Callsenet al., pp. 538–539.

88. Krausnick, *Hitlers Einsatzgruppen,* p. 164.

89. The text of this notice is given in Wiehn, *Die Schoáh von Babij Jar,* pp. 7–8.

90. As reported by the Soviet newspaper *Junost*, cited according to Klee and Dreßen, *"Gott mit Uns,"* p. 119.

91. Rüß, "Wer war verantwortlich für das Massaker von Babij Jar?" p. 493.

92. Ibid., pp. 490–491 and 494–495.

93. See the article "Babi Yar" in Israel Gutman, ed., *Encyclopedia of the Holocaust,* vol. 1 (New York: Macmillan, 1990).

94. Testimony of Kurt Werner, in Adalbert Rückerl, *NS-Verbrechen vor Gericht: Versuch einer Vergangenheitsbewältigung,* 2nd ed. (Heidelberg: C. F. Müller, 1984), pp. 43–45.

95. See Janssen's testimony in the proceedings of the Darmstadt county court against Callsen et al., pp. 503–507.

96. See Bernd Boll, Hannes Heer, Walter Manoschek, and Hans Safrian, "Verwischen der Spuren. Vernichtung der Erinnerung," in Hamburg In-

stitute for Social Research, ed., *Vernichtungskrieg: Verbrechen der Wehrmacht 1941 bis 1944,* exhibition catalogue (Hamburg: Hamburger Edition, 1996), pp. 160–176.

97. Report USSR no. 106, October 7, 1941, cited according to Klee and Dreßen, *"Gott mit Uns,"* p. 132.

98. See, for instance, Joachim Hoffmann, *Stalins Vernichtungskrieg 1941–1945,* 2nd rev. ed. (Munich: Verlag für Wehrwissenschaften, 1995), pp. 187ff.

99. Froreich's first name is unknown. See proceedings of the Darmstadt county court against Callsen et al., pp. 455 and 512.

100. Report of Military Administrative Counselor von Froreich, 454th Security Division, Department 7 (Administration), October 2, 1941, concerning his visit to the headquarters of Field Commander 195 in Kiev on the previous day; in the Bundesarchiv-Militärarchiv Freiburg im Breisgau, RH 26–454/28: supplementary vol. 3 to 454th Security Division's War Logbook 1 (May 15–December 31, 1941), Quartermaster's Department.

101. Ulrich Herbert, "The German Military Command in Paris and the Deportation of the French Jews," in Herbert, ed., *National Socialist Extermination Policies* (New York: Berghahn, 2000), pp. 151–152.

102. Victor Klemperer, *I Will Bear Witness: A Diary of the Nazi Years,* trans. Martin Chalmers, vol. 2 (New York: Random House, 1999), p. 41.

103. Herbert, "The German Military Command in Paris," p. 154.

104. Wiehn, *Die Schoáh von Babij Jar,* p. 106.

105. Ueberschär, *Generaloberst Franz Halder,* p. 95.

106. Ulrich Herbert, "Extermination Policy: New Answers and Questions about the History of the 'Holocaust' in German Historiography," in Herbert, *National Socialist Extermination Policies,* p. 26.

107. *The Einsatzgruppen Case,* vol. 4 of *Trials of War Criminals before the Nuernberg Military Tribunals* (Washington, D.C.: U.S. Government Printing Office, 1950), p. 500.

108. Willi Dreßen, "Befehlsnotstand," in Wolfgang Benz, ed., *Legenden, Lügen, Vorurteile: Ein Wörterbuch zur Zeitgeschichte,* 7th ed. (Munich: Moos, 1995), p. 46.

109. *The Einsatzgruppen Case,* pp. 15–22.

110. United States Office of the High Commissioner for Germany, *Landsberg: A Documentary Report* (Frankfurt, 1951), p. 8.

111. Ibid., p. 19.

112. Proceedings of the Darmstadt county court against Callsen et al., p. 544.

113. See Ulrich Herbert, *Best: Biographische Studien über Radikalismus,*

Weltanschauung und Vernunft, 1903–1989 (Bonn: J. H. W. Dietz, 1996), pp. 495–497 and 507–510.

114. Andreas Hillgruber, "Der Ostkrieg und die Judenvernichtung," in Ueberschär and Wette, *"Unternehmen Barbarossa,"* pp. 225–226.

115. See the excellent study of this topic by Omer Bartov, *The Eastern Front, 1941–1945: German Troops and the Barbarisation of Warfare* (New York: St. Martin's, 1986).

116. For interpretation of this report, see Hans Safrian, "Komplizen des Genozids: Zum Anteil der Heeresgruppe Süd an der Verfolgung und Ermordung der Juden in der Ukraine 1941," in Walter Manoschek, ed., *Die Wehrmacht im Rassenkrieg: Der Vernichtungskrieg hinter der Front* (Vienna: Picus, 1996), pp. 91–93.

117. Report of Lieutenant General Hans Leykauf to General Thomas at OKW, of December 2, 1941, reprinted in Ueberschär and Wette, *"Unternehmen Barbarossa,"* pp. 392–393.

118. Raul Hilberg, "Wehrmacht und Judenvernichtung," in Manoschek, *Die Wehrmacht im Rassenkrieg,* pp. 35 and 33.

119. Hannes Heer, "Killing Fields: The Wehrmacht and the Holocaust in Belorussia, 1941–42," in Heer and Naumann, *War of Extermination,* pp. 55–79; and "The Logic of the War of Extermination: The Wehrmacht and the Anti-Partisan War," ibid., pp. 92–126. For "mopping up the countryside," see "Killing Fields," p. 64.

120. Heer, "The Logic of the War of Extermination," p. 99.

121. Ibid., p. 95.

122. Ibid., p. 97.

123. Hilberg, "Wehrmacht und Judenvernichtung," p. 33.

124. Bartov et al., *Bericht der Kommission zur Überprüfung der Ausstellung "Vernichtungskrieg,"* p. 65.

125. Ibid., pp. 66–67.

126. Ibid., p. 67.

127. Ibid., p. 68.

128. See the report of Major Rudolf-Christoph von Gersdorff on a trip to the front, dated December 9, 1941, in Ueberschär and Wette, *"Unternehmen Barbarossa,"* pp. 397–398.

129. The cases described were taken from a secret order of the personnel office of the Army High Command dated October 21, 1942; see the Bundesarchiv-Militärarchiv, Freiburg, RL 5/793, as well as BA-MA RH 15/186, fol. 107. See also Manfred Messerschmidt, *Die Wehrmacht im NS-Staat: Zeit der Indoktrination* (Hamburg: R. v. Decker, 1969), p. 355;

and Gerhard Schreiber, *Deutsche Kriegsverbrechen in Italien: Täter, Opfer, Strafverfolgung* (Munich: Beck, 1996), pp. 30–31.

130. Dermont Bradley and Richard Schulze-Kossens, eds., *Tätigkeitsbericht des Chefs des Heerespersonalamtes, General der Infanterie Rudolf Schmundt, fortgeführt von General der Infanterie Wilhelm Burgdorf, 1.10.1942–29.10.1944* (Osnabrück: Biblio-Verlag, 1984), p. 16. See also the brief biography of Schmundt, ibid., pp. 15–16.

131. Messerschmidt, *Die Wehrmacht im NS-Staat*, p. 239.

132. Ludger Borgert, "Kriegsverbrechen der Kriegsmarine," in Wolfram Wette and Gerd R. Ueberschär, eds., *Kriegsverbrechen im 20. Jahrhundert* (Darmstadt: Primus, 2001), pp. 309–323.

133. Gerhard Schreiber, *Revisionismus und Weltmachtstreben: Marineführung und deutsch-italienische Beziehungen 1919–1944* (Stuttgart: Deutsche Verlagsanstalt, 1978), p. 382.

134. Schreiber, *Deutsche Kriegsverbrechen in Italien*, p. 29.

135. Ibid.

136. *Trial of the Major War Criminals before the International Military Tribunal, Nuremberg*, vol. 31 (1949; rpt., Buffalo, N.Y.: William S. Hein, 1995), Document 2878-PS, p. 250.

137. Schreiber, *Deutsche Kriegsverbrechen in Italien*, pp. 29–30.

138. Messerchmidt, *Die Wehrmacht im NS-Staat*, p. 356, n. 1201.

139. Schreiber, *Deutsche Kriegsverbrechen in Italien*, p. 34.

140. See Jonathan Steinberg's book based on extensive archival research, *All or Nothing: The Axis and the Holocaust, 1941–1943* (London: Routledge, 1990).

141. See Schreiber, *Deutsche Kriegsverbrechen in Italien*, p. 31. Schreiber cites both Steinberg, *All or Nothing*, and Rainer Eckert, "Die Verfolgung der griechischen Juden im deutschen Okkupationsgebiet Saloniki-Ägäis vom April 1941 bis zum Abschluss der Deportationen im August 1943," *Bulletin des Arbeitskreises "Zweiter Weltkrieg," Heft* 1–4 (Berlin, 1966), 41–69.

142. Schreiber, *Deutsche Kriegsverbrechen in Italien*, p. 31; he cites Steinberg, *All or Nothing*, p. 133.

143. Schreiber, *Deutsche Kriegsverbrechen in Italien*, pp. 32–33; he cites Raul Hilberg, *The Destruction of the European Jews* (Chicago: Quadrangle Books, 1961), p. 443.

144. Schreiber, *Deutsche Kriegsverbrechen in Italien*, p. 32.

145. Ibid., p. 28.

146. Ibid., p. 32.

147. Ibid., p. 33.

148. Ibid., pp. 33–34, with citations from reports of the "German general in Agram" to the OKW.

149. Joseph Goebbels, *The Goebbels Diaries, 1942–1943*, ed. and trans. Louis P. Lochner (New York: Doubleday, 1948), p. 241.

150. For details, see Manoschek, *"Serbien ist judenfrei."* For a summary, see the section "Partisanenkrieg und Genozid: Die Wehrmacht in Serbien 1941," in Manoschek, *Die Wehrmacht im Rassenkrieg*, pp. 142–167.

151. These figures are taken from Schreiber, *Deutsche Kriegsverbrechen in Italien*, p. 217. For the fate of one of these groups, see the same author's standard work on the subject, *Die italienischen Militärinternierten im deutschen Machtbereich 1943 bis 1945: Verraten—Verachtet—Vergessen* (Munich: R. Oldenbourg, 1990), vol. 28 of *Beiträge zur Militärgeschichte*.

4. Generals and Enlisted Men

1. Ralph Giordano, *Die Traditionslüge: Vom Kriegerkult in der Bundeswehr* (Cologne: Kiepenheuer & Witsch, 2000), pp. 175ff.

2. See Wolfram Wette, *Kriegstheorien deutscher Sozialisten: Marx, Engels, Lassalle, Bernstein, Kautsky, Luxemburg: Ein Beitrag zur Friedensforschung* (Stuttgart: Kohlhammer, 1971).

3. Friedrich Wilhelm Foerster, *Mein Kampf gegen das militaristische und nationalistische Deutschland: Gesichtspunkte zur deutschen Selbsterkenntnis und zum Aufbau eines neuen Deutschland* (Stuttgart: Verlag "Friede durch Recht," 1920), p. 35.

4. Ibid., pp. 20–21, 25, and 35.

5. Paul von Schoenaich, *Vom vorigen zum nächsten Krieg* (Fichtenau bei Berlin: Verlag der Neuen Gesellschaft, 1925), p. 24.

6. Letter dated December 11, 1880, in *Gesammelte Schriften und Denkwürdigkeiten des General-Feldmarschalls Grafen Helmuth von Moltke*, vol. 3 (Berlin: E. S. Mittler & Sohn, 1891), p. 154.

7. Compare Manfred Messerschmidt, "Moltke," in *Ostdeutsche Gedenktage 1991: Persönlichkeiten und historische Ereignisse* (Bonn: Bund der Vertriebenen, 1991), pp. 87–90. For more on the discussion surrounding Moltke, see also Stig Förster, "Militär und Militarismus im deutschen Kaiserreich: Versuch einer differenzierten Betrachtung," in Wolfram Wette, ed., *Militarismus in Deutschland 1871 bis 1945: Zeitgenössische Analyse und Kritik* (Münster: Lit, 1999), pp. 63–80.

8. Schoenaich, *Vom vorigen zum nächsten Krieg*, p. 137.

9. Cited according to Theo Schwarzmüller, *Zwischen Kaiser und Führer:*

Generalfeldmarschall August von Mackensen: Eine politische Biographie, 2nd ed. (Paderborn: F. Schöningh, 1996), p. 23.

10. Ibid., pp. 38–39.

11. *Erlass des Chefs des Allgemeinen Truppenamtes an die Generalstabsoffiziere,* October 18, 1919, in Manfred Messerschmidt and Ursula von Gersdorff, *Offiziere im Bild von Dokumenten aus drei Jahrhunderten* (Stuttgart: Deutsche Verlags-Anstalt, 1964), Document 73, pp. 220ff.

12. Ibid., p. 221.

13. Gordon Craig, *The Politics of the Prussian Army, 1640–1945* (Oxford: Clarendon Press, 1955), p. 394.

14. Ibid., p. 413.

15. Ibid., p. 413n.

16. Helmut Donat, "Zur preußischen Wende der deutschen Geschichte: Die Unterredung Bernhardi-Roon im Februar 1862," in Fried Esterbauer et al., *Von der freien Gemeinde zum föderalistischen Europa: Festschrift für Adolf Gasser zum 80. Geburtstag* (Berlin: Duncker & Humblot, 1983), p. 203.

17. Ulrich Kluge, *Die deutsche Revolution 1918–1919: Staat, Politik und Gesellscahft zwischen Weltkrieg und Kapp-Putsch* (Frankfurt: Suhrkamp, 1985), pp. 141–145. According to a different view, Ebert and Groener formed a political "alliance" on November 9, 1918; see, for example, Lothar Berthold and Helmut Neef, *Militarismus und Opportunismus gegen die Novemberrevolution,* 2nd ed. (Frankfurt am Main: Verlag Marxistische Blätter, 1978), pp. 28ff.

18. See the detailed study by Johannes Hürter, *Wilhelm Groener: Reichswehrminister am Ende der Weimarer Republik (1928–1932)* (Munich: Oldenbourg, 1993).

19. Letter from Lieutenant General Wilhelm Groener to President Friedrich Ebert, September 17, 1919, in Federal Archive–Military Archive, Freiburg, Nachlass von Schleicher, N 41/12, fols. 207–208.

20. Adolf Hitler, *Hitler's Second Book: The Unpublished Sequel to "Mein Kampf,"* ed. Gerhard L. Weinberg, trans. Krista Smith (New York: Enigma, 2003), pp. 9 and 37.

21. Ludwig Beck, *Studien,* ed. Hans Speidel (Stuttgart: Koehler, 1955), pp. 247, 251, and 257.

22. See the chapter "Pazifismus und Landesverratsprozesse," in Rainer Wohlfeil and Hans Dollinger, *Die deutsche Reichswehr: Bilder, Dokumente, Texte: Zur Geschichte des Hunderttausend-Mann-Heeres 1919–1933* (Wiesbaden: Englisch, 1977).

23. Hitler's speech to the commanders of the army and navy on February 3,

1933, is reprinted in Thilo Vogelsang, "Neue Dokumente zur Geschichte der Reichswehr 1930–1933," *Vierteljahrshefte für Zeitgeschichte* 2 (1954), 434ff., and in Hans Adolf Jacobsen, *1939–1945: Der zweite Weltkrieg in Chronik und Dokumenten* (Darmstadt: Wehr und Wissen, 1959), pp. 95–96.

24. From the notes of General Liebmann, cited according to Wolfgang Sauer, "Die Mobilmachung der Gewalt," in Karl Dietrich Bracher, Wolfgang Sauer, and Gerhard Schulz, eds., *Die nationalsozialistische Machtergreifung: Studien zur Errichtung des totalitären Herrschaftssystems in Deutschland 1933–34,* 2nd ed. (Cologne: Westdeutscher Verlag, 1962), pp. 719–720.

25. See Andreas Hillgruber, *Großmachtpolitik und Militarismus im 20. Jahrhundert: 3 Beiträge zum Kontinuitätsproblem* (Düsseldorf: Droste, 1974), pp. 7 and 37; Carl Dirks and Karl-Heinz Janßen, *Der Krieg der Generäle: Hitler als Werkzeug der Wehrmacht* (Berlin: Propyläen, 1999).

26. Vogelsang, "Neue Dokumente," pp. 432–433.

27. See Wolfgang Scheel, *Der Tag von Potsdam* (Berlin: Brandenburgisches Verlagshaus, 1996).

28. A photograph capturing the moment appeared in many newspapers; it is reproduced in Rudolf Herz, *Hoffmann & Hitler: Fotografie als Medium des Führer-Mythos* (Munich: Klinkhardt & Biermann, 1994), pp. 206–207.

29. For a summary of research on this subject, see Gerd R. Ueberschär, ed., *Der 20. Juli 1944: Bewegung und Rezeption des deutschen Widerstandes gegen das NS-Regime* (Cologne: Bund-Verlag, 1994).

30. There are two recent collections of generals' biographies: Ronald Smelser and Enrico Syring, eds., *Die Militärelite des Dritten Reiches: 27 biographische Skizzen* (Berlin: Ullstein, 1995); and Gerd R. Ueberschär, ed., *Hitlers militärische Elite,* 2 vols. (Darmstadt: Primus, 1998).

31. See Winfried Vogel, "'. . . schlechthin unwürdig'. Mit hohen Dotationen in Reichsmark oder Immobilien versuchte Hitler, Feldmarschälle und Generäle der Wehrmacht zu korrumpieren," *Die Zeit,* March 28, 1997, p. 44.

32. See Frank Bajohr, "Nationalsozialismus und Korruption," *Mittelweg* 36, no. 1 (1998), 55–77; and Bajohr, *Parvenüs und Profiteure: Korruption in der NS-Zeit* (Frankfurt: S. Fischer, 2001).

33. See Gerd R. Ueberschär and Winfried Vogel, *Dienen und Verdienen: Hitlers Geschenke an seine Eliten* (Frankfurt: S. Fischer, 1999), especially pp. 101ff., 146ff., and the table of gifts to the German field marshals and admirals of the fleet between 1936 and 1945, pp. 202–203.

34. Ibid., p. 195.

35. See Manfred Messerschmidt, "Die Wehrmacht in der Endphase: Realität und Perzeption," in Messerschmidt und Ekkehart Guth, eds., *Die Zukunft des Reiches: Gegner, Verbündete und Neutrale (1943–1945)* (Herford: E. S. Mittler, 1990), pp. 195–222; also the final section of this chapter.

36. See Wolfram Wette, "Deutsche Erfahrungen mit der Wehrpflicht 1918–1945: Abschaffung in der Republik und Wiedereinführung in der Diktatur," in Roland G. Foerster, ed., *Die Wehrpflicht: Entstehung, Erscheinungsformen und politisch-militärische Wirkung* (Munich: Oldenbourg, 1994), pp. 91–106.

37. See Adolf Hitler, *Sämtliche Aufzeichnungen 1905–1924,* ed. Eberhard Jäckel and Axel Kuhn (Stuttgart: Deutsche Verlags-Anstalt, 1980), pp. 214, 218, 583, and 728.

38. See General Liebmann's notes from the meeting, in Vogelsang, "Neue Dokumente," pp. 434–435.

39. Ibid., p. 422.

40. Details can be found in Wilhelm Deist, "The Rearmament of the Wehrmacht," in Deist et al., eds., *The Build-up of German Aggression,* trans. P. S. Falla et al., vol. 1 of *Germany and the Second World War* (Oxford: Clarendon Press, 1990), pp. 375–540; and Hans Jürgen Rautenberg, *Deutsche Rüstungspolitik vom Beginn der Genfer Abrüstungskonferenz bis zur Wiedereinführung der Allgemeinen Wehrpflicht 1931–1935* (Bonn, 1973). See also Rautenberg, "Drei Dokumente zur Planung eines 300 000-Mann-Friedensheeres aus dem Dezember 1933," *Militärgeschichtliche Mitteilungen,* no. 2 (1977), 103–139.

41. The text of the law is contained in the *Reichsgesetzblatt* 1, no. 52 (1935), 103–139.

42. See Michael Salewski, "Die bewaffnete Macht im Dritten Reich 1933–1939," in Gerhard Papke et al., eds., *Deutsche Militärgeschichte in sechs Bänden 1648–1939,* vol. 4 (Herrsching: Pawlak, 1987), pp. 134–140.

43. The full text is reproduced in Adolf Hitler, *Speeches and Proclamations, 1932–1945: The Chronicle of a Dictatorship,* vol. 2, ed. Max Domarus (Wauconda, Ill.: Bolchazy-Carducci, 1990), pp. 652–656.

44. For details, see Wolfram Wette, "Ideology, Propaganda, and Internal Politics as Preconditions of the War Policy of the Third Reich," in Deist, *The Build-up of German Aggression,* pp. 11–155.

45. Hitler, *Speeches and Proclamations,* 2:708.

46. Manfred Messerschmidt, "Das Reichskriegsgericht und die Verweigerer aus Gewissensgründen," in Ernst Willi Hansen et al., eds., *Politischer*

Wandel, organisierte Gewalt und nationale Sicherheit: Beiträge zur neueren Geschichte Deutschlands und Frankreichs: Festschrift für Klaus-Jürgen Müller (Munich: Oldenbourg, 1995), pp. 369–383.

47. See Detlev Garbe, *Zwischen Widerstand und Martyrium: Die Zeugen Jehovas im "Dritten Reich,"* 3rd ed. (Munich: Oldenbourg, 1997).

48. A paradigm for this effort may be seen in an address delivered to this group by a government official named Wilhelm Haegert, "Nationalsozialismus und Allgemeine Wehrpflicht," *Jahrbuch der Deutschen Gesellschaft für Wehrpolitik und Wehrwissenschaften* (1935), pp. 20–25. In it the speaker praised the "right of the German man to defend himself" as "the sacred legacy of our fathers."

49. See Burkhart Mueller-Hillebrandt, *Das Heer 1933–1945,* vol. 1 (Darmstadt: E. S. Mittler, 1954), p. 253. According to Mueller-Hillebrandt, 17,893,200 men were drafted into the Wehrmacht and Waffen-SS between June 1, 1939, and April 30, 1945; 7,590,000 of them were alive at the end of the war. His statistics indicate that 10 million men died in the Wehrmacht. This finding has been called into question by Rüdiger Overmans; see his essay "Die Toten des Zweiten Weltkrieges in Deutschland: Bilanz der Forschung unter besonderer Berücksichtigung der Wehrmacht- und Vertreibungsverluste," in Wolfgang Michalka, ed., *Der Zweite Weltkrieg: Analysen, Grundzüge, Forschungsbilanz* (Munich: Piper, 1989), pp. 858–873.

50. I have here borrowed the concept developed by Ralph Giordano in *Die zweite Schuld oder Von der Last Deutscher zu sein* (Hamburg: Rasch & Röhring, 1987), p. 11.

51. See Wolfram Wette and Gerd R. Ueberschär, eds., *Stalingrad: Mythos und Wirklichkeit einer Schlacht* (Frankfurt: Fischer, 1992). In this collection of essays the battle of Stalingrad is depicted "from below," that is, from the perspective of ordinary enlisted men.

52. Manfred Messerschmidt, "Allgemeine Wehrpflicht: Bürger in Uniform," in *Die französische Revolution: Impulse, Wirkungen, Anspruch: Vorträge im Sommersemester 1989* (Heidelberg: Heidelberger Verlagsanstalt, 1990), pp. 100–101.

53. See Manfred Messerschmidt and Fritz Wüllner, *Die Wehrmachtjustiz im Dienste des Nationalsozialismus: Zerstörung einer Legende* (Baden-Baden: Nomos, 1987); and Fritz Wüllner, *Die Militärjustiz und das Elend der Geschichtsschreibung: Ein grundlegender Forschungsbericht* (Baden-Baden: Nomos, 1991).

54. Paragraph 3.1 of section IIA, "Political Principles," of the Potsdam Declaration of August 2, 1945, in *A Decade of American Foreign Policy: Ba-*

sic Documents, 1941–49, Prepared at the request of the Senate Committee on Foreign Relations by the Staff of the Committee and the Department of State (Washington, D.C. : U.S. Government Printing Office, 1950).

55. These numbers are taken from Garbe, *Zwischen Widerstand und Martyrium,* pp. 484–488.

56. Messerschmidt, "Das Reichskriegsgericht und die Verweigerer aus Gewissensgründen," p. 377.

57. Detlev Garbe, "'Du sollst nicht töten': Kriegsdienstverweigerer 1939–1945," in Norbert Haase and Gerhard Paul, eds., *Die anderen Soldaten: Wehrkraftzersetzung, Gehorsamsverweigerung und Fahnenflucht im Zweiten Weltkrieg* (Frankfurt: Fischer, 1995), p. 92.

58. See Gordon Charles Zahn, *In Solitary Witness: The Life and Death of Franz Jägerstätter,* rev. ed. (Springfield, Ill.: Templegate Publishers, 1986); Erna Putz, *Franz Jägerstätter . . . besser die Hände als der Wille gefesselt,* 2nd ed. (Linz: Veritas-Verlag, 1978); and Norbert Haase, "Gott mehr gehorcht als dem Staat": Franz Jägerstätter vor dem Reichskriegsgericht: Eine Dokumentation, *Tribüne: Zeitschrift zum Verständnis des Judentums* 29, no. 114 (1990), 198–206.

59. See the biography by Eberhard Röhm, *Sterben für den Frieden: Spurensicherung: Hermann Stöhr (1898–1940) und die Ökumenische Friedensbewegung* (Stuttgart: Calwer Verlag, 1985).

60. Manfred Messerschmidt, "Aufhebung des Todesurteils gegen Franz Jägerstätter," *Zoom: Zeitschrift für Politik und Kultur,* no. 7 (1997), 16–22.

61. Garbe, *Zwischen Widerstand und Martyrium,* p. 103.

62. From the Defense Law of May 21, 1935; see *Reichsgesetzblatt* 1, (1935), 609.

63. Garbe, *Zwischen Widerstand und Martyrium,* p. 87.

64. The Reich War Court cited ibid., p. 88; see also p. 104.

65. These sentences were based on the relevant paragraph 69 of the Military Criminal Code. See the decree regarding the revision of this code of October 10, 1940, *Reichsgesetzblatt* 1, no. 181 (October 16, 1940), 1353.

66. These statistics are taken from Fritz Wüllner; see Messerschmidt and Wüllner, *Die Wehrmachtjustiz,* pp. 87 and 91; Wüllner, *Die Militärjustiz: Ein Forschungsbericht,* p. 476; Manfred Messerschmidt, "Deserteure im Zweiten Weltkrieg," in Wolfram Wette, ed., *Deserteure der Wehrmacht: Feiglinge, Opfer, Hoffnungsträger? Dokumentation eines Meinungswandels* (Essen: Klartext, 1995), p. 61.

67. For more on the history of desertion since the early modern period, see Ulrich Bröckling and Michael Sikora, eds., *Armeen und ihre Deserteure: Vernachlässigte Kapitel einer Militärgeschichte der Neuzeit* (Göttingen:

Vandenhoeck & Ruprecht, 1998), and my review in *Die Zeit*, June 25, 1998, p. 36. For more on the Wehrmacht in particular, see the survey of recent research by Dieter Knippschild, "Deserteure im Zweiten Weltkrieg: Der Stand der Debatte," in Bröckling and Sikora, *Armeen und ihre Deserteure*, pp. 222–251.

68. William Bradford Huie, *The Execution of Private Slovik: The Hitherto Secret Story of the Only American Soldier since 1864 to Be Shot for Desertion* (New York: Duell, Sloan and Pearce, 1954).

69. See the comparative study by Christoph Jahr, *Gewöhnliche Soldaten: Desertion und Deserteure im deutschen und britischen Heer 1914–1918* (Göttingen: Vandenhoeck & Ruprecht, 1998), vol. 123 of *Kritische Studien zur Geschichtswissenschaft*.

70. Adolf Hitler, *Mein Kampf*, trans. Ralph Manheim (Boston: Houghton Mifflin, 1943), p. 524.

71. See Peter Riedesser and Axel Verderber, *"Maschinengewehr hinter der Front": Zur Geschichte der deutschen Militärpsychiatrie* (Frankfurt: Mabuse, 2004).

72. The army physician Christian Schöne, for example, who had reported on the killings of Jews in chain letters and thus committed the crime of "undermining morale," received a relatively light sentence from the Central Army Court in Berlin on November 22, 1943. See the documentation "'Daß mit den Erschießungen der Juden aufgehört wird': Kettenbriefe gegen die deutschen Verbrechen im Zweiten Weltkrieg," *Frankfurter Allgemeine Zeitung*, no. 91 (April 18, 1996), 13–14.

73. See Rolf-Dieter Müller, Gerd R. Ueberschär, and Wolfram Wette, eds., *Wer zurückweicht wird erschossen! Kriegsalltag und Kriegsende in Südwestdeutschland 1944–1945* (Freiburg: Dreisam, 1985); Manfred Messerschmidt, "Die Wehrmacht: Vom Realitätsverlust zum Selbstbetrug," in Hans-Erich Volkmann, ed., *Ende des Dritten Reiches—Ende des Zweiten Weltkrieges: Eine perspektivische Rückschau* (Munich: Piper, 1995), pp. 223–257; Hans-Joachim Schröder, "'Ich hänge hier, weil ich getürmt bin': Terror und Verfall im deutschen Militär bei Kriegsende 1945," in Wolfram Wette, ed., *Der Krieg des kleinen Mannes: Eine Militärgeschichte von unten*, 2nd ed. (Munich: Piper, 1995), pp. 279–294.

74. On the variety of motives, see Norbert Haase, *Deutsche Deserteure* (Berlin: Rotbuch, 1987); Stefanie Reichelt, *"Für mich ist der Krieg aus!" Deserteure und Kriegsdienstverweigerer des Zweiten Weltkrieges in München* (Munich: Buchendorfer, 1995).

75. Volker Ullrich, "Den Mut haben, davonzulaufen," in the collection published by the newspaper *Die Zeit, Zeit-Punkte*, no. 3 (1995), *Gehorsam bis*

zum Mord? *Der verschwiegene Krieg der deutschen Wehrmacht: Fakten, Analysen, Debatte,* p. 69.

76. See Bernward Dörner, "'Der Krieg ist verloren!' Wehrkraftzersetzung und Denunziation in der Truppe," in Haase and Paul, *Die anderen Soldaten,* pp. 105–122.

77. For more on the topic of denunciation, see Robert Gellately, *The Gestapo and German Society: Enforcing Racial Policy, 1933–1945* (Oxford: Clarendon Press, 1990); and Manfred Messerschmidt, "Der 'Zersetzer' und sein Denunziant: Urteile des Zentralgerichts des Heeres—Außenstelle Wien—1944," in Wette, *Der Krieg des kleinen Mannes,* pp. 255–278.

78. Quotations are taken from "Warum hat der deutsche Soldat in aussichtsloser Lage bis zum Schluß des Krieges 1939–1945 gekämpft?" an essay written by General Blumentritt included in the "Operational History (German) Section" of the U.S. Army, in the Document Center of the Militärgeschichtliches Forschungsamt, Ms. B-338.

79. Haase and Paul, *Die anderen Soldaten.*

80. See Ortwin Buchbender, *Das tönende Erz: Deutsche Propaganda gegen die Rote Armee im Zweiten Weltkrieg* (Stuttgart: Seewald, 1978); Ortwin Buchbender and Horst Schuh, *Die Waffe, die auf die Seele zieht: Psychologische Kriegführung 1939–1945* (Stuttgart: Motorbuch Verlag, 1983); Buchbender and Schuh, eds., *Heil Beil! Flugblattpropaganda im Zweiten Weltkrieg: Dokumentation und Analyse* (Stuttgart: Seewald, 1974); Staatsbibliothek Preußischer Kulturbesitz, ed., *Flugblattpropaganda im 2. Weltkrieg,* exhibition catalogue 14 (Berlin, 1980). For information on Soviet propaganda, see Hans Heinrich Düsel, *Die sowjetische Flugblattpropaganda gegen Deutschland im Zweiten Weltkrieg* (Ingolstadt, 1985).

81. See Christian Streit, *Keine Kameraden: Die Wehrmacht und die sowjetischen Kriegsgefangenen 1941–1945* (Stuttgart: Deutsche Verlags-Anstalt, 1978), vol. 13 of *Studien zur Zeitgeschichte;* Ernst Klee, Willi Dreßen, and Volker Rieß, *"Gott mit uns": Der deutsche Vernichtungskrieg im Osten 1939–1945* (Frankfurt: S. Fischer, 1989); *Eine Schuld, die nicht erlischt: Dokumente über deutsche Kriegsverbrechen in der Sowjetunion* (Cologne: Pahl-Rugenstein, 1987); Omer Bartov, "A View from Below: Survival, Cohesion, and Brutality on the Eastern Front," in Bernd Wegner, ed., *From Peace to War: Germany, Soviet Russia, and the World, 1939–1941* (Providence: Berghahn, 1997), pp. 325–340.

82. Marlis G. Steinert, *Hitler's War and the Germans: Public Mood and Attitude during the Second World War,* ed. and trans. Thomas E. J. de Witt (Athens: Ohio University Press, 1977), pp. 333–334.

83. Ortwin Buchbender and Reinhold Sterz, *Das andere Gesicht des Krieges:*

Deutsche Feldpostbriefe 1939–1945 (Munich: C. H. Beck, 1982); Wolf-Dieter Mohrmann, ed., *Der Krieg hier ist hart und grausam! Feldpostbriefe an den Osnabrücker Regierungspräsidenten 1941–1944* (Osnabrück: H. Th. Wenner, 1984); Joachim Dollwet, "Menschen im Krieg: Bejahung und Widerstand? Eindrücke und Auszüge aus der Sammlung von Feldpostbriefen des Zweiten Weltkrieges im Landeshauptarchiv Koblenz," *Jahrbuch für westdeutsche Landesgeschichte* 13 (1987), 279–322; Frank Schumann, ed., *"Zieh Dich warm an!" Soldatenpost und Heimatbriefe aus zwei Weltkriegen: Chronik einer Familie* (Berlin: Verlag Neues Leben, 1989); Jens Ebert, "Zwischen Mythos und Wirklichkeit: Die Schlacht von Stalingrad in deutschsprachigen authentischen und literarischen Texten," 2 vols. (Ph.D. diss., Humboldt University, Berlin, 1989); Anatoly Golovchansky et al., eds., *"Ich will raus aus diesem Wahnsinn": Deutsche Briefe von der Ostfront 1941–1945: Aus sowjetischen Archiven* (Wuppertal: P. Hammer, 1991).

84. The Sterz collection in the Library for Contemporary History, Württemberg State Library, Stuttgart, deserves particular mention.

85. It should be kept in mind that the critical voices among the soldiers grew more numerous, a circumstance reflected in the constant increase in charges of "undermining morale." See Messerschmidt, "Der 'Zersetzer' und sein Denunziant."

86. The text of the speech is reproduced in H. Michaelis and E. Schraepler, eds., *Das Dritte Reich: Die Wende des Krieges* (Berlin: Dokumenten-Verlag, 1973), vol. 18 of *Ursachen und Folgen: Vom deutschen Zusammenbruch 1918 und 1945 bis zur staatlichen Neuordnung Deutschlands in der Gegenwart,* pp. 92–99.

87. Sterz Collection, Library for Contemporary History, Württemberg State Library, Stuttgart, Field Post 1943, folder for January.

88. The full text is included in Helmut Heiber, ed., *Goebbels-Reden,* vol. 2 (Düsseldorf: Droste, 1972), pp. 172–208.

89. Sterz Collection, Library for Contemporary History, Württemberg State Library, Stuttgart, Field Post 1943, folder for February.

90. Gotthard Breit, *Das Staats- und Gesellschaftsbild deutscher Generale beider Weltkriege im Spiegel ihrer Memoiren* (Boppard: H. Boldt, 1973); Reinhard Stumpf, *Die Wehrmacht-Elite: Rang- und Herrschaftsstruktur der deutschen Generale und Admirale 1933–1945* (Boppard: H. Boldt, 1982); Messerschmidt and Gersdorff, *Offiziere im Bild von Dokumenten aus drei Jahrhunderten.*

91. Messerschmidt, introduction to Deist, *The Build-up of German Aggression,* p. 3.

92. After the First World War, however, the tone of official histories corresponded to a large extent to that of officers' memoirs. The critical depictions that served as a counterweight tended to be produced by novelists and journalists rather than by academic historians.

93. For more on the popular publications known as *Landserhefte*, see Klaus F. Geiger, *Kriegsromanhefte in der BRD: Inhalt und Funktionen* (Tübingen: Tübinger Vereiningung für Volkskunde, 1974); Geiger, "Jugendliche lesen Landserhefte: Hinweise auf Lektürefunktion und -wirkungen," in Gunter Grimm, ed., *Literatur und Leser* (Stuttgart: Reclam, 1975), pp. 324–341; Walter Nutz, "Der Krieg als Abenteuer und Idylle," in Hans Wagener, ed., *Gegenwartsliteratur und Drittes Reich: Deutsche Autoren in der Auseinandersetzung mit der Vergangenheit* (Stuttgart: Reclam, 1977, pp. 265–283; Gerhard Schneider, "Geschichte durch die Hintertür: Triviale und populärwissenschaftliche Literatur über den Nationalsozialismus und den Zweiten Weltkrieg," *Aus Politik und Zeitgeschichte* 6 (1979), 3–25.

94. For more on developments in modern military history that have taken the subject in new directions, see the survey by Eckardt Opitz, "Der Weg der Militärgeschichte von einer Generalstabswissenschaft zur Subdisziplin der Geschichtswissenschaft," in Hans-Joachim Braun and Rainer H. Kluwe, eds., *Entwicklung und Selbstverständnis von Wissenschaften: Ein interdisziplinäres Colloquium* (Frankfurt: Lang, 1985), pp. 57–78.

95. See the statistics compiled by Rüdiger Overmans, "Die Toten des Zweiten Weltkrieges in Deutschland," and by Bernhard R. Kroener, "The Manpower Resources of the Third Reich in the Area of Conflict between Wehrmacht, Bureaucracy, and the War Economy, 1939–1942," in Kroener et al., eds., *Wartime Administration, Economy, and Manpower Resources, 1939–1941*, pt. 1 of *Organization and Mobilization of the German Sphere of Power* (Oxford: Clarendon Press, 2000), vol. 5 of *Germany and the Second World War*, pp. 787–1170.

96. See Werner Lahne, *Unteroffiziere: Werden, Wesen und Wirkung eines Berufsstandes*, rev. ed. (Herford: Verlag Offene Worte, 1974); Horst Rohde, "Zur Geschichte des deutschen Unteroffiziers," in Manfred Grotzki, Paul Klein, and Horst Rohde, eds., *Unteroffiziere*, vol. 1 of *Soldat: Ein Berufsbild im Wandel* (Bonn, 1989).

97. Several exceptions should be noted: Messerschmidt and Wüllner's studies of desertion, "undermining morale," and military trials, *Die Wehrmachtjustiz*; Gerhard Schreiber's work on Italian internees, *Die italienischen Militärinternierten im deutschen Machtbereich 1943–1945: Verachtet–Verraten–Vergessen* (Munich: Oldenbourg, 1990); and Thomas

Rohrkrämer, *Der Militarismus der "kleinen Leute": Die Kriegsvereine im Deutschen Kaiserreich 1871–1914* (Munich: Oldenbourg, 1990); a more general approach is taken by Hans Dollinger in the excellent collection *Kain, wo ist dein Bruder? Was der Mensch im Zweiten Weltkrieg erleiden musste: Dokumentation in Tagebüchern und Briefen* (1987), new ed. (Cologne: Komet, 2003).

98. See Reinhard Koselleck, "Der Einfluss der beiden Weltkriege auf das soziale Bewusstsein," in Wette, *Der Krieg des kleinen Mannes*, pp. 324–343.

99. Stephen G. Fritz, *Frontsoldaten: The German Soldier in World War II* (Lexington: University Press of Kentucky, 1995).

100. Ibid., p. vii.

101. As Fritz notes, "Given the agonizing nature of combat, some *Landsers* not surprisingly proved unequal to the task of describing the monstrous actualities they experienced"; ibid., p. 37. He quotes soldiers on the nervous strain of being at the front, pp. 62–63.

102. Ibid., pp. 5 and 6.

103. See the chapter "The Bonds of Comradeship," ibid., pp. 156–186.

104. Ibid., pp. 50–59.

105. Ibid., pp. 57–58.

106. Ibid., p. 225.

107. Ibid., p. 55.

108. Hans Joachim Schröder, *Die gestohlenen Jahre: Erzählgeschichten und Geschichtserzählung im Interview: Der Zweite Weltkrieg aus der Sicht ehemaliger Mannschaftssoldaten* (Tübingen: Niemeyer, 1992).

109. See, by Hans Joachim Schröder, "Die Vergegenwärtigung des Zweiten Weltkrieges in biographischen Interviewerzählungen," *Militärische Mitteilungen* 49 (1991), 9–37; "'Man kam sich da vor wie ein Stück Dreck': Schikane in der Militärausbildung des Dritten Reiches," in Wette, *Der Krieg des kleinen Mannes*, pp. 183–198; "Alltag der Katastrophen: Der Kampf um Stalingrad im Erinnerungsinterview," in Wette and Ueberschär, *Stalingrad: Mythos und Wirklichkeit einer Schlacht*, pp. 168–177; and "Ich hänge hier, weil ich getürmt bin."

110. Schröder, *Die gestohlenen Jahre*, p. 317.

111. Ibid., p. 671.

112. See Rolf-Dieter Müller and Gerd R. Ueberschär, *Kriegsende 1945: Die Zerstörung des Deutschen Reiches* (Frankfurt: Fischer Taschenbuch, 1994), pp. 37–41. For an account of one region's experience during this period, see Wilfried Beer, *Kriegsalltag an der Heimatfront: Alliierter Luftkrieg und deutsche Gegenmaßnahmen zur Abwehr und Schadens-*

begrenzung, dargestellt für den Raum Münster (Bremen: Hauschild, 1990).

113. See the survey of aerial attacks on Berlin, "Luftangriffe und deren Auswirkungen auf die Zivilbevölkerung," in Reinhard Rürup, *Berlin 1945: Eine Dokumentation* (Berlin: W. Arenhövel, 1995).

114. For more on German war propaganda in the last months of the war, see Ernest K. Bramsted, *Goebbels and National Socialist Propaganda, 1925– 1945* (East Lansing: Michigan State University Press, 1965); and Ian Kershaw, *The "Hitler Myth": Image and Reality in the Third Reich* (Oxford: Oxford University Press, 1987).

115. Bormann's speech of April 2, 1945, is reprinted in Müller and Ueberschär, *Kriegsende 1945,* p. 168.

116. Recollections of enlisted men on the pressure to hold out in the final months of the war form the basis of Schröder's article "Ich hänge hier, weil ich getürmt bin"; Müller, Ueberschär; and Wette, *Wer zurückweicht wird erschossen!*

117. For details, see Wilhelm Deist, "Die Politik der Seekriegsleitung und die Rebellion der Flotte Ende Oktober 1918," *Vierteljahrshefte für Zeitgeschichte* 14 (1966), 341–368.

118. For more on these events, see Richard Stumpf, *War, Mutiny, and Revolution in the German Navy: The World War I Diary of Seaman Richard Stumpf,* ed. and trans. Daniel Horn (New Brunswick, N.J.: Rutgers University Press, 1967); parts of the original text reproduced in Wette, *Der Krieg des kleinen Mannes,* pp. 168–172.

119. See Dan van der Vat, *The Grand Scuttle: The Sinking of the German Fleet at Scapa Flow in 1919* (Staplehurst: Spellmount, 1994); and Andreas Krause, *Scapa Flow: Die Selbstversenkung der wilhelminischen Flotte* (Berlin: Ullstein, 1999).

120. See Wolfram Wette, *Gustav Noske: Eine politische Biographie,* 2nd ed. (Düsseldorf: Droste, 1988), pp. 470–477.

121. Ibid., p. 488, n. 147.

122. The text of Hindenburg's telegram is reproduced in *Akten der Reichskanzlei: Das Kabinett Scheidemann, 13. Februar bis 20. Juni 1919,* ed. Hagen Schulze (Boppard: H. Boldt, 1971), no. 114, p. 477, n. 5. The same message from the Wolff Telegraph Office also in *Schultess' Europäischer Geschichtskalender* 1 (1919), 263–264. For the political context, see Wette, *Gustav Noske,* pp. 487–488.

123. See Gerd R. Ueberschär, "Stalingrad—eine Schlacht des Zweiten Weltkrieges," in Wette and Ueberschär, *Stalingrad,* pp. 33–34.

124. Wolfram Wette, "Das Massensterben als 'Heldenepos': Stalingrad in der NS-Propaganda," ibid., pp. 43–60.

125. Hans Barth, *Masse und Mythos: Die ideologische Krise an der Wende zum 20. Jahrhundert und die Theorie der Gewalt: Georges Sorel* (Hamburg: Rowohlt, 1959), pp. 68–70.

126. Wette, "Das Massensterben als 'Heldenepos,'" p. 43.

127. Reich Marshal Goering's appeal to the troops was made on the tenth anniversary of the National Socialists' seizure of power, January 30, 1943. The text is reproduced in Michaelis and Schraepler, *Das dritte Reich*, pp. 92–99. For interpretation, see Wette, "Das Massensterben als 'Heldenepos,'" pp. 52–53.

128. Michaelis and Schraepler, *Das dritte Reich*, p. 95.

129. Hitler, *Speeches and Proclamations*, 4:2752.

130. Wette, "Das Massensterben als 'Heldenepos,'" pp. 58–59.

131. Entry in Goebbels's diary for February 3, 1943; see *Die Tagebücher von Joseph Goebbels: Sämtliche Fragmente*, ed. Elke Fröhlich, vol. 7 (Munich: K. G. Saur, 1987–1996), p. 253.

132. This is Bernd Wegner's thesis; see the conference report by Andreas Kunz, "'Untergang' als Erfahrung, Ideologie und Mythos," in *Militärgeschichtliche Mitteilungen* 57 (1998), 313; and Bernd Wegner, "Hitler, der Zweite Weltkrieg und die Choreographie des Untergangs," *Geschichte und Gesellschaft* 26 (2000), 492–518.

133. See Messerschmidt, "Der 'Zersetzer' und sein Denunziant."

134. General von Hengl spoke these words in a lecture to generals and officers during a conference at Sonthofen; cited according to Messerschmidt, "Die Wehrmacht in der Endphase," p. 209.

135. Barth, *Masse und Mythos*, p. 96.

136. Albert Speer, *Inside the Third Reich: Memoirs*, trans. Richard and Clara Winston (New York: Macmillan, 1970), p. 400.

137. Joseph Goebbels, *The Goebbels Diaries, 1939–1941*, trans. and ed. Fred Taylor (London: H. Hamilton, 1982), p. 415.

138. See Josef Folttmann and Hanns Möller-Witten, *Opfergang der Generale: Die Verluste der Generale und Admirale und der im gleichen Dienstrang stehenden sonstigen Offiziere und Beamten im Zweiten Weltkrieg* (Berlin: Bernard & Graefe, 1953).

139. See Messerschmidt, "Die Wehrmacht in der Endphase"; and Messerschmidt, "Die Wehrmacht: Vom Realitätsverlust zum Selbstbetrug," pp. 23–257.

140. Heinrich Schwendemann, "Endkampf und Zusammenbruch im deut-

schen Osten," *Freiburger Universitätsblätter* 130 (1995), 9–27; and Schwendemann, "Strategie der Selbstvernichtung: Die Wehrmacht-führung im 'Endkampf' um das 'Dritte Reich,'" in Rolf-Dieter Müller and Hans-Erich Volkmann, eds., *Wehrmacht: Mythos und Realität* (Munich: Oldenbourg, 1999), pp. 224–244.

141. Percy Ernst Schramm, ed., *Die Niederlage 1945: Aus dem Kriegstagebuch des Oberkommandos der Wehrmacht*, 2nd ed. (Munich: Deutscher Taschenbuch Verlag, 1985).

142. There is a collection of the "Nachrichten des Oberkommandos der Wehrmacht" from September 1944 to February 1945 in German Federal Archives–Military Archives, RW 4/v. 350 and 352.

143. See "Mitteilungen für die Truppe," no. 379 (December 1944) to no. 393 (February 1945), Federal Archives–Military Archives, RW 4/v. 357.

144. Wilhelm Keitel, *The Memoirs of Field Marshal Keitel*, ed. Walter Gorlitz, trans. David Irving (New York: Stein and Day, 1965), pp. 199–200.

145. See the edition of source material, Wolfram Wette, Ricarda Bremer, and Detlef Vogel, eds., *Das letzte halbe Jahr: Stimmungsberichte der Wehrmachtpropaganda 1944–45* (Essen: Klartext, 2002).

5. The Legend of the Wehrmacht's "Clean Hands"

1. Omer Bartov, *Hitler's Army: Soldiers, Nazis, and War in the Third Reich* (Oxford: Oxford University Press, 1991).

2. Omer Bartov, "'Whose History Is It, Anyway?': The Wehrmacht and German Historiography," in Hannes Heer and Klaus Naumann, eds., *War of Extermination: The German Military in World War II, 1941–1944* (New York: Berghahn Books, 2000), pp. 400–416.

3. Norbert Frei, *Adenauer's Germany and the Nazi Past: The Politics of Amnesty and Integration*, trans. Joel Golb (New York: Columbia University Press, 2002).

4. Ulrich Herbert and Olaf Groehler, eds., *Zweierlei Bewältigung: Vier Beiträge über den Umgang mit der NS-Vergangenheit in den beiden deutschen Staaten* (Hamburg: Ergebnisse Verlag, 1992).

5. Gerd R. Ueberschär, "Der Mord an den Juden und der Ostkrieg: Zum Forschungsstand über den Holocaust," in Heiner Lichtenstein and Otto R. Romberg, eds., *Täter—Opfer—Folgen: Der Holocaust in Geschichte und Gegenwart* (Bonn: Bundeszentrale für politische Bildung, 1995), pp. 49–81.

6. Klaus Naumann, "Nachkrieg: Vernichtungskrieg, Wehrmacht und Militär in der deutschen Wahrnehmung nach 1945," *Mittelweg* 36 (1997), 11–25.

7. See also an earlier essay by Klaus Naumann, "Wenn ein Tabu bricht: Die Wehrmachtsausstellung in der Bundesrepublik," *Mittelweg* 36 (1997), 11–25.

8. Erich Murawski, *Der deutsche Wehrmachtsbericht 1939–1945: Ein Beitrag zur Untersuchung der geistigen Kriegführung mit einer Dokumentation der Wehrmachtberichte vom 1.7.1939 bis zum 9.5.1945* (Boppard: H. Boldt, 1962); and Günter Wegmann, *"Das Oberkommando der Wehrmacht gibt bekannt . . ."*: *Der deutsche Wehrmachtbericht: Vollständige Ausgabe der 1939 bis 1945 durch Presse und Rundfunk veröffentlichten Texte*, 3 vols. (Osnabrück: Biblio Verlag, 1982).

9. Bernd Boll, Hannes Heer, Walter Manoschek, and Hans Safrian, "Verwischen der Spuren. Vernichtung der Erinnerung," in Hamburger Institute for Social Research, ed., *Vernichtungskrieg: Verbrechen der Wehrmacht 1941 bis 1944*, exhibition catalogue (Hamburg: Hamburger Edition, 1996), p. 161.

10. Ibid., pp. 164–165.

11. Various sources cited ibid., p. 162.

12. Ibid., p. 161.

13. Sources cited ibid., p. 163. See also Walter Manoschek, *"Serbien ist judenfrei"*: *Militärische Besatzungspolitik und Judenvernichtung in Serbien 1941–42"* (Munich: R. Oldenbourg, 1993), vol. 38 of *Beiträge zur Militärgeschichte;* and Ernst Klee, Willi Dreßen, and Volker Rieß, eds., *"The Good Old Days": The Holocaust as Seen by Its Perpetrators and Bystanders*, trans. Deborah Burnstone (New York: Free Press, 1991).

14. Statements of witnesses on the burning of the corpses in Boll et al., "Verwischen der Spuren," pp. 174–175; see also the section on the massacre at Babi Yar (Chapter 3).

15. See Walter Manoschek, ed., *"Es gibt nur eines für das Judentum: Vernichtung": Das Judenbild in deutschen Soldatenbriefen 1939–1945* (Hamburg: Hamburger Edition, 1995).

16. Franz Dröge, *Der zerredete Widerstand: Soziologie und Publizistik des Gerüchts im 2. Weltkrieg* (Düsseldorf: Bertelsmann-Universitätsverlag, 1970).

17. From the report of Major von Gersdorff on a trip to the front, December 5–8, 1941, in the war log of the High Command of Army Group Central for December 9, 1941. The report is reproduced as document 42 in Gerd

R. Ueberschär and Wolfram Wette, eds., *"Unternehmen Barbarossa": Der deutsche Überfall auf die Sowjetunion 1941* (Paderborn: F. Schöningh, 1984); quoted passage, p. 398.

18. A vivid example is provided by the "Jäger Report," a summary of the murders of Jews and other victims in Lithuania. It is reprinted in Klee et al., *"The Good Old Days,"* pp. 46–58.

19. As reported by the commander of Einsatzgruppe D, SS General Otto Ohlendorf, in April 1942.

20. OKW/WPr Oral Propaganda Campaign, 1944–1945, Federal Archives–Military Archives, Freiburg im Breisgau, Rw 4/v. 266. See also the documentary volume edited by Wolfram Wette, Ricarda Bremer, and Detlef Vogel, *Das letzte halbe Jahr: Stimmungsberichte der Wehrmachtpropaganda 1944/45* (Essen: Klartext, 2001), vol. 13 of *Schriften der Bibliothek für Zeitgeschichte*, n.s..

21. See Bernhard R. Kroener, "Auf dem Weg zu einer 'nationalsozialistischen Volksarmee,'" in Martin Broszat, Klaus-Dietmar Henke, and Hans Woller, eds., *Von Stalingrad zur Währungsreform: Zur Sozialgeschichte des Umbruchs in Deutschland,* 3rd ed. (Munich: Oldenbourg, 1990), vol. 26 of *Quellen und Darstellungen zur Zeitgeschichte,* pp. 651–682.

22. See Heinrich Schwendemann, "Endkampf und Zusammenbruch im deutschen Osten," *Freiburger Universitätsblätter* 130 (1995), 9–27.

23. Klaus-Dietmar Henke, *Die amerikanische Besatzung Deutschlands* (Munich: Oldenbourg, 1995), p. 958.

24. Ibid., pp. 809–814.

25. The German phrase was "bis zum Untergang," meaning until the death or destruction of the leaders—or of the country. For more on the Wehrmacht generals' refusal to acknowledge the reality of their situation in 1944–45, see Manfred Messerschmidt, "Die Wehrmacht: Vom Realitätsverlust zum Selbstbetrug," in Hans-Erich Volkmann, ed., *Ende des Dritten Reiches—Ende des Zweiten Weltkrieges: Eine perspektivische Rückschau* (Munich: Piper, 1995), pp. 223–257.

26. Henke, *Die amerikanische Besatzung,* pp. 964–965.

27. Josef Folttmann and Hans Möller-Witten, *Opfergang der Generale: Die Verluste der Generale und Admirale und der im gleichen Rang stehenden sonstigen Offiziere und Beamten im Zweiten Weltkrieg,* 2nd ed. (Berlin: Bernard & Graefe, 1953), pp. 100ff., 118, 124, 128, 131.

28. For more on the comparison of antiwar sentiment after the two world wars, see Wolfram Wette, "Die deutsche militärische Führungsschicht in den Nachkriegszeiten," in Gottfried Niedhart and Dieter Riesen-

berger, eds., *Lernen aus dem Krieg? Deutsche Nachkriegszeiten 1918 und 1945* (Munich: Beck, 1992), pp. 39–66.

29. Bertrand Perz, "Wehrmachtsangehörige als KZ-Bewacher," in Walter Manoschek, ed., *Die Wehrmacht im Rassenkrieg: Der Vernichtungskrieg hinter der Front* (Vienna: Picus, 1996), pp. 168–181.

30. See Kurt Pätzold, "Der Streit um die Wehrmacht," *Bulletin der Berliner Gesellschaft für Faschismus- und Weltkriegsforschung* 9 (1997), 3–47, and Pätzold's more recent treatment of the same subject, *Ihr waret die besten Soldaten: Ursprung und Geschichte einer Legende* (Leipzig: Militzke, 2000).

31. For details, see Reimer Hansen, *Das Ende des Dritten Reiches: Die deutsche Kapitulation 1945* (Stuttgart: Klett, 1966); Marlis G. Steinert, *Capitulation, 1945: The Story of the Dönitz Regime*, trans. Richard Barry (London: Constable, 1969); and—with an apologetic approach—Walter Lüdde-Neurath, *Regierung Dönitz: Die letzten Tage des Dritten Reiches* (Göttingen: Muster-Schmidt-Verlag, 1964).

32. The report of May 9, 1945, is reprinted in Percy Ernst Schramm, ed., *Die Niederlage 1945: Aus dem Kriegstagebuch des Oberkommandos der Wehrmacht*, 2nd ed. (Munich: Deutscher Taschenbuch Verlag, 1985), p. 404.

33. Manfred Messerschmidt, "Forward Defense: The 'Memorandum of the Generals' for the Nuremberg Court," in Heer and Naumann, *War of Extermination*, p. 382.

34. The astonishing background behind the composition of the generals' memorandum is described by George Meyer, "Zur Situation der deutschen militärischen Führungsschicht im Vorfeld des westdeutschen Verteidigungsbeitrages 1945–1950/51," in Militärgeschichtliches Forschungsamt, ed., *Von der Kapitulation zum Pleven-Plan*, vol. 1 of *Anfänge westdeutscher Sicherheitspolitik 1945–1956* (Munich: Oldenbourg, 1982), 577–726; the quotation is taken from pp. 680–681.

35. Ibid., p. 681.

36. The text is reprinted in Siegfried Westphal, *Der deutsche Generalstab auf der Anklagebank: Nürnberg 1945–1948* (Mainz: Hase & Koehler, 1978), pp. 28–87.

37. Meyer, "Zur Situation der deutschen militärischen Führungsschicht," p. 673.

38. Messerschmidt, "Forward Defense," p. 382.

39. Ibid., p. 390.

40. Meyer, "Zur Situation der deutschen militärischen Führungsschicht," p. 672.

41. Telford Taylor, *The Nuremberg Trials: War Crimes and International Law* (*International Conciliation* 450 [April 1949]) (New York: Carnegie Endowment for Peace, 1949), p. 271.

42. For the problems associated with this, see Telford Taylor, *The Anatomy of the Nuremberg Trials: A Personal Memoir* (New York: Knopf, 1992), chap. 10, "The SS and the General Staff–High Command," pp. 236–261.

43. See Appendix B to the indictment, *Trial of the Major War Criminals before the International Military Tribunal, Nuremberg, 14 November 1945–1 October 1946*, 42 vols. (1947; rpt. Buffalo, N.Y.: William S. Hein, 1995), 1:83–84; and Telford Taylor's summation, 4:395–398.

44. In German military history, the term "general staff" is used to denote, first, the sum of specially trained officers who report directly to the top military leadership, and second, a particular institution. During the German empire, the army supreme command had this function. The Treaty of Versailles abolished it in 1919, but it continued to exist in disguised form and was officially called by this title again from 1935 on. During the Second World War, particular staffs functioned in the OKW, newly created in 1938, and in the High Commands of parts of the Wehrmacht as a general staff (general staff of the Luftwaffe and admiralty staff).

45. The most important sources of law on which the Nuremberg trials rested are reprinted by Telford Taylor, including an excerpt from the charter of the International Military Tribunal, Control Council Law no. 10, and the Military Government of Germany (United States Zone) Ordinances nos. 7 and 11; Taylor, *The Nuremberg Trials: War Crimes*, pp. 356–370.

46. See the judgment, *Trial of the Major War Criminals before the International Military Tribunal*, 1:279.

47. Ibid., pp. 278–279.

48. "Tripartite Agreement by the United States, the United Kingdom, and Soviet Russia Concerning Conquered Countries, August 2, 1945," Pamphlet no. 4, *Pillars of Peace: Documents Pertaining to American Interest in Establishing a Lasting World Peace: January 1941–February 1946* (Carlisle Barracks, Pa.: Book Department, Army Information School, 1946), p. 113.

49. The biographical data on the defendants are taken from the court records and in some cases supplemented with information from other sources: Municipal Archives, Nuremberg, War Crimes Trials, Case 12, Department B (documents of the prosecution), no. 1. Every curriculum vitae has an NOKW (Nuremberg-OKW) number. The trial records contain extensive autobiographical accounts prepared by the accused them-

selves, as well as extracts from the officers' army personnel files. A brief biographical sketch of each defendant is also included in the court's judgment in Case 12.

50. *The High Command Case*, vol. 10 of *Trials of War Criminals before the Nuernberg Military Tribunals* (Washington, D.C.: U.S. Government Printing Office, 1951), p. 3.

51. Georg Meyer, "Soldaten ohne Armee: Berufssoldaten im Kampf um Standesehre und Versorgung," in *Von Stalingrad zur Währungsreform*, p. 709.

52. There is a summary in *The High Command Case*, p. 4.

53. Taylor, *The Nuremberg Trials: War Crimes*, p. 288.

54. Hans Laternser, *Die Verteidigung deutscher Soldaten* (Bonn: R. Bohnemeier, 1950).

55. *The High Command Case* (continued), vol. 11 of *Trials of War Criminals before the Nuernberg Military Tribunals*, p. 491.

56. Meyer, "Soldaten ohne Armee," pp. 709–710.

57. See Frei, *Adenauer's Germany and the Nazi Past*, sec. 2.

58. *Trials of War Criminals before the Nuernberg Military Tribunals* (see note 50).

59. For more on this series and its individual volumes, see Norman E. Tutorow, ed., *War Crimes, War Criminals, and War Crimes Trials: An Annotated Bibliography and Source Book* (New York: Greenwood Press, 1986), pp. 347–350.

60. *Trials of War Criminals before the Nuernberg Military Tribunals*, including vol. 10, *The High Command Case*, and vol. 11, *The High Command* Case (continued) and *The Hostage Case.*

61. Robert M. W. Kempner and C. Haensel, eds., *Das Urteil im Wilhelmstraßen-Prozeß* (Schwäbisch-Gmünd: A. Bürger, 1950).

62. Laternser, *Die Verteidigung deutscher Soldaten.*

63. Jörg Wollenberg, "Das Eliteverbrechen," in Jörg Friedrich and Jörg Wollenberg, eds., *Licht im Schatten der Vergangenheit: Zur Enttabuisierung der Nürnberg Kriegsverbrecherprozesse* (Frankfurt am Main: Ullstein, 1987), pp. 10–25.

64. Ralph Giordano, *Die zweite Schuld oder Von der Last Deutscher zu sein* (Hamburg: Rasch und Röhring, 1987), in particular the section "Wehrmacht und Krieg—die heiligen Kühe: Über das Hauptverbrechen Hitlerdeutschlands," pp. 169–204.

65. Meyer, "Soldaten ohne Armee," p. 713.

66. *Der Nürnberger Prozeß: Aus den Protokollen, Dokumenten und Materialien des Prozesses gegen die Hauptkriegsverbrecher vor dem Interna-*

tionalen Militärgerichtshof, with an introduction by P. A. Steininger, vol. 1, 2nd ed. ([East] Berlin: Rütten & Loening, 1957). This edition contains the indictment, legal foundations, questions of law, and judgment of the IMT trial.

67. *Fall 12: Das Urteil gegen das Oberkommando der Wehrmacht, gefällt am 28. Oktober 1948 in Nürnberg vom Militärgerichtshof V der Vereinigten Staaten von Amerika* ([East] Berlin: Rütten & Loening, 1960).

68. Ibid., "Vorwort," pp. 9–20.

69. Jörg Friedrich, *Das Gesetz des Krieges: Das deutsche Heer in Russland, 1941 bis 1945: Der Prozess gegen das Oberkommando der Wehrmacht* (Munich: Piper, 1993).

70. Gerhard Schreiber, *Deutsche Kriegsverbrechen in Italien: Täter, Opfer, Strafverfolgung* (Munich: Beck, 1996), pp. 214–215.

71. General Vietinghoff-Scheel used these words in a study written for the Historical Division of the U.S. Army titled "Feldzug in Italien" (Campaign in Italy), cited according to ibid., p. 216.

72. These figures are the result of Gerhard Schreiber's research, ibid., p. 217.

73. Oliver von Wrochem, "Rehabilitation oder Strafverfolgung: Kriegsverbrecher-Prozeß gegen Generalfeldmarschall Erich von Manstein im Widerstreit britischer Interessen," *Mittelweg* 36, no. 3 (1997), 26–36.

74. Ibid., pp. 29–31.

75. This last quote is taken from Paget's summing up, reproduced in part in Paul Leverkuehn, *Die Verteidigung Mansteins* (Hamburg: Nölke, 1950); quoted according to Wrochem, "Rehabilitation oder Strafverfolgung," p. 32.

76. Wrochem, "Rehabilitation oder Strafverfolgung," pp. 33–36.

77. Reginald T. Paget, *Manstein: His Campaigns and His Trial* (London: Collins, 1951); in German, *Manstein: Seine Feldzüge und sein Prozess* (Wiesbaden: Limes-Verlag, 1952).

78. Bertrand Russell, "Recht oder Vergeltung?" *Hamburger Abendblatt,* June 27, 1949, cited according to Wrochem, "Rehabilitation oder Strafverfolgung," p. 29.

79. An indication of this omission is provided by the index to vols. 1–22 of the *Trial of the Major War Criminals before the International Military Tribunal.* Under the heading "Jews, Persecution of" the index makes no reference to the Wehrmacht (23:386–402).

80. *Trials of War Criminals before the Nuernberg Military Tribunal,* vol. 4, *Case 9: U.S. v. Ohlendorf (Einsatzgruppen Case)*(Washington, D.C.: U.S. Government Printing Office, 1949).

81. Walter Laqueur, *The Terrible Secret: Suppression of the Truth about Hitler's "Final Solution"* (Boston: Little, Brown, 1980).

82. Thomas E. Wood and Stanisław M. Jankowski, *Karski: How One Man Tried to Stop the Holocaust* (New York: J. Wiley, 1994).

83. While searching the National Archives in 1996, the American historian Richard Breitman found 282 pages of transcripts from German radio transmissions made known to the British government, which kept them secret. See Richard Breitman, *Official Secrets: What the Nazis Planned, What the British and Americans Knew* (New York: Hill and Wang, 1998).

84. Karl-Heinz Janßen identifies a large number of additional channels of information in a newspaper article, "Was wussten die Alliierten vom Holocaust? Warten auf die Retter: Von der Hilflosigkeit der Verfolgten und der Ohnmacht des Westens," *Die Zeit*, no. 5 (January 24, 1997), 46.

85. Bernd Wegner, "Erschriebene Siege: Franz Halder, die 'Historical Divison' und die Rekonstruktion des Zweiten Weltkrieges im Geiste des deutschen Generalstabes," in Ernst Willi Hansen, Gerhard Schreiber, and Bernd Wegner, eds., *Politischer Wandel, organisierte Gewalt und nationale Sicherheit: Beiträge zur neueren Geschichte Deutschlands und Frankreichs: Festschrift für Klaus-Jürgen Müller* (Munich: Oldenbourg, 1995), vol. 50 of *Beiträge zur Militärgeschichte*, p. 287.

86. See Charles Burdick, "Vom Schwert zur Feder: Deutsche Kriegsgefangene im Dienst der Vorbereitung der amerikanischen Geschichtsschreibung über den Zweiten Weltkrieg," *Militärgeschichtliche Mitteilungen*, no. 2 (1971), 69–80; Christian Greiner, "'Operational History (German) Section' und 'Naval Historical Team': Deutsches militärstrategisches Denken im Dienst der amerikanischen Streitkräfte von 1946 bis 1950," in Manfred Messerschmidt, ed., *Militärgeschichte: Probleme—Thesen—Wege* (Stuttgart: Deutsche-Verlags-Anstalt, 1982), vol. 25 of *Beiträge zur Militär- und Kriegsgeschichte*, pp. 409–435.

87. Burdick, "Vom Schwert zur Feder," pp. 71 and 77.

88. Ibid., p. 75. General (ret.) Halder had a decisive influence in West Germany during the 1950s and 1960s on the way the history of the Second World War was written, by virtue of the knowledge he had amassed working on the studies assembled by the Historical Division, which he shared with both professional historians and interested amateurs and veterans. See Gerd R. Ueberschär, *Generaloberst Franz Halder: Generalstabschef, Gegner and Gefangener Hitlers* (Göttingen: Muster-Schmidt, 1991), pp. 92ff.

89. This was a group of German intelligence experts who worked under CIA

auspices after the war gathering information on eastern Europe and the Soviet Union.—Trans.

90. For details, see Christopher Simpson, *Blowback: America's Recruitment of Nazis and Its Effects on the Cold War* (New York: Weidenfeld & Nicolson, 1988).

91. Wegner, "Erschriebene Siege," p. 290.

92. Ibid., pp. 291–292.

93. The papers of General (ret.) Günther Blumentritt in the Federal Archives–Military Archives include a great deal of correspondence in which the former officer of the Wehrmacht provided information on historical events along with the desired evaluation of them in the spirit of the general staff.

94. Ueberschär, *Generaloberst Franz Halder,* p. 96.

95. Wegner, "Erschriebene Siege," pp. 294–295.

96. Ueberschär, *Generaloberst Franz Halder,* p. 95.

97. Peter Reichel, "Zwischen Dämonisierung und Verharmlosung: Das NS-Bild und seine politische Funktion in den 50er Jahren: Eine Skizze," in Axel Schildt and Arnold Sywottek, eds., *Modernisierung im Wiederaufbau: Die westdeutsche Gesellschaft der 50er Jahre* (Bonn: Dietz, 1993), p. 692.

98. Franz Halder, *Hitler als Feldherr* (1949); English-language edition, *Hitler as War Lord,* trans. Paul Findlay (London: Putnam, 1950).

99. Karl Dönitz, *Zehn Jahre und Zwanzig Tage* (1958); English-language edition, *Memoirs: Ten Years and Twenty Days,* trans. R. H. Stevens in collaboration with David Woodward (Annapolis, Md.: Naval Institute Press, 1990).

100. Heinz Guderian, *Erinnerungen eines Soldaten* (1951); English-language edition, *Panzer Leader,* trans. Constantine Fitzgibbon (1952; rpt. New York: DaCapo Press, 1996).

101. Albert Kesselring, *Soldat bis zum letzten Tag* (1953); English-language edition, *A Soldier's Record* (New York: W. W. Morrow, 1954).

102. Erich von Manstein, *Verlorene Siege* (1955); English-language edition, *Lost Victories,* trans. Anthony G. Powell (London: Methuen, 1958); and *Aus einem Soldatenleben, 1887–1939* (Bonn: Athenäum-Verlag, 1958).

103. Siegfried Westphal, *Heer in Fesseln: Aus den Papieren des Stabschefs von Rommel, Kesselring und Rundstedt* (1950); English-language edition, *The German Army in the West* (London: Cassell, 1951).

104. Erwin Rommel, *Krieg ohne Haß* (1950); English-language edition, *The Rommel Papers,* ed. B. H. Liddell Hart, with the assistance of Lucie-Maria Rommel, Manfred Rommel, and Fritz Bayerlein, trans. Paul

Findlay (New York: Harcourt, Brace, 1953). Rommel had died in 1944, and his papers were published by surviving family members.

105. Adolf Heusinger, *Befehl im Widerstreit: Schicksalsstunden der deutschen Armee 1923–1945* (Tübingen: Wunderlich, 1950).

106. Wegner, "Erschriebene Siege," p. 298.

107. Friedrich Gerstenberger, "Strategische Erinnerungen: Die Memoiren deutscher Offiziere," in Hannes Heer and Klaus Naumann, eds., *Vernichtungskrieg: Verbrechen der Wehrmacht 1941 bis 1945* (Hamburg: Hamburger Edition, 1995), pp. 620–633.

108. Manstein, *Lost Victories*.

109. Basil H. Liddell Hart, *The Other Side of the Hill*, rev. ed. (London: Cassell, 1951); *The German Generals Talk* (New York: W. Morrow, 1948).

110. Bartov, "Whose History Is It, Anyway?" p. 401.

111. See Michael Schornstheimer, "'Harmlose Idealisten und drauf-gängerische Soldaten': Militär und Krieg in den Illustriertenromanen der fünfziger Jahre," in Heer und Naumann, *Vernichtungskrieg*, pp. 634–650; and Schornstheimer's monograph, *Die leuchtenden Augen der Frontsoldaten: Nationalsozialismus und Krieg in den Illustriertenromanen der Nachkriegszeit* (Berlin: Metropol, 1995).

112. See Hannes Heer, "Die Bilderwelt der Nachkriegsjahre," in Hamburg Institute for Social Research, ed., *Vernichtungskrieg: Verbrechen der Wehrmacht 1941 bis 1945: Ausstellungskatalog* (Hamburg: Hamburger Edition, 1996), pp. 8–18.

113. Typical of this approach is the book by a former member of the Wehrmacht propaganda staff, Heinz Schröter, *Stalingrad: ". . . bis zur letzten Patrone"* (1953), new ed. (Klagenfurt: Kaiser, 1970). As Gerd R. Ueber-schär was able to ascertain, Schröter also put together the anonymously published work *Letzte Briefe aus Stalingrad* (1950; rpt. Gütersloh: Bertelsmann, 1954).

114. Hans-Jürgen Rautenberg and Norbert Wiggershaus, eds., "Die 'Himmeroder Denkschrift' vom Oktober 1950: Politische und militärische Überlegungen für einen Beitrag der Bundesrepublik Deutschland zur westeuropäischen Verteidigung," *Militärgeschichtliche Mitteilungen* 21 (1977), 135–206.

115. For more on General Hermann Foertsch, see Manfred Messerschmidt, *Was damals Recht war . . . NS-Militär- und Strafjustiz im Vernichtungs-krieg*, ed. Wolfram Wette (Essen: Klartext, 1996). See also Manfred Messerschmidt, *Die Wehrmacht im NS-Staat: Zeit der Indoktrination* (Hamburg: R. von Decker, 1969).

116. The German text of this statement was also read to reporters by a gov-

ernment spokesman in Bonn. See Klaus von Schubert, *Wiederbe-waffnung und Westintegration: Die innere Auseinandersetzung um die militärische und außenpolitische Orientierung der Bundesrepublik 1950–1952* (Stuttgart: Deutsche Verlagsanstalt, 1982), pp. 82–83.

117. Deutscher Bundestag, stenographic reports of the first session, 1951, p. 4984.

118. For details, see Meyer, "Soldaten ohne Armee," pp. 688–689.

119. Frei, *Adenauer's Germany and the Nazi Past.*

120. Norbert Frei, "Das ganz normale Grauen," *Der Spiegel,* no. 16 (April 14, 1997), 64–67.

121. Ibid., p. 67.

122. Alfred Streim, "Saubere Wehrmacht? Die Verfolgung von Kriegs- und NS-Verbrechen in der Bundesrepublik und in der DDR," in Heer and Naumann, *War of Extermination,* p. 577.

123. The judgment handed down in the Einsatzgruppen trial and the extensive material supporting it have been documented by H. G. van Dam and Ralph Giordano, eds., *Einsatzkommando Tilsit: Der Prozess zu Ulm,* vol. 2 of *KZ-Verbrechen vor deutschen Gerichten* (Frankfurt: Europäische Verlagsanstalt, 1966).

124. Adalbert Rückerl, *NS-Verbrechen vor Gericht: Versuch einer Vergangen-heitsbewältigung,* 2nd ed. (Heidelberg: C. F. Müller, 1984), p. 140.

125. See the summary ibid., sec. C.

126. Ibid., p. 143.

127. Ibid., p. 143, n. 90, and pp. 157 and 172. See also Adalbert Rückerl, *Die Strafverfolgung von NS-Verbrechen 1945–1978: Eine Dokumentation* (Karlsruhe: C. F. Müller, 1979), p. 50.

128. Streim, "Saubere Wehrmacht?" p. 578.

129. Ibid., pp. 579, 581, and 593.

130. See Rückerl, *NS-Verbrechen vor Gericht,* pp. 238–239. There Rückerl reports that in the 1960s a prominent former member of the Reich Security Main Office tried to create a centrally coordinated list of arguments for defendants in the National Socialist trials (presumably Werner Best). After this was uncovered, a great deal of information surfaced about his contacts and connections with groups of former officials in various National Socialist organizations and their sympathizers.

131. Ulrich Herbert, *Best: Biographische Studien über Radikalismus, Weltan-schauung und Vernunft, 1903–1989,* 3rd ed. (Bonn: Dietz, 1996), pp. 495–497.

132. Ibid., pp. 496–497.

133. Cited according to ibid., p. 497.

134. Compare the conclusions reached by Frei, "Das ganz normale Grauen."

135. Herbert, *Werner Best,* pp. 507–510.

136. Ibid., p. 508.

137. Ibid., p. 509. See also Helmut Kramer, "Kriegsverbrechen, deutsche Justiz und das Verjährungsproblem," in Wolfram Wette and Gerd R. Ueberschär, eds., *Kriegsverbrechen im 20. Jahrhundert* (Darmstadt: Primus, 2001).

138. Herbert, *Best,* p. 510.

139. Christopher R. Browning, "Wehrmacht Reprisal Policy and the Mass Murder of Jews in Serbia," *Militärgeschichtliche Mitteilungen* 33 (1983), 31–47.

6. A Taboo Shatters

1. Andreas Hillgruber, *Hitlers Strategie: Politik und Kriegführung, 1940–1941* (Frankfurt am Main: Bernard & Graefe Verlag für Wehrwesen, 1965); the expert opinions provided by Krausnick and Jacobsen for trials are included in Institut für Zeitgeschichte (Munich), ed., *Anatomy of the SS State,* trans. Richard Barry, Marian Jackson, and Dorothy Long (New York: Walker, 1968); Manfred Messerschmidt, *Die Wehrmacht im NS-Staat; Zeit der Indoktrination* (Hamburg: R. von Decker [1969]); Klaus Jürgen Müller, *Das Heer und Hitler: Armee und nationalsozialistisches Regime 1933–1940* (Stuttgart: Deutsche Verlags-Anstalt, 1969).

2. Militärgeschichtliches Forschungsamt, ed., *Germany and the Second World War,* 6 vols. (New York: Oxford University Press, 1990–); Gerd R. Ueberschär and Wolfram Wette, eds., *"Unternehmen Barbarossa": Der deutsche Überfall auf die Sowjetunion 1941* (Paderborn: F. Schöningh, 1984); Wolfgang Michalka, ed., *Der Zweite Weltkrieg: Analysen, Grundzüge, Forschungsbilanz* (Munich: Piper, 1989); Bernd Wegner, ed., *From Peace to War: Germany, Soviet Russia, and the World, 1939–1941* (Providence: Berghahn Books, 1997); Wolfram Wette and Gerd R. Ueberschär, eds., *Stalingrad: Mythos und Wirklichkeit einer Schlacht* (Frankfurt am Main: Fischer Taschenbuch Verlag, 1992); Wolfram Wette, ed., *Der Krieg des kleinen Mannes: Eine Militärgeschichte von unten* (Munich: Piper, 1992).

3. Messerschmidt had delivered a lecture at the Protestant Academy Hofgeismar in May 1979; when it appeared in the *Süddeutsche Zeitung* in early 1981, it prompted an unusual number of responses from readers; Manfred Messerschmidt, "Kein gültiges Erbe," *Süddeutsche Zeitung,*

February 21–22, 1979. It has been published elsewhere in different versions: Manfred Messerschmidt, "Das Verhältnis von Wehrmacht und NS-Staat und die Frage der Traditionsbildung," in Klaus-Michael Kodalle, ed., *Tradition als Last? Legitimationsprobleme der Bundeswehr* (Cologne: Verlag Wissenschaft und Politik, 1981); Messerschmidt, "Der Kampf der Wehrmacht im Osten als Traditionsproblem," in Ueberschär and Wette, *"Unternehmen Barbarossa";* and Messerschmidt, "Wehrmacht, Ostfeldzug und Tradition," in Michalka, *Der Zweite Weltkrieg,* pp. 314–328.

4. Manfred Messerschmidt, *Militärgeschichtliche Aspekte der Entwicklung des deutschen Nationalstaates* (Düsseldorf: Droste, 1988), p. 243.

5. Ibid., p. 245.

6. Ibid., p. 248.

7. Julius H. Schoeps, ed., *Ein Volk von Mördern? Die Dokumentation zur Goldhagen-Kontroverse um die Rolle der Deutschen im Holocaust* (Hamburg: Hoffmann und Campe, 1996); Johannes Heil and Rainer Erb, eds., *Geschichtswissenschaft und Öffentlichkeit: Der Streit um Daniel Goldhagen* (Frankfurt: Fischer Taschenbuch Verlag, 1998).

8. This is the upshot of Wolfgang Wippermann's reflections in *Wessen Schuld? Vom Historikerstreit zur Goldhagen-Kontroverse* (Berlin: Elefanten Press, 1997).

9. Dieter Pohl, "Die Holocaust-Forschung und Goldhagens Thesen," *Vierteljahrshefte für Zeitgeschichte* 45 (1997), 1.

10. See Otto D. Kulka, "Die deutsche Geschichtsschreibung über den Nationalsozialismus und die 'Endlösung': Tendenzen und Entwicklungsphasen 1924–1984," *Historische Zeitschrift* 240 (1985), 559–640.

11. Pohl, "Die Holocaust-Forschung," p. 5. See also the same author's excellent survey, which covers the more recent German contributions to the field, *Holocaust: Die Ursachen, das Geschehen, die Folgen* (Freiburg: Herder, 2000).

12. Hamburg Institute for Social Research, *The German Army and Genocide: Crimes against War Prisoners, Jews, and Other Civilians in the East, 1939–1944,* trans. Scott Abbott (New York: New Press, 1999).

13. Gerd R. Ueberschär, "Der Mord an den Juden und der Ostkrieg: Zum Forschungsstand über den Holocaust," in Heiner Lichtenstein and Otto R. Romberg, eds., *Täter—Opfer—Folgen: Der Holocaust in Geschichte und Gegenwart* (Bonn: Bundeszentrale für Politische Bildung, 1995), p. 50.

14. Ibid., p. 58.

15. Ibid., p. 62, with n. 192. See also Ulrich Herbert, "Der Holocaust in der Geschichtsschreibung der Bundesrepublik Deutschland," in Herbert and

Olaf Groehler, eds., *Zweierlei Bewältigung: Vier Beiträge über den Umgang mit der NS-Vergangenheit in den beiden deutschen Staaten* (Hamburge: Ergebnisse Verlag, 1992), pp. 67–86; and Ilya Ehrenburg and Vasily Grossman, eds., *The Black Book: The Ruthless Murder of Jews by German-Fascist Invaders throughout the Temporarily Occupied Regions of the Soviet Union and in the Death Camps of Poland during the War of 1941–1945*, trans. John Glad and James S. Levine (New York: Holocaust Publications, 1981).

16. Omer Bartov, "'Whose History Is It, Anyway?': The Wehrmacht and German Historiography," in Hannes Heer and Klaus Naumann, eds., *War of Extermination: The German Military in World War II, 1941–1944* (New York: Berghahn Books, 2000), p. 401.

17. Andreas Hillgruber, "Der geschichtliche Ort der Judenvernichtung: Eine Zusammenfassung," in Eberhard Jäckel and Jürgen Rohwer, eds., *Der Mord an den Juden im Zweiten Weltkrieg* (Frankfurt: Deutsche Verlags-Anstalt, 1985), pp. 213–224.

18. Ibid., p. 219.

19. See Ulrich Herbert, ed., *Nationalsozialistische Vernichtungspolitik 1939–1945: Neue Forschungen und Kontroversen* (Frankfurt: Fischer, 1998). Dieter Pohl provides another good survey of current research in the field in his previously mentioned book *Holocaust: Die Ursachen, das Geschehen, die Folgen* (see note 11).

20. Thomas Sandkühler, *"Endlösung" in Galizien: Der Judenmord in Ostpolen und die Rettungsinitiativen von Berthold Beitz* (Bonn: Dietz, 1996).

21. Dieter Pohl, *Nationalsozialistische Judenverfolgung in Ostgalizien 1941–1944: Organisation und Durchführung eines staatlichen Massenverbrechens* (Munich: Oldenbourg, 1996); Christian Gerlach, *Kalkulierte Morde: Die deutsche Wirtschafts- und Vernichtungspolitik in Weißrussland 1941 bis 1944* (Hamburg: Hamburger Edition, 1999).

22. Christoph Dieckmann makes this point in a review of the books by Sandkühler and Pohl, "Genaue Beschreibung der 'Hölle hier auf Erden': Neue Forschungen über die Vernichtung der ostgalizischen Juden," *Badische Zeitung*, May 15, 1997.

23. See Ulrich Herbert, "Knappe Formeln erklären den Mord an den Juden nicht: Über die aufklärerische Herausforderung der Geschichte des Holocaust," *Frankfurter Rundschau*, January 25, 1997, p. 7.

24. See Peter Longerich, *Der ungeschriebene Befehl: Hitler und der Weg zur "Endlösung"* (Munich: Piper, 2001); in English, *The Unwritten Order: Hitler's Role in the Final Solution* (Stroud, U.K.: Tempus, 2001.)

25. See Detlef Bald, *Militär und Gesellschaft 1945–1990: Die Bundeswehr der*

Bonner Republik (Baden-Baden: Nomos, 1994), and his bibliography for further reading on the subject.

26. See the survey by Donald Abenheim, *Reforging the Iron Cross: The Search for Tradition in the West German Armed Forces* (Princeton: Princeton University Press, 1988).

27. The German term *Verhaltenssicherheit* was coined by Norbert Wiggershaus, "Zur Debatte um die Traditon künftiger Streitkräfte 1950–1955/56," in Hans-Joachim Harder and Norbert Wiggershaus, *Tradition und Reform in den Aufbaujahren der Bundeswehr* (Herford: E. S. Mittler, 1985), p. 7.

28. See Chapter 4, section 1.

29. Johann Adolf, Count Kielmansegg, "Der Krieg ist der Ernstfall," *Truppenpraxis,* no. 3 (1991), 304–307.

30. The term was used particularly by Gerd Schmückle. For details, see Detlef Bald, "Graf Baudissin und die Reform des deutschen Militärs," in Hilmar Linnenkamp and Dieter S. Lutz, eds., *Innere Führung: Zum Gedenken an Wolf Graf von Baudissin* (Baden-Baden: Nomos, 1995), p. 44.

31. See Chapter 5, section 4.

32. See Harder and Wiggershaus, *Tradition und Reform.*

33. Jakob Knab, *Falsche Glorie: Das Traditionsverständnis der Bundeswehr* (Berlin: Ch. Links, 1995), pp. 54–55.

34. Ibid., pp. 57–59.

35. Biographical sketches of these men and others after whom army bases were named can be found ibid., pp. 72–93.

36. For more on this debate, see Winfried Vogel, "Nun sag, wie hältst du's mit der Tradition . . . ?" ibid., pp. 119–130. For the battle over the naming of Camp Dietl in Füssen, see ibid., pp. 131–144. The battle was ultimately won by Jakob Knab, and the camps named after Dietl and Kübler were renamed in 1995.

37. For the activities of these pro-democracy officers, see the following two collections: Dieter S. Lutz, ed., *Im Dienst von Frieden und Sicherheit: Festschrift für Wolf Graf von Baudissin* (Baden-Baden: Nomos, 1985); and Linnenkamp and Lutz, *Innere Führung.*

38. Hans-Jürgen Rautenberg and Norbert Wiggershaus, eds., "Die 'Himmeroder Denkschrift' vom Oktober 1950: Politische und militärische Überlegungen für einen Beitrag der Bundesrepublik Deutschland zur westeuropäischen Verteidigung," *Militärgeschichtliche Mitteilungen* 21 (1977), 135–206. Also published as a special issue by *Militärgeschichtliche Mitteilungen* (Karlsruhe, 1977), quotation on p. 53.

39. For the discussion that follows in the text, see Detlef Bald, "Kämpfe um die Dominanz des Militärischen in der Bundeswehr," in Detlef Bald, Johannes Klotz, and Wolfgang Wette, eds., *Mythos Wehrmacht: Nachkriegsdebatten und Traditionspflege* (Berlin: Aufbau, 2001), specifically the chapter "Der Gründungskompromiss von 1950: Vorbild Wehrmacht."

40. The "Blank Office," founded in 1950 and named after its head, Theodor Blank (1905–1972), was the semi-secret predecessor of the West German Ministry of Defense. Formed before West Germany had officially rearmed, it was given an innocuous-sounding name as a disguise.—Trans.

41. Gerhard Ritter, "Das Problem des Militarismus in Deutschland," *Historische Zeitschrift* 177 (1954), 21ff.

42. See Wolfram Wette, "Für eine Belebung der Militarismusforschung," in Wolfram Wette, ed., *Militarismus in Deutschland: Zeitgenössische Analysen und Kritik* (Münster: Lit, 1999), pp. 13–37.

43. Knab, *Falsche Glorie*, p. 21.

44. See ibid., pp. 101–106.

45. One notable collector of foreign admirers of the Wehrmacht's effectiveness was General Heinz Karst of the Bundeswehr. See his book *Das Bild des Soldaten: Versuch eines Umrisses* (Boppoard am Rhein: H. Boldt, 1964).

46. Hans-Joachim Harder, "Traditionspflege in der Bundeswehr 1956–1972," in Harder and Wiggershaus, *Tradition und Reform*, p. 119.

47. The full text of this decree is reprinted ibid., pp. 155–160.

48. Bald, "Graf Baudissin und die Reform des deutschen Militärs," p. 43.

49. Ibid., p. 45.

50. The "Guidelines for the Understanding and Cultivation of Traditions in the Bundeswehr" were announced on September 20, 1982, by the German minister of defense (Fü S 13–Az. 35–08–07) and published in *Information für Kommandeure*, no. 1 (1982).

51. For a summary, see Karl Seidl, "Ein Kampf um die Geschichte der deutschen Wehrmacht: Historiker des Militärgeschichtlichen Forschungsamtes in Freiburg unter Beschuss von rechts," *Badische Zeitung*, February 16–17, 1985.

52. See, for example, the article by Colonel (ret.) Rolf Eible, a member of the board of the Federation of German Soldiers, in the organization's newsletter, *Soldat im Volk* (September 1984), 4–5.

53. See an early critical contribution, the reprint of a lecture, "Kein gültiges Erbe," in the *Süddeutsche Zeitung*, February 21–22, 1981.

54. *Soldat im Volk* (September 1984), 4.

55. Rolf Eible, "Uns reicht's jetzt," *Soldat im Volk* (February 1985), 3.

56. "Deutsche Geschichte 'amtlich' gefälscht" (unsigned), *Deutsche Wochen-Zeitung*, January 18, 1985, p. 3.

57. From a letter to the editor of the *Badische Zeitung*, March 8, 1997.

58. This is a reference to the SPD politician Hans-Jürgen Wischnewski.

59. Heinz Karst, "Kampagne gegen die Wehrmacht: Eine zweite Welle der 'Entmilitarisierung,'" *Criticon* 87 (1985), 19–20.

60. Ibid., p. 20. Karst published an expanded version of his *Criticon* article under the title "Wider die Selbstzerstörung: Lanze für eine gerechte Geschichtsbewertung der Wehrmacht," *Alte Kameraden: Unabhängige Zeitschrift deutscher Soldaten* 33, no. 3 (1985), 3–5.

61. *Deutschland Magazin* 20, no. 5 (1988), cover story, "Die Bundeswehr und ihr Trojanisches Pferd."

62. See the book written by the former premier of Baden-Württemberg, Hans Filbinger, *Die geschmähte Generation* (Munich: Universitas, 1987).

63. See, for example, the discussion by the editors of *Die Zeit* in the spring of 1995, accompanied by the booklet *Gehorsam bis zum Mord? Der Verschwiegene Krieg der Wehrmacht* (ZEIT-Punkte, March 1995), of which more than 100,000 copies had been sold by 1999, and the series *Die Zeit des Nationalsozialismus*, edited for Fischer Verlag in Frankfurt by Walter H. Pehle from 1979 on.

64. See the collection by the Hamburg Institute for Social Research, ed., *Krieg ist ein Gesellschaftszustand: Reden zur Eröffnung der Ausstellung "Vernichtungskrieg: Verbrechen der Wehrmacht 1941 bis 1944"* (Hamburg: Hamburger Edition, 1998).

65. Klaus Naumann, *Der Krieg als Text: Das Jahr 1945 im kulturellen Gedächtnis der Presse* (Hamburg: Hamburger Edition, 1998).

66. In Vienna, for example, the Wehrmacht was the subject of an international conference in 1995. See Walter Manoschek, ed., *Die Wehrmacht im Rassenkrieg: Der Vernichtungskrieg hinter der Front* (Vienna: Picus, 1996).

67. Helmut Donat and Arn Strohmeyer, eds., *Befreiung von der Wehrmacht? Dokumentation der Auseinandersetznung über die Ausstellung "Vernichtungskrieg—Verbrechen der Wehrmacht 1941 bis 1944" in Bremen 1996/97* (Bremen: Donat, 1997); Hans-Günther Thiele, ed., *Die Wehrmachtausstellung: Dokumentation einer Kontroverse* (Bremen: Landeszentrale für politische Bildung, 1997). (The latter also appeared as a special issue published by the Bundeszentrale für politische Bildung [Bonn, 1997]).

68. Cultural Affairs Department of the City of Munich, ed., *Bilanz einer Ausstellung: Dokumentation der Kontroverse um die Ausstellung "Ver-

nichtungskrieg–Verbrechen der Wehrmacht 1941 bis 1944" in München (Munich, 1998).

69. Rüdiger Proske, *Wider den Mißbrauch der Geschichte deutscher Soldaten zu politischen Zwecken: Eine Streitschrift* (Mainz: Hase & Koehler, 1996); and *Vom Marsch durch die Institutionen zum Krieg gegen die Wehrmacht* (Mainz: Hase & Koehler, 2002).

70. Heer and Naumann, *War of Extermination;* Hamburg Institute for Social Research, ed., *The German Army and Genocide: Crimes against War Prisoners, Jews, and Other Civilians in the East, 1939–1944,* trans. Scott Abbott (New York: New Press, 1999), the English translation of the exhibit catalogue; and *Gehorsam bis zum Mord? Der Verschwiegene Krieg der Wehrmacht (ZEIT-Punkte* March, 1995).

71. Heribert Prantl, ed., *Wehrmachtsverbrechen: Eine deutsche Kontroverse* (Hamburg: Hoffmann & Campe, 1997).

72. Gottfried Kößler, *"Vernichtungskrieg–Verbrechen der Wehrmacht 1941 bis 1944": Eine Ausstellung des Hamburger Instituts für Sozialforschung. Bausteine für den Unterricht zur Vor- und Nachbereitung des Ausstellungsbesuchs* (Frankfurt: Baur Institute, 1997).

73. Hamburg Institute for Social Research, ed., *Besucher einer Ausstellung: Die Ausstellung "Vernichtungskrieg–Verbrechen der Wehrmacht 1941 bis 1944," in Interview und Gespräch* (Hamburg: Hamburger Edition, 1998).

74. Ruth Beckermann, *Jenseits des Krieges: Ehemalige Wehrmachtsoldaten erinnern sich* (Vienna: Döcker, 1998).

75. Bundesministerium der Verteidigung, Fü S I 3–Az. 50–00–00, April 25, 1995.

76. Ibid., paragraph 14.

77. Ibid., paragraph 16.

78. Cited according to Winfried Vogel, "Die Wehrmacht ist kein Vorbild: Volker Rühes klares Wort zum Selbstverständnis der Bundeswehr," *Die Zeit,* December 1, 1995, p. 16.

79. Raul Hilberg, *The Destruction of the European Jews* (Chicago: Quadrangle Books, 1961); in German, *Die Vernichtung der europäischen Juden: Die Gesamtgeschichte des Holocaust* (Berlin: Olle & Wolter, 1982).

80. Raul Hilberg, *Die Vernichtung der europäischen Juden,* 3 vols. (Frankfurt: Fischer, 1999).

81. This is the title of the 1994 German edition, *Unerbetene Erinnerung: Der Weg eines Holocaust-Forschers* (Frankfurt: Fischer, 1994), of a manuscript Hilberg wrote in English. It was later published as *The Politics of Memory: The Journey of a Holocaust Historian* (Chicago: Ivan R. Dee, 1996).

82. For more on this breakdown of national myths, see Marion Countess Dönhoff, "Wandel der Wahrheit: Wie Nationen sich ihre Geschichte schreiben," *Die Zeit,* Ocotber 31, 1997, p. 1, and articles on the way countries such as Germany, Sweden, France, and Switzerland were dealing with "the burden of the past" in the same issue, pp. 9–13.

83. See the report "Bundeswehr ehrt Widerstandskämpfer," *Frankfurter Rundschau,* March 23, 2000, p. 4.

84. *Frankfurter Allgemeine Zeitung,* March 23, 2000, p. 4.

85. Ingo Preissler, "Die Willensbildung erfolgte von oben: Streit um die Umbenennung einer Kaserne in Rendsburg: Ein Wehrmachtgeneral soll einem Widerstandskämpfer weichen," *Berliner Zeitung,* April 8–9, 2000, p. 7.

86. Hannah Arendt, *Eichmann in Jerusalem: A Report on the Banality of Evil,* rev. ed. (New York: Penguin Books, 1994), p. 230.

87. Ibid., p. 231.

88. From the article on Abba Kovner in Israel Gutman, ed., *Encyclopedia of the Holocaust,* vol. 2 (New York: Macmillan, 1990), p. 823. See also the book by the American journalist Rich Cohen, *The Avengers* (New York: Knopf, 2000).

89. Hermann Adler, *Gesänge aus der Stadt des Todes* (Zurich: Oprecht, 1945), p. 5.

90. From a letter of December 26, 1966, from Hermann Adler to Secretary Katz of the Israeli Embassy in Bern, in the archives at Yad Vashem, in the collection "The Righteous among the Nations," dossier M 31/55. Schmid Anton, fols. 30–32.

91. Hermann Adler, *Ostra Brama: Legende aus der Zeit des großen Untergangs* (Zurich: Helios, 1945), pp. 109–116.

92. The documentary film *Feldwebel Schmid* (Sergeant Schmid), was commissioned by the Zweites Deutsches Fernsehen (ZDF) and made by the Sator Film Company of Hamburg in 1967. It was awarded a prize by a German labor union. Adler's radio script, titled "Der Feldwebel Anton Schmid: Eine Begegnung im Wilnaer Ghetto," was broadcast by the Südwestfunk (Southwest German Radio) on March 9, 1967.

93. The file on Schmid at Yad Vashem, mentioned in note 86, also contains the citation in French and Hebrew so honoring him, dated February 1, 1967, fol. 34. The year 1964, given in the *Encyclopedia of the Holocaust* (4:1333), is an error.

94. *Encyclopedia of the Holocaust,* 4:1333. The article there refers to Yitzhak Arad, *Ghetto in Flames: The Struggle and Destruction of the Jews in Vilna in the Holocaust* (Jerusalem: Yad Vashem, 1980).

95. Simon Wiesenthal, *The Murderers among Us* (New York: McGraw-Hill, 1967), pp. 284–285.

96. Adler, *Ostra Brama*, p. 111.

97. Reichenau's order is reprinted in Ueberschär and Wette, *"Unternehmen Barbarossa,"* pp. 339–340.

98. For more on the mass killings of Jews in Lithuania, see Christoph Dieckmann, "Der Krieg und die Ermordung der litauischen Juden," in Herbert, *Nationalsozialistische Vernichtungspolitik*, pp. 292–329.

99. Michael MacQueen, "Polen, Litauer, Juden und Deutsche in Wilna 1939–1944," in Wolfgang Benz and Marion Neiss, eds., *Judenmord in Litauen: Studien und Dokumente* (Berlin: Metropol, 1999), p. 62.

100. See the chronological table in Benz and Neiss, *Judenmord in Litauen*, p. 178.

101. Józef Mackiewicz's story "Der Stützpunkt Ponary" was first published in 1945; it is reprinted ibid., pp. 165–175; quotation on p. 167.

102. MacQueen, "Polen, Litauer, Juden und Deutsche in Wilna," p. 62.

103. Arad, *Ghetto in Flames*, pp. 216–217.

104. Adler, *Ostra Brama*, p. 111.

105. This information was taken from the entry on Schmid in the *Österreichisches Biographisches Lexikon*, vol. 10 (Graz: H. Böhlau's Nachfolger, 1994), pp. 234–235.

106. From a personal communication received from Major Thomas Vogel of the Research Institute for Military History in Potsdam, who has made a study of Schmid's life.

107. "Anton Schmid," in *Österreichisches Biographisches Lexikon*, 10:234.

108. Arno Lustiger, "Feldwebel Anton Schmid: Um den Preis des Lebens: Die Rettung von Juden aus Wilna und die Hilfe beim jüdischen Widerstand," *Frankfurter Allgemeine Zeitung*, June 3, 2000, p. 3. The entry on Schmid in the *Encyclopedia of the Holocaust*, by contrast, states that the circumstances of his arrest remain mysterious (4:1333).

109. Personal communication from Major Vogel, based on information from the Federal Archives in Aachen-Kornelimünster, where World War II German military personnel records are kept.

110. Friedrich Vogl, *Widerstand im Waffenrock: Österreichische Freiheitskämpfer in der Deutschen Wehrmacht 1938–1945* (Vienna: Europa Verlag, 1977), p. 150.

111. Letter from Fritz Kropp, a Catholic military chaplain, to Stephanie Schmid, ibid., p. 151.

112. The photograph is reproduced in the *Encyclopedia of the Holocaust*, 4:1333.

113. Wiesenthal, *The Murderers among Us,* pp. 284–285.

114. As forced labor.

115. Wiesenthal, *The Murderers among Us,* pp. 285–286.

116. Cited according to Vogl, *Widerstand im Waffenrock,* pp. 150–151.

117. Wiesenthal, *The Murderers among Us,* p. 286.

118. See Wolfram Wette, ed., *Retter in Uniform: Handlungsspielräume im Vernichtungskrieg der Wehrmacht* (Frankfurt: Fischer, 2002).

119. Jakob Knab, "Verklärung und Aufklärung: Von den Heldenmythen der Wehrmacht zur Traditionspflege der Bundeswehr," *S. + F. Vierteljahresschrift für Sicherheit und Frieden* 19 (1999), 105.

120. When the National Socialists divided Germany into administrative regions called *Gaue,* the part of the country where the town of Weiden is located became the Bayerische Ostmark, the "Eastern March of Bavaria." The name "Ostmark" thus has clear associations with the Third Reich.—Trans.

121. "'Schmid-Kaserne' im vierten Versuch: Personalrat der Flugabwehr kritisiert ungleiche Behandlung," *Schleswig-Holsteinische Landeszeitung,* April 20–21, 2000.

7. Conclusion

1. The collection edited by Rolf-Dieter Müller and Hans-Erich Volkmann, *Die Wehrmacht: Mythos und Realität* (Munich: Oldenbourg, 1999), although rich in material, does not devote enough space to the topic of the Wehrmacht and the murder of Jews. Only one of more than sixty contributions, namely, Jürgen Förster's "Wehrmacht, Krieg und Holocaust," expressly deals with the Wehrmacht's part in these crimes.

2. One outstanding work on this topic is Christian Gerlach's *Kalkulierte Morde: Die deutsche Wirtschafts- und Vernichtungspolitik in Weißrussland 1941 bis 1944* (Hamburg: Hamburger Edition, 1999).

3. See Manfred Messerschmidt, "Völkerrecht und 'Kriegsnotwendigkeit' in der deutschen militärischen Tradition," in Messerschmidt, ed., *Was damals Recht war . . . NS-Militär- und Strafjustiz im Vernichtungskrieg* (Essen: Klartext, 1996), pp. 191–229.

4. See the summary of the scholarly literature in Rolf-Dieter Müller and Gerd R. Ueberschär, *Hitlers Krieg im Osten 1941–1945: Ein Forschungsbericht* (Darmstadt: Wissenschaftliche Buchgesellschaft, 2000).

5. See part 2 ("Deutsche Kriegsverbrechen im Zweiten Weltkrieg") in Wolfram Wette and Gerd R. Ueberschär, eds., *Kriegsverbrechen im 20. Jahrhundert* (Darmstadt: Primus, 2001).

6. See, in addition to the studies cited in Chapter 4, section 4, the exemplary study by Klaus Cachay, Steffen Bahlke, and Helmut Mehl, *"Echte Sportler"—"Gute Soldaten": Die Sportsozialisation des Nationalsozialismus im Spiegel der Feldpostbriefen* (Weinheim: Juventa, 2000).

7. A recent study on this subject is Kurt Pätzold, *Ihr waret die besten Soldaten: Ursprung und Geschichte einer Legende* (Leipzig: Militzke, 2000).

8. See Johannes Klotz, ed., *Vorbild Wehrmacht? Wehrmachtsverbrechen, Rechtsextremismus und Bundeswehr* (Cologne: PapyRossa, 1998).

9. The same expectation is voiced by Ralph Giordano in *Die Traditionslüge: Vom Kriegerkult in der Bundeswehr* (Cologne: Kiepenheuer & Witsch, 2000).

10. The Germans' rejection of a martial culture, as embodied in the Wehrmacht among other institutions, which set in after the Second World War was the topic of a conference hosted by the group Historische Friedensforschung. See the proceedings in Thomas Kühne, ed., *Von der Kriegskultur zur Friedenskultur? Zum Mentalitätswandel in Deutschland seit 1945* (Münster: Lit, 2000).

Index

Löhr, Alexander, 135–137
Ludendorff, Erich, xii, 38, 40–42, 45, 56–58, 60, 140, 147, 184
Ludwigsburg, 105, 124, 242–243, 247–248
Luftwaffe. *See* Air Force
Lutherans, xvi, 157, 162–163
Lutsk, 111
Lüttwitz, Heinrich von, 44, 49, 55
Luxemberg, Rosa, 9–10, 44–45, 53

Mackensen, August von, 143, 155
Mackiewicz, Józef, 285
Maercker, Georg Ludwig, 63–64
Mannheim, 35
Manoschek, Walter, 103–104, 252, 254, 256
Manstein, Erich von, 73–76, 95–96, 207, 224–226, 234, 262, 313n145
Manteuffel, Hasso von, 260
Marburg, 270
Marx, Karl, 141, 151
Master race, 99, 135, 137, 194
McCloy, John J., 124, 239–240
Mellenthin, Horst von, 234
Menasse, Robert, 274
Mensheviks, 10
Messerschmidt, Manfred, xv, 26, 76, 86, 176, 207–208, 252–254, 266–267, 349n3
Meyer, Hermann: *Konversations-Lexicon*, 6
Middeldorf, Eike, 234
Milch, Eduard, 81, 155, 209
Militarism, 33, 60, 139, 141, 149, 152, 158–159, 183, 185–186, 194, 212, 262
Militär-Wochenblatt, 42, 76
Military History Research Institute, 28, 92, 252, 255, 266, 268, 305n4
Mittelungen für die Trappe, 98–99
Mölders, Werner, 260
Moltke, Helmuth von, 141–144, 149
Mommsen, Hans, 68–69
Mönchengladbach, 272
Moscow, 20
Moses Mendelssohn Zentrum, 305n4
Mostar, 136
Müller, Klaus-Jürgen, 71, 74, 85, 252, 313n137
Munich, 45, 50, 52, 245, 270, 272–273, 276
Münster, 291

Murr, Wilhelm, 203
Mutiny, 187

Nachkrieg period, 49–62
Napoleon I, 27, 154
National Assembly (Weimar Republic), 47–48, 63
National Defense Department (Wehrmacht), 216
National Democratic Party, 273
National Federation of German Soldiers, 61, 353n52
Nationalism, 6, 11–14, 33–36, 44, 51, 56–58, 62, 66–67, 69, 141–142, 148, 156, 166, 188, 239
National Socialism, vii, ix-xi, xiii, xv-xvi, 25–26, 52, 134, 139, 141, 197, 222, 253, 290, 348n150; and military, 2, 71–89, 150, 152, 154, 156, 158, 166–172, 181, 185, 188–194, 211–213, 235–237, 262, 265, 269–271, 275, 279; and Jewish Bolshevism, 14–17, 42, 48, 91; propaganda, 16, 23, 27, 42, 69, 86–91, 95–96, 98–100, 102–104, 116, 131, 149, 157, 167, 169–175, 181–185, 189–191, 193–194, 198–199, 201–202, 213, 254; anti-Semitism, 28–29, 33, 55, 61, 63, 69–89, 294; and murder of Jews, 91, 98–99, 101, 103, 125, 254–255, 275; and conscientious objectors, 160–161, 164; crimes of, 240–250, 264, 276. *See also* Third Reich
National Socialist German Workers' Party, x, 12, 41, 48, 55–56, 65–66, 68–69, 71–72, 76, 150–151, 154, 157, 191, 193, 203, 207, 210, 213, 216, 241, 294
Naumann, Erich, 124
Naumann, Klaus, 196, 271
Navy, 41, 43–44, 50, 59, 72, 76, 85, 89, 133–134, 151, 176, 186–187, 209–210, 216, 252
Navy High Command, 305n2
Nazism. *See* National Socialism
Nazi-Soviet Pact, 170
Neue Preussische Zeitung, 57
Nibelungs, 189
Normandy invasion, 183
North Atlantic Treaty Organization, 236
Noske, Gustav, 10, 47–48, 52–53, 63, 187–188